# THE FIVE BOOKS
# OF MOSES

A REEXAMINATION OF THE MODERN THEORY THAT THE
PENTATEUCH IS A LATE COMPILATION FROM DIVERSE
AND CONFLICTING SOURCES BY AUTHORS AND EDITORS
WHOSE IDENTITY IS COMPLETELY UNKNOWN

*By*

OSWALD T. ALLIS

*We have found Him, of whom Moses in the law,
and the prophets did write*

**PRESBYTERIAN AND REFORMED PUBLISHING CO.**
**Phillipsburg, New Jersey**

# PREFACE

THE REEXAMINATION of every important and widely accepted theory should be welcomed by friend and foe alike. Theories tend to become systematized and stereotyped. Old problems, difficulties, and objections are likely to be forgotten or ignored, when the theory becomes popular. Doubtful arguments come to be accepted without question because they fit in with or are required by the system whose correctness is regarded as established. Beside this, new light may come from unexpected quarters and challenge the correctness or require the revision of conclusions long regarded as assured. For both of these reasons a reexamination of the higher critical view of the Pentateuch may be regarded as proper and desirable at this time. The history of this theory has been marked by changes and even reversals of position. Some of the points regarding which it is now asserted that they are accepted by all scholars were rejected by men whose names are highly esteemed in critical circles; and the objections raised in the past by opponents of the theory have in many instances lost none of their cogency. Furthermore, the archaeological discoveries of recent years, especially of the last decade, have been so remarkable that they have produced an "archaeological revolution" [1] and have caused not a few who accept in general the viewpoint of the critics to admit or assert that these conclusions must be considerably revised.

One of the reasons this reexamination of the critical theory is needed is that very many have accepted it without careful investigation. The complexity and intricacy of the application of the theory has led them to feel that only those who have very unusual aptitude and special training are competent to pass judgment upon it. Consequently they have accepted it second-hand, on the authority of "experts," because they have not felt able to study it for themselves and were afraid of being lost in its mazes, or because they were unwilling or unable to take the time and make the effort which such a study seemed to demand. But such an attitude is not really necessary. The higher critical study of the Pentateuch had a very simple beginning. Its normative principles are easy to master. It is only their application which is complicated and confusing; and in this very fact, that the application is so complicated, lies the clearest indication that the theory is at fault.

These basic principles are two in number. The first is the claim that variety in diction, style, and subject-matter implies diversity of source and authorship. The second is that the history of Israel, especially the religious history, must have followed in general the same pattern as that of other nations and races, and that the theory of naturalistic evolution must be applied to all without exception. Careful consideration of these two principles will convince the reader that, as applied by the critics, they represent the direct antithesis of the principles which generations of Christians have applied to the Bible in the past.

The time-honored method of interpreting Scripture is the harmonistic method. This means that if the Bible is the Word of God, we are entitled to expect it to be both true and self-consistent. Consequently Scripture is to be interpreted in the light of Scripture with a view to exhibiting and establishing its harmony and unity. The higher criticism, on the other hand, began with variations or differences, the variations in the use of the divine names in Genesis; and it gradually developed into a quest of differences. Scripture has been pitted against Scripture. Variations, however trivial and microscopic, have been magnified into contradictions. The result has been that the Bible instead of being regarded as remarkable for its unity and harmony has become in the hands of the critics a collection of writings, characterized by wide diversity of viewpoint, by discord and contradiction. Such a result is destructive of its divine authority. In fact it tends to deprive it of any authority at all. Conflicting evidence has little if any value.

The Bible manifestly claims to be the record of God's redemptive dealings with mankind and especially with Israel. Israel is represented as a chosen people, the object of special supernatural and providential dealings, that through Israel all the nations of the earth might be blessed. A supernatural redemption is its major theme. But now that naturalistic evolution has cast its spell over much of our thinking, and has become increasingly the standard which is applied to human life in general, consistency seems to demand that its advocates apply it to Biblical history as well. Obviously the attempt to impose upon the Bible a philosophy of history which is radically different from the one which it teaches and exemplifies will lead to drastic and rigorous reconstruction. Whether true or false the redemptive supernaturalism of the Bible is the direct antithesis of the doctrine of naturalistic evolution. And the extreme to which the critics are obliged to go in their endeavor to bring about their reconstruction is conclusive proof that "the new agreeth not with the old."

The design of this "reexamination" is to make these very important matters clear to the reader, and to place him in a position to weigh the evidence, to examine the method, and to test the conclusions of the critics for himself. In order that the evidence may be available to those whose knowledge of the Bible is restricted to the English versions, where the Hebrew is referred to the transliteration given in Young's *Analytical Concordance* (7th edition) is used. Students of Hebrew would naturally prefer a more exact transliteration. But the one used by Young is sufficiently accurate for the purpose of identifying the words which are referred to.

So many books have been written on the subject of the Pentateuch that a writer may well hesitate to add to their

# PREFACE

number. Whether I have been justified in doing so the reader will judge. I have endeavored to treat this subject in a way which will be sufficiently popular and non-technical for the general reader who has neither the time nor the special equipment requisite to the study of a technical treatise. I have also sought to discuss the problem with sufficient fulness and detail to make the book of interest and value to scholars. But my principal aim has been to convince earnest Bible students, both ministers and laymen, that this vitally important question is not one which they must leave to experts and specialists, but that they are quite competent to investigate it for themselves, and to place them in a position to do this. For this reason a number of examples and illustrations have been given under most of the topics discussed. Some are quite simple, others are more or less intricate. The argument is cumulative. But the reader is asked to bear constantly in mind that these examples are given, not primarily with a view to refuting the conclusions of the critics in detail, but for the purpose of exposing the fallacy of the principles on which they proceed, the inconsistency of their application of these principles, and the disastrous results to which they lead inevitably. With a view to assisting the reader to follow the main argument, much of the detailed discussion has been set in smaller type.

It is a great pleasure to avail myself of this opportunity to express my appreciation of the help which I have received in connection with the publication of this book from my friend, Rev. Samuel G. Craig, D.D., the President of *The Presbyterian and Reformed Publishing Company*. Dr. Craig is so well known as an earnest contender for the faith once delivered to the saints, that it seems eminently fitting, and it is especially gratifying to me, that this book which is written in defense of the Mosaic authorship of the Pentateuch should be published under such auspices.

If the great need of the world today is a truly Christian leadership in the conduct of the war in which we are now

## PREFACE

engaged and in planning for the peace to which we look forward with confidence, and if the great need of the Christian Church is a profound conviction that the Bible is "the word of God, the only infallible rule of faith and practice," this book which deals with the seemingly remote question of the authorship of the Pentateuch may be regarded as a contribution to the solution of the most practical and pressing of the problems that confront us. That the Lord may be pleased to use it to this end is the hope and prayer with which the author sends it forth.

*November 18, 1942.*

## PREFACE TO SECOND EDITION

No change has been made in the general form of this discussion of the problem of the Pentateuch. But advantage has been taken of the opportunity to revise and correct, and also to expand to a moderate extent. The most extensive addition is the new chapter in Part III. entitled "Negative and Positive Developments." In the first part of this chapter some further examples are given of the disastrous results of that disintegration of the Pentateuch on which the higher critics are still busily engaged. It is followed by brief discussions of Form Criticism and of Barthianism. These two topics have only an indirect bearing upon the basic problem of the Pentateuch for the reason that both movements accept the general conclusions of the Higher Criticism as well-established and proceed upon that assumption. If it is false and if the Pentateuch is *Mosaic* and its statements are to be taken at their face value and accepted as a thoroughly trustworthy record of the matters with which they deal, then Form Criticism and Barthianism cease to have any real significance because they build upon assumptions which are lacking in any real basis in fact. However, in view of the present interest in these relatively recent movements, it has seemed advisable to include a brief discussion of them in the new edition. The funda-

# PREFACE

mental issue as it concerns the Pentateuch and the entire Bible remains unchanged; and it is as sharply drawn as ever. It is between those who accept the statements of the Bible as true, despite the adverse claims of the critics, and those who accept the claims of the critics as true despite the positive statements of the Bible to the contrary.
*January 25, 1949.*

## PREFACE TO THIRD EDITION

The fifteen years which have elapsed since the appearance of the Second Edition of this book have been busy years in the Old Testament field. There has been increased activity among Conservative scholars; and a number of valuable books and articles have been published in defense of the traditional, or we would prefer to say, the Biblical view of the Old Testament.

Some of the results of the wide-spread and intensive labors of the archaeologist have confirmed the Scriptures in a gratifying way and refuted adverse theories which were confidently proclaimed as fact. But the spade has also uncovered evidence which it is not easy to bring into agreement with the Biblical record; and these differences are being exploited as proving that the Bible is not free from human error. Archaeology has a vast field to explore. We need to remember that its researches can give us at best only a very imperfect picture of the past. It is like a torch in a vast cave, which throws a brilliant light on some objects while casting dark shadows on others and leaving many things hidden which clearer light would reveal. Archaeology has both confirmed and challenged the historical statements of the Bible. We must beware of placing too much confidence in it in our defense of the Scriptures.

In like manner and also as a result of archaeological research, our information regarding ancient religions has been constantly increasing. It shows very clearly the vast difference between the religion of Revelation and the ethnic faiths. But there are many scholars today who are studying these religions from the standpoint of evolution, who stress the similarities and minimize the differences with a view to relating and even deriving Biblical religion from these pagan cults. The uniqueness of the religion of the Bible needs special emphasis today.

The higher critical movement from its inception has been unfriendly to the Supernatural. Natural Science has vastly expanded our knowledge of the material universe. But instead of being led to increased reverence and awe of its Creator, many scientists are disposed to treat the universe as a closed system from which the Supernatural is to be rigorously excluded. The popularity of Tillich and Bultmann is a striking evidence of this. The Christian needs to remember that the Supernatural is of the very essence of the Biblical revelation. He does not need to apologize for it or to minimize its importance. On the contrary, he should glory in it as evidence of the fact that God is neither an unknowable X nor an absentee land-lord, but the almighty Creator of this expanding universe and its sovereign Lord and that it is in Him that we live and move and have our being.

The great problems which concern our faith in the Bible are still with us. The writer has considered the advisability of adding a further chapter dealing with them to this volume as it appears in the new edition. But he has now for a considerable time been working on a new book which he has entitled, *The Old Testament: Its Claims and Its Critics.* It is his hope that in the good providence of God it will make its appearance in a few months. So he ventures to refer the readers of this volume to it for a further discussion of Old Testament problems.

*September 9, 1964*                                    O. T. A.

# NOTE ON BIBLICAL QUOTATIONS

In quoting from the Bible I have used both the Authorized Version (AV) and the American Revised Version (ARV)*; and I have also at times translated directly from the Hebrew. In doing so I have frequently restored or retained the Hebrew word *Elohim* (God); and I have rendered the Memorial Name by *Jehovah* instead of LORD. This was for the sake of clearness in the discussion of a subject in which these two words figure so prominently. The use of LORD in the AV in the Old Testament is justified by the fact that it has the sanction of New Testament usage (cf. Ps. cx.1 with Matt. xxii.44, Mk. xii.36, Lk. xx.42); it is not due to the "Jewish superstition" which regarded the Name as too sacred to be uttered. That the pronunciation *Jehovah* is not correct is generally recognized. It resulted from the attempt to pronounce the Memorial Name (called the Tetragram because of its four letters, *YHWH*) with the vowels of the word "Lord" (*Adonai*) which Jewish scholars were accustomed to substitute for it in reading the Old Testament. The correct pronunciation of the Name may be *Yahweh*. But this is not certain; and *Yahweh* has a decidedly strange and unnatural sound. Since *Jehovah* is familiar to readers of the AV (cf. Ex. vi.3) and is regularly used in the ARV, its use here is doubly appropriate.

* The principal passages quoted from the ARV are the following: Gen. vii.21-23 (p. 98), Ps. xix.7 (p. 108), Ex. xxxiv.6f. (p. 141), Jer. vii.21f. (p. 170), Deut. vi.4f. (p. 175). They are quoted by permission of the *International Council of Religious Education*, which now owns the copyright of this version.

# CONTENTS

# CONTENTS

# INTRODUCTION

## THE TRADITIONAL AND HIGHER CRITICAL VIEWS REGARDING THE PENTATEUCH STATED AND CONTRASTED

"The Pentateuch is the thread of gold which runs —now latent, now prominent—throughout the whole body of the Scriptures. Retain it in its place, and the whole is united by a consistent purpose from end to end; take it away, and all the rest of revelation becomes a mass of inextricable confusion" (EDWARD GARRETT, article "Pentateuch" in KITTO's *Cyclopaedia of Biblical Literature,* Third Edition, 1861).

# INTRODUCTION

HIGHER CRITICISM is, strictly speaking, the counterpart of lower criticism. The field of lower criticism is documentary evidence, the investigation of the text of a document with a view to ascertaining its true and original form. It uses for this purpose printed editions, manuscripts, translations, quotations, allusions, everything bearing on the text of the document. Hence it is often called textual criticism. The higher criticism may be said to begin its work where the lower criticism ends. Assuming that the correct text of the document has been determined, the higher critic seeks to ascertain whether the claims which are made regarding it, by the document itself or by other evidence which bears upon it, are well grounded in fact, whether its alleged authorship and date are correct, whether its statements are trustworthy and credible.

So defined it is obvious that there is an important difference between these two forms of criticism. The word criticism implies the formation and expression of a judgment or estimate; and since this judgment is expressed by a person it cannot be altogether free from personal bias. But the work of the textual critic is more objective and less likely to be influenced by subjective considerations than that of the higher critic. His aim is to determine the correct text, not to pass judgment upon its origin or value. But when the higher critic undertakes to decide whether the claims made by or for the document as to date, authorship and value are credible, there is far more likelihood that the subjective element will influence his conclusions to a considerable extent, perhaps even control them.

One of the best illustrations of this difference is the controversy which has been waging for nearly a century around the question of the authorship of the *Plays of Shakespeare*. The problems of the textual critic are neither simple nor unimportant despite the fact that the First Folio Edition dates from 1623, less than a decade after Shakespeare's death. But the question which has excited the most widespread interest, has been that of authorship. Did Shakespeare write the *Plays of Shakespeare?* A vigorous opponent of the theory that "Bacon wrote Shakespeare" does not hesitate to say of it, "In all forms it appears to proceed upon *a priori* belief that the 'Stratford actor' *could not* have possessed the scholarly and other qualifications supposed to be revealed in the works ascribed to him."[2] Whether there is basis in fact for this *a priori* belief is the question at issue between the "Stratfordians" and the "anti-Stratfordians." And the ardor with which the Baconian theory has been defended is an illustration of the weight attached by its advocates to this decidedly theoretical argument. Objective evidence that Bacon wrote the plays of Shakespeare there is none. His name was never connected with them until two centuries or more after his death.

If the lover of Shakespeare's *Plays* regards the question whether they come to him from the pen of the bard of Avon as of importance, for the lover of the Bible the question whether "Moses wrote the Pentateuch" is of far greater importance. This is due partly to the superior character of the evidence which supports the Mosaic authorship. But it is also due, as in the case of the authorship of Shakespeare's *Plays*, to the importance attached by the gainsayers to an *a priori* judgment, which is that Moses was not qualified to write the Pentateuch and that the early history of Israel must have been very different from what the Pentateuch would lead us to suppose. In both cases the presumptive evidence is strongly in favor of the generally accepted authorship. History may be wanting in generosity in its treatment of the career of William Shakespeare. But of

Francis Bacon as the author of the *Plays,* history knows nothing. In like manner history may not tell us all we would like to know about Moses, but of another than Moses as author of the Pentateuch history knows absolutely nothing.

## I. THE MOSAIC TRADITION AND THE CONSEQUENCES OF REJECTING IT

Until comparatively recent times, the practically universal view among both Jews and Christians was that "Moses wrote the Pentateuch." Josephus, the Jewish historian, in speaking of the sacred books of the Jews declares: "and of them five belong to Moses, which contain his laws and the traditions of the origin of mankind till his death."[3] That these words refer to the Pentateuch, that they attribute it to Moses, and that they represent the accepted opinion of Jewish scholars of the past is undeniable. The acceptance of this belief in the Christian Church is shown by the fact that in Luther's translation of the Bible each of the books of the Pentateuch is entitled a "book of Moses," and that a similar statement appears in the 1611 Version of the English Bible. The question whether a tradition which is so ancient and so universal is correct is important in itself. But it becomes especially important when we consider the three matters closely connected with it which have already been alluded to: (1) the basis of this tradition, (2) the consequences of rejecting it, and (3) the methods used by the critics to disprove the Mosaic authorship.

### 1. The Basis of the Mosaic Tradition Is Four-fold

#### a. The Claims of the Pentateuch Itself

The quotation from Josephus given above states that the Pentateuch contains "his [Moses'] laws." This is borne out by the statements of the document itself. As to the Decalogue, it is expressly declared that all the arrangements for that most impressive scene at Mount Sinai when the Law was given were made by Moses, and that the Ten Words were uttered in his presence (Ex. xx.19f.); later he was told to write them (xxxiv.27). Regarding the laws of Ex. xxi.-xxiii., we are expressly told that "Moses wrote all the words of Jehovah" (xxiv.4); and the document containing them is clearly the "book of the covenant" referred to in vs. 7. All of the laws regarding the erection of the tabernacle and its worship recorded in Ex. xxv.-xxxi. are given in the form of personal communications to Moses; and the account of the construction of the tabernacle and of its erection is accompanied by the oft-repeated refrain, "as Jehovah commanded Moses."[4] In Leviticus the words, "Jehovah spake (said, called) unto Moses" (or less freq., "unto Moses and Aaron"), occur about 35 times, 19 of which are at the beginning of a chapter; and xxvi.46 and xxvii.34 definitely connect the giving of these laws with Sinai. Numbers closely resembles Leviticus in this respect. Nearly half of the chapters begin in the same way; and the last verse of the book brings us down to the time when Israel was encamped in Moab. Deuteronomy is largely made up of elaborate discourses declared to have been delivered by Moses, the primary aim of which is to rehearse the laws already given and apply them to the new conditions under which Israel will shortly live, and to exhort the people to loyalty and obedience. Chap. xxxi.9, 24 tells us that Moses wrote the law in a book; and vs. 26 tells us that he commanded the Levites to place this book beside the ark. The meaning and scope of the word "law" in these statements is a matter of dispute, but the natural inference would be that it at least included all the legal portions of the Pentateuch.

What applies to the laws is also true to some degree of the historical portions of the Pentateuch. Of the events of his own day we are told that Moses was commanded to write God's judgment upon Amalek "in a book" (Ex. xvii.14).

It is also stated that Moses wrote the itinerary recorded in Num. xxxiii. And there is force in the argument that the writer of this itinerary would naturally be the author of the narrative which describes the history of which it is only a summary.[5] We are also told that Moses gave as a parting legacy to Israel the Song and the Blessing recorded in Deut. xxxii.-xxxiii. The fact that these chapters are expressly attributed to Moses favors the correctness of Josephus' phrase "and the traditions of the origin of mankind till his death."[6] They show that Moses was interested in the past history of his people (xxxii.7, 8); and the author of Deut. xxxiii. might well be the recorder of Gen. xlix.[7] It is true that the Book of Genesis nowhere claims to have been written by Moses. But an account of the origin of mankind or at least of the ancestors of Israel such as is given there is required to make the other four books intelligible. Furthermore, the "and" (or, now) with which Ex. i.1 begins is an indication that this book is a continuation and only in Genesis do we find the history recorded which Exodus continues.[8]

*b.* The Testimony of the Rest of the Old Testament

References to Moses are about as numerous in Joshua as in all the other books of the Old Testament taken together. They show that Joshua derived his authority from Moses and appealed constantly to what Moses had commanded. These references serve to define the task assigned Joshua after the death of Moses. Chap. i.7 is typical: "Only be thou strong and very courageous, that thou mayest observe to do according to all the law, which Moses my servant commanded thee." We speak at times of Joshua as Moses' successor. But such an expression is misleading. Moses was the Law-giver: it was the duty of all who came after him to keep that law and instruct others to do so. In his farewell to Israel Joshua passed on to the elders (xxiii.6) the obligation to obey the law of Moses, which had been

solemnly laid upon him. This involved "all that is written in the book of the law of Moses." Moses had, strictly
speaking, but one successor: the One who said of Himself,
"A greater than Moses is here."

Occasional references to Moses are found in 14 other
books. In Judges iii.4 it is declared that certain nations
were left in the land after the death of Joshua for the purpose of testing whether Israel "would hearken unto the
commandments of Jehovah, which he commanded their
fathers by the hand of Moses." The books of Kings,
Chronicles, Ezra, Nehemiah, all refer to the law of Moses.

The prophets only occasionally mention Moses by name.
They refer more frequently to "the law." But that by this
they mean "the law of Moses" is indicated by the fact that
his is the only name ever connected with the law, Aaron
being merely his mouthpiece.[9] The final word of the last
of the prophets is "Remember the law of Moses my servant." Just what is covered by the word law may be a matter
of dispute, but that the Old Testament attributes the law
of God which was Israel's most precious possession to Moses
and to no one else is so obvious that detailed discussion is
here unnecessary.

### c. The Testimony of the New Testament

The New Testament makes it quite clear that Jesus did
not dispute the Old Testament canon as accepted by the
Jews, but fully accepted it as the Word of God. He challenged only their misinterpretation of it and failure to follow its teachings (e.g., Lk. xx.37, Jn. vii.19). This is made
especially clear by Luke xxiv.27, 44, which indicates that
Jesus recognized as already in existence the divisions of the
Old Testament as later defined by Josephus, and that the
"writings" of Moses (Jn. v.47, cf. Lk. xvi.29, 31) to which
He referred were the Pentateuch. He quoted the Decalogue (Ex. xx.12, Deut. v.16) with the words "Moses said"
(Mk. vii.10) and added a quotation taken from Ex. xxi.17

and Lev. xx.9. When the Pharisees raised the question of easy divorce (Mt. xix.3), He appealed first to Gen. ii.24; and then, when the appeal was made to Moses' "command" (Deut. xxiv. 1-4), He declared that Moses permitted divorce because of the hardness of their hearts. When the question of levirate marriage (Deut. xxv.5) was placed in a ridiculous light by the Sadducees for the purpose of making the resurrection seem absurd, Jesus appealed to the words uttered at the Bush (Ex. iii.6) which in Mk. xii.26 are referred to "the book of Moses" and in Mt. xxii.31 ascribed directly to "God." That Paul held the same view is indicated by Acts xxviii.23. Such passages as Rom. x.19, 1 Cor. ix.9, 2 Cor. iii.15, indicate clearly the viewpoint of the New Testament on this question, which is that "Moses" and "law" are equivalent expressions.

### d. The Voice of Tradition

Since the higher critics do not deny the antiquity and practical universality of the tradition that the Pentateuch is Mosaic,[10] but rather affirm that their own view is essentially a modern discovery, it is not necessary to prove this in detail. A few facts, however, may be noted. The earliest extra-canonical witness to the Old Testament canon is Ecclesiasticus (written about 250 B.C.). There we read, "He [Jehovah] made him [Moses] to hear his voice and brought him into the dark cloud, and gave him commandments before his face, even the law of life and knowledge, that he might teach Jacob his covenants and Israel his judgments."[11] Second Maccabees speaks of the "commandment of the law which was given . . . by Moses" (vii.30). Philo, who was an older contemporary of Josephus, attached such importance to the books of Moses that he assigned the Pentateuch a unique place among the Old Testament books. In the Talmud it is declared that any departure from the teaching that Moses wrote the Pentateuch would be punished by exclusion from Paradise.[12] Among Christian scholars, one of the first to refer to the "five books of Moses" is Melito, Bishop of Sardis (*cir.* 175 A.D.). In all of the lists of the Canonical Scriptures given by the Church Fathers the Five Books of the Law are given a unique position; and they are frequently called the "books of Moses."[13] The simplest explanation of this tradition is that it represents the teachings of the Bible itself.

2. *The Consequences of the Rejection of the Claim that the Pentateuch Is Mosaic Are Very Serious*

*a.* The first consequence is the rejection of all the positive external evidence, both Biblical and extra-Biblical, as to the authorship of the Pentateuch. This is to be done, not on the authority of older and better evidence, as no such evidence has been produced. It is to be done in the interest of a theory, the correctness of which has never been proved. And since this rejection of external evidence necessarily involves and includes the rejection of the testimony of the New Testament and, most important of all, the testimony of Jesus as recorded in it, the question of the Mosaic authorship of the Pentateuch becomes a matter of very vital concern to the New Testament Christian. Unless he is prepared to treat it as of no importance whether Jesus is correctly quoted in the New Testament, or whether He accommodated Himself to Jewish prejudices and accepted traditions which He knew to be false, or whether He was in such a sense a "man of his age" that He was as ignorant as were His contemporaries of the "facts" which the critics claim to have discovered, the Christian of today must regard the question of the Mosaic authorship of the Pentateuch as no less important than it was held to be before the rise of the higher criticism first called it into question, and then positively rejected it.

*b.* The second consequence of the rejection of the Mosaic authorship of the Pentateuch is the admission that the account of the "Mosaic" age given us in it is a fundamentally erroneous one. Moses is the outstanding figure. He is mentioned more than 500 times in Exodus to Deuteronomy. But, if all the legal codes of the Pentateuch date from long after Moses' time, and if the history is late and unreliable, Moses becomes a decidedly elusive figure; and it becomes difficult if not impossible to account for the prominent rôle assigned him. His reputation is vast, but the deeds which serve as the basis for it are no longer to be regarded as his. He becomes a kind of legal fiction.

c. The third consequence of the acceptance of this theory is the adoption of a low view of the authority and credibility of the Bible as a whole. For, as will appear in the course of the discussion, it is only by rejecting or amending the statements of Scripture that the evidence cited above can be overthrown.

### 3. The Method Employed by the Critics Is Responsible for These Radical Consequences

a. It is characteristic of this method that it is divisive and destructive of the unity and harmony of Scripture. The slightest variations in diction, style, viewpoint or subject-matter are seized upon as indicative of difference in author, date, and source. Differences are frequently magnified into contradictions. A book which is full of contradictory statements cannot speak with the authority of truth and cannot be in a unique and special sense the Word of the God of truth.

b. It is characteristic of this method that it largely rejects the claim of Scripture that the children of Israel were in a unique sense the object of divine guidance. The tendency is to substitute for the uniqueness of God's dealings with Israel, the uniqueness of Israel herself, her special genius for religion.

c. It is characteristic of this method that it minimizes or rejects the redemptive supernaturalism of Biblical history and endeavors to reconstruct it in terms of naturalistic evolution. The miraculous element is viewed with suspicion and regarded either as evidence of the late date and unreliability of a narrative, or as proof that it represents a primitive and unscientific account of phenomena in which a modern writer would see only the operation of natural processes.

In view, therefore, of the strength of the Mosaic tradition, the serious consequences of rejecting it, and the drastic methods made use of by those who do this, the question whether Moses wrote the Pentateuch should be of vital concern to everyone who has any knowledge of the Bible or any interest in it. Before entering upon the discussion of this question, we must ask ourselves exactly what is to be understood by the words, "Moses wrote the Pentateuch."

### What Does "Moses wrote the Pentateuch" Mean?

These words have been understood in several different ways:

*a.* Some have taken them to mean that Moses wrote, or at least dictated, every word in the Five Books. A serious objection to this view is the account of Moses' death given in Deut. xxxiv. Some have held that even this chapter must have been written by him.[14] Others have argued that Moses could not have written it and that if he did not write it, there may be many other passages of which he was not the author. Neither of these extreme positions is justified by the facts. Deut. xxxiv. is clearly a unique chapter. It stands at the very end of the Pentateuch. It is written as history, not as prophecy. Its contents seem obviously to require another author than Moses. The inclusion of the account of a man's death in his autobiography would not prove that he did not write the account of his life. The two are so different that such an inference would be unjustified.

*b.* Some have taken the tradition that "Moses wrote the Pentateuch" to mean that everything in it was given to Moses so directly by God that to raise the question of sources is unnecessary and even irreverent. This is not the case. It confuses the important difference between revelation and inspiration. As far as facts of history which were available to him are concerned, Moses did not need a special divine revelation. He needed only the guidance and illumination (inspiration) of the Holy Spirit to enable him to ascertain the facts and record them correctly. Moses doubtless knew the oral traditions current in his day; and he may also have had access to written documents of great antiquity. We may well believe that he made such use of them as was appropriate and necessary. We have no reason to think that God made known to Moses by special revelation facts which he could readily ascertain by ordinary means.

c. Whether the words, "Moses wrote the Pentateuch," will permit us to recognize the presence of any post-Mosaic additions to it is a matter which has been much discussed. Long before the rise of the higher criticism the claim was made that there are anachronisms in the Pentateuch. These anachronisms were regarded by some writers, e.g., sceptics like Hobbes and Spinoza, as proving the Pentateuch to be post-Mosaic. Some defenders of the Mosaic authorship have held that these alleged anachronisms are in the nature of editorial additions made by Ezra or some other inspired man, and that this is not incompatible with the view that the Pentateuch is substantially and essentially Mosaic.[15] Others have emphatically denied that there are any proved anachronisms in the Pentateuch. They claim that such alleged anachronisms as "Dan" (Gen. xiv.14), "beyond the river," "the Canaanite was then in the land," "before there reigned a king in Israel," were satisfactorily explained by Carpzov, Witsius, and others, several centuries ago and that subsequent research has discovered no new ones.[16]

Until the presence of post-Mosaic elements in the Pentateuch is established beyond reasonable doubt, the question whether their presence in it is compatible with its essential Mosaicity is a rather academic one. Certainly all would agree that to assert that Moses wrote the Pentateuch and at the same time admit that there is any considerable post-Mosaic material in it would be quite inconsistent. The Pentateuch cannot be both Mosaic and non-Mosaic. It is to be noted, therefore, that the great argument for the late date of the Pentateuch, according to the critics of today, does not consist in such alleged anachronisms as the ones mentioned above. These are all made use of. But the greatest anachronism of all is, they tell us, the entire Mosaic law which they hold to have been practically unknown, because practically non-existent, until centuries after the time of Moses. This amounts to saying that we should no longer speak of "the law and the prophets" (e.g., Mt. xxii.40), but rather of "the prophets and the law." For if this view is correct the "law of Moses" did not precede by many centuries, but was itself later than, the golden age of prophecy. Such a view makes it quite impossible to speak of the Pentateuch as Mosaic. Consequently this question of the law is the great issue between the critics and those who believe that Moses wrote the Pentateuch.

## II. The Higher Critical Theory of the Origin of the Pentateuch

The history of the higher critical theory of the origin of the Pentateuch is a long and complicated one, and much has been written upon it.[17] But it is generally recognized that there are three main steps or stadia to be distinguished in it.

### 1. The Documentary Hypothesis of Astruc, Eichhorn, and Hupfeld

#### a. As Proposed by Astruc and Eichhorn

In 1753 a French physician by the name of Astruc made an attempt to analyze the Book of Genesis into two main documents (an Elohist and a Jehovist) primarily on the basis of the variations in the use of the divine names *Elohim* (God) and *Jehovah* (AV, "Lord") which occur in it.[18] While distinguishing sources in the book, Astruc did not deny that Moses was its author. On the contrary he argued for the Mosaic authorship. Eichhorn has been called "the father of the higher criticism." His source analysis and his attitude toward the Mosaic authorship of Genesis was in 1787 and in 1803 much the same as Astruc's. Neither of them carried the documentary analysis beyond the early chapters of Exodus. But a couple of years later (1805) De Wette challenged the Mosaic authorship of the Pentateuch and assigned Deuteronomy to the time of Josiah.[19] This precipitated an animated controversy and a number of writers came forward in defense of the traditional view. In 1823 Eichhorn no longer insisted upon the Mosaic authorship of the Pentateuch.[20] And the extension of the source analysis to Joshua by Bleek (1822) and others served to confirm the critics in the conclusion that the Pentateuch could not be the work of Moses. For obviously if the sources of which it was composed extended into the post-Mosaic period, Moses could not have been the author of the Pentateuch. This left it an open question how much of the source material could be attributed to him.

Acceptance of the view that the Book of Genesis and the Pentateuch as a whole is composite necessarily raised the question as to the nature of the sources of which it is composed. The original theory as proposed by Astruc and elaborated by Eichhorn was, as we have seen, a two-document theory since only two main sources were recognized by them.[21] Several other theories were subsequently proposed, the most important of which are known as the Fragment, the Crystallization, and the Supplementary, Hypotheses. While of interest to the student of the history of the higher critical movement, they need not be discussed here, since the hypothesis generally accepted today is directly related to the Documentary Hypothesis of Astruc and Eichhorn. Aside from the extension of this hypothesis to the entire Pentateuch and Joshua, two important steps are to be noted. The first was proposed by Hupfeld, the second is usually associated with the names of Graf and Wellhausen, especially the latter.

### b. Hupfeld's Modified Documentary Hypothesis

In 1853, just a century after the appearance of Astruc's book, Hupfeld proposed an important modification of the documentary hypothesis.[22] He stressed three points which are of great importance:

(1) The Composite Character of the Elohist. Hupfeld maintained as against Astruc and Eichhorn that there are two Elohistic documents in Genesis. The first he called the *Urschrift* (basic document). In the first 19 chapters of Genesis his *Urschrift* is much the same as the Elohist of Astruc and Eichhorn. Astruc assigned to it 164 verses, Eichhorn 176, Hupfeld 184. But with chapter xx. according to Hupfeld a second or "younger" Elohist begins. To this document Hupfeld gave much of the material regarded by Astruc and Eichhorn as Elohistic. In fact he assigned to his *Urschrift* less than 100 verses in chapters xx.-l.

(2) The Continuity of the Several Documents. Hupfeld held that the most convincing evidence of the correctness of the Documentary Hypothesis was to be found in the proof of the continuity of the several documents. Consequently he regarded it as a major objective of criticism to establish a connection between the various parts of these three documents.

(3) The Redactor. Hupfeld attached great importance to the rôle of the redactor who combined the sources. He pointed out that sometimes the redactor showed the utmost fidelity in dealing with the sources, preserving their exact phraseology with meticulous care, while at other times he exercised the rights and duties of an editor and made such changes in them as he deemed advisable.[23]

These three points were generally accepted by the critics and have long been recognized as basic principles of the documentary analysis. With regard to the relative order of the sources Hupfeld's theory of two Elohists made little change. It had been customary to regard the Elohist as the earlier of the documents and to assign it to the time of the United Monarchy. Hupfeld simply subdivided the Elohist. Consequently his relative order was the following:

HUPFELD'S ARRANGEMENT OF THE DOCUMENTS
First Elohist *(Urschrift)*
Second Elohist
Jehovist
Deuteronomist

With regard to this sequence it is especially important to observe that the generally accepted view that the priestly legislation of the middle books of the Pentateuch (Ex.-Num.) was Elohistic was not affected by Hupfeld's theory of two Elohists, since he assigned this legislation to his *Urschrift*.

## 2. *The Development or Graf-Wellhausen Hypothesis*

The second important modification of the Documentary Hypothesis was proposed about a decade after the appearance of Hupfeld's epoch-making work. It accepted Hupfeld's claim that there are two Elohists. But it proposed a radical change in the order of the sources. It was asserted by Graf (1865) and Wellhausen (1878) that according to the historical and prophetical books of the Old Testament the priestly legislation of the middle books of the Pentateuch was unknown in pre-exilic time, and that this legislation must therefore be a late development. This seemed to necessitate the conclusion that the First Elohist *(Urschrift)* which contained this legislation, instead of being the earliest of the Pentateuchal documents must be regarded as the latest. This change was so drastic that it has been called a "Copernican revolution." But despite its radical nature, it soon gained general acceptance in critical circles. Since the late dating of the priestly legislation made the names *Urschrift* and *First Elohist* inappropriate for the document to which it belonged, the symbol P (priestly document) came to be generally used to describe it and E was used for the *Second Elohist*. So according to the Graf-Wellhausen school, the order of the documents is the following:

THE GRAF-WELLHAUSEN REARRANGEMENT OF THE SOURCES
J (the Jehovist)
E (the Second Elohist)
D (the Deuteronomist)
P (the First Elohist, Hupfeld's *Urschrift*)[24]

This hypothesis aside from minor variations is the one most widely accepted among those who deny that the Pentateuch is Mosaic. While the Development Hypothesis is in a sense only a modification of the Documentary Hypothesis, the two can very properly be considered separately because the Documentary Hypothesis preceded the Development Hypothesis in point of time and also because the questions as to the extent of the documents and as their relative order and date, while closely related, are also in a sense quite distinct. The extent of the documents is determined primarily by a study of their diction, style, and subject-matter. Their relative order and date is determined by ascertaining the period in the actual course of Israel's history which accords most fully with the customs, beliefs, institutions, and laws, which they describe, assume, enjoin, and enforce; and by events to which they refer. Broadly speaking then, the one subject is mainly literary, the other mainly historical.

PART I

THE DOCUMENTARY HYPOTHESIS

". . . the Scripture cannot be broken . . ."
(JOHN x.35)

# THE DOCUMENTARY HYPOTHESIS

SINCE THE SOURCE ANALYSIS of the Pentateuch has been governed from the time of Hupfeld to the present by the general principles which he formulated nearly a century ago, it is not necessary for us to consider the subsequent history in detail. Probably no presentation of this theory has enjoyed wider popularity than that given in Driver's *Introduction to the Literature of the Old Testament*. And since Driver accepted Hupfeld's modification of the Documentary Hypothesis, it will suffice if we contrast this three-document theory of Hupfeld, as set forth by Driver in his *Introduction*,[1] with the two-document theory of Astruc and Eichhorn.[2] By so doing the drastic character of the change which Hupfeld made in it will become evident. The following points are to be noted:

1. The claim that the First Elohist (P) has a distinctive style is constantly stressed today. It is recognized that the Second Elohist (E) which begins at chapter xx. (or at xv.) resembles the Jehovist (J) much more closely than it does the First Elohist, and that the analysis of JE into its component parts may be difficult or even impossible. In Gen. i-xix. there is no important difference between Hupfeld's *Urschrift* and Driver's P. Both assign about 185 verses to P. In the rest of Genesis Hupfeld gave only about 85 verses to P, while Driver's P has more than twice that number. The result, in terms of Driver's analysis, for chaps. xx.-l. is this: P (First Elohist) 175, E (Second Elohist) 361, J (Jehovist) 500. According to these figures, the two Elohists (P and E) taken together are less extensive in these chapters than the one Elohistic document as defined by Astruc and Eichhorn; and the Second Elohist which resembles J is twice as extensive as the First Elohist which

has a distinctive style. This is especially noteworthy for it means that the distinctive style of the Elohist can be recognized only in a comparatively small part, about one-sixth, of the last 31 chapters of Genesis.

2. The attempt to establish the continuity of the documents has led to great emphasis on the theory of doublets, i.e., allegedly parallel and conflicting accounts of the same event. For the JE analysis variations in the subject-matter are especially stressed, and are considered fully as important for the analysis as are variations in phraseology. In many instances they are regarded as furnishing the principal clue, in some cases the only clue, to the analysis.

3. The indispensability of the redactor to the working out of the theory has become increasingly clear; and the two-sidedness of the rôle assigned to him appears again and again. When appeal is made to the exact phrasing of a passage as indicative that it belongs, let us say, to P, this presupposes that the redactor has copied this source, at least at this point, with meticulous care. On the other hand, the attributing to the redactor of the traces of J or E, which the critic finds in a passage which he wishes to assign to P, can only be justified on the assumption that the redactor made changes in his sources when he deemed it advisable to do so.

When we proceed to examine the evidence which is appealed to in support of the Documentary Hypothesis we find that there are four main points to be considered:

1. The Variations in the Divine Names in Genesis;
2. The Secondary Variations in Diction and Style;
3. The Parallel or Duplicate Accounts (Doublets);
4. The Continuity of the Various Sources.

The first two of these topics have to do primarily with questions of diction and style, and the last two deal more especially with the content or subject-matter.

# CHAPTER I

# THE VARIATIONS IN THE DIVINE NAMES

THE VARIATIONS now to be considered are of prime importance in the study of the Documentary Hypothesis because they supplied the key to this modern theory regarding the Pentateuch. But aside from that the variations are noteworthy in themselves and are calculated to attract the attention of any thoughtful reader. That *Elohim* occurs 33 times in the first 34 verses of Genesis and is followed by *Jehovah Elohim* 20 times in the next 45 verses, and then by *Jehovah* 10 times in the 25 verses which follow is a remarkable fact, so noticeable that it demands explanation. Several matters are to be noted with regard to it.

## 1. Very Marked Variation Is Rare

Such marked variation in the use of the divine names as occurs in the opening chapters of Genesis is rare.[3] The divine names do not occur sufficiently frequently in the Book of Genesis to form the basis of a detailed analysis of the entire book.[4] There are four chapters in which the Deity is not mentioned.[5] In the last twenty chapters the name *Jehovah* occurs only 15 times, 11 of which are found in two chapters.[6] Yet J passages or traces of J are found in all of the twenty. *Elohim* does not occur in 15 chapters, and only once in each of 7 others.[7] Yet one of these chapters (xxiii.) is assigned as a whole to P and portions of twelve of the others. In the last 30 chapters of Genesis *Elohim* occurs 85 times, of which only 10 (or 11) are assigned to P. Of these, half occur in a single passage (xxxv.9-13, 15), the others being xxi.2*b*, 4, xxiii.6, xxv.11*a*, and xxviii.4.[8] Obviously then, any detailed analysis must be based largely

on other data than the variation in the use of the divine
names.

## 2. The Name Jehovah Elohim

Even more remarkable than the alternation between *Elohim* and *Jehovah* in these opening chapters is the fact already alluded to, that these two names are joined together
20 times in chaps. ii. and iii.[9] This is especially significant
because the combination *Jehovah Elohim* is quite rare, occurring elsewhere in the Pentateuch only once (Ex. ix.30)
and less than 20 times in all the rest of the Old Testament.
This favors the view that there must be a special reason for
the use of this compound name here and that it is to identify *Elohim* as God of creation with *Jehovah* as God of redemption.[10] It is also significant that, while *Jehovah Elohim* occurs 20 times in chaps. ii.4-iii.24, *Elohim* is used 4
times in the conversation between the serpent and the
woman (iii.1-5). This fact favors the view that these names
are sometimes used significantly. The name *Jehovah* would
be quite inappropriate in the mouth of the serpent, the
enemy and seducer of mankind.

## 3. Names May Be Used Significantly

There are a number of instances where the usage seems
clearly due to a preference based on difference in meaning
and application. One of the clearest examples is Gen. ix.26
(J) where *Jehovah* is declared to be the God of Shem,
while it is stated that *Elohim* will enlarge Japheth. Similarly we read of "calling on the name of *Jehovah*" (iv.26,
xii.8, xiii.4, xxi.33, xxvi.25, cf. xvi.13—all J) and of altars
erected for the worship of *Jehovah* (viii.20, xii.7, 8, xiii.18,
xxvi.25—all J).[11] These examples do not prove that the
variation can always be regarded as due to the meaning.
But they suffice to show that before the claim is made that
variation in the use of the names is indicative of diversity
of source, care should be taken to determine whether the

variation can properly be explained as due to the difference in the usage of the names based upon their meaning and significance. The tendency of the critics is to ignore this possibility entirely.

### 4. Source Analysis Mutilates the Text

The variations in the occurrence of the divine names are of such a nature that they cannot be made the basis of an extended analysis without drastic mutilation of the text.

*a.* In Gen. vii.16 the words "and *Jehovah* shut him in" follow immediately on the statement "as *Elohim* had commanded him." Ex. iii.4 states that "When *Jehovah* saw that he turned aside to see, *Elohim* called unto him out of the midst of the bush." These statements seem definitely intended, like the use of the compound name *Jehovah Elohim* in Gen. ii., to identify *Jehovah* and *Elohim*. Consequently, short passages, even single verses or parts of verses, have at times to be cut apart or cut out of the context in which they stand because of the divine names which occur in them.

Note especially Gen. v.29; vi.22-vii.1; xix.29; xxi.1-2; xxvii. 27, 28; xxviii.16, 17, 20, 21; xxx.23-24; xxxi.49, 50; Ex. iii.15; vi.2; xiii.16f.; xiv.18f.; xix.3; xx.1f., 21f.; xxiv.11f. If the critics were thoroughly consistent in applying their principles, the mutilation of the text would be even greater than it is. *Elohim* occurs, as we have seen, three times in Gen. iii.1-5 and also in iv.25. If the critics are right in claiming *Elohim* as characteristic of P, these verses should belong to P or to some other Elohistic source.[12] To ignore these variations and assign all of ii.4b-iv.26 to J, as is usually done, is decidedly inconsistent. The same inconsistency is shown in assigning ix.27 to J despite the fact that *Elohim* is used in it.

*b.* The serious mutilation of the text, which results from the attempt to analyze a connected narrative on the basis of the divine names which occur in it, appears especially clearly in the narrative which tells of Jacob's marriages and of the birth of all of his sons, except Benjamin (Gen. xxix.15-xxx.24).

The name *Jehovah* occurs 5 times in this passage, *Elohim* 8 times. *Jehovah* occurs in the account of the birth of the first four of Leah's sons, Reuben, Simeon, Levi, and Judah (xxix. 31-35), *Elohim* in that which speaks of the birth of Dan and Naphtali to Bilhah (xxx.1-8), and of Issachar and Zebulun to Leah (vss. 17-20). Both *Elohim* and *Jehovah* appear in the account of the birth and naming of Joseph (vss. 22-24). This narrative is divided between J, E, and P. Only a very small part is given to P. Consequently P does not record the birth of any sons. E knows that Bilhah had two sons (xxx.6, 8) and that Leah had a fifth and a sixth son (vss. 17-20*a*), but says nothing about the birth of the first four. E also knows that Rachel had a son, but does not know his name (vss. 20*c*-22 [except last clause], 23). J records the birth of four sons of Leah (xxix. 32-35), of two unnamed sons of Bilhah (xxx.3*b*-5, 7), of the two sons of Zilpah (vss. 9-13), and apparently the birth of a fifth son of Leah who is said to make six (vss. 14-16, 20*b*), also the birth to Rachel (?) of a son called Joseph (vss. 22 [last clause], 24). In short, P records the birth of no sons, E of 4 sons, J of 10 sons. Yet the fact that Jacob had 12 sons (including Benjamin, Gen. xxxv.16-20, E) is referred to again and again in the Old Testament and no one knows this better than P (e.g., xxxv.22f.), who records the birth of none of them. It is perfectly plain that what each of the three documents needs to complete it and make it intelligible is exactly what has been cut away and given to the other two. And the defenders of the analysis must either hold that each source originally contained all of this information or that the idea that Jacob had twelve sons was the result of the attempt to combine traditions which were more or less conflicting and contradictory.

## 5. *Exodus vi.3 Is Misinterpreted by Critics*

After Ex. vi.3 the divine names cease to be a criterion for the analysis. The great preponderance of the name *Jehovah* over *Elohim* in the last four books of the Pentateuch makes the conclusion inevitable, either that in Exodus-

Numbers P frequently uses *Jehovah,* or else that P is very scantily represented in these books. The former alternative has been adopted by the critics.

The facts are these. In Genesis the simple names, *Jehovah* and *Elohim,* occur with nearly equal frequency *(Jehovah* 146 times, *Elohim* 164 times). In the rest of the Hexateuch, *Jehovah* occurs about 1,800 times while *Elohim* occurs about 125 times. Yet the bulk of P is found in the middle books of the Pentateuch in which *Jehovah* occurs about 1,000 times and *Elohim* less than 100 times. Consequently the name *Jehovah,* which has been rigorously excluded from P in Genesis, occurs hundreds of times in P in Exodus-Numbers, while *Elohim* which is characteristic of P in Genesis occurs but rarely in that document in these three books. Such an anomaly obviously calls for a satisfactory explanation.

According to the critics the anomaly in P's use of the divine names is fully explained by Ex. vi.3; which may be rendered as follows: "And *Elohim* spake unto Moses and said unto him, I am *Jehovah:* and I appeared unto Abraham, unto Isaac, and unto Jacob, as *El Shaddai* [God Almighty]; but by my name *Jehovah* I was not known to them." This verse definitely asserts, according to the critics, that the writer of P believed that the name Jehovah was first made known to Israel in the time of Moses. Consequently the inference is drawn that he avoided its use up to this point in order to be historically accurate and not guilty of using an anachronism. If this explanation is correct, it must be regarded as giving a reasonable explanation of the apparent anomaly in P's use of the divine names. But there are serious objections to the acceptance of the interpretation placed by the critics on this verse.

*a.* The expression "and they shall know (or, 'that they may know') that I am Jehovah" occurs many times in the Old Testament. It is used frequently in Exodus: of the Israelites (vi.7, x.2, xvi.12, xxix.46, xxxi.13), of the Egyptians (vii.

5, xiv.4, 18) of Pharaoh (vii.17, viii.22); and its use clearly implies that what is meant by "to know Jehovah" is to know and appreciate the nature and character of Jehovah. Certainly it did not require all the plagues of Egypt to convince the Israelites, the Egyptians, and Pharaoh that the God of Israel was called Jehovah. What they needed to know was who Jehovah was. This is confirmed by the fact that in Ezekiel, centuries after the Exodus, this expression is used so often that it is like a refrain.[13] Did the exiles in Babylon need to be told that their God was called Jehovah? Certainly not! "To know Jehovah" meant, for the exiles in Babylon as for the bondsmen in Egypt, to know who Jehovah their God really was. And the implication everywhere is that such knowledge will or should result in obedience to His will.

b. This interpretation is favored by the emphasis placed in Ex. vi.3 on the word "name": "I appeared unto Abraham, unto Isaac and unto Jacob as El Shaddai, but (as, or in) my name Jehovah I was not known unto them." The word "as" apparently means "in the capacity, or nature of." And the force of the preposition may properly be regarded as carrying over to the word "name." The contrast is between "in the capacity of El Shaddai" and "in the capacity of my name, Jehovah." *Name* is clearly the important word. Consequently it is to be noted that in Hebrew a name is more than a mere vocable. Names in the Old Testament are frequently significant. The change of the name Abram to Abraham and of the name Jacob to Israel was intended to mark an important epoch in the lives of these patriarchs. And when the God of Sinai proclaims His name to Moses, He does not stop with the words "Jehovah, Jehovah," but goes on to describe in some detail the character of its Bearer (Ex. xxxiv.6-7) and its implications for Israel. The statement in vs. 14, "for Jehovah, whose name is Jealous, is a jealous God" shows that the name is expressive of the nature. Consequently, the declaration that *Elohim* was not known to the patriarchs in the significance of the name *Jehovah* may properly be taken to mean that the redemptive significance of the name was not known or had not been made clear to them. It was this which the enslaved Israelites needed to know and the deliverance from Egyptian bondage is often referred to as the great illustration of Jehovah's redemptive power.[14]

c. The view that Ex. vi.3 (P) implies that the name Jehovah was known, but rarely used by the patriarchs and relatively meaningless to them, because the great redemptive work of the Exodus which was to make its significance evident had not yet taken place, finds support in the record itself. The use of the divine names in the history of Joseph (Gen. xxxvii., xxxix.-l.) favors such an inference. The Deity is not named in chap. xxxvii. In chap. xxxix. the historian uses *Jehovah* 8 times, but Joseph in vs. 9 uses *Elohim*. In chapters xl.-l., Joseph uses *Elohim* about 20 times, Joseph's brethren use it 3 times, Pharaoh uses it twice. Jacob uses *Elohim* in xlviii.11, 15$^{bis}$, 20, 21, God Almighty *(El Shaddai)* in xliii.14, xlviii.3; *El* alone in xlvi.3 and *El* and *Shaddai* separately in xlix.25. Yet Jacob uses *Jehovah* in xlix.18 in an exclamation, "I have waited for (or await) thy salvation, O Jehovah," which shows that the name was not unknown to him and that perhaps he realized prophetically something of the meaning which would attach to it in future days.[15] Such facts as these are quite in harmony with the view that in the days of the patriarchs and earlier the name *Jehovah* was known and therefore could properly be used by Moses in writing of that period, but had not acquired the importance which was to attach to it in later times.

d. The explanation of this important passage as implying that while the name Jehovah was known to the patriarchs it was perhaps rarely used and its meaning was relatively unknown to them, finds support in the fact that in Scripture a statement is sometimes made in absolute terms in order to bring out and emphasize an important relative truth. "The law was given by Moses, grace and truth came by Jesus Christ" (Jn. i.17) is a familiar illustration of this. In 1 Cor. ix.9f. Paul emphatically denies the primary intent of Deut. xxv.4 (the care of the ox) in the interest of an important secondary implication.[16]

e. The claim of the critics that Ex. vi.3 implies that the name Jehovah was first used in the time of Moses is opposed by the fact that such an interpretation of the words, "I was

not known unto them," is contradicted by other plain statements of Scripture:

(1) The document P is brought into sharp conflict with J
which asserts definitely that God was worshipped by the name
Jehovah even before the Flood (Gen. iv.25), that He revealed
Himself by that name to Abram (xv.7) and Jacob (xxviii.13),
and that Noah (ix.26), Abraham (xv.2, xviii.31, xxii.14, xxiv.
3), Abraham's servant (xxiv.12), Isaac (xxvi.25), Esau (xxvii.
20), Jacob (xxviii.21), Leah (xxix.32f.) and Rachel (xxx.24),
knew Him by that name.[17]

(2) This interpretation also makes P self-contradictory.
We are twice told in P (Ex. vi.20, Num. xxvi.59) that the name
of Moses' mother was Jochebed (which means "Jehovah is
glorious"). Since Moses was eighty years old when he appeared
before Pharaoh (vii.7), this would imply that names compounded with Jehovah were used by the Israelites a century
or more before the name was "known" to them. Otherwise
we should have to assume that the name Jochebed was a new
name given to Moses' mother in her old age and used propleti-
cally in Ex. vi.20. Of this there is not the slightest evidence.

(3) The same contradiction appears in the interpretation
given by the critics to the passage in Ex. iii. which they regard
as giving E's account of the origin of the name Jehovah and
which they claim supports their view that according to the
Elohists the name *Jehovah* was first used in the days of Moses.
Ex. iii. uses *Elohim* frequently. But *Jehovah* occurs 7 times
(vss. 2, 4, 7, 15, 16, 18[bis]). In vss. 2, 4, 7, the language is that
of the writer of the account. But in vss. 15-18 where the words
of *Elohim* are recorded, *Elohim* orders Moses to tell the people
that "Jehovah the God of your fathers, the God of Abraham,
the God of Isaac, and the God of Jacob" has sent him (vs. 15).
This command is amplified in vss. 16-17. Then it is declared that the Israelites will believe it (vs. 18) and that Moses
and the elders are to demand of Pharaoh in the name of "Jehovah, the God of the Hebrews" that he let them go to sacrifice in the desert. This repeated declaration that Jehovah is
the *God of the fathers* is not discredited by the fact that Moses
inquires what name he is to give the God of the patriarchs in
speaking to their enslaved descendants. His question may

mean simply that Moses knew the God of Israel by several names *(El, Elohim, El Shaddai, Elyon, Jehovah)* and did not know which of these names he was to use in speaking to Israel. But the fact is not to be overlooked that Moses was extremely reluctant to undertake the mission assigned him by God. His question may mean that he was playing for time, unwilling to go, unwilling to refuse to go. It may also mean that Moses, like Gideon, wanted additional proof that the One who had described Himself as the *Elohim* of Abraham, Isaac, and Jacob (vs. 6) was really *Jehovah,* and adopted this indirect way of reassuring himself, by suggesting that the people might inquire the name of the Deity who had commissioned him to promise them deliverance. It is especially to be noted that the analysis which is quite generally accepted (it assigns vss. 1, 4*b*, 6, 9-15, 19-22 to E) requires the splitting up of a verse. Vs. 4 reads, "And when *Jehovah* saw that he turned aside to see, *Elohim* called unto him out of the midst of the bush, and said, Moses, Moses. And he said, Here am I." The aim of the writer seems to be unmistakable. It is to indicate that *Jehovah* and *Elohim* are the same. The critics are forced to assign the first clause to J in order to nullify this obvious aim of the writer.[18]

*f.* The above discussion justifies the conclusion that the interpretation of Ex. vi.3 adopted by the critics is not demanded by the verse itself or by other relevant data in Scripture, but is forced upon them by the exigencies of their theory. They can only account for the anomaly in P's use of the names *Elohim* and *Jehovah,* by insisting that Ex. vi.3 means that the name Jehovah was unknown until the time of the Exodus. This is borne out by the history of interpretation. It is a significant fact that Astruc and Eichhorn did not take this view of Ex. vi.3. They were not prepared to deny that Genesis was early or to assert that its author used documents which were contradictory, and they did not carry their analysis beyond the opening chapters of Exodus. It was not until the critics were prepared to insist that Genesis is made up of sources which are late and contradict one another even on important points and that these documents extend through the Pentateuch (and Joshua) that the now popular interpretation of Ex. vi.3 was adopted. For only on the assumption that the author of P re-

garded the use of Jehovah as an anachronism before Ex. vi.3
can they account for his avoidance of it in Genesis and his constant use of it in the rest of his document. And if P was right,
we have of course a flat contradiction between P and J.[19] The
following statement by a prominent critic is significant. He
tells us:

"A signal instance of the gradual way in which God leads His people into
a fuller understanding of His word is afforded by the fact that it is only
in the last 150 years that the attention of students has been arrested by
these verses. How is it that though God here says that up to this point
His name Yahweh has not been known, yet in the Book of Genesis the
patriarchs appear to know it well and use it freely? The question cannot
be answered except by the recognition that varying traditions have been
incorporated from different sources."[20]

The first part of this statement is quite incorrect and decidedly
misleading. Poole's *Synopsis* (1669-74), published nearly a
century before Astruc's work appeared, gives a number of
different interpretations of this passage, and shows clearly that
its difficulties were recognized long before the rise of the higher
criticism.[21] What is significant in the above quotation is this:
it claims for the critics the credit of having made the discovery
that Ex. vi.3 must be interpreted in such a way as to bring it
into irreconcilable conflict with other passages of the Pentateuch and so to necessitate the acceptance of the theory that
the Pentateuch is made up of diverse and mutually contradictory sources. This was the discovery made by the higher critics
regarding the interpretation of this verse. It may seem to be
a rather doubtful tribute to the critics to say that their great
achievement in the interpretation of this verse is one that makes
the Pentateuch self-contradictory. But they claim the honor
of having made this discovery.

## 6. Variations Occur after Exodus vi.3

Despite the fact that according to the theory of the critics
variation in the use of the names *Jehovah* and *Elohim*
ceases at Ex. vi.3 to be significant for the analysis, it is to be
noted that variations in the use of the divine names strikingly similar to those found before Ex. vi.3 do occur occasionally beyond that point in Exodus.

*a.* A striking example is furnished by Ex. xviii. Verse 1 reads as follows: "Now Jethro, the priest of Midian, Moses' father-in-law, heard of all that *Elohim* had done for Moses, and for Israel his people, how that *Jehovah* had brought Israel out of Egypt." In the rest of the chapter, *Elohim* occurs 5 times without the article and 5 times with it; and *Jehovah* also occurs 5 times. Yet the critics usually assign Ex. xviii. as a whole to E, making little effort to find other sources in it.

*b.* In the Balaam story (Num. xxii.-xxiv.) *Elohim* is used 10 times,[22] *Jehovah* 19. These chapters are assigned to JE and since E according to the critics was aware that the name *Jehovah* was known in the time of Moses, some other explanation must be found for the variation in these chapters than for similar variations which occur before Ex. iii.15 and vi.3.[23]

## 7. Similar Variations Occur Elsewhere in Old Testament

It is especially to be noted that such variation as we find in the use of the divine names in Genesis is not at all a unique phenomenon in the Old Testament.[24] Many examples can be cited of variation in the use of proper names. In some cases the reason for the variation is simple and obvious. In others it is not. These variations fall into two classes:

*a.* Cases where a Change of Name is announced or referred to:

(1) The change in the names of Abram and Sarai to Abraham and Sarah is announced (xvii.5, 15) and the change is at once made. Here no difficulty arises.

(2) The change of Jacob's name to Israel is announced twice. Yet neither after the first announcement nor after the second is the new name employed uniformly. Why this is the case we do not know. But the significant fact is that the documentary analysis based primarily on the divine names does not account for or accord with the variations in the use of the two names of the patriarch. J announces the change in xxxii.28 and then proceeds to use both names (e.g., xxxiii.1; xxxv.21). P announces it in

xxxv.10; yet with one exception (xlvi.8) continues to use Jacob exclusively. E which knows nothing of the change of name uses both; and it does this after it has been announced by both J and P (e.g., xxxv.5; xlvi.2).[25]

(3) We have a somewhat similar instance in the case of Gideon, who received the sobriquet Jerubbaal. The origin of the name *Jerubbaal* is stated in Judg. vi.32. But the name Gideon is almost exclusively used in chaps. vii. and viii., while *Jerubbaal* is used exclusively in chap. ix.[26] The facts are obvious. The explanation is not.

*b.* Cases where no Explanation of the Variations is given:

(1) The king of Egypt is usually called "Pharaoh" in the Pentateuch, only rarely is he referred to as "the king of Egypt" (11 times), still more rarely as "Pharaoh king of Egypt" (8 times). In Ex. i.11 (J) it is "Pharaoh"; in iii.18 (also J) it is "king of Egypt"; in v.1, 2, 4 (E), "Pharaoh" occurs twice (vss. 1, 2), "king of Egypt" once (vs. 4); in i.15-22 (E, except vs. 20*b*), "king of Egypt" occurs 3 times (vss. 15, 17, 18), "Pharaoh" twice (vss. 19, 22); in vi.2-vii.13 (P), "Pharaoh" occurs 12 times, "Pharaoh king of Egypt" 4 times. Here we have in J, E, and P variety in the course of the same document, despite the fact that variety in phraseology is supposed to indicate diversity of source.[27]

(2) Similar examples occur outside the Pentateuch, in the use of two different names for the same king, or of two different spellings of the same name: (*a*) The son of Amaziah is called both *Azariah* and *Uzziah* in 2 Kgs. xiv.-xv. (b) The son of Jehoram of Judah is called *Ahaziah* in Kings (16 times) and in 2 Chr. xxii. (9 times); in 2 Chr. xxi.17, xxv.23 he is called *Jehoahaz*. (*c*) The son of Jehoiakim is called *Jehoiachin* (twice), *Jeconiah* (4 times), *Coniah* (3 times), all in Jeremiah, it being assumed that the reader will understand. (*d*) The name of Tiglath-pileser is mentioned three times in 2 Kgs. xv.-xvi.; in chap. xv. he is twice called *Pul*. (*e*) The name of Saul's eldest son occurs 25 times in 1 Sam. xiv. It is usually

spelled *Jonathan*, but in vss. 6, 8 the longer form *Jehonathan* is used. In chap. xix.1-7, the longer form occurs 7 times, the shorter once. (*f*) In Kings, the son of Jehoshaphat of Judah is called *Joram* (4 times) and *Jehoram* (5 times); the son of Ahab of Israel is usually called *Joram* (16 times) but also *Jehoram* (4 times). (*g*) In 2 Kgs. xi.-xiv., the son of Ahaziah of Judah is called *Joash* (8 times) and *Jehoash* (8 times), while the son of Jehoahaz of Israel is called *Joash* (9 times) and *Jehoash* (9 times). (*h*) In Jer. xxxv. the son of Rechab is called *Jehonadab* in vss. 8, 14, 16, 18, and *Jonadab* in vss. 6, 10, 19. (*i*) The name of king Hezekiah is spelled three different ways in 2 Kgs. (*j*) Jeremiah usually calls the greatest of the kings of Babylon Nebuchad*r*ezzar; occasionally the name is spelled Nebuchad*n*ezzar as elsewhere (except Ezek.). Since such variations as the above could easily have been avoided, they indicate clearly that the writers of Old Testament history regarded them as not only permissible but desirable, even though they are at times confusing to the modern reader.

### 8. Variations Admit of Several Explanations

While the fact of the occurrence of such variations as we have been considering is perfectly obvious, the reason is not always so obvious; and various explanations may be given.

*a*. Variety in the use of names avoids the monotony of identical repetition. The use of the expressions "house of Jehovah" and "house of God" in 1 and 2 Chr. is a particularly good example of this. The former occurs about 100 times, the latter about one-third as often. There are 8 verses in which both expressions occur: e.g., 2 Chr. xxiv.7, "For the sons of Athaliah, that wicked woman, had broken up the house of God [the *Elohim*]; and also all the dedicated things of the house of Jehovah did they bestow upon Baalim" (cf. 2 Chr. xxviii.24). It does not seem that any more probable explanation of such variations can be given than the desire to avoid monotony, although here the word "Jehovah" may perhaps be emphatic.

*b.* In 1 Sam. iii.3 we read of ". . . the lamp of God . . . in the temple of Jehovah, where the ark of God *was.*" In chaps. iv.-vi. the expressions occur, "ark of the covenant of Jehovah (of hosts) . . . ark of the covenant of God . . . ark of God . . . ark of Jehovah . . . ark of the God of Israel," etc. Whether there is any intention in these passages to identify Jehovah as the God of Israel, or whether variety is the main or only object is not clear.

*c.* In some cases the use of a variety of names seems clearly intended to bring out various aspects and relations of the Deity. (1) In 2 Sam. vii. the Deity is mentioned about 25 times. Six different words or combinations are used: Elohim, the Elohim, Jehovah, Jehovah of hosts, Lord Jehovah, and Jehovah Elohim. These variations in a prose passage are very interesting. (2) Such variety is more common in poetry. Eight names are used in Ps. lxxviii., several of which are unusual: "Most High," "God Most High," "Holy One of Israel." In Ps. lxviii. "God" (Elohim) is used 23 times, and along with it 7 other designations are used which justifies the remark that "the whole cornucopia of divine names has been poured out upon it."[28]

*d.* On the other hand, while exact and frequent repetition may become monotonous, it may also be impressive and emphatic. (1) The great theme of Gen. i. is "God the Creator of all." The constant repetition of the one word *Elohim* (32 times) tends to impress this primary emphasis upon the mind of the reader.[29] (2) This is even more true of the occurrences of *Jehovah Elohim* in Gen. ii.4-iii.24. Had the combined name been used only in ii.4 and Jehovah appeared alone in the rest of chapters ii. and iii., the intention of the writer to identify *Jehovah* with *Elohim* would have been clearly indicated. But the use of it twenty times serves to emphasize this important fact.

*e.* It is also to be recognized that there is a quite evident tendency in Scripture for a given expression to become stereotyped. Of this we find some striking illustrations.

Two of the best and most familiar, despite the fact that neither occurs in Genesis, are the titles "man of God" and "servant of Jehovah."

(1) "Man of God (*Elohim*)" occurs about 75 times in the Old Testament: "man of Jehovah" never occurs. This perhaps accounts for the fact that while "Jehovah" occurs 18 times in 1 Kgs. xiii., the prophet is called as usual "man of God" (14 times) not "man of Jehovah." Note such a statement as 2 Chr. xi.2, "But the word of *Jehovah* came to Shemaiah the man of *Elohim*, saying" (cf. 1 Kgs. xiii.5, xvii.24; but 1 Kgs. xii.22 has "word of *Elohim*"). Moses is called "the man of *Elohim*" (5 times), as also is David (twice).

(2) "Servant of Jehovah" occurs less frequently than "man of God." It is used of Moses (19 times), but also of Joshua (Jgs. ii.8) and of David (in the titles of Pss. xviii. and xxxvi.). "Servant of God [*Elohim*]" is used only twice, both times of Moses (Neh. x.29, Dan. ix.11).

(3) "Angel of Jehovah" is much more frequent in the Old Testament than "angel of Elohim" (about 5 to 1). This may account for the fact that in Gen. xxii. "angel of Jehovah" is used in both vss. 11 and 15, despite the fact that Elohim occurs 5 times in vss. 1-12.[30] It is noteworthy that while "Elohim" (or *El*) and "Jehovah" occur with almost equal frequency in Num. xxii.-xxiv., "angel of Jehovah" occurs 10 times in this passage, while "angel of Elohim" does not occur at all.

(4) Lord Jehovah (*Adonai Yahweh*) occurs 293 times in the Old Testament. The title is an old one occurring already in Gen. xv.2*a*, 8 (J?). But it is found most frequently in Ezekiel. It occurs there 217 times which makes it Ezekiel's favorite designation of the Deity. The reason for this is apparently to be found in the fact that this name is used in the passage which describes Ezekiel's call: "And thou shalt say unto them, Thus saith the Lord Jehovah" (ii.4, iii.11, 27). This is a natural and sufficient explanation of its frequency in Ezekiel. But Ezekiel does not use it to the exclusion of other names, of which he uses eight. A frequent expression on the lips of the prophets was this: "And the word of Jehovah came (was) unto me saying." Ezekiel uses this expression

about 40 times and in the usual form, "word of Jehovah"; he does not once use "word of the Lord Jehovah." The same is true of the expression, "ye (they) shall know that I am Jehovah," which occurs 60 times in Ezekiel. This expression goes back to early times (e.g., Ex. vii.17 J); and here also Ezekiel uses the ordinary form: he does not say "that I am the Lord Jehovah." But in the case of another expression, "saith Jehovah" (lit., "utterance [*neum*] of Jehovah"), which occurs about 80 times, Ezekiel almost always uses his favorite title and says "saith the Lord Jehovah."

(5) "Holy One of Israel" occurs 31 times in the O.T. It is largely confined to the Book of Isaiah (25 times). Yet "Holy One of Jacob" occurs in Isa. xxix.23; and nowhere else in the Bible.

Such examples as the above show how difficult it is to account for, and how impossible it is to predict the exact form of a passage in cases where there is no hard and fast rule to determine good usage, but two or more equally valid principles may apply.

## 9. *The Appeal to the Redactor*

Finally, it is to be noted that what cannot but be regarded as a major defect of the critical analysis appears already quite plainly in connection with the use of the divine names: it cannot be carried through without appeal to a redactor or redactors. This means that where simple, even if hair-splitting, partitioning of the text will not give the source analysis desired by the critics, it is alleged that a redactor has altered or edited the sources. If *Jehovah* is regarded as the name of Deity characteristic of J, the addition of *Elohim* in the title *Jehovah Elohim* in Gen. ii.4b-iii.24 has to be attributed to a redactor.[31] The occurrence of *Elohim* in J (iv.25, vii.9, ix.27), of *Jehovah* in P (xvii.1, xxi.1b) and in E (xx.18, xxviii.21), of *El Shaddai* in xliii.14 (J or E), and of "angel of Jehovah" in xxii.11 (E), being quite contrary to the theory, has to be explained as due to the redactor who in these instances altered the sources which elsewhere he is supposed to have combined without change. For if chap. xvii is to be assigned as a whole to P, the fact that it begins with the words, "And when Abram was ninety and nine years old, *Jehovah* appeared unto Abram," must be regarded as a serious blunder of the redactor, since P could not have used "Jehovah." If the second part of xxi.1 "And *Jehovah* did unto Sarah as he had spoken" is P, the redactor must have made a "slip of the pen." If xxviii.20-22 is E, the words "then shall *Jehovah* be my God" must be a gloss or interpolation. Whenever the theory will not work the critic has recourse to the vagaries of this unknown and purely hypothetical redactor (R) who must bear the blame. It is to be noted, therefore, that every appeal to the redactor is a tacit admission on the part of the critics that their theory breaks down at that point.[32]

In view of the difficulties with which the attempt to analyze Genesis, or the Pentateuch as a whole, on the basis of the primary criteria, the names *Jehovah* and *Elohim,* is confronted, it is not to be wondered at that the advocates of this theory attach great importance to other indications of composite authorship. We pass on therefore to the consideration of the secondary criteria.

# CHAPTER II

# THE SECONDARY VARIATIONS IN DICTION AND STYLE

IT FOLLOWS from the fact of the infrequent occurrence of the divine names, *Elohim* and *Jehovah,* in the greater part of Genesis and from the further fact that this variation ceases to have value for the analysis after Ex. vi.3, that very much of the analysis of the Pentateuch must be based by the critics on other data. If we examine the two passages, Gen. i.1-ii.4*a* and ii.4*b*-iv.26, which for convenience we shall call Section I and Section II, and if, regarding them as being respectively the first Elohistic (P) and Jehovistic (J) passages, we compare them with a view to determining and explaining their differences of diction, we observe at once that the difference is marked. Some words are common to both, but a large number of words occurs only in one. It would be easy to jump to the conclusion that a careful tabulation of all the words in three groups— those found in both Sections, those found only in Section I, those found only in Section II—would lead at once to the solution of the problem. But we do not have to carry our investigation far to convince ourselves that an analysis based simply on words will be arbitrary and misleading unless due regard is paid to the subject-matter of the passage in which they occur.

The two accounts of creation given in these two Sections are in no respect contradictory.[33] But they differ in many ways. The account in Section I is cosmic. It tells of the creation of the universe. It speaks of heaven, a firmament, luminaries, stars, seas, dry land, sea animals, birds, land animals and mankind (generic man, male and female). Section II describes the planting of a garden to be the abode of man, the forming of one man, and of one woman from the man, of a probation and fall, of expulsion from the garden, of sacrifice, of murder and its results. Obviously the subject-matter differs considerably. The fact that the negative particle *lo* (no, not) occurs 13 times in Section II, and never in Section I, is wholly due to the subject-matter. The word occurs scores of times in P as in J. "Stars" are not necessarily characteristic of P because mentioned only in Section I. They are referred to in the Pentateuch only 11 times; and all of the remaining 10 occurrences are assigned to JE or D, not one of them to P. Section II mentions the "offering" *(minchah)* of Abel. Elsewhere in Genesis this word is used only of a "present" to men. Yet *minchah* is the technical word for "meal-offering" in P.[34] Death is not referred to in Section I. "Die" occurs 3 times in Section II (ii.17, iii.3, 4). Yet chap. v. with its mournful refrain "and he died" (8 times, cf. ix.29) is referred to P (except vs. 29). "Cherubim" are referred to once in Section II (iii.24). The other 18 occurrences in the Pentateuch are all P. Such examples as these show that, as it is to be expected, the subject-matter of a passage largely determines its phraseology. The failure of a word to occur in a given passage is significant only if the subject-matter makes its use either natural or necessary, and its non-use of especial significance. With this in mind we proceed to examine some of the words and groups of words which appear in these two Sections.

## I. THE VOCABULARIES OF SECTION I AND II

*1. Verbs of Making*

    *a. Asah* (make, do), 10 times in Section I, 8 times in Section II, and frequently elsewhere; cannot be regarded as characteristic of any one document or period.

    *b. Banah* (build, make), only in Section II (ii.22, iv.17). Elsewhere in Gen. 14 times: all J, except two, E (xxii. 9, xxxv.7). All or most of the 15 occurrences in Ex. and Nu. are E, or JE. (According to some critics, one or all of 5 occurrences in Num. xxxii. are P.) Also found 10 times in Deut. (usually D).

*c. Bara* (create), seven times in Section I (i.1, 21, 27*ter*; ii.3, 4*a*), also in v.1, 2 (P); vi.7 (J); and elsewhere in Pent. only Ex. xxxiv.10 (RJE) and Deut. iv.32 (a reference to the creation of man).

*d. Yatsar* (form), in Section II (ii.7, 8, 19) but nowhere else in the Pentateuch; a noun from this root occurs in J (vi.5, viii.21) and in Deut. xxxi.21.

### 2. Verbs of Putting, Placing, Setting, Appointing

*a. Nathan* (in sense of "set"), once in Section I (i.17). Elsewhere in Pent. Gen. ix.13 (P), xviii.18 and xxx.40 (J), xli.41 (E), Ex. (5 times, P), Lev. (6 times, P or H), Deut. (10 times).

*b. Nuach* (in causative stem [*hiphil*], put; literally, cause to rest), once in Section II (ii.15), also xix.16 (J), Lev. xxiv.12 (H), Nu. xv.34 (P).

*c. Sim* (put, set, appoint), twice in Section II (ii.8, iv.15); in rest of Gen. J or E (about 45 times), P (vi.16).

*d. Shith* (set, put, appoint), twice in Section II (iii.15, iv.25), elsewhere in Pent. (16 times) either J (e.g., Ex. vii.23, x.1) or E (e.g., Ex. xxi.22, 30) or JE.

### 3. Verbs of Dividing

*a. Badal,* 5 times in Section I (i.4, 6, 7, 14, 18), nowhere else in Gen.; 11 times in Ex., Lev., Num. (all P), 5 times in Deut. (D).

*b. Parad,* once in Section II (ii.10), elsewhere P (x.5, 22, xiii.11*b*), J (xiii.9, 14 [?], xxv.23, xxx.40) and Dt. xxxii.8.

### 4. Verbs of Ruling

*a. Mashal,* once in Section I (i.18, cf. vs. 16), twice in Section II (iii.16, iv.7); also J (xxiv.2), E (xxxvii.8, xlv.8, 26, Ex. xxi.8), and Dt. xv.6.

*b. Radah,* twice in Section I (i.26, 28), and also P or H (4 times in Lev.), JE (Nu. xxiv.19).

### 5. Verbs of Increase

The combination, "be fruitful (*parah*) and multiply (*rabah*) and fill (*male*)" occurs in Section I (i.22, 28) and also ix.1. "Be fruitful and multiply, bring forth abundantly (*sharats*)" occurs in ix.7 and in different form in viii.17 and Ex. i.7. "Be (make) fruitful and multiply" occurs alone or in other combinations in Gen. xvii.20, xxviii.3, xxxv.11, xlvii.27*b*, xlviii.4, Lev. xxvi.9. All are assigned to P, though the phrasing except in i.22, 28 and ix.1 is never twice exactly the same. Note, therefore, that these four verbs all occur elsewhere in Genesis outside of P:

*a. Parah* (be fruitful), in P (xvii.6), J (xxvi.22), E (xli.52).

*b. Rabah* (multiply), in J (vii.17*b* + 10 times), P (vii.3 + 4 times), E (xv.1*b*, xli.49).

*c. Male* (fill, replenish), P (vi.11, 13), J (xxv.24, l.3), E (xxix.21).

*d. Sharats* (bring forth abundantly, creep): (1) Verb, in Section I (i.20, 21) also P (vii.21, viii.17, ix.7, Ex. i.7, Lev. xi. [5 times]), J (Ex. viii.3);

(2) Noun, in Section I (Gen. i.20), P (vii.21, Lev. [12 times]), Deut. xiv.19 (D).

### 6. Verbs of Speaking

*a. Amar* (say) and *qara* (call) occur frequently in both Sections and in all documents of Pent.

*b. Dabar* (speak), first in viii.15, (P), often found in P, J, E, and D. The phrase "spake saying" occurs in P (viii.15, xvii.3, xxiii.3, 8, 13, [xxxiv.8, 20]), in J (xxxix.17, 19, l.4), in E ([xxxiv.8, 20], xli.9, xlii.14).

*c. Tsawah* (command), 3 times in Section II; elsewhere in Gen P (vi.22, vii.16a + 5 times), J (vii.5, 9 + 7 times), E (xxxii.17 + 5 times).

*d. Barak* (bless), 3 times in Section I, elsewhere in Gen. P (v.2, vii.20, ix.1 *et pass.*), J (xii.2, 3, xxiv. [6 times], xxvii. [12 times, J or E?]).

*e. Arar* (curse), 3 times in Section II, 6 times elsewhere in Genesis; all J or JE; but v. 29 is cut out of a P context.

*f. Tsaaq* (cry out), once in Section II (iv.10), elsewhere in Pent., J (4 times), E (7 times), JE (twice), D (3 times), P (once, Ex. xiv.15, unless the words, "wherefore criest thou unto me" are cut out of the P Section [vss. 15-18] and given to E).

### 7. The Two Forms of the Pronoun "I"

*a. Anoki,* Section II (iii.10, iv.9). Of the 55 occurrences in Genesis, 35 are J., 18 are E, 1 is P (xxiii.4), xv.14 is J, E, or R.

*b. Ani,* first in vi.17 (P). Of the 40 occurrences in Genesis, 15 are J, 17 are E, 7 are P and 1 is in Gen. xiv., which the critics assign to an independent source.

### 8. Words of Resemblance

*a. Demuth* (likeness), Section I (vs. 26) and v.1, 3 (P), nowhere else in Pent.

*b. Tselem* (image), Section I (vss. 26, 27) also in v.3, ix.6 and Nu. xxxiii. 52, all P.

*c. Ke negdo* (meet for him, i.e., corresponding to him, his counterpart), Section II (ii.18, 20), nowhere else in this sense.

### 9. Words for Land, Earth, etc.

*a. Erets* (the most usual word), 22 times in Section I, 10 times in Section II, characteristic of neither.

*b. Adamah* (ground, or earth), Section I (i.25), Section II (14 times), 28 times in rest of Gen., all of which are given to J (or E) except P (vi.20, ix.2).

*c. Yabbashah* (dry ground), Section I (i.9, 10), not elsewhere in Gen.; in Ex. 5 times, P (xiv.16, 22, 29, xv.19), J (iv.9). Another word for "dry ground" *(charabah)* occurs in J (Gen. vii.22, Ex. xiv.21b).

*d. Sadeh* (field), Section II (seven times), elsewhere in Gen. J (xxiv. 63, 65, xxv.27, 29), P (xxiii. [8 times], xxv.9, 10), also xiv.7.

*e. Gan* (garden), Section II (12 times), also Gen. xiii.10 (J), elsewhere only Deut. xi.10.

*10. Some Miscellaneous Words Found in These Sections*

*a. Basar* (flesh), Section II (ii.21, 23, 24). Its next occurrence is vi.3 (J). Then it appears 20 times in P. The last 8 occurrences in Gen. are J or E. Very frequent in Lev. (P or H).

*b. Maqom* (place), Section I (i.9). Of the nearly 50 occurrences in Gen. only three are P (xxxv.13, 15, xxxvi.40), elsewhere in Pent. in all four sources.

*c. Ereb* (evening), Section I (6 times). Not one of the seven other occurrences in Gen. is P, found elsewhere in Pent. in all 4 sources.

*d. Boqer* (morning), Section I (6 times). None of the remaining 13 occurrences in Gen. are P; in Ex.-Dt. found in all four sources.

*e. Laqach* (to take), Section II (10 times), then in v.24 (P); occurs about 150 times in Gen., usually in J, less frequently in E, about 20 times in P.

*f. Zakar* and *neqebah* (male and female), Section I (i.27), also P (v.2, vi.19, vii.16a), J (vii.3, 9); similar expressions in rest of Pent. P (5 times), D (once).

*g. Tsela* (rib), Section II (twice), elsewhere only P (in Ex. xxv.-xl.).

*h. Min* (kind), Section I (10 times), also P seven times in vi.20 and vii. 14. Elsewhere only in Lev. xi. (9 times), Dt. xiv. (4 times) and Ezek. xlvii.10.

*i. Yalad* (bear, beget), three forms of this verb are used in Section II:

(1) The simple form (*qal*) is used of parenthood, both maternal (bear, iii.16, iv.1, 17³⁵, 20, 22, 25) and paternal (beget, iv.18). In the former sense (bear) it is found also in E and P; in the latter (beget) it occurs 6 times in chap. x. (four times in J, twice in vs. 24, R) and 4 times elsewhere in the Pent. (J [Gen. xxii.23, xxv.3], JE [Num. xi.12] and Deut. xxxii.18).

(2) A passive form (*niphal*) occurs in iv.18, elsewhere in Gen. it is P (x.1 + 5 times).

(3) Another passive (*pual*) occurs in iv.26: elsewhere in Gen., J (vi.1, x.21, 25, xxiv.15), P (xxxv.26, xxxvi.5 [?], xlvi.22, 27), E (xli.50, l.23). These passive forms (2) and (3) describe parenthood usually with reference to the father (comp. Gen. xvii.17, xlvi.20, and xli.50, xlvi.22).

(4) Three other expressions are to be noted:

(*a*) The causative (*hiphil*) of this verb occurs first in Gen. v. (28 times), then vi.10, xi.10-27 (26 times), xvii.20, xxv.19, xlviii.6, Num. xxvi.29, 58—all P; also Deut. iv.25, xxviii.41 (D).

(*b*) The expression, "the sons of _____ (were)," or "these are the sons of," is found repeatedly in Gen. x., and is regarded as characteristic of P, where it also occurs in the genealogies in Gen. xxxv., xxxvi., xlvi., Ex. vi., Num. xxvi. But in Gen. xxv.3, 4, it is J.

(*c*) *Toledoth* (generations), Section I (ii.4a) and also in v.1, vi.9, x.1, xi.10, xi.27, xxv.12, xxv.19, xxxvi.1, xxxvi.9, xxxvii.2, Nu. iii.1. All of these verses are assigned in whole or part to P and regarded as headings.

*j. Derek* (way), Section II (iii.24) and 30 times elsewhere in Gen.: J (18 times), E (10 times), P (vi.12, xlviii.7*bis*).

*k. Moed* (season), Section I (i.14); P. (Gen. xvii.21, xxi.2), J (Gen. xviii.14, Ex. ix.5, xiii.10 [or JE]), E (Ex. xxiii.15). Beginning at Ex. xxvii. 21 very frequent in P.

*l. Yereq* (green [thing]), Section I (i.30), P (Gen. ix.3), E (Ex. x.15c, Num. xxii.4?).

*m. Reshith* (beginning), Section I (i.1), elsewhere J (Gen. x.10, xlix.3), E (Ex. xxiii.19), J or JE (Ex. xxxiv.26). Also in Num. and Deut.

*n. Ramas* (move, creep): (1) Verb, Section I (4 times), also P (Gen. vii.14, 21, viii.17, 19, Lev. xi.45, 46), J (Gen. vii.8), D (Deut. iv.18); (2) Noun, Section I (3 times), also P (Gen. vi.20, vii.14, viii.17, 19, ix.3), J (Gen. vi.7, vii.23).

*o. Yare* (fear), Section II (iii.10), elsewhere about 100 times in Hex., of which about 40 are in Deut., 20 in E, 8 in Lev. (H), 1 in P (Ex. xxxiv. 30), the rest J or JE.

*p. Qaton* (little, small), Section I (i.16). Elsewhere in Hex. words from this root occur 26 times, 3 of which are in Deut. and the rest about equally J or E; P never.

*11. A Few Words Occurring in Early Chapters of Genesis, but not in Sections I or II*

*a. Mizbeach* (altar), J (Gen. viii.20^bis, xii.7, 8, xiii.4, 18, xxvi.25); E (13 times up to Ex. xxiv.6); beginning Ex. xxvii.1 very frequent in P.

*b. Olah* (burnt offering), J (Gen. viii.20, Ex. x.25); E (9 times up to Ex. xxiv.5); beginning Ex. xxix.18 very frequent in P.

*c. Riach nichoach* (sweet savour), J in Gen. viii.21, then beginning with Ex. xxix.18, 38 times in P.

*d. Mabbul* (flood), 11 times in Genesis: P (vi.17 + 8 times), J (vii.7, 10).

*e. Rekush* (substance), P (Gen. xii.5, xxxi.18, xxxvi.7, xlvi.6); but xv.14 is J, E, or R.

*f. Berith* (covenant), P (vi.18, repeatedly in ix.1-17 and xvii.), J (xv.18, xxvi.28), E (xxi.27, 32, xxxi.44).

*g. Zakar* (to remember), P (viii.1, ix.15, 16, xix.29, xxx.22a?), E (xl.14, 23, xli.9 and xlii.9).

*h. "X years old"* (Hebrew, "son of X years"), P (v.32 + 16 times), E (l.26).

The above list includes 64 words or phrases. Of these 44 occur in only one Section (23 in Section I, and 21 in Section II). Six which occur in both Sections and six which occur in neither Section are included because they are synonymous expressions. Eight others are added under No. 11 because they are of special interest. The list is not exhaustive, but adequate we believe to serve as a basis for the following observations regarding the variations in diction and style in the various parts of the Pentateuch, especially Genesis.

## II. Observations on the Vocabularies of Sections I and II

### *1. The Complexity of the Analysis*

The most obvious feature of the analysis is that the farther it is carried the more complicated it becomes. It is a simple, even if tedious, matter to take Sections I and II and arrange their vocabularies in three groups with a view to determining which words are common to both, which are found only in Section I, and which occur only in Section II. A large number of words would be assigned to each group. But when we endeavor to ascertain what words are characteristic of each Section, regarded as the beginning of a Pentateuchal document, the problem at once becomes complicated and difficult in the extreme. The farther the analysis is carried the more certain it is to prove confusing or conflicting. Words which do not occur in Section I are almost certain to occur sooner or later in P; and words which do not appear in Section II are almost certain to occur sooner or later in J or E, unless these words are of such rare occurrence that no inference can properly be drawn from their use. Of the 23 words found in Section I, and not in Section II, except for two which occur nowhere else in the Pentateuch, all except "generation" are found sooner or later in J, E, or D, sometimes in all of them. Similarly in the case of the 21 words found in Section II but not in Section I, except for three rare words, all are found subsequently in one or more other sources. Consequently it must either be admitted that words which, on the basis of Sections I and II, might be regarded as characteristic of P or of J, are proved as a result of a fuller induction not to be distinctive, or else drastic measures must be employed to make them so.

That a word which is of frequent occurrence in the Old Testament is practically certain to appear in all the sources recognized by the critics is illustrated especially clearly by the word "fear" *(yare)*. It occurs 378 times in the Old Testament, in every book except 5 (Ezra, Esth., Cant., Obad., Nah.), and about 100 times in the Hex. That it is used in Section II but not in Section I is readily explained by the subject-matter. It is found in Deut. about 40 times, is nearly as frequent in E as in J, and appears 8 times in H and *once* in P (Ex. xxxiv.30). The critics try to explain its presence in P by saying that P and H use the word only in the sense of "revere" or "feel awe." But such a rendering is decidedly forced in Ex. xxxiv.30; and the fact that the word is used in Chron. and Neh. in the sense of "be afraid" makes its occurrence in that sense in P entirely appropriate.

In some cases the conflict in usage is quite startling:

*a.* The word "place" occurs in Section I and then appears elsewhere in P only in three out of nearly fifty occurrences in Genesis.

*b.* "Commanded" occurs 3 times in Section II. Elsewhere in Genesis it is found 9 times in J, 6 times in E, 7 times in P. With Deity as subject it is: *"Jehovah Elohim commanded"* (ii.16), *"Jehovah* commanded" (vii.5), *"Elohim* commanded" (vi.22, vii.9, 16a, xxi.4). Consequently ii.16 and vii.5 are assigned to J, and vi.22, vii.16a and xxi.4 to P. But vii.9 (*"Elohim* commanded") has to be given to J or to R.

*c.* The combinations of words used to express the command to increase or the promise of increase are especially interesting. The three-fold combination, "be fruitful and multiply and fill," is a striking one. That it should occur twice in Section I (i.22, 28) is quite natural. It is equally natural that it should be repeated in ix.1, where owing to the flood a similar situation exists. But this exact combination of words occurs nowhere else, and all of the three words that compose it are found in other documents. Furthermore the combinations which do occur are quite varied in form. All that they have in common with the expression in i.22, 28, is the fact that synonyms are heaped up for the sake of emphasis. Yet the attempt is made to assign them all to P, even at the cost of splitting a verse (Gen. xlvii.27).

d. The long form of the pronoun "I" (*anoki*) occurs twice in Section II. The critics regard the short form (*ani*) as characteristic of P. Yet *anoki* occurs in vs. 4 of Gen. xxiii., one of the few chapters in Genesis which the critics assign as a whole to P.[36]

e. The same complexity appears in the case of the words not found in Sections I and II:

(1) "Covenant" occurs first in Gen. vi.18 (which is assigned to P, where *Elohim* is used in vss. 11, 12, 13, 22). It occurs 7 times in ix.1-17 and 13 times in chap. xvii., both of which passages are assigned to P because it is *Elohim* who makes the covenant. But in xv.18 we read, "In the same day *Jehovah* made a covenant with Abram"! Consequently "covenant" cannot be distinctive of P.

(2) The words "Elohim remembered" are assigned to P in Gen. viii.1. Consequently in chap. xix. the *one* verse which contains this expression (vs. 29) is cut out of a J narrative and assigned to P with the result that P tells us that *Elohim* remembered Abraham and sent Lot out of a destruction of which P has made not the slightest mention. In chap. xxx. the words "and *Elohim* remembered Rachel" (vs. 22a) are assigned by some critics to P. But as a solitary phrase cut out of a JE context, they are quite unintelligible; and the addition of vss. 4a and 9b does not contribute materially to the intelligibility or continuity of P.

(3) Expressions which are regarded as characteristic of P occur first in J: e.g., "sweet savor" (38 times in P and 4 times in Ezekiel) is found first in J (Gen. viii.21); the idea of "clean" animals occurs first in J (Gen. vii.2, 8; viii.20); the first mention of altars is in J (Gen. viii.20 and always J or E up to Ex. xxvii.); "burnt offering" is first mentioned in J (Gen. viii.20 and always J or E up to Ex. xxix.).

## 2. The Importance and Significance of E

About half of the words listed above as occurring in Section I but not in Section II are later found in E and in some cases are more frequent in E than in P. This is significant in view of two facts which have been already mentioned: (1) that the distinction between the two Elohists (P and E) was, relatively speaking, a late development in the history of the higher critical movement, and (2) that E is said by the critics to resemble J much more than it does the other Elohist, P.

## 3. The Drastic Methods Used by the Critics in Making Their Analyses

Only a detailed examination of the data given above would suffice to illustrate this point adequately. One of the best examples is verse 4 of chapter ii. It is a significant fact that Section I ends with ii.4a and Section II begins with ii.4b. This means that the dividing line between these two important passages has to be made in the middle of a verse.

The history of the critical treatment of this verse is very illuminating. The word "generations [*toledoth*]" occurs in headings 11 times in Genesis (usually in the form: "these are the generations of"). Consequently we might expect this word to figure prominently in any analysis of the book. Astruc assigned four of these headings (ii.4, x.i, xi.27, xxv.19) to the Jehovist, four (v.1, vi.9, xi.10, xxxvii.2) to the Elohist, and three (xxv.12, xxxvi.1, xxxix.9) to secondary sources. Eichhorn assigned two (x.1, xxv.12) to the Jehovist, six (v.1, vi.9, xi.10, xi.27, xxv.19, xxxvii.2) to the Elohist, and three (ii.4, xxxvi.1, xxxvi.9) to the passages which he called "insertions." Hupfeld vigorously defended the view that ii.4 is the heading of the first J passage despite the fact that he assigned nearly all the other headings to his *Urschrift* (P). But, of course, if similarity or identity of language proves identity of source, all of these headings should belong to the same document. This had been asserted by Ilgen in 1798, when he divided ii.4 into two parts, treated the first part as the misplaced original heading of the first Elohistic Section, and assigned all the other headings to the same Elohist. This drastic but consistent proposal was revived by Noeldeke in 1869 and soon became the generally accepted view of the critics; and they have been asserting ever since with growing positiveness that the "framework" of Genesis, as determined by these headings, belongs to P, the latest of the sources of Genesis.[37]

There are three main objections to this view:

*a.* Since all the other headings precede the passages which they *head,* this should be the case with ii.4a. To assert that the redactor found it at the beginning of chap. i. and transferred it to its present position is to admit that he felt this position was the more suitable of the two. This constitutes a strong initial presumption in favor of the view that it originally stood there.

*b.* There is no sufficient warrant for dividing verse 4. It reads as follows: "[a] These are the generations of the heaven and the earth when they were created, [b] in the day that Jehovah Elohim made earth and heaven." There is in this verse an element of repetition which is often found in the Old Testament. 4b repeats and enlarges on the last clause of 4a. The words "heaven" and "earth" appear in both. "Made" is not, as we have seen, distinctive of Section II. It occurs more often in Section I. Compare especially vs. 26 ("let us make") with vs. 27 ("and Elohim created"). "Create" is not used exclusively in P; we find it also in J (vi.7). "Generations" does not occur elsewhere in Section I. But the root from which it comes ("bear" or "beget") occurs 9 times in Section II. If the words "Jehovah Elohim" are proof that the second part of this verse must be J, it would be a simple matter to assign the whole to that source. Splitting the verse after the word "created" leaves only a temporal clause to begin the first J section of Genesis.

*c.* The claim that all of these headings belong to P is not favored by the contents of the passages which they introduce. (1) In the short *Toledoth* (the Fifth, Seventh, and Ninth) which begin at xi.10, xxv.12, xxxvi.1 respectively, no divine name occurs and the subject-matter is mainly genealogical. (2) In the Fourth (x.1-xi.9) *Elohim* is not used, but *Jehovah* occurs six times. The entire passage should be J (so Astruc, Eichhorn, Hupfeld). But four sections totaling a dozen verses are cut out of it and given to P, which badly mutilates the genealogies of Ham and Shem. (3) In the remaining four *Toledoth* both *Elohim* and *Jehovah* occur. The Second (v.1-vi.8 begins with a P section and ends with a J section. The Third (vi.9-ix.29) begins with a P section and then J and P alternate. In the Sixth (xi.27-xxv.11) the first name to occur is *Jehovah* (xii.1) and this name occurs in all but one of the chapters: *Elohim* does not occur until xvii.3 and is found in only seven of the chapters. In the Eighth (xxv.19-xxxv.29) *Jehovah* occurs four times near the beginning and 24 times in seven other chapters. *Elohim* does not occur until xxvii.28 and then 37 times in 8 chapters. In the last of the *Toledoth* (xxxvii.2-l.26) the heading is immediately followed by an E section (xxxvii.2b-11) and the bulk of the passage is given to J and E. P does not appear until xli.46.

This all serves to show how precarious is the claim that the words "these are the generations of" belong properly or exclusively to P. It was a long while before the critics felt able to assert confidently: "The framework of Genesis belongs to P"! The fact that Hupfeld, who discovered the "distinctive style" of P, assigned all of ii.4 to J is an inconvenient fact which has to be ignored when it is claimed that all critics are agreed as regards the extent of this document.

### 4. The "Distinctive Style" of P

This point is especially stressed by the critics as convincing proof that Genesis is composite. They tell us that, while J and E may be at times hard to distinguish, the style of P is unmistakable. Consequently this claim needs careful consideration.

*a.* "Lived" and "was . . . years old." As an illustration of what is meant by the distinctive style of P the following example is both interesting and informing. We have seen that the critics only gradually reached the conclusion that all of the headings (*toledoth*) in Genesis should be assigned to P and that this conclusion necessitated the splitting of ii.4 into two parts. The second of these headings (v.1) begins a chapter which was one of the first to be assigned to an Elohistic source. The most obvious reason for assigning this chapter to P is that vss. 1-2 refer to and almost quote from chap. i.26-28 (P). Yet it is chap. iv.25-26 (J) which first mentions Seth. Gen. v. is largely genealogical. So it was inferred that the writer of this (Elohistic) source was fond of genealogy. The word "lived" occurs often in it (16 times in vss. 3-30). But in vs. 32 we meet for the first time a different expression, "years old" ("Noah was 500 years old," which is literally "Noah was a son of 500 years"). Since the usual expression in this chapter is "lived," we would expect the critics to regard this new phrase "years old" as indicative of another source (J or E?). On the contrary, they consider it so characteristic of P that they assign all but one of the 18 occurrences in Genesis to P, even in the case of vii.6, xii.4*b*, xxv.26*b*, xxvi.34, xxxvii.2*a*, xli.46, cutting short passages varying in length from half a verse to two verses out of a J or E context to give them to P.[38] In fact the only verses in the Hexateuch not assigned to P in which this phrase occurs are: E (Gen. l.26, Josh. xxiv.29), JE (Ex. xxxii.11, Josh. xiv.7, 10), D (Deut. xxxi.2).[39] The principal reason the critics want to assign this phrase to P is apparently because it occurs a number of times in such passages as Gen. xvii., Lev. xxvii., and Num. i.-x. But the obvious explanation of its occurrence in them is simply because they deal with questions of age (age at parenthood, circumcision, census-taking, death). Unless it is to be argued that P alone could have been interested in ages, it is difficult to see why the expression "years old" should be distinctive of P. The arbitrary way in which passages which refer to age are cut out of J, E, or D contexts and the fact that even then the critics have not succeeded in eliminating it wholly from those sources is a clear indication that there is no sufficient basis for regarding this phrase as distinctive of P. This example is especially instructive because it shows how misleading and contradictory the clues appealed to by the critics often are. The natural assumption, according to critical principles, that "years old" (vs. 32) must belong to a different source from "lived" (vss. 1-30) is contradicted by its frequent occurrence in P elsewhere in the Pentateuch.

*b.* Another example of this distinctive style is the use of the word "kind." In Gen. i., vi.20, xii.14, it occurs 17 times and is always P. It occurs 9 times in Lev. xi., also P. Yet we find it 4 times in Deut. xi., the only other passage in the Pentateuch where the distinction between clean and unclean animals is discussed. This shows that this word is just as characteristic of D as of P where the subject treated is the same.[40]

*c.* Gen. xli.46 is especially noteworthy, because it is the *only* verse between xxxvii.2*b* and xlvi.6 which the critics assign definitely to P. It reads as follows: "And Joseph was thirty years old when he stood before Pharaoh king of Egypt. And Joseph went out from the presence of Pharaoh, and went throughout all the land of Egypt." Many critics, e.g., Wellhausen, limit P to the first half of the verse. Obviously it is assigned to P primarily because it contains the expression "years old." But this sentence also contains the expression, "Pharaoh king of Egypt." This title is unusual. The king of Egypt is usually called simply "Pharaoh" in the Pentateuch. Consequently if "years old" is distinctive of P, it might be argued that "Pharaoh king of Egypt" is distinctive also. And the fact that five of the seven remaining occurrences are found in P might seem to favor such a conclusion. But the facts indicate otherwise. In Ex. vi.2-vii.13 (P) where "Pharaoh king of Egypt" occurs four times (vss. 11, 13, 27, 29), "Pharaoh" is used 16 times. Similarly in the portions of Ex. xiv. which are assigned to P (about half of the chapter), "Pharaoh" is used 9 times, "Pharaoh king of Egypt" only once (vs. 8). The natural explanation is emphasis. This is especially clear here in Gen. xli.46. It was after he had been a slave in Egypt for 13 years that Joseph suddenly and unexpectedly "stood before *Pharaoh king*

*of Egypt."* The fact that the full expression occurs in Deut.
vii.8, xi.3 indicates clearly that it cannot be regarded as distinctive of P.

*d.* The critics regard the name "Padan Aram" as distinctive of P. E.g., Addis remarks, "So always in P. The older
documents have Aram Naharaim [AV, Mesopotamia]."[41] The
facts are these: (1) Aram Naharaim occurs only *twice* in the
entire Pentateuch. It is used in Gen. xxiv.10 (J) of the abode
of Abraham's kin, in Deut. xxiii.4 (D) of Balaam's home.
(2) Padan Aram is mentioned 10 times in the Pentateuch (Gen.
xxv.20, xxviii.2, 5, 6, 7, xxi.18*b*, xxxiii.18*a*, xxxv.9, 26, xlvi.15)
and Padan once (xlviii.7). All of these passages are assigned to
P. But xxxi.18*b* and xxxiii.18*a* are the only passages (each less
than a verse) in three entire chapters (xxxi.-xxxiii.) which
are assigned to P. These chapters belong in other respects
wholly to the "older documents" (J and E). It is only when
a part of a verse is cut out of chapter xxxi. and part of a verse
out of chapter xxxiii., that the statement can be made "So
always in P."[42]

*e.* An example of the distinctive style of P, viewed *nega-
tively,* would be the almost entire absence (cf. Nu. xxxv.20)
from this document of the ordinary words for "love" and
"hate." Such words and ideas were certainly not unknown to
P. We must conclude, therefore, that the subject-matter has
been divided up between the sources in such a way as to bring
about this rather remarkable result. This appears, for example
in the complicated analysis of Gen. xxxiv. According to Driver
this chapter is composed of J and P sections and vs.3 is
assigned to J. It reads as follows: "And his soul clave unto
Dinah the daughter of Jacob, and he loved the damsel, and
he spake kindly to the damsel." Here is a verse which might
easily be regarded not merely as a doublet but as a triplet,
part of which could certainly be given to P. Yet Driver (like
Wellhausen) assigned it all to J.[43]

It is by such methods and by building up such an intricate chain of differentia that the style of P is made distinctive and characteristic. This "distinctive style" of P is a
striking illustration of arbitrary analysis. It is largely due

to the character of the material assigned to this document. "Generations" or genealogies and statements as to age are nearly always given to P; and various statistical data are largely assigned to P. This fact will help to explain how the style of P becomes "distinctive."

## 5. *The Uncertainty of the JE Analysis*

It has been already pointed out that Hupfeld divided the Elohistic document into two sources, and that he did this on the ground that, except for its use of *Elohim,* the Second Elohist (E) resembles the style of the Jehovist rather than the distinctive style of the First Elohist (P). This explains the fact that the critics not seldom differ as to whether a given passage should be assigned to J or to E and that they find the disentanglement of JE narratives difficult and at times impossible. To distinguish between sources which they admit resemble one another in style must be much harder than to recognize a source whose style is regarded as "distinctive" and "unmistakable." All that they can be sure of in many instances is that as far as style is concerned a passage does not belong to P. They are agreed, for example, that Gen. xv. does not contain any P sections. But there has been much difference of opinion as to whether it belongs to J as Hupfeld maintained or just how much of it is E or R. One of the most intricate of the partitionings of this chapter (that of Gunkel as used by Skinner) divides it into about twenty-five fragments and assigns 11 to J, 8 to E and 6 to R. The reason the attempt to analyze JE is carried to such extremes will appear more clearly later. But it cannot be too strongly emphasized that this recognition of E as a source distinct from P on the ground that it resembles J, is a significant admission that a large part of the "Elohistic" document lacks many of the features which properly belong to it. The appearance of E at Gen. xv. or xx. is a confession that at least as early as that the distinctive style of the Elohist ceases to be distinctive. A second Elohist whose style is not distinctive appears at that point.

The complexity of the JE analysis is clearly indicated by the fact that the critics have long regarded J as itself composite. Wellhausen, Kuenen, and Budde recognized a second J source in the early chapters of Genesis, especially in the Flood narrative. Smend (1912) endeavored to trace this double source throughout the Pentateuch, as did also Eissfeldt (1922) who distinguished between an older document L ("lay" source) and a younger which he called J. Pfeiffer (1941) finds in the J document (as ordinarily defined) a source which he regards as of Southern or Edomite origin and designates by S (South or Seir). Unlike Smend and Eissfeldt he limits it to Genesis. He also subdivides it into S and $S^2$. He finds the beginning of both of these sources in Gen. ii. and divides the J material in chaps. i.-xi. nearly equally between them, giving J's account of the flood to $S^2$ *in toto*. Pfeiffer traces S as far as the end of chap. xxxviii.; $S^2$ ends with xxv.4. Despite the fact that the general opinion among critics since Astruc has been that J begins in Gen. ii., Pfeiffer declares that "In thought and form $S$-$S^2$ is totally at variance with J." One of the notable results of this analysis is that it makes J begin as abruptly in Gen. xii. as E does in chap. xv. or xx.[44] On the other hand, Mowinckel has endeavored to remedy this defect in E by assigning the second J source to it, thus making this document begin in Gen. ii.

## 6. *The Inconsistencies of the Critics*

The general thesis of the critics is that differences in style, especially the use of different words to express the same idea, is an indication that a passage is composite. But their application of this principle is arbitrary and inconsistent. A few examples will serve to illustrate this.

*a.* At times the critics resort to drastic measures to secure a verse or fragment of a verse for the "right" source.

(1) This is shown as we have seen in their partitioning of Gen. ii.4. They defend it on the ground that the heading must belong to P; and they point out that "create" is used in 4*a*

and "make" in 4*b*. But in chap. i. we find "make" used in vs. 26 and "create" (3 times) in vs. 27. Yet both verses are assigned to the same source. And if the use of "create" is to be regarded as distinctive of P in Gen. ii.4*a*, its occurrence in vi.7 (J) has to be ignored or explained as the work of the redactor.

(2) Similarly, the use of two different words for "dry ground" in Ex. xiv. is regarded as proof that vss. 16, 22, 29 in which the one word occurs are P; so the middle part of vs. 21 (P) is cut out and assigned to J because the other word appears in it. But in Ex. iv.9, P's word appears in J.[45]

(3) "Male and female" is regarded as characteristic of P in Gen. i.26, v.2, vi.19 and vii.16*a;* and it is pointed out that in vii.2-3 (J) another expression is used for male and female (literally, "a man and his wife"). Consequently the fact that the very expression which is distinctive of P in i.26, v.2, vi.19 and vii.16*a* also occurs in vii.3, 9, which is assigned to J has to be ignored or it must be said that it was "borrowed by the redactor from P." Such analyses are all based on the assumption that the use of different expressions to convey the same idea implies difference in source.

*b.* On the other hand, the occurrence in the same passage of two different words with the same or approximately the same meaning is sometimes simply ignored.

(1) The use of two words for "earth" or "ground" *(erets,* 22 times; *adamah,* once, vs. 25) in Section I is simply ignored, despite the fact that "ground" *(adamah)* is in Genesis almost always assigned to J or E.

(2) Similarly the fact that in Section I we find two verbs for "rule" and in Section II three verbs for "set, place, appoint" is ignored. There would be just as much warrant for assigning Gen. ii.8*a* ("and He placed [*sim*] there the man") and vs. 15 ("and Jehovah Elohim took the man and put him [*nuach*] in the garden of Eden") to different sources[46] as for many other partitionings which are undertaken by the critics.

(3) If difference in diction means difference in source, iv.18*a,* "and unto Enoch *was born* Irad: and Irad *begat (qal)*

Mehujael," should be split up and given to different sources, especially since "was born" is found in P.

(4) The sudden appearance of the expression, "and Noah was five hundred years old" (Gen. v.32), in a chapter where the formula "and—lived—years" has been used 9 times of the age of a man at parenthood is as remarkable as almost any variation to be found in Genesis. But, as has been pointed out above, this verse is given to P and the phrase is even regarded as distinctive of P.

(5) In Gen. x. the analysis is largely determined by the words "begat" (6 times, J) and "the sons of—— (were)" (8 times, P). Yet Gen. xxv.3, 4, where both expressions occur in a genealogy which is too brief to be divided, is usually assigned to J or the hand of the redactor is seen in it.

(6) In Gen. xxiv. the word "draw (water)" occurs frequently. In Ex. ii.16, 19, a different verb is used to express the same idea. Both passages are assigned to J.

(7) Gen. xxv.1-7 is assigned to E in the main. Three different expressions are used of the same event: vs. 1, "the God (El) that appeared" (raah); vs. 3, "the God (El) that answered" (anah); vs. 7, "there God (Elohim) appeared" (galah). In these three verses two different divine names are used and three different verbs. Yet all three verses are given to E.

(8) Two words are used for "assembly" or "congregation" in the Hexateuch. Qahal occurs 35 times and in all six books; edah is used nearly four times as often, but is not found in Gen. or Deut. Qahal occurs in J (Gen. xlix.6), in E (Num. xxii.4), in JE (Num. xvi.33), in D (11 times), and in D² (Josh. viii.35). That is, 15 out of 35 occurrences are not in P. This would suggest that qahal is to be regarded as an early (non-P) word. Edah on the other hand is frequently used in P. Consequently the following facts are significant. All but three of the remaining 20 occurrences of qahal are found in ten chapters in which edah also occurs. Six of these chapters (Ex. xii. and xvi.; Num. x., xiv., xvi., and xx.) are regarded as composite by the critics; and Driver assigns considerable portions of each to JE. This would at least suggest that these words would figure in the analysis: qahal being JE, edah being P. But Driver

assigns all the passages in these chapters in which either one or both of these words occur to P (Ex. xvi.33 is JE, as stated above). The variation in diction is especially noticeable in Num. xx., where *qahal* occurs in vss. 4, 6, 10, 12 and *edah* in vss. 1*a*, 2, 8*bis*, 11, 22, 27, 29. Yet, although Driver assigns ten verses of this chapter to JE, even splitting vs. 1, he gives all four of the verses in which *qahal* occurs to P. Note particularly Num. xvi.3, where both words occur. The remaining four chapters (Lev. iv. and xvi.; Num. xv. and xix.) are assigned in their entirety to P.

Such passages as the above[47] make it clear that variations in diction and style are not necessarily indicative of diversity of source, the critics themselves being judges. When they fit into the analysis, they are appealed to as proving that a narrative is composite. When they do not do this, they are ignored.

## 7. *The Prominent Rôle of the Redactor*

As in the case of the divine names a great weakness of this analysis is to be found in the prominent rôle which the redactor or redactors play in it. The main function of these redactors was according to the critics to combine their sources, using passages or excerpts from each and combining them as they saw fit. Sometimes, we are told, they quoted them *verbatim;* and the exact words used in a verse are pointed to as clear evidence of the source to which it is to be assigned. Sometimes they edited them, making intentional changes. Sometimes they blundered, making mistakes which the critics feel at liberty to correct.

(1) The fact that Gen. ii.4*a* stands at the end of Section I indicates very clearly that it is not the heading of that section. To say that it originally stood at the beginning but was transferred by the redactor to the end, is simply to attribute one of the first major difficulties encountered by the analysis to an editor who did not hesitate to make radical changes in the sources at his disposal, and blundered in the attempt.

(2) The critics are insistent that *yalad* (*qal*) in the sense of "beget" belongs to J. But in Gen. x.24 where it occurs twice they either assign the verse to the redactor, since Arphaxad is mentioned only in vs. 22 (P), or ignore the inconsistency.

(3) It may seem very simple and easy to account for the presence in a passage which the critics regard as J (Gen. vii.7-10) of three expressions ("two and two," "male and female," and "God") which they consider to be characteristic of P by saying "borrowed by the redactor from P."[48] But it is a confession of weakness the significance of which should be obvious to every reader.

It has already been pointed out, but in view of its importance the point cannot be too much stressed, that in assigning to the redactor the rôle of editor and making him responsible for all the cases where the analysis does not work out as they think it should, the critics resort to a device which is destructive of their whole position. For the critics to blame the failure of the analysis to work out satisfactorily on an unknown redactor who has changed the text of his sources is equivalent to changing the actual text which the critics have before them in the interest of their theory as to what that text originally was. To put it bluntly, it is what is called "doctoring the evidence." By such means any theory can be proved or disproved.

# CHAPTER III

# CONCLUSIONS REGARDING THE DICTION OF THE PENTATEUCH

IN VIEW of the importance attached by the critics to the diction and phraseology of the Pentateuch and the prominent rôle it has played in the documentary analysis, it will be well for us, before passing on to consider the last two arguments for this analysis, to state and defend our conclusions regarding this argument against the unity of the Pentateuch. These are three in number: (1) that the diction of the Pentateuch is good and effective; (2) that the critical analysis rests on a fundamentally false basis; and (3) that the critics attempt the impossible.

## I. THE STYLE OF THE PENTATEUCH IS GOOD AND EFFECTIVE

The fact that there are other marked differences in diction and phraseology in the Pentateuch besides the variations in the divine names is obvious, and it is generally recognized. The important point to notice is that they are in accord with good usage, especially Semitic usage. The three features which were noted in the case of the divine names appear also in the use of other words and expressions: sameness and variety and the use of stereotyped expressions.

### *a.* Sameness or Uniformity of Diction

Frequent repetition of a word, a phrase, or a passage tends to become monotonous. Monotony is a serious fault which good writers seek to avoid. But identical repetition

may also be impressive and emphatic. It is also characteristic of what may be called a business, legal, or official style.

(1) The frequent repetition of the words "lived" (16
times) and "died" (8 times) in Gen. v. is in harmony with
the simple genealogical or tabular form of the chapter; and
the oft repeated "and he died" is like the solemn tolling of a
bell, a tragic confirmation of the word of Jehovah Elohim (ii.
17) and a terribly conclusive refutation of the serpent's lie
(iii.4). To use two or three different words here would be
stilted, and would weaken the emphasis and be out of keeping with the character of the passage.

(2) The close resemblance between the phraseology of
fiat and fulfilment in Gen. i. almost amounts to tautology.
But it serves to stress the all-important fact, that what God
commanded He also brought to pass: "He spake and it was
done." And the slight variations in phrasing which occur are
significant in themselves and perhaps intended to keep the
reader from skipping hastily over what might seem to be mere
repetition.

(3) The account of the making of the tabernacle and of
its erection and dedication (Ex. xxxv.-xl. P) follows closely
the exact phraseology of the instructions given to Moses (chaps.
xxv.-xxxi. P). The writer might have contented himself with
saying simply that the instructions were carried out "as the
Lord commanded Moses." But the repetition is designed to
stress this important fact by detail and specification.

(4) Num. vii. (P) is the longest chapter in the Pentateuch
(89 verses). This is due to the fact that the list of the gifts
of each of the 12 princes of Israel is given in full, despite the
fact that they are identical. These identical lists are repeated
12 times and 6 verses are given to each list, 72 verses in all.
It is easy to say that this simply means that the 12 lists were incorporated in Numbers. But why the repetition? Some descriptions in the Pentateuch are very brief and concise, e. g., that of
the ark in Gen. vi. Why not this one? Apparently the intention was to make it perfectly clear that for the service of the
altar each of the twelve tribes through its prince made exactly
the same contribution. No tribe was to have any superior

claim to the altar of God: all of the tribes were to share equally in its privileges.

(5) Exact repetition is especially characteristic of lists and statistics. In Num. xxxiii. the Hebrew uses only one word for "pitched" and one for "journeyed." Each occurs 42 times. The constant recurrence of the same words is quite natural and appropriate in such a list. And the monotony of the repetition may even suggest how long and tedious was the journey from Egypt to the land of promise.

## b. Variety

There are many passages in the Pentateuch which show that the writer had at his command, when needed, a wide and varied vocabulary. Such variety of phrasing is necessary when an idea is to be amplified or emphasized.

(1) The account of Abraham's death is a good example of such variety: "And Abraham gave-up-the-ghost *(gawa)* and died in a good old age, an old man and full (of years) and was gathered to his people (kinsmen) and Isaac and Ishmael his sons buried him" (xxv.8f. P). Almost exactly the same phraseology is used of Isaac's death (xxxv.29) and the expressions "gave-up-the-ghost" and "was gathered to his people" are used of Ishmael (xxv.17), of Jacob (xlix.33, cf vs. 29), and of Aaron (Num. xx.29, cf. vs. 24). That this unusual phrasing is due to the special dignity of the persons whose decease is here described is indicated by the fact that the deaths of Deborah (xxxv.8) and of Rachel (vs. 19) are described by the simple words, "and she died and was buried." There is no reason why the brief accounts of the deaths of Deborah and Rachel (E) cannot be from the same pen as the elaborate obituary of Isaac (vs. 29). Yet the critics insist on assigning the account of Isaac's death and all the passages where "gave-up-the-ghost" and "was gathered to his people" occur to P.

(2) Similarly, the obituary on Abraham's life is recorded in xxvi.5 in a combination of words which is unique in the Book of Genesis, yet most appropriate to his unique career: "because Abraham obeyed my voice, and kept my charge, my commandments, my statutes, and my laws" (xxvi.5 J).[49]

(3) Of the Israelites we read, "And the children of Israel were fruitful, and teemed, and became many, and became mighty, exceedingly exceedingly, and the land was filled with them" (Ex. i.7, P).

(4) Of Pharaoh's chariots and horses we are told, "The enemy said, I will pursue, I will overtake, I will divide spoil, my desire shall be satiated on them, I will draw out my sword, my hand shall despoil them" (Ex. xv.9, E).

In the four passages just quoted the heaping together of synonymous or nearly synonymous expressions occurs in close connection, in single verses. But it is not at all necessary that it should be so restricted. If, for example, P can use the words "give-up-the-ghost" and "die" in the same verse in describing the death of eminent individuals (Gen. xxv.8, 17, xxxv.29), there is no apparent reason why in Gen. vii.21f. "died" (vs. 22) should be J and "gave-up-the-ghost" (vs. 21, AV and ARV, "died") should be P.

(5) The Hebrew language expresses the idea of "destroy" in many different ways.[50] In Gen. xviii.-xix. four different verbs are used to express this idea. One is used nine times, another four, another three times, a fourth is used one.[51] Note especially xviii.22-32 where "spare," the opposite of "destroy," occurs twice as does also the colorless word "do." Yet the whole of this passage (except xix.29) is assigned to J;[52] and two of these words appear in the one verse (xix.29), which the critics assign to P. This means that in the use of words for "destroy" J is permitted a varied style which in the case of many other words is rigidly denied him.

(6) Gen. xxiv. (J) is marked to a considerable extent by repetition and there is a certain sameness in the repetition due to the desire of the servant of Abraham to make it clear how carefully he carried out his master's command and how wonderfully God heard and answered his prayer for manifest guidance (compare especially vss. 34-48 with vss. 1-33). Yet along with the repetition there is much variety in statement. This appears quite clearly in the words which are used to describe Rebekah. She is referred to as an *ishshah*, i.e., a "woman" (vss. 5, 8, 39, 44) who is to be a "wife" (vss. 3, 4, 7, 37, 38, 40, 51, 67). She is called a *naarah* ("damsel," vss. 14, 16, 28, 55,

57). Once she is called a *bethulah*, i.e., a "virgin" (vs. 16) and once an *almah* (vs. 43, cf. Isa. vii.14) which means the same thing. Eleven times she is called "Rebekah" (vss. 15, 29, 30, 45, 51, 53, 58, 59, 60, 61, 67), the name being introduced proleptically at vs. 15. Her relatives, for example, call her "Rebekah" (vs. 51), "the damsel" (vss. 55, 57), "our sister" (vs. 60).

(7) As a study in Hebrew style Ex. iii.-xv. is very interesting. The deliverance of Israel from Egyptian bondage is its great theme. "Let my people go" (v.1) is the demand of Jehovah. "I know not Jehovah, neither will I let Israel go" is Pharaoh's bold retort. So "Let go" becomes the slogan which meets us 40 times in these chapters (in J, E, and P). The frequent repetition of this one word is clearly emphatic. On the other hand there is much variety in expression in these chapters. Three different verbs are used to describe the obstinacy of Pharaoh's heart, and each describes it both as a condition for which Pharaoh is himself responsible and as an act of Jehovah. One word means "strong" *(chazaq)* and is given to P and E. The second word means "hard" *(qashah)* and is P and JE. The third word is "heavy" *(kabed)* and it is assigned to J.[58] We read also that he "was unwilling" (Ex. x.27 E), that he "refused" (3 times, J). Consequently this passage is marked both by variety and by sameness of expression, and judging by the passages already cited there is no reason why the variety in diction should be regarded as evidence that this group of chapters is of composite authorship.

(8) The ark is referred to about 30 times in Josh. iii.-viii. It is variously described as: *(a)* "the ark" (6 times), *(b)* "the ark of Jehovah (your God)" (8 times), *(c)* "the ark of the covenant" (6 times), *(d)* "the ark of the covenant of Jehovah (your God)" (7 times), *(e)* "the ark of the testimony" (iv.16), *(f)* "the ark of Jehovah the Lord of all the earth" (iii.13). In chap. iv., where the ark is mentioned 7 times, five of these six expressions occur. Especially noteworthy is the expression "the ark of the testimony" (vs. 16). Since elsewhere this phrase occurs frequently in P, this verse is assigned to P or R. But "testimony" occurs also in E (Ex. xxxii.15). We have here a good illustration of a varied style, which avoids the monotony

of identical repetition. When chap. vi.6 refers to "the ark of the covenant" and then to "the ark of Jehovah" the intention of the writer is especially plain (cf. 1 Sam. iv., especially vs. 4). That "the ark of the covenant of Jehovah" should be referred to both as "the ark of Jehovah" and as "the ark of the covenant" is natural and eminently proper.

### c. Stereotyped Expressions

That frequently used phrases tend to become stereotyped has already been noted in the case of the divine names. But it is equally true of other expressions:

(1) A very instructive illustration of this is the use of the two forms of the pronoun "I." The critics point out that the short form (ani) occurs 138 times, in Ezekiel, 130 times in P, 30 in Chronicles, while anoki occurs but once in each (Ezek. xxxvi.28, Gen. xxiii.4, 1 Chr. xvii.1). This they regard as conclusive proof that the longer form is early and the shorter late.[54] At first glance these figures are very impressive. But a little scrutiny of them reveals the following significant facts: (a) The expression "(and ye [they] shall know that) I am Jehovah" occurs 60 times in Ezekiel and nearly 50 times in P (and H). In this expression ani is always used. This means that nearly half of the occurrences of ani in Ezekiel and more than one-third of those in P and H are found in this one expression. (b) This formula, as we may call it, "I am Jehovah," occurs in what the critics regard as early literature (Gen. xv.7, J, E, or R; xxviii.13, J; Ex. vii.17a, J); and in all of these three instances anoki occurs two or three times in the context. This indicates that the use of ani in this expression was regarded as appropriate by J no less clearly than by P.

(2) "Levites" is the name usually given to the descendants of Levi; "sons of Levi" is comparatively rare. "Levites" occurs more than 50 times in Numbers, "sons of Levi" only 6 times. In chap. iii. "Levite" occurs 12 times, "sons of Levi" once (vs. 15); in chap. xviii. the former expression occurs 5 times, the latter once (vs. 21). Since "Levites" is the usual expression in P, and since "sons of Levi" occurs in J (Ex. xxxii.26, 28), D (Deut. xxi.5, xxxi.9) and JE (Deut. xxx.8),

it might well be argued that this latter expression is characteristic of the earlier sources and that the 7 other occurrences in
the Hexateuch (Num. iii.15, iv.2, xvi.7, 8, 10, xviii.21; Josh.
xxi.10) should be cut out of P and given to JE or D. This
would apply especially to Num. xvi. a considerable portion of
which is given to JE.

(3) "Spake . . . saying" is a phrase which appears first
in Gen. viii.15 (P). It occurs occasionally elsewhere in Genesis
in J, E, and P. It is very frequent in the rest of the Pentateuch.
"Spake . . . and said" occurs but rarely (Gen. xix.14, xliii.
19f. [cf. xviii.29] in J; xlii.7 in E). It is usually "spake unto
. . . saying," less frequently "spake with . . . saying." Yet
we find that P uses the former in viii.15, xx.3, 13, xxxiv.20 and
the latter in xvii.3, xxiii.8, xxxiv.8, xli.9. Why does P use
"unto" in xx.3, 13 and "with" in vs. 8 of the same chapter?

Such an example as the one just given illustrates the fact
that even in the case of expressions which occur so frequently
as to become stereotyped, the monotony of style which results
from exact repetition can be avoided to some extent.

## II. The Critical Analysis Rests on a False Basis

Careful examination, in the light of the preceding discussion, of the basic contention of the critics that variation
in diction and style implies diversity of authorship justifies
the conclusion that the critical analysis rests on a fundamentally erroneous principle. We have already observed
that it is generally regarded as a mark of a good writer that
he has command of an ample vocabulary. A meagre vocabulary suggests paucity of ideas and slight ability to express them. The vocabulary of the average man and average writer of today may be counted in the hundreds. In
the case of a great writer it is counted by the thousands. A
good violinist does not do all his playing on one string, or
a pianist use only one finger. A good writer shows his mas-
tery of language by the varied and precise use which he
makes of words. Yet the theory of the critics is that variety
in diction and style indicates diversity of authorship. This

means that the vocabulary of the Pentateuch, aside from what we might call the "small change" of speech, is to be divided between four different authors or sources. The Pentateuch is not a large book. In the average octavo edition of the Authorized Version it is not over 250 pages long. Its vocabulary is not immense. The reader of ordinary intelligence can read it easily and aside from archaisms and technical terms there are comparatively few words that send him to the dictionary. Yet we are asked to believe that except in the case of words which occur frequently and are widely distributed in it, the vocabulary of the Pentateuch is to be divided between four main writers or schools of writers who have to be assisted by several redactors. The tendency of this is to restrict the vocabulary of each of these sources: to put a premium on meagreness of vocabulary and monotony of style and to regard variety as a liability, a suspicious feature suggesting diversity of authorship. This we believe to be a fundamental error. And the proof that this is the case lies in the fact that if applied to many other documents which are of considerable length, deal with a variety of subjects, and use that variety of diction which is the mark of a good writer, yet are known to be the work of a single author, they could be divided up in the same way as the critics divide the Pentateuch, into a number of conflicting documents.

The inconsistency with which the critics apply this principle that variety in diction implies diversity of source is a clear indication of the uncertainty of this alleged criterion. Examples of this inconsistency have been given above. Deut. xxv.5-10 will serve as a further illustration. This brief passage contains the law of levirate marriage. Three different words are used to describe the unwillingness of the husband's brother to fulfil his obligation: viz., "refuse" (*maan,* vs. 7), "like (not)" (*chafets,* vss. 7, 8), "will (not)" (*abah,* vs. 7). Three different expressions are used to indicate the intent of the law: viz., "that his name be not

blotted out of Israel" (vs. 6), "to raise up unto his brother
a name in Israel" (vs. 7), "build up his brother's house"
(vs. 9). Emphatic repetition is especially noticeable in
vs. 7: "My husband's brother *refuseth* to raise up unto his
brother a name in Israel; he *will not* perform the duty of
a husband's brother unto me." This passage is given as a
whole to D. But the variations in phrasing and the emphatic repetition are essentially the same as are made the
basis of source analysis in such "test passages" as the Flood
Narrative. If such a passage as this is not composite—
Driver, for example, does not even raise the question—
there is no reason why many similar passages should be par-
titioned by the critics; there is no warrant for such hairsplitting analyses as they often indulge in. If this passage
is a good example of Hebrew writing, it shows that the use
of a variety of words and expressions to emphasize and
elaborate a rule or regulation, or to describe an event, is
as natural and proper in the Hebrew of the Pentateuch as
it is admitted to be in many other types of literature.

## III. The Critics Attempt the Impossible

The difficulties which the literary analysis of the Pentateuch encounters at many points and the arbitrary and inconsistent way in which the difficulties are solved by the
critics is also a clear indication that the task they have set
themselves is an impossible one. In the case of the secondary criteria as in that of the divine names, it is very easy to
call attention to variations in diction and style. It is not so
easy to explain them. The old saying, "A fool can ask
questions which a wise man cannot answer," has its application to many of the problems and difficulties raised by
the critics. The problems of literary style are complex
because the personal equation figures so markedly in them.
It is quite obvious that when the same idea is to be expressed several times there are two ways of doing this, by
repeating the same words or by using different words, by

identity or variety of expression. But when is the one to be employed and when the other? This is a question as to which experts may well differ.

What living writer, if called upon to account for his use of a particular word or phrase, would be able in every case to give a reason for his preference? Yet in the case of a document written centuries ago and under quite different circumstances from those in which the modern critics find themselves, these critics claim that they are able to decide exactly what a writer could or could not say, and on this basis to determine what part of the document belongs or does not belong to him. We may admire the courage of the critics, but we cannot commend them for their common sense. There is in literary style an elusive, imponderable something which defies analysis. Of this we shall give several illustrations.

### 1. Buchan's Defense of Sir Walter Scott

John Buchan was a great admirer of Sir Walter Scott. In a paper read to the English Association in 1923 and published in his *Homilies and Recreations* (1926), Buchan says in answering the critics who denounce the unevenness of Scott's style: "Let us grant that he could write abominably. But is there any great writer, especially any great novelist, who does not sometimes nod? Dickens has appalling lapses of style; so has Thackeray; so has George Meredith, though his habit of twisted language often disguises their feebleness." For an illustration Buchan turns to "a very great modern" [Thomas Hardy]. He declares that the last two paragraphs of *The Woodlanders* are "the most beautiful passage written in our day by any novelist." "It is so beautiful that I am almost ashamed to pick a hole in it." He quotes two-thirds of a sentence and says, "Could anything be better?" Then he quotes the rest of the sentence and says, "Could anything be worse?"[55] Had Buchan been a devotee of the higher criticism he might have gone a step farther and declared that only the first part of the sentence quoted from *The Woodlanders* could come from the pen of "a very great modern" and that the rest must be an interpolation from a second source, the work of a bungling editor or redactor. The reader may agree with Buchan or differ with him in his estimate of the sentence he quoted from Hardy. That is quite immaterial. The important point is that a writer of no mean ability as a critic could express such a conflicting estimate of a single sentence the authenticity of which no one would dream of questioning.

2. *A Parallel from Robertson's* History of Scotland

Several years after the appearance of Astruc's *Conjectures,* a book was published in Scotland which might well have sufficed to expose at the outset the dubious character of the theory that variety in the use of the divine names in Genesis is indicative of composite authorship. In 1758-59 William Robertson published his *History of Scotland during the Reign of Queen Mary and of King James VI. till his Accession to the Crown of England.* This work was enthusiastically received and passed through many editions. Soon after its appearance the author was elected Principal of the University of Edinburgh, a position which he occupied for thirty years.

In the Harper edition [1836] of the *History,* 35 pages (pp. 126-160) are devoted to that brief but tragic episode in the life of Mary, Queen of Scots, her connection with Darnly. Darnly is introduced to the reader as "Henry Stewart, lord Darnly, eldest son of the earl of Lennox" (p. 126). Up to the time of his marriage with Mary (p. 136) he is called "Darnly" 26 times and "lord Darnly" three times (p. 129, where he is also twice called "Darnly"). The usage after the marriage is especially interesting. From that point on the references to the new monarch are as follows: p. 137 ("lord Darnly . . . Darnly"); p. 141 ("the king"); p. 142 ("Darnly . . . Darnly"); p. 143 ("the king . . . Henry . . . Darnly . . . king . . . king . . . king . . . Henry"); p. 144 ("the king," 5 times, "Henry," once); p. 145 ("the king," four times); p. 146 ("the king"); p. 148 ("Darnly . . . Henry"); p. 150 ("Henry"); p. 151 ("Darnly . . . Henry"); p. 152 ("king . . . Darnly . . . king"); p. 155 ("king . . . king . . . Henry"); p. 156 ("king"); p. 157 ("king"); p. 158 ("king," 8 times); p. 159 ("king . . . Henry . . .

king . . . king . . . Henry"); p. 160 ("king," 4 times, and "Henry Stewart lord Darnly," once).

Two matters of especial interest emerge from the above summary: (1) The suddenness with which the name "Henry" is introduced on p. 143. This is in connection with the murder of Rizio. The explanation is apparently that Robertson considered "Henry" a more suitable name for the *king* than Darnly and therefore employed it as a variant.[56] But the introduction of the name is so abrupt that the reader may be pardoned if the question occurs to him whether "Henry" means "Darnly," "the king" (both names are used in this and the preceding paragraph), whose name Henry has only appeared once, viz., when "Henry Stewart lord Darnly" was first introduced upon the scene (p. 126) or whether another Henry is meant. (2) The concluding paragraph begins with the words: "Such was the unhappy fate of Henry Stewart lord Darnly, in the twenty-first year of his age" (p. 160). The rest of the paragraph speaks briefly of the tragedy of Darnly's career But the failure of this sentence to go beyond the introductory statement on p. 126, "Henry Stewart lord Darnly," is rather surprising. From these data it might be plausibly argued, according to higher critical principles, that the account of the career of Darnly given us in Robertson's *History* was written by two men, one of whom was willing to call Darnly king, while the other was unwilling to do this and spoke of him as Darnly or Henry. And the sentence quoted above from p. 160 might be cut out of its context and taken to mean that Henry Stewart was never really king, but died as "lord Darnly" at the early age of twenty-one. Such conclusions would be manifestly absurd. Robertson's literary style and his clear and logical presentation of facts were highly praised by able critics of his own day and apparently no one ever raised the question whether the entire work came from his pen. But it may be doubted whether he could have given any convincing justification or explanation of many of the variations in the use of proper names which appear in his treatment of the tragic career of Darnly in his *History of Scotland,* except the natural desire to avoid the monotony of constantly repeating the same word.

And we may well ask the further very pertinent question, What right have we to expect him to be able to do so? The "rule of thumb" cannot be rigidly applied to matters of literary style and expression.

Many other examples might be given. Froude in his *History of England* refers to Mary Queen of Scots scores of times. He nearly always calls her either "Mary Stuart" or "the Queen of Scots." In some cases there is an evident appropriateness in the use of one or the other designation. But in many cases the explanation seems to be simply the desire for variety.[57] Similarly, Motley in *The Rise of the Dutch Republic* refers to William the Silent by several names: most frequently as William, William of Orange, the Prince, the Prince of Orange, Orange. Such parallels as these make the attempt to treat the variations in the Pentateuch in the use of proper names and titles as indicative of diversity of source appear quite impracticable to say the least. If the critics are prepared to insist that the Bible is to be studied as "literature," they should apply to it tests which are applicable to literature in general and not insist on judging it by standards which are clearly inapplicable to other literary works.

## 3. The Methods of Bible Translators

A still better way of illustrating the fallacy and futility of the method of the higher critics is by applying it to the standard translations of some well-known work. For in the case of a translation we have, unless the original from which the translation was made has been lost, the means of knowing exactly what it was which the translator wanted to express, insofar at least as the language of the original makes this clear. So we can study his translation with a view to determining his literary standards and methods and comparing them with those of other translators of the same original. Bible translations are especially suitable for this purpose. So we shall examine the renderings of several Pentateuchal passages in eight well-known versions, four ancient (Septuagint [LXX], Targum of Onkelos, Peshitto Syriac, Vulgate) and four modern (Luther, Authorized Version of 1611, American Revised, Moffatt).

### a. Genesis xxiv

We have seen that the story of the obtaining of a wife for Isaac is regarded as a splendid example of Hebrew narrative prose and is assigned to J. In this chapter Rebekah is referred to five times as a "damsel" *(naarah,* vss. 14, 16, 28, 55, 57) and twice as a "virgin" (vs. 16, *bethulah,* vs. 43 *almah);* and *naarah* is also used of her servants (vs. 61).

> (1) Renderings of *naarah*
> > (*a*) LXX renders by three words: "virgin" *(parthenos,* vss. 14, 16, 55), "child" *(pais,* vss. 28, 57), and "servants" *(abra,* vs. 61).
> > (*b*) Targum of Onkelos uses only one word.
> > (*c*) Peshitto Syriac, two words (one in vss. 14, 16, 55, 61, the other in vss. 28, 57).
> > (*d*) Vulgate, one word *(puella).*
> > (*e*) Luther, one word *(Dirne).*
> > (*f*) AV and ARV, one word *(damsel).*
> > (*g*) Moffatt, two words: "maiden" (vss. 14, 61), "girl" (vss. 16, 28, 55, 57).

As to these eight versions we observe:

> (*a*) Five render the one Hebrew word by one word. Two use two words. One, the earliest of them all, uses three words.

> (*b*) Only one version uses a different word to describe Rebekah's "damsels" who were clearly servants, i.e., slaves, viz. the LXX. Yet this is the only one of the six occurrences where the use of a different word seems justified or demanded by the usage.

> (*c*) Of the three which use more than one word, no two are in agreement as to how the rendering should be varied.

> (2) Rendering of *bethulah* (vs. 16)

All of the eight versions render by "virgin." This has the result that in the LXX we read that the "virgin" was a "virgin" which is decidedly tautological.

> (3) Rendering of *almah* (vs. 43)

LXX, Vulgate, Luther, AV, render by "virgin" (cf. vs. 16), Onkelos and Peshitto by the same word as in vs. 14, ARV and Moffatt by "maiden."

### b. Genesis xxxiv

This chapter is regarded by the critics as composite and divided between J and P (or E). Dinah is referred to as a *naurah* (vss. 3[bis] and 12, J) and as a *yaldah* (vs. 4, P or E).

> (1) LXX renders in vs. 3 by "virgin" and in vss. 4 and 12 by "child" *(pais).*
> (2) Onkelos uses the same word in all four places.
> (3) Peshitto, same.

(4) Vulgate renders by *puella* (vss. 4, 12) and has no nouns in vs. 3.
(5) Luther uses *Dirne* (vss. 3 and 12), *Mägdlein* (vs. 4).
(6) AV uses *damsel* in all four places.
(7) ARV does the same.
(8) Moffatt uses "girl" (vss. 3, 4, 12) and "her" (vs. 3).

We observe:

(1) The only version which renders *yaldah* differently from *naarah* is Luther's.
(2) Six versions render *yaldah* by the same word as *naarah*.
(3) LXX renders *naarah* by two words, but uses one of them also to render *yaldah*.
(4) AV and ARV render both words by one.

### c. *Amah* and *Shiphchah* in Genesis

Gen. xxiv. deals with a freeborn maiden who is a virgin. Yet the word most frequently used in speaking of Rebekah can also be used of slaves (vs. 61), and of women who are not virgins (e.g., Judg. xix.3f.). The two words which are most frequently used of the maidservant or slave are *amah* and *shiphchah*. *Amah* occurs 56 times in the Old Testament and *shiphchah* is slightly more frequent. But *amah* is used only 7 times in Genesis (xx.17, xxi.10*bis*, 12, 13, xxx.3, xxxi.33), while *shiphchah* occurs 26 times (xii.16; xvi.1, 2, 3, 5, 6, 8; xx.14; xxiv.35; xxv.12; xxix.24, 29; xxx.4, 7, 9, 10, 12, 18, 43; xxxii.5, 22; xxxiii.1, 2, 6; xxxv.25, 26). Confining ourselves to Genesis we note that the usage of our eight versions is the following:

(1) LXX uses one word to render both.
(2) Targ. of Onkelos uses one word except in xxxi.23, xxxii.22, xxxiii.1, 2, 6, where the word for *concubine* is used.
(3) Peshitto uses only one word.
(4) Vulgate renders *amah* by two words (*ancilla* and *famula*) and *shiphchah* by three words (*ancilla*, except xxix.29 [*serva*] and xxxiii.1 [*amba*]).
(5) Luther uses one word.
(6) AV renders *amah* by three words (*maidservant, bondwoman, maid*) and *shiphchah* by five words (*maidservant, maid, maiden, womenservants, handmaid*) and uses two plurals of handmaid (*handmaids* and *handmaidens*).
(7) ARV renders *amah* by three words (*maidservant, handmaid, maid*) and *shiphchah* by four (*maidservant, handmaid* [plural, *handmaids*], *womenservants, maid*).
(8) Moffatt renders *amah* by three words (*concubine, slave-girl, maid*) and *shiphchah* by three (*female slave, maid-servant, maid*).

Here we observe:

(1) Three versions (LXX, Pesh., Luther) use only one word to render both Hebrew words. This is remarkable since all three languages possessed more than one word to describe a female servant. Furthermore, both LXX and Peshitto use more than one word to render the one word *naarah*.

(2) The AV uses the greatest number of words. The ARV reduces this number slightly.

(3) Not one of these versions follows the Hebrew exactly, viz., in using only two words, one to render *amah*, the other to render *shiphchah*.

(4) All of the versions which use more than one word to render both Hebrew words, sometimes use the same word or words to render both Hebrew words. E.g., in the Vulg. *ancilla* and *famula* render both *amah* and *shiphchah;* in AV and ARV maid-servant and maid are used in the same way.[58]

### d. Numbers xxxiii

It has been pointed out above that the itinerary in this chapter is characterized by simplicity of phrasing. The Hebrew uses one word for journey, and one word for encamp. The usage of the versions is especially interesting.

(1) All but two of the eight versions follow the Hebrew usage, using a single word to render each Hebrew word.

(2) The Vulgate uses a variety of words to render each of the Hebrew words. The AV resembles the Vulgate in using a variety of renderings.[59] But it has its own method of introducing the various words. That is, it adopts the principle of variety of rendering but applies it differently. It is not a translation of the Vulgate. Consequently were we to analyze these two versions of Num. xxxiii on the basis of diction, the documents in the Vulgate and in the AV would not correspond.

There seems to be only one conclusion which can be drawn from the evidence which has just been given. In the case of words which are synonymous or nearly so, no hard and fast rules can be made as to when or how such words are to be used. Versions which are regarded as good and reliable and which have enjoyed wide popularity differ with one another and have no consistent policy as regards themselves. In the same version we may find one Hebrew word rendered in two or more ways or two or more Hebrew words rendered in the same way. Thus, the LXX renders *naarah* in Gen. xxiv. by three different words, but renders *amah* and *shiphchah* in Genesis by only one word. The AV renders *naarah* in Gen. xxiv. by one word, but uses three different words to render *amah* in Genesis.

Especially interesting is the Moffatt translation. This version is, we are told, specially designed to introduce the methods and results of the higher criticism into Bible translation. Consequently we would expect it to reflect the usage of the Hebrew as closely as possible. It does not do this. In Gen. xxiv, *naarah* is rendered by "girl" four times; and "maiden" is used both of the free-born Rebekah (vs. 14) and of her servants (vs. 61). In Gen. xxx. Bilhah is once called *amah* (vs. 3), in vss. 4-18 *shiphchah* is used (6 times) of her and of Zilpah. Moffatt renders both words by "maid." In Gen. xxxiv. Dinah is called *naarah* (vs. 3*bis*, 12) and *yaldah* (vs. 4). Moffatt renders both Hebrew words by "girl." Yet according to the critics *amah* in Gen. xxx. is E and *naarah* J; and in chapter xxxiv. *naarah* is J and *yaldah* is either P or E. Such disregard of critical principles on the part of a higher critic is singular, to say the least.

Now the question is this. What right have the critics to demand that we recognize in and apply to the Pentateuch a theory of literary style which is clearly inapplicable to standard translations and to other standard forms of literature? We know far more about the English language when the 1611 Version was made than we do about the Hebrew language between 1500 B.C. and 500 B.C. Yet there are many questions regarding the AV which we cannot answer. Thus the word "wench" occurs about 80 times in Shakespeare's *Plays*. It is used once in the AV (2 Sam. xvii.17) where it renders *shiphchah*. Why is it used once in 2 Sam. which elsewhere (6 times) renders *shiphchah* by "handmaid"? Why is it used only once in this book? Why is it used only once in the entire AV? The word "girl" occurs about 65 times in the *Plays*. In the AV we find it twice (Joel iii.3, Zech. viii.3) as the rendering of *yaldah*. But in Gen. xxxiv.4 (the only other occurrence of this word in the Old Testament) the AV has "damsel" (the usual rendering of *naarah*). Why does the AV use "girl" at all? Why does it use it only twice? Why does it use it to render *yaldah* in two only of its three occurrences?[60]

These are questions which it is easy to ask, but hard to answer. To many of them the old saying would apply: "There is no accounting for tastes," or as it is somewhat more tersely stated, "many men, many minds." While in some cases the question of usage may be of interest and even of importance if accuracy of statement is involved, the problems raised by the use of synonyms are in many ways idle and unprofitable. We are frank to confess that we do not know, nor are we greatly concerned to find out, why "wench" occurs only once in the AV. What we are concerned to make clear is that it is to just such questions as these that the critics attach great importance, and also and especially that they have relatively meagre data, in many cases no data at all, to enable them to answer them. If the critics had an extensive body of extra-Biblical literature covering the entire period from 1500 B.C. to 500 B.C. to serve as a standard of comparison, they might appeal to it to substantiate their claim that words which appear in J are early and words which appear in P are late. As it is, the argument for early date or late date is often based solely on the fact that a given word occurs in a document which the critics, for other than literary reasons, assign to an early or to a late date. This is arguing in a circle. The critics have no means, certainly no adequate means, of determining when or how long the two words for "assembly" or "congregation" (*qahal* and *edah*) were used in Biblical times. Yet they regard both as appropriate to P as we have seen. They do not know when or how long the word "give-up-the-ghost" (*gawa*) was good Hebrew usage. All they know about it is that it is a rarely used synonym of *muth* (the usual word for "die"). In Num. xvii.13f. (P) it is placed in the mouths of Israelites of the wilderness period. In Lam. i.19 and Zech. xiii.8 it is exilic or post-exilic. That it is a poetic and perhaps unusual word is favored by the fact that it occurs repeatedly in Job, the date of which is uncertain. Yet the critics arbitrarily treat it as characteristic of P and regard it as indicative of late date.

How dangerous such arguments are is illustrated by such significant facts as the following. The critics, as we have seen, regard the two forms of the pronoun "I" as indicative of date, *anoki* being early, *ani* late. Both occur in poetic parallelism on a recently discovered tablet from Ras Shamra dating from about the time of Joshua. Two words for "window" are used in the Flood Narrative. *Arubbah* (vii.11, viii.2a) is assigned to P, *challon* (viii.6) to J. Both occur together on the same Ras Shamra tablet.[61] Where no facts are available, it is easy to make very dogmatic assertions. Where there are facts to appeal to, they indicate clearly that the Documentary Hypothesis is both unsound in theory and unworkable in practice.

It should not be necessary to add, in concluding this discussion of the argument from diction, that what has been pointed out above is not to be understood as indicating any lack of appreciation of the importance of careful study of words with a view to determining their exact meaning and the differences, even though minute, which distinguish synonymous expressions. The aim has been simply to show that the use which the critics make of these differences is unwarranted. It is perfectly proper for them to endeavor to ascertain the exact meaning of each of the words rendered "window" in the Flood Narrative. This is essential to that accurate knowledge of words upon which their correct interpretation must ultimately rest. But it is quite a different matter when they assume that these two words, each of which occurs only twice in the Pentateuch, belong to two different documents, the assumption being that one and the same author (or editor) could not, should not, or would not have used both. When the critics proceed on this assumption they are leaving the field of exact philological and literary criticism and proceeding on the basis of assumptions, the precariousness of which should be apparent to every competent student of language and literature.

# CHAPTER IV

## VARIATIONS IN VIEWPOINT AND SUBJECT-MATTER

THE ATTEMPT to divide the Book of Genesis into two main documents on the basis of the names *Elohim* and *Jehovah* led at once as we have seen to the recognition of other words and expressions as characteristic of these documents and to the attempt to show that each document was marked by a distinctive style. A further and no less natural result of the analysis was the claim that the documents also showed characteristic differences in viewpoint and subject-matter. Thus Eichhorn, having assigned Gen. v.1-28, 30-32, xi.10-32 to the Elohist and x.1-32, xi.1-9 to the Jehovist, pointed out that the former constructed his genealogies according to "chronological," the latter according to "cosmological" principles. And having given iv.1, v.29, xi.9, etc., to the Jehovist, he was able to declare that in his history of ancient times this writer was interested in recording "etymologies." Consequently Eichhorn could give two reasons for assigning v.29 to the Jehovist: a literary reason, the use of the word *Jehovah*, and a "characteristic" reason, the explanation of the name Noah, which he regarded as an illustration of the Jehovist's *penchant* for etymologies. Similarly, the partitioning of the Flood Narrative into a Jehovist and an Elohist account produced many such differences. E.g., the former makes a distinction between clean and unclean beasts, bringing seven of the former into the ark, while the latter knows of no such distinction and brings the animals to Noah only by pairs. Consequently the search for and stressing of such differences in representation — differences which might easily be magnified into contradictions—was a natural and inevitable result of an analysis based primarily on differences in diction and style.[62]

It is an interesting and significant fact that when Hupfeld in 1853 endeavored to define more precisely the limits of the true Elohistic document (the *Urschrift*) and to establish the existence of a younger Elohist which was distinct from both the *Urschrift* and the Jehovist, he paid much attention to these alleged differences in subject-matter. Making a beginning with the history of the life of Jacob, Hupfeld pointed out that in xxviii.19, xxxv.7, and xxxv.9-15 there are three different accounts of the name Bethel, and that the first two place the naming before Jacob's sojourn with Laban, the third after it. He assigned the third to the *Urschrift* (P) and the others to the Jehovist and the Second Elohist (E) respectively; and from these passages and others of a similar nature he drew the inference that the Second Elohist not only differed from the *Urschrift*, but stood in closer relation to the Jehovist. In his endeavor to develop and establish his thesis, Hupfeld did not of course ignore or minimize stylistic differences. He was insistent that the *Urschrift* (P) had a distinctive and unmistakable style. But his admission that the Second Elohist (E) did not differ markedly from the Jehovist in its literary style made it inevitable that in the effort to distinguish between E and J he should appeal particularly to such differences in viewpoint and factual representation as the above and use matters of diction and style to confirm them wherever possible. The acceptance of Hupfeld's further contention that the proof of the existence of these three distinct sources lay in establishing the continuity of each, led necessarily to the stressing of the "characteristic" differences and to the attempt to find as many parallel accounts or doublets in the Pentateuch as possible. According to the critics there are in the Pentateuch many instances where two or more accounts, either separate or combined, are given of the same event; and it is claimed that this duplication can only be the result of the combining of two or more documents, and is therefore proof that the Pentateuch is composite. To evaluate this claim correctly it is necessary to draw certain important distinctions.

It is, of course, to be recognized that the Old Testament, like the New Testament, does in a number of cases contain more than one account of the same event, or deal more than once with the same subject. There are many parallel accounts in Samuel-Kings and in Chronicles; e.g., the great Messianic promise to David (2 Sam. vii. and 1 Chr. xvii.). Sennacherib's threat against Jerusalem is described three times in detail in 2 Kgs., 2 Chron., and Isaiah; and the phraseology is often identical. The destruction of Jerusalem by Nebuchadnezzar is described in 2 Kgs. xxv. and Jer. xxxix. and lii. Similarly the Book of Acts gives three accounts of the conversion of Paul.

The Old Testament also contains markedly different accounts of the same thing. The two accounts of the creation in Genesis are markedly different. One is cosmic, deals with the universe, and reaches its climax in man: the other is particularistic and centres about man. The prose account of the crossing of the Red Sea (Ex. xiv.) is quite different from the poetical account given in the next chapter, and the reason is to be found in this very fact: one is prose, the other poetry. There are two accounts in 1 Samuel of David's youth and of the way in which he became acquainted with Saul. There are two accounts of Saul's death, one by the historian who wrote or compiled 1 Samuel, the other quoted from the lips of an Amalekite who obviously distorted the facts in his own interest. Whether in such cases the difference between the two accounts is of such a nature as to require the theory that two or more different sources have been used is certainly a debatable question. But at least we are entitled to assume that the author or editor who used these sources and incorporated them in his work, regarded them as true and harmonious the one with the other.[63] The difficulties we find in reconciling them may be apparent rather than real and due very probably to ignorance on our part of essential or relevant facts which were known to the writer or editor.

The duplicates upon which the critics rely to establish the continuity of the documents of which they believe the Pentateuch to be composed are of two kinds: (1) Narratives of distinct but similar events are claimed to be varying accounts of the same event; (2) Apparently homogeneous accounts of a single event are alleged to be composed of two or more conflicting accounts of that event.

## I. Accounts of Different Events Alleged to be Different Accounts of the Same Event

In such cases the claim that the narratives deal with the same event is refuted by the express statements of the narratives themselves.

1. We read in Genesis that Abram twice practised deceit regarding his relationship to his wife. That he did this once (xii.10f.) is regrettable. But there is no reason in the nature of things why, if he did it once, he could not have done it a second time (xx.1-18). The very fact that the first subterfuge was successful might account for its repetition. Yet the critics insist that we have here two different accounts of the same event, and they assign the one to J, the other to E. Genesis tells us further that Isaac followed in the footsteps of his father (xxvi.1-11). It was natural that he should do so. There is an old saying, "Like father, like son." The critics assign this to J. Consistency would rather require that it be assigned to a third source (P).[64] In all three there are important differences which prove the incidents to be distinct.

2. The same applies to the two expulsions of Hagar (xvi. and xxi.8-21), which are assigned to J and E respectively. The one was followed by her return and submission to her mistress: the other was final. The one occurred before Ishmael was born: the other when he was a lad of some 16 years of age.

The one occurred before the birth of Isaac, the other after and as a result of it. The differences between the two accounts could hardly be more obvious.[65] To speak of such passages as "parallel narratives of an event which can only have happened once"[66] is highly arbitrary; and is contradicted by the fact that history abounds in such instances, a fact which has given rise to the proverb, "History repeats itself."

3. The birth of Isaac was so remarkable an event and so momentous that it is quite natural we should have three references to the significant name which was given him: one telling that Abraham laughed when the promise was made to him (xvii.17-19); a second, that Sarah laughed when it was repeated in her hearing (xviii.12); a third, that when Isaac was born, Sarah declared that God had caused her to laugh and all who heard of Isaac's birth would laugh (xxi.6). In all three cases, the circumstances are different. There is no reason for regarding them as three conflicting accounts of the name Isaac and assigning them respectively to P, J and E.

4. It is an obvious fact that Genesis twice records the changing of the name of Jacob to Israel. It is easy to assert as Hupfeld did that, "It must be admitted, according to the laws of universal logic, that a name that has been already given cannot be given a second time."[67] If this be so, the redactor who clearly treated these narratives as distinct offended against the laws of universal logic in doing so. But the really difficult problem is not that the name is changed twice. The fact that the name Israel is rarely used (xxxii.32; xxxiv.7) between xxxii.28 and xxxv.10 may be intended to indicate that Jacob did not understand the significance of the first announcement and seldom used the new name during that interval; and this would explain the repetition of the command. The really difficult question is why after xxxv.10 the name Jacob continues to be used along with Israel, in the rest of Genesis, throughout the Old Testament and even in the New Testament. Of this fact the documentary theory offers no solution.

The claim which underlies the attempt to find doublets of a single event in such narratives as have been mentioned, viz., that such an event "can only have happened once," would have, if consistently applied, the most far-reaching consequences. Thus, the bringing back to life of the son of the woman of Shunem by Elisha, of the son of the widow of Nain, of Lazarus, of Eutychus, would all be doublets of Elijah's raising of the son of the widow of Zarephath. Is not the very fact that David spared Saul's life on one occasion an excellent reason for believing that he might have done so also on another?[68]

## II. The One Account of an Event Alleged to be Made up of Several Divergent Accounts of It

A more radical form of this theory consists in the claim that what appears to be a simple, self-consistent account of an event is to be regarded as composite, that is, as made up of two or more distinct and even contradictory accounts of the same event. The best known example of this, as it was the first to be discovered by the critics, is the alleged double account of the Flood in Gen. vi.-viii., which we shall shortly examine in some detail. The extreme to which the search after doublets has been carried and the great array of variations which have been discovered is calculated to surprise and amaze the "uncritical" reader of the Bible.

1. It is seriously maintained by some critics (not by Driver) that in the fact that Rebekah used two means (xxvii.15, 16) to insure the success of the deception practised upon Isaac, there is evidence that the narrative is composite; and the use of Esau's garment is assigned to J and of the skins of the goats to E.[69] This is in defiance of the familiar axiom that it is better to have "two strings to one's bow," and so to make "doubly sure" of success.

2. Shechem's unbridled passion for Dinah (Gen. xxxiv.) with all that it involved for the future relations of the Shechemites and Jacob's household was a matter of such moment that it is quite natural that Shechem should have first appealed to his father to negotiate for him and then have himself taken an active part in the negotiations. The attempt to find two ac-

counts, a "Shechem" narrative (J) and a "Hamor" narrative (E or P) leads to hairsplitting analysis.[70]

3. Two reasons are given for the attitude of Joseph's brethren to him, his father's preference (xxxvii.3f.) and his own dreams (vss. 5-11). The one is assigned to J, the other by some critics to E (Driver also J). Yet both may be true and equally important.

4. Two accounts are discovered of the cruelty of Joseph's brothers: "In one account [J], Joseph is *sold* to *Ishmaelites* on the advice of *Judah;* in the other [E] he is kidnapped by passing *Midianites,* unknown to the brethren, and to the dismay of *Reuben,* who had hoped to save him."[71] This startling evidence of conflicting accounts is secured by dividing chap. xxxvii. between J and E and especially by partitioning vs. 28. This verse is made up of four brief statements joined together loosely by "and." It reads as follows:

"Then [and] there passed by Midianites, merchantmen; and they drew and lifted up Joseph out of the pit, and they sold Joseph to the Ishmaelites for twenty pieces of silver: and they brought Joseph into Egypt."

Taken in their context (vss. 26f.), the words "and they sold Joseph" seem clearly to mean that his brothers (vss. 23, 25), who had put Joseph in the pit, were the ones who drew him out of it and sold him into slavery. Joseph's words to them, "I am J. whom ye sold" (xlv.4f.) definitely support this interpretation; and the explanation which he gave to the chief butler, "I was stolen away" (xl.15) may simply mean that he viewed or wished to represent the whole dastardly business as the stealing of his father's son by his own brothers, family pride preventing him from naming them or mentioning their part in it. But when the words, "and they sold Joseph to the Ishmaelites for twenty pieces of silver," are taken out of vs. 28 (E) and assigned to J, the rest of the verse then reads:

"And there passed by Midianites, merchantmen; and they drew and lifted up Joseph out of the pit . . . And they brought Joseph into Egypt."

This would naturally mean that the Midianites simply found Joseph and stole him. This mutilation of the verse consequently changes its meaning very materially, and makes the narrative a combination of mutually contradictory elements.

And, of course, if two different stories are to be found in combination in this narrative, they must also be found in those other passages which bear directly upon it. Yet chapters xl. and xlv. are both predominantly E, which would seem to indicate that E saw no difference between the alleged "sale" and "kidnap" versions of the story. But by cutting xlv.4b, 5a out of its E context and giving it to J (according to Driver this chapter is E "with traces of J") two conflicting versions can be discovered in these chapters as in chap. xxxvii.

5. Gen. xlviii. deals with the blessing by Jacob of Joseph's sons. This is a matter of importance because it explains how his grandsons, Ephraim and Manasseh, attained to the status of sons (tribes) and how the younger took precedence over the elder. The narrative is divided by the critics between P (vss. 3-6, 7) and E or JE. The main difficulty is that only one verse in the chapter (vs. 19) explains Jacob's determination to prefer Ephraim over Manasseh. If this is assigned to J (together with vss. 13-14, 17-18), the statement of E (vs. 20b), "and he set Ephraim before Manasseh," makes Jacob's act seem arbitrary. Some explanation seems to be required by the fact that E knows (vs. 1) that Manasseh is the older. But in the case of P, although the order of names, "Ephraim and Manasseh," in xlviii.5 reverses xlvi.20 and Num. xxvi.28, just as vs. 20b (E) reverses vs. 1 (E), P unlike E says nothing about it. It is far simpler to accept the narrative as it stands. The fact that Jacob referred to Joseph's sons, before he saw them, as "Ephraim and Manasseh" (vs. 5) indicates that he already knew God's will and explains Joseph's attempt to correct what he doubtless regarded as a lapse of memory on his father's part, first by presenting his sons in proper order to Jacob (vss. 12-14) and then by endeavoring to reverse his father's action (vss. 17-18), all of which prepares for and leads up to the explanation given in vs. 19.

6. The account of the Crossing of the Red Sea (Ex. xiv.) describes a momentous event in Israel's history and is strongly marked by that emphatic amplification which makes it readily susceptible to partitionment. Vs. 21 is especially interesting. It consists of four sentences joined by "and":

"And Moses stretched out his hand over the sea; and Jehovah caused the sea to go *back* by a strong east wind all the night, and made the sea dry land, and the waters were divided."

The first clause tells what Moses did (cf. vss. 16, 26, 27), the next two state what Jehovah did (cf. vss. 24, 25, 30, 31), the last tells the result. The critics assign the first and last sentences to P and cut out the middle part and give it to J. The result is that P reads as follows:

"And Moses stretched out his hand over the sea . . . and the waters were divided,"

while according to J,

". . . [and] Jehovah caused the sea to go *back* by a strong east wind all that night, and made the sea dry land. . . ."

P makes Moses the agent; and the only means referred to is his hand, which to some of the critics suggests magic. J says nothing of Moses, describes the drying up of the sea as an act of God, and gives as the means the "strong east wind" that blew all that night. In this way two conflicting and even contradictory accounts of the passage through the Red Sea are secured. But such mutilation of the text is quite unnecessary. It is perfectly obvious that it was when Moses at the command of God stretched out his hand that Jehovah sent the strong east wind. When some of the critics go still farther and distinguish between the "hand" version of P and a "rod" version secured by assigning the first six words of vs. 16 and parts of several other verses to E, they give us an example of disintegrative analysis which illustrates very clearly the extremes to which the "doublet" theory can be carried.

Such examples as the above serve to show that, unless a narrative is very elaborate and says the same thing over two or three times in practically the same words, the alleged "parallel" accounts into which the critics divide it will necessarily be partial and seemingly contradictory, because each account requires the data contained in the others to complete it and make it intelligible. The extreme to which the attempt to find conflicting statements in Scripture can easily be carried is strikingly illustrated by the comment made by G. B. Gray in his Commentary on Numbers on the statement in x.33, which says simply that the ark "went before" Israel when they departed from Sinai. This succinct statement is adequate and appropriate since Num. iv. has described in detail how it was to be made possible that the ark and the other sacred vessels might be carried by the Kohathites without injury to themselves. Any one accustomed to interpret Scripture by Scripture would infer from that passage that, when Num. x.33 says "the ark went before them," it means that the priests or Levites carried it before the host of Israel. No one but a critic in search of varying and conflicting accounts would venture to suggest that this verse may mean that in JE the ark "is conceived of as moving by itself," and point to this verse as indicating that we have here a conflict between JE and P (Num. iv.). Such extreme interpretations expose most plainly the fallacy of this divisive and antithetic method of interpreting Scripture.

### III. Inconsistent Application of the Doublet Theory

While absolute consistency cannot be expected in every case and what seems to be inconsistency may be at times more apparent than real, it is important to keep the fact constantly in mind that if consistently applied the principles and methods of the higher criticism would lead to the complete disintegration of the Pentateuch and that it is only the failure on the part of the critics to apply them in thoroughgoing fashion which prevents this fiasco from occurring.

1. We shall see presently that in the Plague Narrative in Exodus it is the fact that the story is told in terms of threat and execution, which makes it possible to divide this account between two or three documents, with the result that no two of them agree as to the number or order of the

plagues. It would be a much simpler matter to divide Genesis i. into two narratives: and for the same reason, the elaborateness of the language. This appears especially in the fact that the fulfilment of the divine fiat is in nearly every case given in three forms: (1) by repeating the terms of the fiat in the language of fulfilment, e.g., "and Elohim said, Let light be (fiat), and light was (fulfilment)"; (2) by the words, "and it was so" (vss. 7, 9, 11, 16, 24, cf. 30); and (3) by the words "and *Elohim* saw that it was good" (vss. 10, 12, 18, 21, 25, cf. 31). It would be a simple matter to treat the words of (2) or (3) or both (2) and (3) as recording the fulfilment of the fiat and to cut away the (1)'s and construct of them with the aid of certain other words and phrases an account of creation which, like Ps. civ., knows nothing of fiats or of six creative days. But while the critics have recognized certain indications of elaboration in the account and Von Rad has recently proposed an analysis along the line suggested above, they have been all but unanimous in giving it as a whole to P. And there is a beautiful symmetry in this chapter which is prima facie evidence of its unity and self-consistency.

2. The two dreams of Joseph in Gen. xxxvii.5-11 and the two dreams of Pharaoh in xli.1-8 (together with their rehearsal in vss. 17-24 and their interpretation in vss. 25f.) are all assigned by Skinner and most critics to E. Yet according to the doublet theory it might very properly be argued that Joseph and Pharaoh each had only one dream and that the two dreams are merely two divergent accounts of an event that "can only have happened once."

3. Similarly in chap. xxxix., vss. 1-6 tell of Joseph's *attaining to favor* with Potiphar who bought him when he was brought down to Egypt. Vss. 21-23 tell how he *attained to favor* with the keeper of the prison, after Potiphar's wife had slandered him and he had been cast into prison. According to the theory of doublets, these should be "parallel narratives of an event which can only have

happened once." Yet Skinner, like Driver and others of the critics, assigns both of these passages to J and says of the second: "Here again he wins the favor of his superior and is soon charged with the oversight of the prison." "Again" is a dangerous word for an advocate of the "doublet theory" to use. These should be two accounts of the same event!

4. Two censuses are recorded in Numbers. The one described in chap. i. was taken at Sinai, the other (chap. xxvi.) in Moab. Some critics (e.g., Driver) speak of the latter as a "second" census. Others consider the two as only variant accounts of one census. Yet they seem to be unanimous that both accounts belong to the same document (P). When Driver speaks of a "second" census, he is taking the position that these events do not belong to the category of events which "can only have happened once." By what right then is it asserted that Abram could only have lied once about his relationship to Sarah?

5. Three passages in Numbers, because they occur in what Driver calls "a long extract from P, extending from i.1 to x.28," are of especial interest in appraising the doublet theory. These passages are i.1-54, ii.1-34 and x.11-28 and we shall refer to them as A, B, C.

A deals primarily with a census taken on the first day of the second month by Moses and Aaron with the help of twelve "princes" or "captains" (nasi) who were famous men, "heads of thousands" (vs. 16). It was entirely on a tribal basis, according to generations, families, fathers' houses, names (and polls); and only those twenty years old and upward, capable of military service, were to be included. The census begins with Reuben. The totals are given for each tribe with a grand total at the end. The Levites are excluded from this census. They are to minister at the "tabernacle of the testimony" (mishkan ha-eduth). The camp is described only with reference to the distinction between non-Levites, who encamp by their "standards," and the Levites, who are to encamp around the "tabernacle of the testimony," and to whom the taking down, carrying and setting up of the "tabernacle" (mishkan) is assigned.

B has to do primarily with the camp. It groups the twelve tribes under four "standards" *(degel)* and gives the location of each standard relatively to the "tent of meeting" *(ohel moed,* vs. 2). It repeats the names of the twelve "princes." It repeats the census enumeration for the tribes and the grand total, adding a total for each of the standards; and declares that it does not include the Levites. It places Judah first. It also gives the order of march of the four standards, stating that the "tent of meeting" (vs. 17) goes "with the camp of the Levites" between the second standard and the third.

C describes the order of march from Sinai, when the cloud was taken up from off the "tabernacle of the testimony" *(mishkan ha-eduth)* on the twentieth day of the second month. It places Judah first. It repeats the names of the twelve "princes." It mentions the Gershonites and Merarites as bearers of the "tabernacle" *(mishkan,* vs. 17, cf. vs. 21) and the Kohathites as bearers of the "sanctuary" *(miqdash,* vs. 21). It gives no statistical figures of any kind.

Comparison of A, B, and C brings out some interesting points: (1) Repetitions: All three passages give the names of the same twelve tribal leaders. All three refer to the moving and pitching of the camp. All three refer to the Levites or their three sub-divisions in connection with the moving or pitching of the tabernacle. B repeats the statistical figures given in A, adds the totals for the standards, and repeats the exclusion of the Levites. C repeats the order of march given in B. (2) Omissions: A does not group the tribes in standards, but mentions the standards (i.52) as already known; B says nothing about the method of the census-taking or of an age limit, "twenty years old and upward"; C says nothing about a census. (3) Variations: A gives as the date, the first day of the second month, C the twentieth day. C mentions the same twelve leaders as are named in A and B, but describes them merely as "over the host," and does not speak of them as "princes." A begins with Reuben, B and C with Judah.[72] B mentions "the tent of meeting" *(ohel moed)* as setting forth with the camp of the Levites between the second and third standards. According to C the "tabernacle" *(mishkan),* carried by the sons of Gershon and of Merari, followed the first standard, while the "sanctuary" *(miqdash)*, carried by the Kohathites, followed the second. B refers only to the "tent of meeting" *(ohel moed)*, C distinguishes the "tabernacle" *(mishkan)* from the "sanctuary" *(miqdash)*. A refers to the "tabernacle" *(mishkan)* and to "the tabernacle of testimony" *(mishkan ha-eduth)* in a revelation made in the "tent of meeting" *(ohel moed,* vs. 1), and makes no reference to a "sanctuary" distinct from the "tabernacle."

The repetitions in these three passages are sufficient according to critical principles to indicate that we have here at least two (A & B) and perhaps three parallel accounts. The omissions and variations, judged by the same principles, indicate diversity of source. Critics who can split up such chapters as Gen. xv., xxxiv., etc., into minute fragments should not assign these three passages to the same source. Yet they do assign all three to P. This is quite inconsistent. On the other hand, considered from the standpoint of the unity of the Pentateuch, these three passages are an excellent illustration of the recapitulatory and progressive character of the Biblical style, with its tendency to repeat, expand, omit, to anticipate and to rehearse, to give details only as they are required. The most obvious "contradiction" is found in the statements in B and C as to the transportation of the tabernacle. But there is no real difficulty. B speaks in general terms of the "tent of meeting," but in placing it between the second and third standards has in mind particularly the most precious part, the sacred vessels which according to C are to be carried by the sons of Kohath. They constituted the tabernacle in the strict sense. Everything else was accessory. Chapter iv. goes into full details as to the respective duties of Kohathites, Gershonites and Merarites. But only in C (chap. x.) are we told the order (relative to the standards) in which they march.

6. The long P section (Num. i.-x.28) ends with the account of the departure from Mount Sinai. If two conflicting accounts of the crossing of the Red Sea are to be found in Ex. xiv.21, the critics should find here two conflicting accounts of the setting forth from Sinai. According to the one (x.11-12), the Israelites journeyed when the *pillar* was removed. According to the other (vs. 13), they journeyed "according to the command-

ment of Jehovah by the hand of Moses." Yet all of these
verses are assigned to P.

7. Num. xx.14-21 deals with Moses' negotiations with Edom
for passage through their land. Two requests are recorded.
Each is refused; and a concluding statement is added to emphasize the fact of refusal. One request declares that Israel
will not drink of the water of the wells; according to the other
they will pay for what they drink. Should not these be regarded as parallel and conflicting accounts of one request (cf.
xxi.22)? Yet the critics give both to the same source, usually
E.

8. Three statements are made in Numbers regarding the
death of Moses and Aaron. (1) Chap. xx.24 declares that
Aaron is to die because Moses and Aaron sinned, but says nothing of Moses' death; (2) chap. xxvii.13 says that Moses shall
die as Aaron did and for the same reason; (3) chap. xxxi.2
declares that Moses shall die, but gives no reason of any kind.
It would be easy to assert that the first passage belongs to a
source which knew only of Aaron's death as a punishment for
their joint act of disobedience, that the second source knew of
the death of both and the reason for it, that the third knew
of Moses' death but of no reason for it unless it be that his
work was finished. But all are given to P. This is especially
noteworthy because the critics cite as proof that Num. xiii.-
xiv. is composite the fact that xiii.30 and xiv.24 do not mention Joshua along with Caleb, while xiv.6, 30, do mention him.
So they assign these passages to JE and P respectively.

9. Gen. xxxi.1-3. Here three reasons are given for Jacob's
departure from Padan Aram: (1) the resentment of Laban's
sons, (2) the alienation of Laban himself, (3) the command
of Jehovah. Should not three reasons suggest three sources?
But the critics give (1) and (3) to J and (2) to E.

10. Ex. xv.25a, "And he cried unto Jehovah, and Jehovah
showed him a tree, and he cast it into the waters, and the
waters became sweet." Here, as in Ex. xiv.21, we have four sentences joined by "and." They are all assigned to J, or E, or JE.
Yet it would be easy to cut away the second and third and give
them to another source. We would then have two contradictory accounts of the healing of the waters. According to the

one, the sweetening of the waters would be solely due to prayer: "And he cried unto Jehovah . . . and the waters became sweet." According to the other, a simple means was made use of: "And Jehovah showed him a tree, and he cast it into the waters." Such analysis is quite as simple as the one resorted to in the case of Ex. xiv.21. The failure of the critics to partition the one is as inconsistent as their insistence on partitioning the other is arbitrary.

11. The words, "and he ministered unto him (them)," occur in Genesis only in xxxix.4 and xl.4. Since chap. xxxix. is usually assigned to J and xl. to E, the presence of this verb in both chapters might be appealed to by the critics as an illustration of the similarity of style which is admitted to characterize JE. But this clause is not essential to the sense in either verse (xxxix.4 consists of four "and clauses," xl.4 of three). Consequently it is a simple matter to cut this phrase out of the J passage and assign it as a fragment to E, as many critics do (not Driver). This helps, though only to a very small extent, to bridge the gap in E between xxxvii.36 and xl.1. But it is purely arbitrary. "Minister" occurs so rarely in E (Ex. xxiv. 13, xxx.11; Num. xi.28) that it can hardly be regarded as characteristic of E as over against J. In the Hexateuch it is usually P (19 times). Here again, as in many other passages, the uninitiated may marvel at the skill with which the critics can carve up a verse. But once the principle is clearly understood, both the marvel and the mystery disappear; and it all becomes quite simple.

Such examples as the above make it difficult for the critics to deny that their conclusions as to the documentary sources of the Pentateuch are not based on a careful and impartial examination of all the variations, but result from the use of such variations as accord with their theories and the ignoring of other and quite similar variations, which do not.

# Chapter V

# THE EXPLANATION OF THE ALLEGED DOUBLETS

IN VIEW of the claim that many of the narratives of the Pentateuch are composite and that, when the different elements of which they are composed are separated into their sources, these documents are more or less complete and continuous, it is important to observe that this seemingly cogent argument for the Documentary Hypothesis finds to a very large extent its natural explanation in two very marked features of the Biblical (Hebraic) style.

The first of these features is syntactical: the frequency with which loosely compounded sentences (complete sentences joined by "and") occur in the Old Testament. Genesis i. is an illustration of this. Nearly all of the 31 verses of this chapter consist of complete sentences; some of them contain more than one complete sentence. But these sentences are loosely joined together by "and." The Hebrew not infrequently uses dependent clauses as the English does. But it very often coordinates clauses by "and" where we would subordinate one to the other. In narrative prose it is also the rule that the verb should stand at the beginning of the sentence. This gives Hebrew narrative style a simplicity and uniformity which is markedly different from the complex periodic sentences of which some English writers are fond, sentences in which many dependent clauses and qualifying phrases are used and the thought is not complete until the end is reached. It is to be noted, therefore, that this tendency to join complete sentences together loosely by "and" may make it appear that the writer is repeating himself; and these loosely connected sentences which all refer to the same event or topic may seem more or less repetitious and to be lacking in strictly logical or chronological sequence. And the very simplicity of the syntax makes it a relatively easy matter to cut apart such sentences, to assert that they describe the same event from different and even conflicting viewpoints and must be assigned to different sources. Were the Biblical narratives written in complicated periodic sentences in the style of an Addison, such analysis would be far more difficult if not impossible.

The second feature of the Biblical style which readily lends itself to source analysis is the frequency with which elaboration and repetition occur in the Bible. It is true that the style of the Bible is often marked by brevity and compactness. A great deal is often said in remarkably few words. But the Bible is a very emphatic book. Its aim is to impress upon the hearer or reader the great importance of the themes of which it treats. The most natural way of securing emphasis in a narrative is by amplification or re-iteration. Consequently the Biblical style is often decidedly diffuse and characterized by elaborateness of detail and by repetition. A few examples will suffice to illustrate these important features and the way in which they have been made use of by the advocates of this theory.

## I. Elaboration and Repetition in Biblical Prose

### 1. The Flood

As this is the first considerable narrative to follow Sections I and II in Genesis, and also because it is the first passage which has to be split up in order to make it comply with the documentary analysis, it is especially worthy of careful consideration. The theme of the narrative is the punishment of man by the flood and the saving of a remnant of grace. Especial emphasis is laid on three things:

a. The sinfulness of man was the cause of the flood.

This we may call the primary emphasis; and it is introduced by the exceedingly impressive statement: "And
Jehovah saw that the wickedness of man was great in the
earth, and that every imagination of the thoughts of his
heart was only evil continually" (vs. 5). We are told further
that the earth was corrupt (vs. 11), that God looked on
it and saw that it was corrupt (vs. 12), and that He told
Noah it was corrupt (vs. 13). This is further emphasized
by the declaration that God repented making man (vss.
6, 7.)

b. The second great emphasis is that the aim of the
flood was to destroy "all flesh." This is stressed by the frequent and detailed references to it (vi.7, 13, 17, vii.4, 21-
23, viii.21) and also by the detail with which the coming,
duration, and abating of the flood are described. The account of the destructiveness of the flood given in vii.21-23
is especially interesting. It reads as follows:

"[21] And all flesh died (*gawa*) that moved (*romes*) upon the earth,
both birds, and cattle, and beasts, and every creeping thing (*sherets*) that
creepeth (*shorets*) upon the earth, and every man: [22] all in whose nostrils was the breath of the spirit of life, of all that was on the dry land,
died (*meth*). [23] And every living thing was destroyed that was upon the
face of the ground, both man, and cattle, and creeping things (*remes*), and
birds of the heavens; and they were destroyed from the earth: and Noah
only was left, and they that were with him in the ark."

In these three verses the utter destruction produced by the
flood is so stressed by detailed repetition that each of the
verses might be regarded as forming a complete statement
and might, on critical principles, be assigned to a distinct
source.[78] The only exception would be the last clause of
vs. 23, which relates to the third of the emphatic features of
the narrative.

c. The third great emphasis is on the saving of a thoroughly representative remnant of man and beast. First
Noah is referred to (vi.8) as the object of the divine favor.
Then vs. 18 speaks of his family and vss. 19-20 refer to the
animals which are to be saved. These specifications are re-

peated in connection with the command to enter the ark
(vii.1-3), in the brief description of the entering (vss. 7-9),
in a fuller description of the same (vss. 13-16), in the command to leave it (viii.16-17), and in the carrying out of
the command (vss. 18-19). Noah, his family, and the animals are referred to six different times, and always with
some detail, as the objects of divine mercy. The purpose
of this detailed repetition is clearly to emphasize the two
sides of the tremendous statement in vii.23: "And every
living thing was destroyed that was upon the face of the
ground, both man, and cattle, and creeping things, and
birds of the heavens; and they were destroyed from the
earth: and Noah only was left, and they that were with
him in the ark." Amazing blending of mercy with judgment!

These three major themes are stressed both by emphatic
statement and by frequent repetition. Obviously then, in
view of these repetitions it should be a relatively simple matter to divide this narrative into at least two accounts, each of which will contain a statement of these
three important truths. To assign vi.5-8 to J and vss. 9-13
to P is, for example, a very simple matter, because the subject-matter is so similar, despite the fact that, as we have
seen, the use of the word "create" in vs. 7 is the occasion
of difficulty. But at this point a greater difficulty arises.
The verses which follow (vss. 14-16) deal with the command to make the ark. The account is brief, for the description of the ark is of secondary importance. So there
is no elaboration or repetition, and the account cannot
readily be divided. The critics do not attempt to divide it,
but assign it all to P. The consequence is that while the J
account refers to the ark it tells us nothing about the ark.
We are left in doubt as to whether J did not know anything
about this great boat, or whether his description of it was
simply discarded when the documents were combined.
Aside altogether from the question of sources, the fact that

the writer has so little to say about the size of the ark and so much to say on the three subjects we have been considering indicates the relative importance which he attached to them.

There is perhaps no better illustration of repetitive style in the Old Testament than this flood narrative in Genesis. Eichhorn, who regarded "repetitions" as a clear evidence that Genesis is composite, appealed to the flood narrative in particular as proving this. He insisted that in a number of cases the same thing is told twice; and he arranged these repetitious statements in two columns which he placed side by side. He insisted that these repetitions could not be accidental nor due to the inexperience of the narrator. He pointed especially to three things: (1) the frequency of the repetitions, (2) their appearance in all parts of the narrative, and (3) to the fact that when arranged in two columns, each forms a continuous narrative. These three arguments were to Eichhorn conclusive evidence that we have two accounts of the flood which have been combined into one. But it is to be noted:

(1) The repetitions are not meaningless. They bear directly upon the great emphases which have been pointed out above. The repetitions are there, whether they be attributed to a single author or to a compiler or editor. The fact that they serve to bring out these emphases is the sufficient warrant for their presence, however they be explained.

(2) The repetitions do not appear in every part of the narrative. There is only one account of the size of the ark (vi. 14-16), the sending out of the birds (viii.6-12),[74] the offering of sacrifice (viii.20-21 [to *savor*]), the command regarding shedding blood and eating with the blood (ix.3-6), the bow of promise (ix.12-16). None of these appear in Eichhorn's columns. In fact of the 83 verses in Gen. vi.5-ix.16, only 36 (less than half) find a place in his parallel columns. Furthermore, all of the verses given in his Elohist Column (vi.9, 12, 13, 17-20, 22, vii.11-16, 18, 21, 22, ix.8-11) and in his Jehovist Column (vi.5, 7, vii.1-9, 17, 23, viii.21-22) bear on the three great topics which, as we have seen, are the vitally important

features of the narrative. This certainly suggests that the explanation of the repetitions is emphasis.

(3) The fact that two fairly continuous narratives can be made by dividing the repetitions into two groups is not in itself conclusive proof that they represent two distinct documents. The fact that the repetitions bear in general only on certain emphatic features of the story would seem to indicate design, a design which might as readily be attributed to an author as to an editor. It is also to be noted that the repetitions are not limited to *two* statements on the same topic. Astruc found three sources in vii.18-20 and three in vss. 21-23; and it would be easy to find other passages in this narrative (e.g., vi.11, 12, 13, vii.9, 15, 16) in which the repetition is three-fold.[75] Yet it would be rather difficult to find three narratives in Genesis vi.-ix.

Finally, it is not to be overlooked that, on critical principles, a quite different analysis of these chapters might be made from that which is generally adopted by the critics. The stress that is placed on the utter destructiveness of the flood in features *a.* and *b.* might be regarded as flatly contradicting feature *c.* which describes the saving of the remnant. It could then be asserted that *c.,* instead of stating a vitally important exception to *a.* and *b.,* is in irreconcilable conflict with them: *a.* and *b.* declare that there were no survivors of the flood, while *c.* insists that Noah, his family, and a representative remnant of beasts and birds were preserved. The aim of the writer is, manifestly, to represent *c.* as an exception to *a.* and *b.* But the critics would of course regard this as simply the result of the combining of mutually contradictory sources.

## 2. *The Plagues*

An impressive illustration of the way in which emphatic repetition lends itself to documentary analysis is the account of the ten plagues. A noteworthy feature of the account is that in some cases it is much fuller than in others. It is fullest in dealing with the Frogs, the Hail, and the Locusts. E.g., in the case of the Frogs (Ex. viii.1-15), six distinct steps are recorded: plague threatened (vss. 1-4, J), command to Moses (vs. 5, P), execution of command (vss. 6-7, P), petition for removal (vss. 8-11, J), removal (vss. 12-14, J), result (vs. 15, JP). It will be noted that, if the command-execution sections (vss. 5-7) are cut out of the record and assigned to a different source and this source is given half of vs. 15, two relatively complete accounts are obtained. The one account (J) tells us the plague was threatened and then, assuming that the threat was executed, tells of its removal; the other (P) tells of the command to bring the plague and of the execution of the command and then, assuming that a plea was made for its removal, tells us that this was done.[76] This is relatively simple; and if all the ten plagues were described with the same fulness we could make out two accounts of them all. But they are not told with the same fulness.

The plagues of Lice and Boils are described very briefly, merely in terms of command, execution, and result. If these sections are assigned to P, as in the case of the Frogs, nothing remains to be assigned to J. Consequently, J must be regarded as ignorant of these two plagues. And since three sources are recognized here by the critics the result of this attempted analysis is, as in the case of Gen. xxix.-xxx., exceedingly complicated and mystifying. The Bible mentions and describes *ten* plagues. But J knows only of seven, P of five, and E of four (and a fifth as threatened merely). All three make the Nile the first plague. J and P make the second plague Frogs; E knows nothing of Frogs and makes it Hail. J makes the third Flies, a plague unknown to P and E; P makes it Lice, a plague unknown to J and E; E makes it Locusts. J makes the fourth plague Murrain, which is unknown to P and E; E makes it Darkness, unknown to J and P; P makes it Boils, likewise unknown to the other two. J makes the fifth plague Hail; E has made it the second; P knows nothing of it. J makes the sixth plague

Locusts, which is E's third plague, and unknown to P. J's seventh plague is the smiting of the First-born; P makes it the fifth plague; E also knows of it as the fifth plague but only as threatened. No two accounts agree as to the number, order or nature of the plagues. Such is the result of the attempt to analyze the narrative of the plagues into three accounts. Where the Biblical account is sufficiently full and elaborate it can be dissected. Where it is brief this cannot be done. The result is confusion and conflict. No two of the documents agree because each needs to complete it just what the others have taken away from it.[77]

### 3. Genesis xv.2-3

In these verses we read that, in response to a "word of Jehovah"[78] which declared His peculiar love of Abram and implied that Abram might expect some signal token of His favor, the patriarch asked a very natural question:

Vs. 2. "And Abram said, Lord Jehovah, what wilt thou give me, when I am going childless and he that shall be possessor of my house is Eliezer of Damascus?"

The force of the question seems clearly to be that nothing would so evidence the love of Jehovah for Abram as the birth of a son which would end this intolerable situation. So, to make it clear that he believed Jehovah was responsible for his deplorable condition and could remedy it, Abram went on to speak more definitely:

Vs. 3. "And Abram said, Behold to me thou hast given no seed: and, lo, one born in my house is mine heir."

This statement is not superfluous. The first part adds point to the question which precedes it, and prepares for the second "word of Jehovah"—"not this one shall be thine heir"—which immediately follows; and there is no reason why Abram should not reiterate in different words his chief complaint that one who was not his son was nevertheless his *heir*. As far as phraseology is concerned there is no warrant for source analysis. Yet the critics insist that we have "obvious doublets" (Skinner) in vss. 2-3; and for many years they have been disposed to divide these verses between J and E. And instead of simply assigning vs. 2 to J and vs. 3 to E, which would be relatively simple, they have complicated matters by dividing each verse in half and giving vss. 2a and 3b to J and vss. 3a and 2b (reversing the order) to E. This is regarded as probable by Driver. J then reads as follows: "(2a) And Abram said, O Lord Jehovah, what wilt thou give me, seeing I go childless . . . (3b) and, lo, one born in my house is my heir," while E tells us, "(3a) And Abram said, Behold to me thou hast given no seed . . . (2b) and he that shall be possessor of my house is Eliezer of Damascus." In this alleged doublet many critics find "the first traces in the Hexateuch of the document E." Yet no sufficient reason is apparent why these verses should be regarded as a doublet, why they should be divided in this awkward way, and why E should begin just here.

### 4. Genesis xxiv.58-61

The critics have often commended the fine literary quality of the document J. They consider it a very admirable specimen of narrative prose. In chap. xxiv. they find the writer of this document at his best. "The chapter is one of the most perfect specimens of descriptive writing that the Book of Genesis contains."[79] Such being the case it should be appropriate for study as a masterpiece of Hebrew narrative and descriptive prose. Regarding it as such, we observe that it is markedly characterized by that tendency to reiteration which has been referred to above. How the servant recognized Rebekah as the divine choice for Isaac is told in prospect (vss. 12-14), in actuality (vss. 15-20), and in retrospect (vss. 42-48). There is both sameness and variety in the three accounts. Yet all are given to J. Especially interesting is the account of Rebekah's departure

(vss. 59-61). It consists of a number of sentences of varying length, loosely connected by "and," and reads as follows:

"59 And they sent away Rebekah their sister, and her nurse, and
Abraham's servant, and his men.

"60 And they blessed Rebekah, and they said unto her, Thou art our
sister, be thou *the mother of* thousands of ten thousands, and let thy seed
possess the gate of those which hate them.

"61 And Rebekah arose, and her damsels, and they rode upon the
camels, and followed the man: and the servant took Rebekah, and went."

These three verses describe the departure of Rebekah
from her home to go to the far country to be the wife of
Abraham's son. It is an event of great interest and emo-
tional appeal; and the historian lingers over it as if he
would make us see it from every angle. He describes it
from three points of view; the family, Rebekah herself,
and Abraham's servant. The first description (vss. 59-60)
is the longest. Verse 59 is a kind of summary. It tells us
of the sending away of Rebekah and describes the size of
the caravan, as consisting of Rebekah, her nurse, Abraham's servant and his men. To it is added as a kind of after-
thought the important fact that her family sent her away
with their blessing and with the highest hopes for her future. Then we are told about Rebekah. "Rebekah arose
and her damsels, and they rode upon the camels and followed the man" (vs. 61a). This statement shows us that
Rebekah went willingly (vs. 58), and that she was worthily
attended. Lastly, we are told of the servant: "And the
servant took Rebekah and went" (vs. 61b). This is the
briefest of all the pen-pictures. But in some respects it is
the most vivid. In the fewest possible words it tells us that
the servant got what he went for and was off. There is in
it a note of triumph which thrills us!

There are several things to notice about this narrative.
One is that the first account is not strictly chronological.
It places the blessing of Rebekah by her family after they

had sent her away, while it of course preceded it.[80] Furthermore, the details are different. The family sent away Rebekah and her *nurse;* Rebekah took her *damsels* with her; the servant took *Rebekah.* If these statements are taken as mutually supplementary, there is no difficulty whatsoever with the narrative. The writer tells the story from different angles, adds here a little and there a little, and even goes back to the beginning several times as if he had forgotten a point which he wished to mention. But if these accounts are regarded as distinct and each is thought of as complete, then they become conflicting and contradictory. Consequently we must take one or other of two attitudes toward it. We may hold that this chapter is as we are told a fine example of Hebrew historical prose-writing and therefore regard these features which we have been examining, and of which many other examples might be given, as characteristic of it;[81] or we must say that the narrative is composite, that its apparent unity is the result of the blending of conflicting and discordant elements, and that J instead of being a great historical writer was simply a bungling compiler. Skinner has endeavored to do both. He praises J's splendid narrative style; and yet he finds in these verses and elsewhere in the chapter evidence that the narrative is composite. Thus he tells us, "in vs. 59 Rebekah is sent away with her *nurse,* in 61*a* she takes her own *maidens* with her; her departure is twice recorded (61*a*, 61*b*)." Such criticism is petty and captious and shows an eagerness to pick flaws which is far from commendable.

### 5. *Genesis xli.14*

Genesis xli. is assigned by the critics in the main to E. But verse 14 has caused them considerable difficulty. It consists of six short sentences joined together by "and":

"And Pharaoh sent, and he called Joseph, and they brought him hastily [literally, "caused him to run"] from the dungeon, and he shaved himself, and he changed his garments, and he came in unto Pharaoh."

Obviously, several of these brief sentences could be omitted without destroying the sense, although there is not one of them which can be regarded as superfluous. In the words, "and they caused him to run from the dungeon," Driver finds "traces of J." Skinner speaks of it as "a clause inserted from J." This is remarkable. According to the critics, "run" is J in Gen. (9 times), but "dungeon" [or, "pit," *bor*] is E (6 or 7 times). That is, the two words point in opposite directions.[82] Driver and Skinner assign the rest of the verse ("and he shaved himself," etc.) to E. Some critics assign it to J. This is inconsistent. The word "shave" *(galach)* occurs nowhere else in J or E. It occurs once in D (Deut. xxi.12). The other 7 occurrences in the Pent. are all P or H. So if the third of these sentences is cut out and given to J, consistency would seem to require that the fourth be assigned to P or at least be regarded as a late interpolation. Yet we know quite well that the mention of "shaving" is historically correct, since "shaving" was practiced by the Egyptians in early times.[83]

### 6. *Joshua ix.15*

The way in which narratives which are characterized by diffuseness of expression lend themselves to source analysis and the extremes to which such analysis can be carried is well illustrated by the compound sentence in Josh. ix.15:

> "And Joshua made peace with them, and he made a covenant with them, to let them live: and the princes of the congregation sware unto them."

The three parts of this sentence are not identical or strictly synonymous. But all three cover much the same ground. The first two describe the covenant as the act of Joshua; and the second may be regarded as a perfectly proper amplification of the first. The third part describes the covenant as also the act of the "princes of the congregation," thereby bringing out the relevant and important fact that these leaders ratified or joined in Joshua's act. There is nothing in the phrasing of the verse to indicate that it is composite,[84] unless the very fact that the sentence is compound is to be regarded as proof of this.[85] Consequently if the phrase "the princes of the congregation" is regarded as characteristic of P, the whole verse might be claimed for that source. But this would make the transition from vs. 14 to vs. 16 abrupt, and since the critics find only very slight traces of P in Josh. i.-xii., it is a simple matter to cut away the last part of vs. 15 and treat it, together with vss. 17-21 which closely resemble it in phraseology, as an insertion from P. This does not seriously affect the narrative as a whole. But the assigning of vss. 15c and 17-21 to P is of importance to the critics since it helps them to defend their claim that the expressions, "prince," "congregation," and "princes of the congregation," all belong to P. A further step in the analysis of vs. 15 is to assign the first two parts to E and J respectively. If this is done, the critics have succeeded in dividing a single short verse about equally between three sources; and the doublet theory is applied to the fullest possible extent.[86] Such microscopic analysis of a single verse which in the Hebrew has only 12 words (4 are given to E, 4 to J, 4 to P) may impress the uninitiated with the amazing skill of the critics. But it is really quite simple, and we believe also quite absurd.

## II. Repetitive Parallelism Characteristic of Poetry and Elevated Prose

In dealing with the question of repetitions, it is important to note that repetition or parallelism in phraseology and content *(parallelismus membrorum)* is a characteristic feature of Hebrew poetry. This is so obvious that proof is unnecessary. A familiar illustration of practically synonymous parallelism is the following:

> "The law of Jehovah is perfect, restoring the soul,
> The testimony of Jehovah is sure, making wise the simple"
> (Ps. xix.7).

During the last half century much attention has been given to the subject of Hebrew poetry. A thorough study of its metrical forms has been made as exhibited in such strictly poetical books as the Psalms. An attempt has also been made to discover poetical passages in much of the prose of the Old Testament, especially in the Prophets.

This has been carried to such an extreme by some scholars that they have insisted on altering the text in order to make it conform to a given metrical scheme. But, while this use of metrics is unwarranted, it has been clearly shown that the dividing line between prose and poetry is not fixed and sharply defined but that elevated or impassioned prose may approximate very closely to poetry, especially that it is often marked by that basic characteristic of Hebrew poetry, balanced repetition or parallelism.[87] A score or more of such poetical passages have been pointed out by the critics in Gen. i.-xx. Several of them are in the first two Sections. We quote one from each Section:

"And Elohim created — the man in his image — in the image of Elohim — he created him — male and female — he created them" (Gen. i.27);

"Cursed be the ground on thine account,
In pain shalt thou eat it all the days of thy life;
And thorns and briars shall it produce for thee — and thou shalt eat the herb of the field.
In the sweat of thy brow — thou shalt eat bread,
Until thou return to the ground — for from it thou wast taken;
For dust thou art — and unto dust thou shalt return" (Gen. iii.17-19).

Obviously it is the repetition, the balanced repetition, which gives these passages that poetical form which they are alleged to have. In the first, the word "created" is used three times and the words "Elohim" and "image" twice. In the second, "eat" is used three times, "ground," "return," and "dust" twice; "pain," "thorns and briars," and "sweat of thy brow," all stand in relation to one another, as do also "all the days of thy life" and "until thou return unto the ground." These and other features which might be mentioned show how natural it is for emphasis to express itself in repetition and for such repetition, whether of words or ideas, to assume a balanced form which is markedly poetic.

We would not assert that balanced repetition by itself entitles a passage to be called poetry. But the very fact that such parallelism is so marked a feature of poetry would naturally lead us to expect it to occur in prose, especially in elevated or impassioned prose.

*a.* The plea made in behalf of the daughters of Zelophehad in Num. xxxvi. is not poetry. We might even regard it as coldly matter of fact. But the opening sentence shows how easily a formal argument can assume the form of almost poetical parallelism:

"And they said:
Jehovah commanded my lord to give the land in inheritance by lot to the children of Israel;
And my lord was commanded by Jehovah to give the inheritance of our brother Zelophehad to his daughters."

Here the two statements are closely parallel: the one gives the general ground for the plea, the other the particular. And the desire to vary the form while keeping the two statements closely parallel is responsible for the almost unique form of expression, "my lord was commanded by Jehovah," the active form of statement being followed by the rarely used passive.[88]

*b.* A passage which has caused the critics some difficulty is Gen. xxi.1-2:

"And Jehovah visited Sarah as he had said,
And Jehovah did unto Sarah as he had spoken.
And Sarah conceived and bare Abraham a son in his old age,
At the set time of which Elohim had spoken to him."

This passage seems to be simple narrative prose. But it is to be noted that like the ones which have just been considered it is clearly marked by a balanced parallelism which makes it quite as poetic, as far as form is concerned, as any one of them. It is we believe a good illustration of the fact that, in good Hebrew narrative style, emphasis is often secured by repetition and this repetition tends to assume that balanced form which is characteristic of formal poetry. Obviously, however, such a passage lends itself very easily to the critical theory of "doublets."[89] And it has long been customary to assign the first half of each verse to J

and the second to P. This is simplicity itself, except for
the fact that in the first verse the parallelism is so close that
the word "Jehovah" appears in both halves of the verse.
Consequently, if vs. 1*b* is to be P, it has to be assumed that
the redactor made a slip of the pen, or intentionally
changed the *Elohim* (or *El Shaddai*) of his P document
to *Jehovah*. If he did this intentionally, he was guilty of
what, according to the critics, he regarded as the gross
anachronism of making P use the name Jehovah before Ex.
vi.3. Furthermore there is not the slightest evidence of the
allegedly distinctive style of the document P in either
vs. 1*b* or vs. 2*b*.[90]

*c*. Gen. xxi.6 exhibits a rhythmic parallelism which
makes it quite as poetic as many passages which the critics
treat as poetry:

"And Sarah said,
    *Elohim* has made laughter for me;
    Every one hearing will laugh over me."

The thought-sequence is quite logical. The second statement follows naturally from the first. The phrasing of the
two parts of the sentence is so similar as to give no ground
for partition. Yet Cornill and other critics assign the first
line to E and the second to J.

*d*. A somewhat similar example is the account in Gen.
xxx.23f. of the naming of Joseph:

"And she conceived and bare a son and said,
    '*Elohim* has taken-away my reproach';
And she called his name Joseph saying,
    'May *Jehovah* add to me another son.' "

Structural and rhythmic balance and parallelism is marked;
and there is a play on the words "take away" (*asaph*) and
"may he add" (*yoseph*), which binds the two verses together. Rachel's first thought was of gratitude that the
reproach of barrenness had been taken from her. Quite
naturally it was followed by desire and hope for a second
blessing. The use of the two divine names, *Elohim* and

*Jehovah,* is quite natural and proper; but according to the theory of the critics it necessitates the partition of the verses. So vs. 23 is given to E and vs. 24 to J; and it is argued that we have here two different and conflicting accounts of the name Joseph. Yet the incident as it stands in Genesis is exactly what we might expect in the case of one who like Rachel had waited long for the blessing of motherhood and whose reproach had been especially hard to bear because of the fruitfulness of a rival wife.

*e.* Ruth's immortal words to Naomi (i.16-17) are usually treated as simple prose. But they show a balance and parallelism which makes them decidedly poetic:

> "Intreat me not to leave thee,
>   To turn back from after thee,
>   For whither thou goest, I will go,
>   And where thou lodgest, I will lodge,
>   Thy people my people, and thy God my God.
>   Where thou diest, I will die,
>   And there will I be buried.
>   Jehovah do so to me, and so may he add
>   If death should part between thee and me."

There is so much emphatic elaboration in these words that it would be a simple matter to divide them into two protestations of loyalty: (1) a promise to return with Naomi to Bethlehem and "lodge," i.e., sojourn with her for a time; and (2) a more thoroughgoing promise, to become an Israelite by accepting Naomi's people and her God. Since vs. 10 tells us that both daughters-in-law declared they would return with Naomi, while vs. 14 states that only Ruth actually did this, it might be argued, in accordance with the theory of doublets, that the one promise represents the words of Orpah, the other the words of Ruth, and that this difference reflects the two conflicting traditions which have here been merged into one, the words of Orpah being given to Ruth in accordance with the tradition which dominates the story in the Book of Ruth and makes Ruth the heroine, the only one who returned. No critic has proposed to partition the Book of Ruth after this fashion. But it would be quite in accord with the theory of doublets and quite as simple as some of the examples which they have discovered in the Pentateuch. Quite as simple, and quite as absurd.

Such examples as have been given here and in Chapter IV should serve to make it abundantly clear, that the very characteristics upon which the critics depend so largely in endeavoring to prove that certain passages are composite appear quite as plainly in other passages the homogeneity of which they do not question. The only proper inference would seem to be that they have made inconsistent use of these characteristic features of Biblical style to prove a theory which, if worked out consistently, would so disintegrate the Bible, as it would any other book, that the result would be the *reductio ad absurdum* of the theory itself.

# CHAPTER VI

# THE CONTINUITY AND EXTENT OF THE DOCUMENTS

WE HAVE SEEN that the work of Hupfeld was especially important in two respects: he insisted on the recognition of the continuity of the documentary sources of Genesis, and he recognized a Second Elohist (E) which was quite distinct from the First Elohist (P) and resembled the Jehovist (J). To this Second Elohist he assigned the greater part of the material in Gen. xx.-l., which had been previously assigned to the one Elohistic document. These two principles were mutually antagonistic. The recognition of a third source of the Book of Genesis increased the difficulty of proving the continuity of the sources; and the restricting of the First Elohist (P) to only a small part of the Elohistic material tended to destroy that continuity, which was the very thing which Hupfeld regarded it as of the utmost importance to establish. This led as we have seen to increased emphasis on the theory of doublets.

Stated in terms of Driver's analysis, we have the following noteworthy facts. Driver assigns about 780 of the 1,534 verses of Genesis to J and about 730 to the Elohistic writings P and E. Of the 730 assigned to P and E, nearly 200 are in Gen. i.-xix. and are assigned to P.[91] This leaves to P and E in the rest of Genesis about 550 verses of which about two-thirds are assigned to E and only one-third to P. In other words, of the 1,036 verses in Gen. xx.-l. only 175 are assigned to P, as against the 600 or more verses assigned to their one Elohist by Astruc and Eichhorn.

## I. The Continuity of P

It appears then that of the three sources (P, E, and J) recognized as occurring in Genesis, P is the most meagre. This is especially noteworthy since P is claimed to have a distinctive and unmistakable style. It is also noteworthy that of the 186 verses assigned to P in Gen. i.-xix., one-half are found in three chapters or connected narratives (i.-ii.4a, v.[except vs. 29], xvii.) while in chaps. xx.-l., nearly one-half are found in three other chapters (xxiii., xxxvi., xlvi.6-27). This not merely has the effect of leaving only relatively few verses to P in the rest of Genesis, but it serves to call attention to the remarkable fact that several extended narratives (e.g., chaps. i, xvii., xxiii.) are given to P, despite the fact that a marked feature of this document is its fragmentariness.[92] It would be strange that a document which deals with certain matters so fully should be so exceedingly sketchy as a whole. On the other hand, if the P document dealt with other matters as fully as with these, it is singular that the editor omitted the great bulk of the P document in favor of the material given in J and E. It raises the question whether the so-called distinctive style of P is not largely due to the subject-matter instead of being characteristic of a distinct document.

How markedly fragmentary the document P is in Genesis, considered as a whole, the following facts will show. There are thirteen chapters in Genesis in which P has only five or less verses and these are often widely separated: xii.4b, 5; xiii.6, 11b, 12a; xvi.1a, 3, 15, 16; xix.29; xxi.1b, 2b-5; xxvi.34, 35; xxix.24, 29; xxxi.18f.; xxxiii.18a; xxxvii.1, 2a; xli.46; xlviii.3-7; l.12-13. The number of single verses or half-verses in P is quite large. Thus in chap. vii., P has six fragments (vss. 6, 11, 13-16a, 17a, 18-21, 24), in chap. viii. four fragments (vss. 1-2a, 3b-5, 13a, 14-19), in chap. xxxiv. eight fragments (vss. 1-2a, 4, 6, 8-10, 13-18, 20-24, 25 [partly], 27-29).[93] It is only necessary to read consecutively such passages as Gen. xvii.22-27, xix.29, xxi.1*b*, 2*b*-5 and xxiii.1-20, or xxv.19-20, 26*b*, xxvi.34, 35, xxvii.46, xxviii.9, xxix.24, (28*b*), 29, (xxx.22*a*), xxxi.18*b* and xxxiii.18*a*, or xxxvii.1-2*a*, xli.46*a* and xlvi.6-27, to see how markedly lacking in continuity the P narrative really is. Again and again it appears with perfect clearness that P is unintelligible because statements which it presupposes have been assigned to J or E.

Especially noteworthy is Gen. xix.29. It is the only verse in chaps. xviii.-xx. which is assigned to P. It refers to the overthrow of the cities of the plain and the sending forth of Lot, because God remembered Abraham. Yet P knows nothing of this overthrow, the entire acount of which is given to J. Practically every word or phrase in the verse can be found in J or E passages; and were it not that the critics are concerned to find here evidence of the continuity of P, even at the cost of making P allude to an event which he does not describe, it would be far simpler for them to attribute the *Elohim* of this verse to the redactor (as in iv.29 and ix.27) or to assign the verse to E, which according to many critics begins in chap. xv. and resembles J in style, than to assign it to P.

## II. The Continuity of J and of E

In the case of J and E it might be expected that the admission that the style of E resembles that of J would make the critics cautious in the attempt to distinguish between them. It is true that in some cases they do not attempt this and speak of such doubtful passages as JE. But, while admitting the difficulty of the analysis, they have often carried it to such an extreme as to make J and E passages quite as fragmentary as P. How extremely fragmentary a seemingly self-consistent narrative can become through the attempt to analyze it into two or three parallel accounts is illustrated by the treatment accorded to Gen. xxxvii. As to the analysis of this chapter there is, according to Skinner, "substantial agreement amongst critics." The 36 verses are divided by him into 35 fragments, 19 of which consist of half a verse or less than half. Of these fragments 3 are given to P, 14 to

J, and 18 to E. Yet this is a chapter in which the primary criteria, the divine names *Jehovah* and *Elohim,* do not occur once. The entire chapter was assigned by Astruc and Eichhorn to a single document (the Elohist). The primary object of such an analysis must be to establish the continuity of the alleged sources by proving the narrative to be composite and to contain diverse and conflicting accounts of the same event: e.g., a "sale" and a "kidnapping" version of Joseph's carrying off to Egypt. But it illustrates in a striking and convincing way the destructively disintegrative character of the critical method.

Despite an analysis which is often hairsplitting the continuity of J and of E, like that of P, leaves very much to be desired. Thus, J introduces Noah with great abruptness (v.29). J tells of Abram's marriage (xi.28f.), without saying who he is. J tells of Isaac's birth (xxi.1*a*), but leaves him nameless and does not refer to him again until chap. xxiv., when he tells at great length of the way in which he was provided with a wife. J introduces Moses as "grown up" (Ex. ii.11), merely intimating that he was an Israelite ("he went out unto his brethren"), or as on the point of fleeing from Pharaoh (vs. 15, Driver). Equally striking is the abruptness with which Joshua is introduced. If all the allusions to Joshua up to Num. xxxii. are given to E or P (Driver insists that the mention of Joshua in xxxii.12 is a mark of P), Joshua is in J an unknown quantity and no reason is given for the prominent rôle he plays after Moses' death.

The same discontinuity appears in E. According to most critics, E begins abruptly with chap. xv. or xx. Why this is the case is purely a matter of conjecture. E does not mention Isaac's birth but tells of his weaning and of the casting out of Hagar and Ishmael (xxi.8-21). E does not know of the birth of Esau and Jacob. Some critics give part of the account of the "blessing" (chap. xxvii.) to E; Driver's E skips from xxii.19 to xxviii.11 (Jacob at Bethel). In Ex.

i-xiv., E is meagre and fragmentary: e.g., v.1-2, 4; vii.15*b*, 17 (in part), 20*b;* ix.22-23*a,* 24*a,* 25*a,* etc. (See Appendix I). There is no real continuity in such disconnected fragments. Finally, it is to be remembered regarding both J and E that after Exodus the analysis of JE is admitted to be difficult and uncertain.

Such examples as the above will suffice to show that the documents J and E are markedly fragmentary and lacking in any real continuity. To regard them as originally possessing continuity, it is necessary to assume that each contained such data as are found in the other documents and that wherever material essential to the continuity of the document is omitted, the editor did this to avoid needless duplication. This does not account for the fact that according to the critics duplication is one of the clearest evidences that the Pentateuchal narratives are composite. Consequently both the duplication and the fragmentariness or lack of duplication must be explained as due to the more or less arbitrary policy pursued by the redactor in including or excluding material contained in the sources which he made use of.

### III. The "Hexateuch" a Modern Invention

Closely related to the question of the continuity in the Pentateuch of the documents of which it is alleged to be composed, is the further question whether these sources extend beyond the Pentateuch and if so how far they can be traced. It has been pointed out that while Astruc and Eichhorn did not carry their analysis beyond the early chapters of Exodus, by about 1822 it had been extended to include not only the rest of the Pentateuch but also the Book of Joshua. Consequently in critical circles the word Hexateuch has largely replaced the ancient and familiar word Pentateuch. This is significant. It suggests that these six books constitute a historically verifiable group analogous to the Pentateuch. But such is not the case.

The "Five Books" of Moses or of the Law can be traced back to early times. We have seen that they are clearly referred to by Josephus. In the Hebrew Bible the Massoretic note at the end of the Pentateuch begins with the words: "The five-fifths of (the) Law are concluded."[94] From ancient times the Law has been read in the weekly service of the Jewish synagogue, either according to a yearly or a tri-yearly system. This Law never included Joshua. But there was early added to the reading of the Law the reading of selections (*Haphtaroth*) from the Prophets which were regarded as appropriate. Among the *Haphtaroth* we find selections from Joshua. This is added proof that Joshua was never regarded as part of the Pentateuch. Furthermore, it is to be remembered that the Samaritans accepted the Pentateuch, regarding it as Mosaic, but did not accept Joshua. This is very remarkable, for Joshua would seem to be a book which they would have been particularly eager to claim. It made Shechem one of the cities of refuge (xx.7), a Levitical city (xxi.21), the scene of Joshua's farewell to *all* the tribes (xxiv.1), and the final resting place of Joseph (vs. 32). Yet the Samaritans did not claim or accept the Book of Joshua. This can only mean that they regarded it as no part of the Law of Moses, the authority of which they recognized.

These facts place the critics in a decidedly awkward and difficult position. If they insist that all of the main sources of the Pentateuch (J, E, D, and P) are present in Joshua, and especially if they use this as an argument for the late date of the Pentateuch, it becomes exceedingly difficult to account for the sharp line of demarcation drawn in later times between the Pentateuch and Joshua. If in all of the sources of the Pentateuch the conquest under Joshua was regarded as the proper continuation (or completion) of the history of the Mosaic age,[95] why should this account have been cut away from the combined record in its complete and final form? How could Joshua come to be

regarded as so different, so distinct, and, we may say, so inferior to the Pentateuch, that it had to be placed in a separate group of books, if in all the sources it was originally
an integral part of it? How could it come to be regarded
as so inferior in authority that the Samaritans refused to
accept a book which was so flattering to their pretensions?
It is easy to assert that sometime during the last three or
four centuries before our era, "the book of Joshua was dis-
jointed from the Pentateuch."[96] But where is there any
real proof of such a drastic procedure?

On the other hand, if the critics, while recognizing a
general similarity, draw a distinction between the sources
of Joshua and those of the Pentateuch and connect Joshua
more directly with the rest of the Former Prophets, the continuity of the sources, which since Hupfeld has been so
stressed by the advocates of the Documentary Hypothesis,
is largely destroyed and there ceases to be any sufficient
reason for speaking of a Hexateuch. Thus it is significant
that G. B. Gray in his *Critical Introduction* (1924) while
largely following Driver's analysis of the "Hexateuch" obviously himself preferred to speak of the "Pentateuch,"
as an indication that he was by no means sure that such a
document as the Hexateuch ever really existed.[97] The
theory of a Hexateuch is for the critics a decided liability,
not an asset. It may seem to strengthen the case against
the Mosaic authorship of the Pentateuch, but in doing this
it loads the theory with the further task of explaining how
this Hexateuch came to be broken up into a Mosaic Pentateuch and a non-Mosaic Joshua. For if Genesis which never
mentions Moses could be a part of the Pentateuch, why
could not Joshua which refers to him constantly have remained among the Five (in that case, six) Books of Moses,
if it was originally one of them?

## Chapter VII

## CONCLUSIONS AS TO VARIATIONS IN VIEW-POINT AND SUBJECT-MATTER

THE FIRST REACTION of one unfamiliar with the methods and results of the higher criticism to the theory of doublets is likely to be bewilderment at the multitude of variations and contradictions produced by the critics, and amazement at the industry and ingenuity which they have expended in their detection. It is to be noted, therefore, that the quest for such differences is a relatively simple and easy one. It would be a simple matter to break a crystal ball into a number of fragments and then to fill a volume with an elaborate description and discussion of the marked differences between the fragments thus obtained, and to argue that these fragments must have all come from different globes. The only conclusive refutation would be the proof that when fitted together they form once more a single globe. After all is said it is the unity and harmony of the Biblical narratives as they appear in the Scriptures which is the best refutation of the theory that these self-consistent narratives have resulted from the combining of several more or less diverse and contradictory sources.

Two points are, therefore, especially to be noted in regard to this theory of doublets:

1. The great importance attached to the theory of duplicates is due to the fact that, as we have seen, stylistic differences do not suffice for the analysis. After chap. xix. the bulk of the book of Genesis, about four-fifths, is given to J and E and it is admitted that the stylistic differences between these two sources are slight. Consequently other means have to be discovered for distinguishing them. And

the most important of these is the theory of doublets. The situation has been stated thus: J and E are distinguished from each other "by their use of the divine names, by slight idiosyncrasies of style and by quite perceptible differences of representation."[98] Apparently the order of statement is intended to be climactic, the "quite perceptible differences of representation," or doublets, being the most serviceable guide in distinguishing between these sources.

But the theory of duplicates is not used merely in distinguishing J and E. It serves at times to determine the presence of P. The writer just quoted does not hesitate to make this rather sweeping statement:

> "No critical operation is easier or more certain than the separation of this work [P], down even to very small fragments, from the context in which it is embedded. When this is done, and the fragments pieced together, we have before us, almost in its original integrity, an independent document, which is a *source,* as well as the framework of Genesis."[99]

This would seem to mean that the distinctive style of P can be recognized even in "very small fragments." But such is not actually the case. The same critic in commenting on Gen. xxi.1b tells us: "Since the continuity of P is seldom sacrificed, 1b is usually assigned to that source (Jehovah, a scribal error)." It was pointed out above that there is not a word in this half-verse which is characteristic of P. But since vs. 1b can be regarded as a doublet of vs. 1a, this half-verse is "usually assigned" to P for the sake of the continuity of that document. And, be it especially noted, the one word in this half-verse which is characteristic, the word *Jehovah,* which should suffice to give this half-verse to J, is treated as a "scribal error." This shows very clearly how much reliance the critics are obliged to place upon duplicates in working out their documentary analysis and establishing the continuity of their sources.

2. It is also to be noted that the theory of doublets is much more destructive of the credibility of the Pentateuch than is the theory of diversity of style. Aside from the fact

that according to the critical interpretation of Ex. vi.3 the name Jehovah is an anachronism in J, very considerable differences in style may be recognized in the Pentateuch without impairing its credibility and reliability as a record of actual fact. These differences may be accounted for as due in part to the sources used by the author. But when the critics divide a document into two or three distinct and conflicting accounts, the credibility of the whole is seriously undermined. The result is that the critics find themselves obliged to give the reader such advice as the following:

"Toward the question of the precise historical accuracy of the stories of the books of Genesis and Exodus we ought to take somewhat the same attitude that the editor of the books took when he gave us parallel and conflicting accounts of the same event, and thereby confessed that he was not sure which of the two was exactly right."[100]

From the standpoint of the critics this advice is sound. But it is obviously so worded as to avoid shocking the reader and it does not go far enough. The differences recognized by the critics as proving the existence of parallel accounts, do not concern unimportant details only. They may make a vast difference in the whole tenor of a narrative. Whether Joseph's brethren sold him to the Midianites or he was kidnapped by them is not an unimportant detail. The words "exactly right" do not apply to such a difference. If one account was right the other was wrong, very wrong. And what are we to think of the reliability of an editor who, having two conflicting accounts before him, tried to combine them in a way which would do full justice to neither? If he used both because he was not sure which was true, how can we be sure that either was true? In higher mathematics two minuses are equal to a plus. But it does not follow that in the case of divergent traditions the adding together of two false accounts will make one true account. If the editor combined two conflicting accounts because he was not sure "which of the two was exactly right," have we any good warrant for accepting either of them as cor-

rect? The whole trend of such criticism is directly toward
scepticism. The critics often try to disguise the fact that
their method of interpreting the Pentateuch is destructive
of its credibility as a historical record, or to minimize the
significance of this fact. They tell us that, "It is a suicidal
error in exegesis to suppose that the permanent value of
the book [of Genesis] lies in the residuum of historic fact
that underlies the poetic and imaginative form of the
narratives."[101] But such an appeal from "historic fact" to
"poetic and imaginative form" shows clearly that the critical method is destructive of the credibility of the Bible.
Truth is not secured by combining errors. A very enthusiastic higher critic rather naively admitted this when,
after pointing out several examples of apparently contradictory statements, he said of them, "Criticism has a simple
solution of these contradictions, but though it can explain
them, it cannot remove or explain them away."[102] This
means that the critics can account for these apparent con-
flicts by assigning the conflicting accounts to two or more
conflicting traditions. But how these traditions arose and
how much truth, if any, is contained in each, that they
cannot tell us. They can "explain" the difficulties, they
cannot "explain them away." Their explanation is destructive, not constructive.

Such being the case, all those who wish to believe that the
Pentateuchal history is made up of more substantial stuff
than poetry and imagination, that its narratives are statements of simple truth and not plausible combinations of
dubieties, must ask themselves seriously the question
whether the critics have proved their case. So destructive a
theory should have an extremely compelling basis in fact. Is
there any such basis? We believe there is not. Many of the
repetitions which are adduced as proof of duplicate accounts can be explained as due simply to the frequent use
of compound sentences, to the desire to secure emphasis by

elaboration and amplification, and to the fondness for a balanced style which finds its fullest development in poetry. The differences in statement are in many cases supplementary: they are only contradictory when treated as mutually exclusive.[103] The contradictions which are alleged to prove the theory of composite authorship would largely disappear if the critics would follow the harmonistic method of interpreting Scripture. That method proceeds upon the natural and proper assumption that the Pentateuch was intended to give a true and self-consistent account of the matters of which it treats and that the student of Scripture should therefore interpret Scripture in the light of Scripture, instead of pitting Scripture against Scripture, chapter against chapter, verse against verse, phrase against phrase. The critics decry the harmonistic method of interpretation as unscientific and unscholarly. We believe that, on the contrary, this old and time-honored method of interpretation is quite as scientific and scholarly as any other which can be proposed and that the destructive conclusions to which the divisive method of the critics leads are a cogent argument in favor of the older and better method. Critics of the Bible would do well to bear in mind the advice of Coleridge: "When we meet an apparent error in a good author, we are to presume ourselves *ignorant of his understanding,* until we are certain that we *understand his ignorance.*"[104]

That there is logically no stopping-place for the thoroughgoing critic in the application of his divisive principle of interpretation is strikingly illustrated by the comparatively recent capitulation of the Book of Ezekiel. In 1907 Redpath made the following remarkable statement: "Scarcely any doubt has ever been cast even by the extremest critic upon the unity and authenticity of the book, though a few glosses and interpretative words or notes may have found their way into the text."[105] But why should Ezekiel be exempted from the application of the critical method? Pfeiffer points out in his *Introduction* that in 1914 Hölscher "still maintained substantially the traditional views" regarding this book, but that in 1924 Hölscher "regarded more than six-sevenths of the book as editorial supplement (1,103 out of a total of 1,273 verses)." As an illustration of what an enterprising critic can accomplish in a decade, the case of Ezekiel supplies us with much food for thought. It is not surprising that Ezekiel should have at last succumbed. Rather is it surprising that it so long enjoyed practical immunity from attack. Disintegration must result inevitably from the application of a disintegrative method of interpretation, whether the variations or differences appealed to are found in the form or in the content of the document to which it is applied.

# PART II

# THE DEVELOPMENT OR GRAF-WELLHAUSEN HYPOTHESIS

"Did not Moses give you the law, and *yet* none of you keepeth the law?" (JOHN vii.19)

# THE DEVELOPMENT HYPOTHESIS

T HE ACCEPTANCE of Hupfeld's contention that the Elohistic document is composite constituted, as we have seen, a very important modification of the Documentary Hypothesis. On the one hand, by recognizing a Second Elohist it changed a relatively simple two-document theory into a far more complicated three-document one. For the opponents of the theory this was especially significant because it amounted to a confession that the analysis based on purely literary criteria breaks down very early: at chap. xx. or even xv. where the Second Elohist appears whose style closely resembles that of the Jehovist. On the other hand, by insisting on the continuity of these documents it led to a hairsplitting dissection of chapters and verses which was not calculated to inspire confidence in the correctness of the theory. But despite these marked weaknesses this three-document hypothesis assumed great importance in connection with the Development Hypothesis which was soon to arise.

A serious weakness in the Documentary Hypothesis during the first century of its history lay in the fact that it furnished no definite clue to the date of the documents which its advocates claimed to have discovered. Of one thing only were they sure: the documents are post-Mosaic. It was generally assumed that the Elohistic document, having most of the ten Headings (*toledoth*) assigned to it, furnished the structural outline of Genesis and must be older than the Jehovist, while both were regarded as older than the Deuteronomist. Hupfeld's revolutionary discovery that the greater part of the Elohistic document belonged to another source did not alter this view, since the headings were nearly all given to the First Elohist. So the Second

Elohist was regarded as the "younger" of the two, but as older than the Jehovist. The order of sources was, therefore, First Elohist, Second Elohist, Jehovist, Deuteronomist. But, very soon after Hupfeld announced his Modified Hypothesis, a school arose which, while accepting in principle his conclusions as to the documentary analysis, shifted the emphasis to questions of historical development, to the study of the origin of the customs, institutions, and laws, described in these documents, for the purpose of determining their relative date. In view of the great importance which it attaches to questions of history, or to speak more accurately, of historical development, it is often called the Historical School. But since, as we shall see, it is more interested in proving its theory of development in history than in history *per se,* it rather deserves the name Development Hypothesis.[1] This new school may be regarded as founded by Graf whose *Untersuchungen* appeared in 1865; and the publication of Wellhausen's *Prolegomena* in 1878 gave it great popularity. But although commonly known as the Graf-Wellhausen hypothesis, it cannot be said to have originated with them.[2]

The most important feature of this new theory in its relation to the Document Hypothesis was, as we have seen, the claim that the history of Israel as exhibited in the Old Testament shows no evidence of the ritual laws (the Priest Code) contained in the middle books of the Pentateuch being in existence before the Babylonian Captivity, and that therefore these laws must be assigned to a late date. This proposal, which required that the First Elohist[3] be regarded as the latest instead of the earliest of the documents, was so revolutionary that the attempt was first made to draw a distinction between the historical and the legal portions of the First Elohist and assign only the latter to a late date. But it was soon shown that this could not be done; and the radical conclusion that the entire First Elohist was not the earliest but the latest of the Pentateuchal sources speedily gained general acceptance. This left only very little legal material for the earlier sources. There had been difference of opinion as to the source to which the Decalogue (Ex. xx.1-17) and the Book of the Covenant (xxi.1-xxiii.19) belonged. Hupfeld had given both to his *Urschrift*. Others of the critics had assigned the Book of the Covenant to J. Since Hupfeld's day the view has gradually prevailed that the Decalogue and the Book of the Covenant belong to the Second Elohist (E),[4] and that the only legal code in J is to be found in Ex. xxxiv., which some critics call the Decalogue of J.

As regards the order and date of the Pentateuchal sources there has been considerable difference of opinion. According to Driver there is general agreement on three points: (1) that neither J nor E is later than 750 B.C.; (2) that D dates from the time of Josiah's reform, 622 B.C.; and (3) that P belongs to the exilic and post-exilic periods. As to the relative order and date of J and E, Wellhausen and his followers placed J at 850-800 B.C. and E cir. 750 B.C. But others have maintained the earlier view that E is older than J. P in its completed form dates, according to many critics, from as late as 450-400 B.C. The earliest part of P, the Holiness Code (H), is regarded by some as later than Ezekiel (e.g., Cornill), by others as earlier (e.g., Driver).

With regard to these sources and the symbols which are assigned to them several things are to be noted, in addition to those which have been already referred to.

J stands for Jehovist. In Genesis this document is characterized by the use of the word *Jehovah*. But the symbol J is also appropriate because the document is generally regarded as of Judean origin, dating from about the reign of Jehoshaphat. The J document is historical. It is our fullest source for the patriarchal period. After the Exodus it becomes rather meagre. It has no code of laws unless such a code is found in Ex. xxxiv.

E represents the Second Elohist. It is scarcely entitled to

this symbol since the name *Elohim* is far more distinctive of the First Elohist in Genesis. But the symbol is appropriate since a more distinctive name has been found for the First Elohist, viz., P (the Priestly writing). The symbol E is also suggestive because the critics regard this document as originating in the Northern Kingdom and therefore describe it as Ephraimite. It begins at Gen. xx. (or chap. xv.) and is less full in dealing with the patriarchal period than is J. Like J its interest is historical. But the Book of the Covenant is usually assigned to it.

Both J and E are regarded as dating from before the beginning of the great prophetic movement of the 8th and 7th centuries (Amos, Hosea, Micah, Isaiah), i.e., before 750 B.C. But the critics are not agreed as to the truthworthiness of these documents. Some regard J and E simply as compilers of the myths, legends, hero-tales, etc., of the past. To them these documents are "pre-prophetic," both in the sense of having been written before the prophetic period began and also as correctly representing the life and ideals of the period they describe. Others hold that the authors of these documents wrote under the influence of the prophetic movement which culminated in the writings of the prophets just mentioned and that their own writings were colored by it. Such critics are therefore disposed to apply the word "prophetic" to both J and E, and to contrast them as the prophetic histories with the priestly history recorded in P. Consequently there is considerable difference of opinion among them as to the reliability of J and E as writers of *history*.

D, the Deuteronomist, is usually connected directly with the reform of Josiah. It is held that the book found by Hilkiah in the temple was at least the nucleus of Deuteronomy, and that it was prepared and placed in the temple for the express purpose of being discovered and made the basis of a so-called reform. D is often spoken of as representing the "prophetic movement." Thus Deut. vi.4-5 is the essence of "prophetic" religion. But there is also a pronounced "priestly" element in it as shown by the emphasis placed on sacrifice (cf. xii., especially). Broadly speaking the bulk of Deuteronomy (v.-xxvi.) may be described as an exposition of the Decalogue, which stands at its beginning (v.6-21). But it is claimed that D introduced important innovations, notably the centralization of the worship at the one sanctuary. This law of the one sanctuary has since De Wette (1805) been regarded as proving that this code belongs to the time of Josiah. And since the book purports to be very largely composed of addresses made by Moses shortly before his death, it has often been called "a pious fraud."[5]

P stands for the Priestly writing. It may also suggest post-exilic, since it is usually regarded as introduced by Ezra. To P the bulk of the laws of the Pentateuch is assigned; viz., the greater part of Ex. xxv.-xl. (except xxxii.-xxxiv.), Lev. (the whole), Num. i.-x., xv.-xx., and xxv.-xxxvi. P is consequently in several respects the antithesis of J and E. It is mainly legal; they are mainly historical. They are the earliest documents: it is the latest. As earlier, they should be the more reliable witnesses regarding the period with which they purport to deal. P also differs from D in that the legislation in P is on the whole more technical and ritualistic than that in D which is of a more general character.

It is to be noted that this revolutionary theory regarding the date of P was prepared for and in a sense made possible by the adoption of Hupfeld's distinction between the *Urschrift* and the Second Elohist. This distinction made it unnecessary to transfer the entire Elohistic material to a post-exilic date. The bulk of the history, being assigned to a Second Elohist which resembled the Jehovist more than it did the *Urschrift* (P), could be allowed to remain at a pre-exilic date when P was declared to be post-exilic. This simplified the task of the advocates of this "Copernican revolution" to no small degree.

The Biblical argument for the acceptance of the Development Hypothesis has been well stated by G. B. Gray as follows:

"The now prevalent critical opinion that P is the latest of the three main documents rests largely on a comparison of the three codes with *the actual course of history,* so far as that is known. Such a comparison shows (1) that the practice of the Hebrews prior to the seventh century follows the laws in JE (*i.e.* mainly Ex. xx.-xxiii.); (2) that the practice of the Jews at the reformation of Josiah, and subsequently, changes from the earlier practice in the direction of the laws of D, where they differ from those of JE; and (3) that the practice of the Jews from the time of Ezra onwards follows P, where this is in conflict with the laws of JE or D."[6]

This statement seems at first sight both logical and cogent. It would seem to offer a perfectly proper and practicable means of ascertaining the dates of these documents; and the critics regard the results which they arrive at as conclusive evidence of the correctness of their theory that the Pentateuch cannot be Mosaic but represents a long development which was not completed until a century or more later than the Babylonian Exile. Two important caveats are therefore to be introduced as preliminary to its discussion. The first is, to direct attention to the fact that the italicized words *"the actual course of history,"* are immediately qualified by the significant addition, "so far as that is known." This qualification is especially noteworthy since the following paragraph begins with the words: "Our knowledge of the history is incomplete; and consequently it is impossible to find records of practice in regard to innumerable details of the laws." This can only mean that the test proposed by the advocates of this hypothesis must be regarded as, to no slight degree, inconclusive and even misleading, because conclusions based on incomplete testimony can never be absolutely reliable. The second caveat is based on the fact that it is asserted again and again in the Old Testament with mournful and even monotonous iteration and reasserted in the New Testament that the history of Israel was largely one of apostasy from the laws given to the people by God through Moses.[7] If this be true, then failure to "practice" the laws, especially those laws which differed most markedly from the customs and practices of other nations, would be a conclusive proof of disobedience or culpable forgetfulness, but not necessarily a proof that the laws had not been long in existence. These two important caveats bear upon the whole subsequent discussion.

By the dates which it assigns to these three legal codes (or four, if we recognize a J Decalogue), this hypothesis divides the history of Israel broadly speaking into three great periods—Pre-prophetic Religion, Prophetic Religion and the Reform of Josiah, Priestly Religion—each of which requires careful consideration.

# CHAPTER I

## THE RELIGION OF ISRAEL IN THE
## PRE-PROPHETIC PERIOD

ACCORDING to the statement quoted above, "the practice of the Hebrews prior to the seventh century
followed the laws in JE (i.e., mainly Ex. xx.-xxiii.)." This
statement might easily be taken to mean that the simple
laws of the Decalogue and the Book of the Covenant constituted the moral and religious code of the Hebrews from
the days of Moses down to about 700 B.C., or we may say, to
the fall of Samaria. Since the Decalogue is recognized by
both Jew and Christian as the great basic law, this would
mean that the great fundamentals of ethical and spiritual
monotheism as enunciated in the Ten Commandments and
elaborated in the Book of the Covenant were reflected in
"the actual course of history" for many centuries, "prior
to the seventh century." But this is not the meaning which
the words "prior to the seventh century" are really intended to convey. What is meant is that the influence of
the JE laws can be traced in the period to which the critics
assign the J and E documents, i.e., from about 850 B.C.
down to the time of Josiah. The earlier period, especially
the patriarchal and the Mosaic, they regard as largely pre-
literary and pre-historical.

Three questions are raised by this statement: (1) What
are the laws of JE?, (2) When did they first become operative in Israel?, (3) What was the form of Israel's religion
"prior" to the enactment of these laws?

### 1. The Laws of JE

#### a. The Decalogue of J

According to many critics, as we have seen, the laws of J as distinguished from E are given in the so-called Decalogue of J as contained in Ex. xxxiv. As to the exact form of this decalogue, there is considerable difference of opinion among the critics. This is unavoidable since there are more than ten commands in this message.[8] It is here given for convenience in the form advocated by Wellhausen:

I. Thou shalt worship no other god.
II. Thou shalt make thee no molten gods.
III. The feast of unleavened bread thou shalt keep.
IV. All that openeth the womb is mine.
V. Thou shalt observe the feast of weeks.
VI. (Thou shalt observe) the feast of ingathering at the end of the year.
VII. Thou shalt not offer my sacrifice with leavened bread.
VIII. The sacrifice of the feast of the passover shall not be left unto the morning.
IX. The first of the first-fruits of thy ground thou shalt bring unto the house of Jehovah thy God.
X. Thou shalt not seethe a kid in its mother's milk.

#### b. The Decalogue of E

The Decalogue of E (Ex. xx.) is regarded as having had originally the following form, all the rest being looked upon as later expansions.

I. Thou shalt have no other gods before me.
II. Thou shalt not make unto thee a graven image.
III. Thou shalt not take the name of Jehovah thy God in vain.
IV. Remember the sabbath day to keep it holy.
V. Honor thy father and thy mother.
VI. Thou shalt not kill.
VII. Thou shalt not commit adultery.
VIII. Thou shalt not steal.

IX. Thou shalt not bear false witness against thy neighbor.

X. Thou shalt not covet.

While this decalogue is usually called the Decalogue of E, there is a decided difference of opinion as to whether it formed a part of the original E document (e.g., Driver), or is to be regarded as a later insertion in it. The view of the more radical critics, e.g., Pfeiffer, is that it is a later insertion, perhaps taken over from Deut. v. This would make it very much later than the E document itself, since the Deuteronomic Code was promulgated, according to the critics, as late as 622 B.C.

These two decalogues are contrasted by the critics as the "ritual" and the "ethical" decalogues. This distinction is a proper one, if we accept the Decalogue of J as in any sense an adequate code of behavior, at all comparable to the Decalogue of E. It is to be noted, however, that such a comparison is both impossible and preposterous. To prove this, it is only necessary to note the following fact. The Decalogue of E has two parts: it defines man's duty first toward God and then to his fellowmen. The Decalogue of J deals exclusively with the former. Of man's duty to man it says nothing. It would be absurd to argue that laws dealing with respect for parents, murder, adultery, theft, falsehood, covetousness, were unknown as late as 850 B.C. Such laws are found in Egypt and Babylon centuries before that time and even the most primitive peoples have them and enforce them, sometimes with remarkable strictness. Since this decalogue is only half a decalogue as compared with Ex. xx. and since it cannot be claimed that there are only ten commands given in this passage or that the ten given above or any other ten are clearly intended to be a decalogue, it is only natural that a good many critics refuse to recognize this so-called decalogue.[9] It is to be noted, therefore, that the inadequacy of this Decalogue of J and the skeleton form in which the Decalogue of E is accepted by the critics have an important bearing upon their estimate of the laws of JE. Two points are especially important:

(1) There is difference of opinion among the critics as to whether J—we refer especially to J since it is generally regarded as earlier than E—is monotheistic. Some would admit this. But others insist that the words of J, "Thou shalt worship no other god," definitely recognize the existence of such gods; and it is claimed that it was only the "jealousy" of Jehovah which prevented Israel from having a pantheon such as many other peoples had. If such be the case, the same would seem to apply to the command of E, "Thou shalt have no other gods before me," which might be construed in the same monolatrous fashion.

(2) It is claimed that the words of J, "Thou shalt make thee no molten gods," do not prohibit the use of all images in the worship of Jehovah, but only the making of expensive images of metal (gold or silver). Those who hold this view maintain that "graven images" of wood, stone, or clay were permitted by J and were first prohibited considerably later by E. As to this it is to be noted that, if J prohibits only a certain form of idolatry, the use of molten images, it would be proper to interpret E as merely prohibiting another form, the use of graven images. For it is the rest of the Second Commandment, "or any likeness of anything," etc., which makes the prohibition of idolatry thoroughgoing and comprehensive, and this the critics regard as a later addition to the command as originally found in E.

The interpretations placed on the first two commands of J by the critics are arbitrary, and imply that neither the Decalogue of J nor that of E was, in its original form, strictly monotheistic or definitely opposed to idolatrous practices as such. Such a conclusion is so startling that we shall test it first in the light of the teachings of the document J and then in the light of the history of the pre-prophetic period as given in the historical books.

### c. J's Conception of Jehovah

J, being regarded as the oldest document of the Pentateuch, should give us valuable information regarding the religious faith of ancient Israel. Without going into great detail certain outstanding features may be noted:

(1) Jehovah is described as almighty and supreme. He is maker of earth and heaven (Gen.ii. 4$b$), of man (vs. 7), of the animals (vs. 19) and of woman (vs. 21f.). He was known to Abraham as "the judge of all the earth" (xviii.25), as "the God of heaven and the God of the earth" (xxiv.3). In the days of Moses, he showed that His sovereign power extended to foreign nations by delivering His people from Egyptian bondage, even declaring that He had raised up mighty Pharaoh in order to show in him His power and declare His name throughout the earth (Ex. ix.16). Even if the word earth as used here refers only to Egypt, this passage shows that the God of Israel was no mere local or tribal God. Pharaoh had never heard of this God (Ex. v.2, E) who claimed sovereign power over his land, his people and himself. If J does not expressly deny the existence of other gods, it does assert the unique sovereignty of Jehovah in a way which makes it a declaration of practical monotheism.

(2) Jehovah is a holy and righteous God. In Gen. ii-iv. He is represented as requiring absolute obedience. For one transgression Adam and Eve are driven out of the garden. The flood is the penalty for sin (Gen. vi.5-8), the confusion of tongues is the rebuke to man's arrogance (xi.1-9), the destruction of Sodom and Gomorrah is because of outrageous sin. The Egyptians are punished for keeping Israel in cruel bondage.

(3) Jehovah is good and merciful. He clothes Adam and Eve with skins. He gives the rainbow of promise. He is ready to spare Sodom if ten righteous are found there. After the sin of the golden calf, He promises to cause all His good-

ness to pass before Moses (Ex. xxxiii.19) and declares His sovereign grace and mercy.

The character of the God of Israel according to J may be summed up in the words of Ex. xxxiv.6-7: "And Jehovah passed by before him, and proclaimed, Jehovah, Jehovah, a God merciful and gracious, slow to anger, and abundant in lovingkindness and truth; keeping lovingkindness for thousands, forgiving iniquity and transgression and sin; and that will by no means clear *the guilty,* visiting the iniquity of the fathers upon the children, and upon the children's children, upon the third and upon the fourth generation." These words which are declared to be a description of the Name, i.e., character, of Jehovah, give a very high conception of Deity. Jehovah is a God of righteousness, of goodness, and of grace, terrible to the disobedient, gracious to the obedient and repentant. Such a statement compares favorably with descriptions found in other parts of Scripture and may properly be regarded as a declaration of ethical monotheism. And it is to be noted that it occurs in close connection with the passage from which the critics derive the Decalogue of J.

### d. J's Attitude toward Idolatry

While the use of images is not referred to in J, it is asserted that J's conception of Jehovah is anthropomorphic, even crudely so. Jehovah "walks" in the garden (Gen. ii.). He appears as a "man" to Abraham (Gen. xviii.) and a "man" wrestles with Jacob (xxxii.24). It is also claimed that expressions are used in J which originally referred to idolatry. This is asserted of the expressions "appear before" (Ex. xxxiv.23) and "besought" (xxxii.11 JE).[10] It is to be noted therefore that

(1) Anthropomorphic language is unavoidable if man is to form any definite conception of God. It is justified by

the fact that man was made in the "image" of God (Gen. 1.27, P), and became a "living soul" through the inbreathing of Jehovah (ii.7, J). It is perverted when man attributes bodily form, human limitation or sinfulness to God (Rom. i.23). The statements in Gen. i. that God "saw," "said," "called" are in a sense quite as anthropomorphic as the statement in Gen. ii. that He "walked." The language of the Psalms is often highly anthropomorphic. The eyes, ears, hands, feet of God are referred to. Yet the Psalter is the great treasury of devotion of the Christian Church. We understand these expressions as figurative and we believe they were always intended to be such. The words of the Priestly Blessing in Num. vi.24f., "Jehovah make his face to shine . . . lift up his face" are as anthropomorphic as any used in J. Yet they are found in P which is regarded as representing a far more spiritual point of view.

The statement in Ex. xxiv.9 (J), "they saw the God of Israel," might seem to indicate that the God of Israel was regarded as having a material form. But the words which follow indicate that all Aaron and the elders really saw was the heavenly glory which hid Him from mortal eyes. This was like a sapphire pavement under the feet of the Heavenly King. That is, they saw no likeness (cf. Deut. iv.15) of God, but only caught a glimpse of the glory that surrounded Him. Centuries later when Isaiah "saw Jehovah" (vi.1) in the temple, he recalled only that the "train" of His flowing robe filled it completely. Such passages enable us to understand Ex. xxxiii. 18-23 (J). What Moses asked to see was God's "glory." What he was permitted to see was not God's "face," but His "back." The word rendered "back" (achor) means what is "after" or "behind." It may properly be regarded as describing the "afterglow" of the glory of the Divine Presence. The Hebrew has two other words for "back" (gab and gaw), which are used in the physical or anatomical sense. Either of these words would be appropriate in the description of Moses' vision, if the crude meaning which many critics find there were really the one intended. Instead a word is used which need not have such a meaning at all. Such being the case it is to be noted that the former of the two words just mentioned is used in the "writing" of king Hezekiah (Isa. xxxviii.17) in the expression "Thou hast cast all my sins behind thy back (*gab*)," to which only the more extreme critics would think of appealing as evidence that Hezekiah was an idolater.

(2) The Old Testament theophanies are clearly intended to be preliminary to and preparatory for the Incarnation. The exact relation in which the Angel of Jehovah stands to Jehovah Himself is not always clear. But it cannot be maintained that these theophanies are crudely anthropomorphic without reflecting upon the significance of the Incarnation and their close typical connection with it.

## 2. *When Did the Laws of JE Become Operative in Israel?*

Certain statements in the Historical Books are appealed to as proving that the religion of Israel could not have reached the level of spiritual monotheism until at least as late as the time of Jehoshaphat or considerably later.

*a.* The use of the plural noun *Elohim* in speaking of the God of Israel is treated as the survival of primitive polytheism; and the few instances where, when so used, it is construed as a plural instead of as a singular, are appealed to as proving this. But the use of the plural of majesty is so clearly recognized in the Hebrew of the entire Old Testament, as well as in other languages both ancient and modern, that such an explanation is highly improbable. The instances where *Elohim* is construed as plural when used of the God of Israel are so exceptional as to serve only to emphasize the rule.

*b.* Jephthah's comparison of Jehovah with Chemosh (Jgs. xi.24) is appealed to as proving that, in the time of the Judges, Jehovah was regarded as merely a tribal or national god like any other Semitic deity. But two other explanations of Jephthah's words are quite possible. We may hold either that he was using an *ad hominem* argument which would appeal to the king of Moab, without intending to assert that Jehovah was really on a par with Chemosh, or that in view of his birth and

upbringing, or rather the lack of it, Jephthah was in no position to speak as an expert on theological questions, and that
even if he was at best a monolater, this would not prove that
such was the faith of the true followers of the God of Israel of
his day. To reject the express statements of the Pentateuch
and appeal to Jephthah shows the extremes to which the advocates of this theory are obliged to resort in order to defend it.

*c.* When David declares that his enemies have tried to drive
him forth from the heritage of the Lord saying, "Go serve
other gods," (1 Sam. xxvi.19), this may suggest the idea that
Jehovah was in such a sense a local deity that one banished
from the land and nation could not serve Him. But David's
own view, as set forth in Ps. cxxxix. is a quite different one;
and Solomon's prayer at the dedication of the temple shows
that a God, who dwells in heaven and whom the heaven of
heavens cannot contain, could also have a local earthly abode.

*d.* The fact that Absalom asked permission to go to Hebron
to pay a vow at the place where he had made it (2 Sam. xv.7f.),
does not prove that the Jehovah of Hebron was different from
the Jehovah of Jerusalem. Absalom was merely offering an
excuse for leaving Jerusalem in order to perfect his plans for
treasonable revolt. Whether the reason he gave had any foundation in fact we cannot say.

*e.* The men of Babylon, Cutha, and Arva (2 Kgs. xvii.) who
were brought to Samaria to repopulate the country, are even
poorer witnesses. It was natural that they should try to combine the worship of Jehovah with that of their ancestral idols.
But they were the ancestors of the Samaritans of the time of
Ezra and Nehemiah who were not allowed to have any part in
the rebuilding of the temple at Jerusalem.

*f.* Hos. iii.4 is appealed to as implying that image-worship
was lawful or at least permissible as late as the 8th century.
But this inference is by no means necessary. The six things
of which Israel is to be deprived,— king, prince, sacrifice, pillar, ephod, teraphim,—are all, with the exception of the last,
used in both a good sense and a bad. They had a legimate
and an illegitimate use. Israel's demand for a king was evil: yet
Israel had been promised a king. Princes had proved both a
blessing and a curse. Sacrifice, pillar and ephod had proper

uses, but could be used in idolatry. Of the teraphim we know very little. Their use is never approved in the Old Testament.[11] The meaning of the prophet may be simply this, that for her sins Israel is to be deprived of all the civil and religious institutions, both legitimate and illegitimate, with which she was familiar. This need not imply that the prophet regarded the use of teraphim as legitimate. Otherwise the implication would be that he looked forward to a time when such an institution would be restored, an inference which would be quite contrary to the claim of the critics that the prophets of the 8th century were the discoverers of a non-idolatrous and spiritual monotheism.

Such arguments as the above have little weight against the claim that the religion taught by Moses was ethical monotheism and are easily refuted, if the frequent denunciations of the worship of other gods and of the use of images which occur in the Pentateuch and in the Historical Books are given the weight to which they are entitled. It is only when the Decalogue is assigned to a late date and these denunciations of idolatry and polytheism are rejected as representing the viewpoint and estimate of a later age that these arguments acquire any importance. This is illustrated especially clearly by the worship of Jeroboam's calves which continued in Northern Israel from the time of the Schism to the fall of Samaria.[12] This worship has been correctly described as "the stronghold of the case for image-worship."[13] But this is true only if the denunciations in the Books of Kings which occur with such ominous iteration are regarded as representing the viewpoint of a later age. The careful and detailed account of the reason for the overthrow of the Northern Kingdom given in 2 Kgs. xvii. must be rejected as at least a misstatement, if not a deliberate falsification of history, if the worship of the calves was a legitimate part of the worship of Jehovah until near the close of the eighth century B.C.

### 3. What Was the Religion of Early Israel?

If according to the critics the religion of Israel did not cease to be idolatrous and did not reach the level of ethical monotheism until about the year 700 B.C., the question as to the nature of her religion in Mosaic and patriarchal times becomes a pressing one. Where are we to go for an answer? An answer which would find wide acceptance in critical circles is the following:

"Our knowledge of the faith and practice of the ancestors of Israel depends on three sources: (i) archaeology; (ii) comparative religion; and (iii) the traditions of Israel herself as preserved in the book of *Genesis,* with occasional hints and references in other portions of the Old Testament. The last of the three is that which is best known among us, but we are compelled to admit that the record has been colored and, perhaps, modified by the theology of later days. We have to confess that we do not know for certain whom or what Israel worshipped in pre-Mosaic times, and must depend to some extent on conjecture based on the statements supplied to us in the Bible."[14]

In this statement three sources are given for knowledge of the religion of Early Israel. Genesis is mentioned last; and while nothing is said about the value of the other two sources, it is carefully pointed out that the Biblical source is unreliable and not to be accepted at its face value. Archaeology and comparative religion, apparently, are entitled to speak authoritatively and to receive a respectful hearing. The testimony of the Bible is discounted and discredited at the very outset. This animus against the testimony of Scripture is significant. It is significant because of the fact which makes it necessary: the testimony of the Book of Genesis and of the Pentateuch as a whole cannot be accepted at its face value if the theories of the critics as to the religion of Early Israel are to be regarded as correct.

This is too obvious to require proof. If it is true that "we do not know for certain whom or what Israel worshipped in pre-Mosaic times," then surely very little value can be attached to the record of the pre-Mosaic period as given to us in J and E. Certainly J and E tell us very plainly that the patriarchs worshipped a God whom they called Jehovah or Elohim; and they tell us not a little about the God of Abraham, Isaac, and Jacob. If then it is to be asserted that "we do not know for certain whom or what Israel worshipped in pre-Mosaic times," it is putting it mildly to say that "we are compelled to admit that the record has been colored and, perhaps, modified by the theology of later days," and that we "must depend to some extent on conjecture based on the statements supplied to us in the Bible." It would be more correct to say that the records which are regarded by the critics as giving the earliest and fullest account of the beliefs and practices of pre-Mosaic Israel have been so colored and modified that their statements even as to matters of the utmost importance cannot be accepted as true, but may be used only as the basis for conjectures which, even if based to some extent on statements contained in the Bible, derive their real value and authority from the other sources mentioned, archaeology and comparative religion.

The confession "we do not know whom or what Israel worshipped in pre-Mosaic times" is a striking illustration of the agnostic attitude toward Scripture which is the result of the method of criticism which we are considering. If all the Old Testament records are late and so colored and modified as to be unreliable, then as far as the Bible is concerned the pre-Mosaic period has become a *terra incognita,* a land of myth, legend, and conjecture. The necessary conclusion is, We do not know (*ignoramus*). But such a conclusion is highly unsatisfactory, even to those whose critical theories have forced them to it. So the critics have recourse to the first two sources referred to in the quotation given above, archaeology and comparative religion. These must test and pass judgment upon the Biblical data: they must fill the gap which is left when the Biblical evidence has been largely discredited.

The evidence to the contrary having been brushed aside as "colored and, perhaps, modified by the theology of later days," the ground is prepared for a statement such as this: "There is no reason to believe that Yahweh in this early Kenite period differed materially from other Semitic gods." This statement is supported by another, "In the thirteenth century B.C. the spiritual period of religious and ethical conception had not yet begun. We do not find it in any race until about the eighth century B.C."[15] These statements are startling. For we do know something from the Bible and from archaeology of the nature of the gods of the Semitic peoples. They are so different from the God of Israel as portrayed in the Old Testament that we ask for the proof that the God of Israel was regarded in the days of Moses or earlier as a being who did not differ materially from Chemosh or Molech. If the claim that the religion of Israel must originally have been essentially the same as that of other Semitic peoples is to be regarded as axiomatic, it may be accepted as self-evident by all who so regard it. But allusion has been made to "conjecture based on the statements supplied to us in the Bible." What are the conjectures based on Scripture which are appealed to as supporting this claim that Jehovah did not originally differ materially from Chemosh or Molech?

This method of conjecture is applied in several different ways: by "reinterpreting" the narrative, and attaching to it a meaning which is in harmony with the theory of the critics; by "expanding" the narrative and reading into it ideas which are not there; and by "correcting" it, which usually means declaring its statements to be "late" and substituting others which are regarded as "primitive" and therefore as in accord with the theory of the development of Israel's institutions held by the critics. The following examples will illustrate the method and the result of its application.

### a. Animism

Among the theories regarding the origin of religion advocated by those who deny the teaching of Genesis that monotheism was the original faith of man and that all other beliefs are a departure from it, none has enjoyed greater popularity than the Animistic,[16] according to which the religion of primitive man originated in a belief in spirits (*animae*). This view was set forth by E. B. Tylor in his *Primitive Culture* (1871) and exerted a powerful influence on Wellhausen, Stade, Kautzsch, and many others of the higher critics. It is still widely influential today.

(1) As an illustration of animism in Genesis, Jacob's dream at Bethel (Gen. xxviii.) is often referred to by the critics. The narrative tells us that Jacob "lighted upon a certain place,"[17] and took "from the stones of the place and set (it) as his pillows."[18] The narrative seems to stress the casualness of Jacob's preparations. He was tired. It was dark or nearly so. He made the best of things, even using a stone as a pillow, and fell asleep. Then, in a dream, Jehovah the God of his fathers spoke to him. This is what the narrative clearly states. That the stone had any connection with the dream is not even hinted. Jehovah stood at the top of a "ladder" which reached up to heaven. But the critics find here clear traces of animism. They tell us that the stone was indwelt by a *numen* and that when Jacob placed his head on it, the spirit which dwelt in the stone revealed itself to him (incubation). In view of the casualness of the event, the usual view seems to be that it was only through the dream that the sacredness of the stone and of the locality was made known to Jacob.[19] But some even hold that Jacob went to a well-known Canaanite shrine and slept with his head on the sacred stone which was the abode of the presiding *numen* of that heathen sanctuary.[20] In either form the explanation of the critics

is simply an attempt to trace the religion of the Hebrew patriarchs back to a crude animism, because this is regarded as a very primitive form of religion.

(2) A survival of animism has been discovered in the law that an altar was to be made of unhewn stone (Ex. xx.25). According to Kittel, "This altar law assumes that the stone had life or rather that it was the dwelling place of a deity. To hew the stone might injure the deity; to mount it might injure its feelings."[21] Having adopted this primitive interpretation, which is quite gratuitous and even absurd, Kittel could argue that "The law originated in a pre-Mosaic time; Israel adopted it and transferred its application to Yahweh."

(3) Many other illustrations could be given of this "quest of the primitive" as we may call it. The fact that Jacob when returning from Haran (Gen. xxxi.) set up a memorial stone and that Laban said "'this stone is witness" does not prove that either one of them regarded the stone as alive (animatism) or as indwelt by a numen (animism). When the two and a half tribes set up an altar, they said, "It is witness." But they declared most emphatically that this altar was not a shrine for worship. Consequently the Deity did not dwell there. When Samuel set up a memorial stone and called it "Ebenezer," some of the people may have superstitiously regarded the stone as the cause of their deliverance.[22] The name "stone of help" might suggest this. But the explanation of the name is this, "Hitherto hath Jehovah helped us." The stone was simply to serve as a memorial.

(4) Since the ancient Semites, like other peoples, attached sacredness to trees and wells, attempts have been made to find primitive tree worship in Genesis. The suggestion that Abram's worship was connected with sacred trees, Isaac's with sacred wells, Jacob's with sacred stones, is called "a brilliant generalization."[23] Thus we are told that "oak of Moreh" means "oak (or terebinth) of the teacher" and that this oak must have been connected with soothsaying and divination. Confirmation of this is sought in the fact that Deborah "dwelt

(or, sat) under the palm tree of Deborah." So it is claimed that these trees were oracle-trees where, perhaps as at the sacred oak at Dodona, the deity was supposed to speak to his devotee through the rustling of the leaves. Yet there is no proof that *moreh* means teacher. Several other meanings are equally possible,[24] and even if this were the true meaning, this pagan interpretation is not established by it.[25]

(5) An illustration of the extremes to which this quest can be carried is furnished us by the interpretation placed on Lev. xix.9-18 (H), which states the law regarding gleaning. It expressly declares that the corners of the field are not to be gleaned. The reason for the command is given: "Thou shalt leave them for the poor and stranger." The explanation is a good and sufficient one, quite in accord with the humanitarian spirit of the religion of Israel. But the quest of the primitive can furnish another reason. Since this humanitarian rule is found in P (or rather H), it is regarded as representing a late development. So we are told, "It may well be that the corners of the field were originally left so as to avoid driving out the vegetable spirit. That motive is now forgotten; the practice remains, and a new motive characteristic of the codifier and the period is found."[26]

### b. The Passover

One of the best and most familiar examples of the determination of the critics to give an explanation of the institutions of Israel different from the one stated in the Old Testament is the passover. The deliverance from Egypt was a signal and in a sense unique event in the history of Israel. It is referred to scores of times. The rite which signalized and commemorated it was the passover. The very first mention of the passover connects it with the slaying of the first-born of Egypt and the "passing over" of Israel, and the statement follows at once: "And this day shall be unto you for a memorial" (Ex. xii.14, P). The fact that this event took place in the spring, in the month Abib, is definitely stated and this month is made the first month of the year (vs. 2). But the seasonal significance is clearly secondary to the historical. The critics have long maintained that this is contrary to fact. According to Wellhausen, "The only view sanctioned by the nature of the case is that the Israelite custom of offering the firstlings gave rise to the narrative of the slaying of the first-born of Egypt"; and he claimed that "the elaboration of the historical motive of the passover is not earlier than Deuteronomy."[27] This means that the connection of the passover with that great historical event of which the Old Testament makes so much, the deliverance from Egypt, was not "elaborated," or to put it bluntly was not *invented* until shortly before the Babylonian Captivity many centuries later. This illustrates how great historical facts dissolve when placed in the crucible of the critics.

Such being the case it is to be noted that, on the basis of the critics' own reconstruction of the Pentateuch, it is the "early" sources (Ex. xii.25f., xiii 3-9, xxiii.15, xxxiv.18 are J. E., or JE) which connect the passover and the feast of unleavened bread with Egypt. Deut. xvi.1-3 merely repeats what these other passages have already stated. This is significant. But what is still more important is the fact that in the allegedly late sources where according to the Wellhausen theory we should expect to find the *historical* explanation "elaborated" (Lev. xxiii., Ex. xii.1-20, 28, 43-51, Num. ix.1-4, xxviii.-xxix.) there is only one mention of Egypt (the date in Num. ix.1). This as Orr pointed out is just the opposite of what we should expect if this theory of the passover were the true one.[28]

## c. Idolatry

One of the best illustrations of the attitude of the critics toward image-worship in Israel is their conjectural interpretation of the story of the apostasy of the golden calf as recorded in Exodus xxxii. which they assign to JE. A recent statement of this interpretation reads as follows:

"Bull-worship in Israel is first mentioned as an act of apostasy which took place at Sinai itself. The story, as recorded in Exod. xxxii., tells how the people grew anxious at the prolonged absence of Moses on the mountain, whither he had ascended to receive instructions from Yahweh. They had been brought out of Egypt by Moses in order to come into contact with Yahweh, and they had lost their leader without finding their God. Accordingly they applied to Aaron, who bade them bring their golden jewels, which he melted down and made into a calf, telling Israel that this was the God who had brought them out of Egypt. While the revelry in connexion with its worship was at its height, Moses returned, investigated the facts, and strongly condemned the action of Aaron, who defended himself by throwing the blame on the people, and suggesting that the calf form taken by the molten metal was not deliberately planned by him, but was the result of chance. He himself seems to have escaped punishment, but numbers of Israelites fell by the hand of the Levites, who took the sword to avenge the insult put upon Yahweh.

"Now we may suspect that at the great bull sanctuaries, such as Bethel, a story rather like this was told to explain the origin of the cult. But it would have been Moses, not Aaron, who was its author, and the pouring of molten metal into water would be a method whereby men could ascertain the exact form under which Yahweh preferred to be worshipped. A later generation, with the prohibition of images in mind, could not endure the slur on Moses, and while they could not eliminate the tradition, they transferred the odium of it to Aaron, a man who elsewhere is little more than a lay figure with no independent personality of his own. Possibly we have a relic of a cult connected with Horeb and transferred to northern Israel. It is significant that Elijah, for whom Yahweh's dwelling was in Horeb, made no protest, as far as we know, against the cult of the bull."[29]

The first of these paragraphs summarizes the Biblical account. According to it, the bull worship was an apostasy from the covenant just ratified at Sinai; it was denounced by Moses, and the people were severely punished for their "great sin." According to the second paragraph the original story, arrived at through comparative religion's quest of the primitive, must have been just the opposite. Moses tried by magical means, by pouring molten metal into water (hydromancy), to find out the special form under which Yahweh wished to be worshipped. This interpretation assumes that Moses was himself an idolater; and the bull worship was the result of the experiment, as we may call it, which he performed at Sinai. This must have been, we are assured, the original story. And such a story was current, so we are told, at Dan and Bethel, the sanctuaries of the golden calves worshipped by the Northern Tribes. It is sufficient to call the attention of the reader to the fact that these two accounts flatly contradict one another. The critics must admit that the narrative in Ex. xxxii. represents the making of the golden calf as "a great sin" against God. Yet they endeavor to show that in its original form it represented a commendable effort to interpret the mind of God regarding the material form under which He wished to be worshipped.

The interpretation of Ex. xxxii. which has just been considered enables us to understand the estimate which the critics are disposed to form of Jeroboam and the calf worship which he made the state religion of the Northern Kingdom. We have already seen that this worship is denounced in the Books of Kings with the utmost severity. Again and again, more than a score of times, we meet as a mournful refrain such words as these: "He departed not from the sins of Jeroboam the son of Nebat, who made Israel to sin." According to this historical record, which is our principal source of information regarding this worship, the institution of the worship of the golden calves at Dan and Bethel was a terrible act of apostasy which was participated in and perpetuated by every king of the Northern Kingdom and led finally to the destruction of that kingdom. Yet we are told by the critics regarding this act: "Jeroboam, when he said: 'Behold thy God, O Israel, who brought thee up out of the land of Egypt' (1 Kgs. xii.28), was not a religious innovator, but a religious conservative."[30] This means that even as late as the time of the Schism, idolatry was simply regarded as old-fashioned, not as unlawful and morally heinous.

Since the interpretation of the bull worship of Northern Israel just given is in such obvious conflict with the statements of the account in Exodus, it is to be noted that this explanation has recently met with vigorous opposition. According to Albright the Mosaic religion was non-idolatrous (aniconic) in character; and he assures us that "there is no basis whatever for the idea that Yahweh was worshipped in bull form by the

Northern tribes at Bethel and Dan."[81] The reason given for this contention is a startling one:

"The golden calf simply formed the pedestal on which the invisible Yahweh stood, just as in the Temple of Solomon the invisible Glory of God was enthroned above the cherubim; conceptually the two ideas are virtually identical."

The main argument advanced in support of this amazing statement is that "Among Canaanites, Aramaeans, and Hittites we find the gods nearly always represented as standing on the back of an animal or as seated on a throne borne by animals—but never as themselves in animal form." There are two serious objections to this view. The first objection is that the Biblical narratives directly connect this idolatrous worship with Egypt where, as is well known, the bull (Apis) worship had flourished for centuries. The incident of Ex. xxxii. took place shortly after the Israelites left Egypt, where they had sojourned for generations; and we are told that Jeroboam had only just returned from an enforced sojourn in that country when he was made king of Israel. It is also natural to find in his words, "Behold thy gods, O Israel, which brought thee up out of the land of Egypt," an echo of the words of Aaron, despite the fact that Aaron's act was so severely punished. Consequently, it would seem that Egyptian influence predominated in both of these acts of apostasy from the spiritual monotheism of the Decalogue.[32] The second objection to this theory is that it completely stultifies the whole prophetic protest against the idolatry of Jeroboam and the idolatrous practices of the apostate Israelites from the time of the Exodus. If the prophets could not discriminate between the calves as objects of worship and the calves as pedestals above which the invisible Yahweh stood or sat enthroned, they were too dense, too thick-headed, to play the tremendous rôle of religious leadership which was theirs. The unanswerable logic of Hosea's characterization of the golden calf: "The workman has made it and it is not god" would have been demolished by the reply: "What did the workman make? The calf is only the pedestal of the invisible Yahweh. Of course it is not God. None but a fool would confound the pedestal and the invisible being enthroned upon it." But where is there the slightest hint that such an answer ever was made or could be made to the passionate denunciation of idolatry which meets us again and again on the pages of the Old Testament? It is only when these narratives are treated as late and unreliable that such theoretical reconstructions of Old Testament religion as these can be regarded as in any sense plausible or possible. The great and sufficient warrant for asserting the religion of Moses was aniconic is found in the second commandment of the Decalogue as uttered by the voice of Jehovah at Mount Sinai! When it is curtailed and treated as late, the door is opened for the most diverse and antithetical theories as regards the worship of Israel in the Mosaic age.

*d.* The Ban or Curse (*cherem*)

The "devoting" of human beings, cities, and nations to utter destruction has frequently been pointed to as proving that the religion of Israel was originally essentially the same as that of other Semitic peoples; and the command to exterminate the Canaanites has been likened to Mesha's destroying the 7,000 inhabitants of Nebo at the behest of Ishtar (and) Chemosh. Two things are to be noted: (1) In the Old Testament the ban had a moral purpose. The same reason and justification is given for it as in the case of the flood. It was the punishment visited by a righteous God on flagrant and incorrigible sin. The Canaanites were to be destroyed because of their abominations which merited punishment. There was the further reason, that Israel might not be corrupted by them. We have no warrant for attributing such a purpose to Mesha's act. (2) The ban is referred to in the Hexateuch most frequently in Deut. and in D passages in Joshua. It is pronounced against Edom in Isa. xxxiv. and against Israel in Isa. xliii.28 (both assigned by Driver to the "closing years of the exile") and by Malachi (iv.6) on all the earth or land as a penalty for failure to remember the law of Moses. It is in accord with the teachings of the entire Bible that the wages of sin, unrepented of and unexpiated, is death. The destruction of Jerusalem by Titus which was foretold by Jesus as a day of vengeance was as terrible an illustration of it as was the destruction of the Canaanites many centuries earlier.

### e. Religious Prostitution

One of the most striking features of the religion of Israel, when viewed in the lurid light of the religions of her Semitic neighbors,[33] is the unique way in which it preserves the golden mean between asceticism and sensuality. The Old Testament lends no support to the idea that celibacy for either sex represents a superior state. The high priest occupied a unique position in Israel's worship. He alone of all Israelites might enter the Most Holy Place. Yet it was expected that he would marry and that one of his sons would succeed him in office. On the other hand, while the God of Israel was recognized as the Author and Giver of life, the Source of fruitfulness and of blessings of every kind, nothing which savored of the licentious fertility cults of the ethnic religions was tolerated in His worship. The most careful provisions were made to prevent the sex relationship entering into the rites of religion. Such provisions as Ex. xix.15, xx.26, and Deut. iv.16 illustrate this, as do also the laws regarding ceremonial uncleanness (Lev. xv., cf. 1 Sam. xxi.5).[34]

How necessary such provisions were is shown by the history of Israel. It seems clear that the worship of the golden calf at Sinai (Ex. xxxii.) was accompanied by immoral rites.[35] It is highly probable that Jeroboam's choice of the bull as the symbol for his idolatrous worship at Dan and Bethel was partly due to the fact that the bull was used in the fertility cult of the Canaanite Baal worship. If, according to the new version of Ex. xxxii., the use of the bull symbol was supposed to go back to Moses and Sinai, it would naturally follow that the religious prostitution which accompanied it was also ancient and legitimate. Some critics find an allusion to it in Ex. xxxviii. (P). If the making of the calf is to be assigned to Moses, the license

which Aaron allowed the people would also be attributed
to him. We find that such rites are definitely prohibited
in D (Deut. xxiii.17, 18). This is quite understandable if
D is Mosaic. But if D belongs to the time of Josiah and
represents the triumph of the prophetic viewpoint,[36] and
if this is the first mention of such a prohibition in the Pentateuchal codes as arranged by the critics, it would be natural, according to critical principles, to infer that up to
that time such rites were at least tolerated and that the
attitude shown toward them in 1 Kgs. xiv.24, xv.12, xxii.46,
is colored by the viewpoint of a later age (2 Kgs. xxiii.7)
when the new code was put into operation.[37] It is no wonder, then, that these critics and many students of comparative religion resent the characterization of such rites as
"abominations of the heathen." They insist that they were
only primitive and not to be judged by the higher moral
standards of later times.[38] By this means they attempt to
hide the moral hideousness of what they regard as the
primitive form of the religion of Israel.

### f. Infant Sacrifice

Archaeology has shown quite clearly that infant sacrifice
was widely practiced by the ancient Semites. It has not,
however, produced the slightest evidence which directly
connects it with the true worship of Israel. Yet it is natural
for the student of comparative religion to argue that so
wide-spread a custom must have formed a part of the religion of Israel in early times. Consequently some of the
critics are disposed to interpret the words of Ex. xxii.29
(E), "the first-born of thy sons shalt thou give unto me,"
as referring to the sacrifice of infants.[39] This interpretation is made slightly plausible by the fact that the following
verse orders the same procedure regarding oxen and sheep
and concludes with the words: "seven days it shall be with
its dam: on the eighth day thou shalt give it to me." This
we are told represents the oldest practice and was originally

taken literally. The first-born of man, as of ox and sheep, was to be sacrificed. But it is to be noted that according to many critics this law of E was not the first one dealing with this subject. In Ex. xiii.13-15 which is usually assigned to J or JE and therefore held to be as old as or older than xxii.29, it is expressly declared: "and all the first-born of man among thy children shalt thou redeem." This important exception is stated also in Ex. xxxiv.20 which some of the critics make one of the commandments of the Decalogue of J. As these laws stand in Exodus, the brevity of xxii.29, its failure to mention this all-important qualification, is explained by the fact that this qualification had according to xiii.13f. already been made a short time previously under most impressive circumstances. Furthermore, if xxii.29 (E) is interpreted as justifying infant sacrifice, xiii.1-2 (P) which likewise makes no distinction between man and beast would bear a similar construction. And this would make this horrid rite an element in the religion of Israel even in post-exilic times. Yet Num. iii.42-51 speaks plainly of the redemption of all the first-born of Israel, a narrative which is given to P by the critics.

It is by such means as those of which illustrations have been given above that the God of Abraham, Isaac, and Jacob is metamorphosed into a nature god, the god of the smoking mountain, who is as ruthless and implacable as Hadad or Chemosh. Having appeared at Sinai he is regarded as the local deity of the mountain, and it is only gradually that he is prevailed on to remove to Canaan.[40] Being regarded as non-ethical his treatment of his enemies is ruthless and blood-thirsty, his attitude toward his friends is fickle and captious.[41] The only thing which distinguishes him from other gods is that not being originally the god of the Israelites in the sense of being their (deified) progenitor or actual begetter, but having become their god by covenant at Sinai, his relationship to them is a voluntary instead of a necessary one. In this the critics are disposed to find the basis of that ethical relationship out of which as a feeble beginning the lofty conception of Jehovah as supremely moral was gradually evolved.

The books which are written today on the subject of Old Testament religion and represent the higher critical viewpoint,[42] usually begin with a more or less elaborate sketch of "primitive Semitic" or "primitive Israelitish" religion, or what is sometimes called "Yahwism." This sketch does not begin with Genesis i. It has little to say about the patriarchs or Moses. It gives an account of the beginnings of Israel's religion so totally different from what the simple reader of the Old Testament would naturally expect, that said reader is often tempted to wonder where the writer has obtained it. What has been said in this brief sketch of pre-prophetic religion as conceived of by the critics, is intended to show him how this feat of *legerdemain* has been accomplished.

In view of the prevalence of these evolutionary theories which find the origin of religion in animism, fetichism, totemism, magic or other low and crude superstitions, it is significant that evidence has been accumulating during the last forty years to show that among many widely scattered "primitive" peoples, e.g., the pygmies in Africa, the Amerindians, and the Australian aborigines, there is to be found the belief in a "high god," who is the Supreme Being, the creator of the world. Andrew Lang (in 1898) was the first to confront the animistic theory with this evidence in favor of primitive monotheism, and he has been followed by a number of others, notably Schmidt of Vienna. Among the more recent defenders of the Biblical doctrine of a primitive monotheism was the Assyriologist Stephen Langdon.[43]

# CHAPTER II

# PROPHETIC RELIGION AND THE REFORM OF JOSIAH

THE PICTURE which we have been examining of the pre-prophetic religion of Israel as painted for us by the evolutionary critics is not a pleasant one. Starting out with the assumption that the religion of Israel was originally very similar to, if not identical with, the religions of other Semitic peoples, they give us a picture of Yahweh which closely resembles Molech or Chemosh. This picture is so crudely abhorrent that the question at once arises, How could the lofty ethical monotheism of Israel have developed from or in spite of such a base and unworthy beginning? The answer given us is this: through the work of the great prophets of the 8th and 7th centuries. To offset the low picture of pre-prophetic religion which they give us after rejecting the claim of the law to be Mosaic, the critics are obliged to assign to these prophets a far more important rôle than the Old Testament gives them. The rôle which it assigns them is to teach, expound, and enforce that ethical monotheism which had long before been made known in the law of Moses. The critics make them the virtual discoveries of that ethical monotheism.

Perhaps no one has stated this in more unqualified terms than has a representative of that Reformed Judaism which has accepted fully the radical conclusions of the higher criticism. Lewis Browne tells us:

"They [the prophets of the 8th century and later] reformed Yahvism from end to end, so that when they were done it was no longer Yahvism at all — it was Judaism. They transformed a jealous demon who roared and belched fire from the crater of a volcano, into a transcendent spirit of Love. They took a bloody and remorseless protector of a desert people, and without realizing it, changed him into the Merciful Father of all mankind. In fine, they destroyed Yahweh and created God!"[44]

The language is so shocking and blasphemous that we hesitate to quote it. But it calls attention in drastic fashion to the importance which the critics assign to the Prophets in the development of the religion of Israel: to their low regard for the religion of the time of Abraham, Moses, and David, and their high regard for the prophetic religion which these prophets "discovered." Two matters demand especial attention: the prophetic doctrine of God, and the prophetic teaching regarding sacrifice.

## I. THE PROPHETIC DOCTRINE OF GOD

In view of the amazing statement just quoted, which ends with the assertion that the prophets "destroyed Yahweh and created God," the first thing to be noted is that Jehovah (Yahweh) is the usual and favorite name given by the prophets to the God of whom they represented themselves as the spokesmen. If the god whom they "destroyed" was such an atrocious antithesis to the God whom they proclaimed, it is passing strange that they used the old familiar name in describing him. To say that they "destroyed Yahweh and created God," is a misstatement at the very outset. The most that could be asserted would be that they "destroyed Yahweh and created Yahweh." This would mean, unless two distinct deities are referred to by the same name, that they replaced one conception of Yahweh by another and markedly different one. In other words, they replaced a conception of Yahweh which regarded him as being, we may say, the twin-brother of Molech or Chemosh, by the conception which is given to us by Hosea who is often referred to as "the prophet of the love of Yahweh," as if Hosea were the discoverer of a "hitherto unsuspected aspect of Yahweh's character," of a "new motive to righteous living,"[45] of the real meaning of the word *chesed* (loving-kindness, mercy, goodness) as applied to the relation between God and man. If the prophets of Israel really accomplished this, it should be regarded as the most amazing feat ever performed, the greatest transformation ever brought about in the course of human history. It would indicate that Job was greatly in error when he answered the question, "Who can bring a clean thing out of an unclean?" by saying, "Not one." According to the theory we are considering the answer should have been: "The great prophets, who changed a Chemosh-like Yahweh into a Yahweh who was a 'transcendent spirit of Love.'" And Jeremiah should not have implied in his rhetorical question, "Can the Ethiopian change his skin, or the leopard his spots?", that it was just as impossible for wicked Israelites to make themselves good. Rather should he have held up their God as a ground for encouragement. If their prophets could make such a wonderful change in their *god,* change him from a Chemosh whom any decent man should abhor and shun to a Being whom all men should love and obey, surely it ought not to be too much to expect of the people that they should be able to change *themselves.* This change in Yahweh, from the old Yahweh to the new Yahweh, is so tremendous that to call them "supermen" would hardly do justice to these mighty prophets, if they really performed the task assigned them by the critics.[46] So the question we must face is this, Was the lofty conception of Jehovah proclaimed by the prophets original with them? As to this the following points are to be noted:

1. The prophets are not pictured to us anywhere in Scripture as supermen, profound theologians and philosophers. Amos, Isaiah, Jeremiah, and Ezekiel may be taken as representative; and they all speak of their own unworthiness and inadequacy and attribute their office of prophet to a distinct and compelling call from God. Jehovah promised to qualify them to be His spokesmen by putting His word into their mouths; and we constantly find them using such expressions as these to introduce their message: "Thus

saith Jehovah," "The word of Jehovah came unto me saying." The difference between the true prophet and the false consisted in this very thing, that the one spoke a message received directly from God, the other a word out of "his own heart" (Jer. xiv.14; xxiii.16, 26). The prophets were not supermen; they were very human men with a superhuman, a divine message.

2. The conception of their God which is given us by the prophets is unquestionably a high one. Jehovah is the "living God": idols are "the work of men's hands" and things of naught, "vanities." This living God is a great God. He has made and controls the stars (Amos v.8), the mountains, the wind (iv.13). He is not a local deity: He controls the nations. He brought the Philistines from Caphtor and the Syrians from Kir (Amos ix.7). He brought Israel out of Egypt (Hos. xii.9; Amos ii.10). And the time is coming when many nations shall seek Him (Isa. ii.3). He is a God of holiness and justice (Amos v.14ff.). He is the protector of the poor, the needy and the orphan (Isa. i.17, 23, xxix.19, Jer. vii.6). He is a God of love (Hos. xi.1, xiv.4, Jer. xxxi.3).

3. According to the prophets, this God whom they represent and who has these lofty and glorious attributes is the God of the Israel of their day by virtue of the fact that He was the God of their fathers. He is the God of Abraham, Isaac, and Jacob (Isa. xxix.22, Mic. vii.20). His especial claim to their allegiance is found in the fact that He delivered them from the bondage of Egypt (Hos. xi.1, xii.9, 13, Amos ii.10, ix.7, Mic. vi.4, vii.15). The prophets are not ignorant of Israel's past. They know the deliverance from Egypt was through Moses (Isa. lxiii.11f., Mic. vi.4). They know of Balak and Balaam (Mic. vi.5), of Samuel (Jer. xv.1), and of David as Israel's great king. In the coming of a king of the Davidic line they predict the future blessing of their people (Hos. iii.5, Amos ix.11, Isa. ix.7, Jer.

xxiii.5). In short, the God whom they represent is the God who was known to the fathers as their God.

4. Especially noteworthy is it that this attitude of the prophets, their belief that they were the spokesmen of the God of the fathers, finds confirmation in the "earlier" writings in the Old Testament. That wonderful "untranslatable" word *chesed* (mercy, loving-kindness, goodness, etc.) which is used by Hosea in ii.19 and is regarded as expressing his conception of Jehovah as "a transcendent spirit of Love" is no new word which he has discovered. According to the "early" sources (J and E) it describes God's relation to Abraham (Gen. xxiv.12, 27), Jacob (xxxii.10), Joseph (xxxix.21) and especially to Israel at the time of the Exodus (Ex. xv.13, xx.6, xxxiv.6, 7, Num. xiv.18, 19). And Hosea himself, as do other of the prophets, recognizes clearly that Israel was the object of the "love" of God when as a "child" he was called out of Egypt.[47]

5. It is hardly necessary, then, to ask the question, Were the prophets conscious of any change in this Jehovah whom they declared to be the God of Israel from days of old? This question is answered by a striking passage which occurs in Jer. ii.5f., "Thus saith Jehovah, What iniquity have your fathers found in me, that they are gone far from me, and have walked after vanity, and are become vain?" This question is a very pertinent one. For, if the God proclaimed by the prophets was so utterly different from the one whom past generations in Israel had known, that the "old Yahweh" could be likened to Chemosh, the people might well have answered, "There was so little difference between the God of our fathers and Chemosh that they were quite excusable for worshipping him; and the god you proclaim is so different from our fathers' god that you have no right to call him their god." Is there any hint of such an answer or of the possibility of such a retort being given? The true answer is given in vss. 11f. and it is a

crushing one: "Hath a nation changed their gods, which are yet no gods? but my people have changed their glory for that which doth not profit." Jehovah declares that His people "have committed two evils: they have forsaken me, the fountain of living waters and hewed them out cisterns, broken cisterns, that can hold no water." It is because, however much they may change, their God "changes not" that there is hope for Israel (Mal. iii.6).

The claim has often been made that the two estimates of the career of Jehu given us in the Old Testament are a clear example of the gradual change which the conception of Jehovah underwent in the course of time. According to 2 Kgs. x.30, Jehu's zeal in exterminating the house of Omri was commendable and received the approval of God. According to Hosea (i.4) Jehovah will "avenge the blood of Jezreel upon the house of Jehu and will cause the kingdom of the house of Israel to cease." Here, they tell us, the difference between the pre-prophetic and the prophetic conceptions of Jehovah is clearly set forth. The prophet of the 8th century denounces, as a crime so heinous that Jehovah will avenge it by frightful judgment, an act which a century earlier had been regarded as directly commanded by God. This is a serious charge, but it is a wholly mistaken one. Jehu's warrant for destroying the house of Omri was the terrible sin which had characterized it (1 Kgs. xxi. 21-26). He was made the executioner of Jehovah's judgment upon that wicked house. When Jehu followed in the steps of his victims and worshipped the calves as they had done, he invoked upon himself a like punishment; he signed his own death warrant. The principle involved is stated clearly in 1 Kgs. xvi. in the brief indictment of Baasha, who had already performed as regards the house of Jeroboam the rôle of Jehovah's executioner. The sin of Baasha was two-fold: "in being like the house of Jeroboam and because he slew him" (vs. 8). By "being like" the men whom they slew, Baasha and Jehu proved themselves to be merely self-seeking rebels who merited the death they had inflicted on their victims only that they might reign in their stead. His own deeds belied the claim of Jehu that his zeal was for the God of Israel. It was for himself.

6. Not only do the prophets fail to indicate in any way that the God whom they proclaim has changed or become different from the God whom their fathers worshipped. What they do insist upon is that the attitude of the people toward their God was then, as it had been in the past, far different from what it should have been. They accuse the people of disobeying their God and following after other gods; and they declare that in this respect they have but followed in the steps of their fathers. They assert further and most emphatically that this has never been due to any longing after something higher, better, more spiritual than what they found in the religion of Jehovah, but that in forsaking Jehovah they have forsaken "their glory" for that which was "unprofitable." How unprofitable the worship of the strange gods has been the prophets illustrate by many striking figures. Hosea declares that "Ephraim feedeth on wind, and followeth the east wind" (xii.1). Of the calf of Samaria he declares, "The workman made it; therefore it is not god" (viii.6). In Isa. xl.-xlviii. the major theme is the utter folly of idolatry and the incomparable uniqueness of Jehovah. In the Song of Moses (Deut. xxxii.) it is declared that the people have forsaken the God which made them and have gone after "new gods that came newly up, whom your fathers feared not." This tragic situation is responsible for the fact that the prophets tell us repeatedly that Jehovah has a "controversy" with Israel (Hos. iv.1, Mic. vi.2, Jer. xxv.31) and exhort Israel again and again to "return" unto the Lord their God (Hos. xiv.1, Amos iv.6, Mic. v.3, Isa. xxi.12, Jer. iii.12). The proneness of the people of Israel to follow the "strange" gods of the neighboring peoples is denounced as apostasy and the things which attracted them in the cults of these peoples are stigmatized as "abominations"; they are declared to have gone a "whoring" after other gods.

Since we are hearing so much today about the importance of the study of comparative religion, it is well to observe that the Old Testament prophets were profound students of this subject. They knew the religions of Israel's neighbors, to which so many in Israel had turned aside, not as a subject of academic or antiquarian interest, but as a matter of the most lively concern. A vital issue was involved. No compromise or straddling was permissible or possible. Elijah stated it bluntly: "If Jehovah be God, follow him: but if Baal, then follow him." And they met the issue thus raised, by a most candid and fearless comparison of the God of Israel with the gods of the heathen, and of the worship of Jehovah with the worship of the strange gods. The comparison is devastating. Jehovah stands forth as the incomparable One. And this unique and incomparable Being is known to the prophets as the God of their fathers, the God of the Abrahamic covenant, the God who brought Israel out of Egypt and into the land of promise where they then dwelt.

The horrible Yahweh of the pre-prophetic period is a figment of the imagination of the evolutionary critic, who proceeds upon an assumption which is the direct antithesis of the teaching of the prophets. The critic proceeds upon the assumption that Jehovah must have been originally like the gods of the heathen: the prophets emphatically assert that He always was essentially different. If a living dog is better than a dead lion, what must be the difference between the "living God" who made the heavens and the earth and those idols of wood and stone which are "the work of men's hands"? "The workman made it, and it is not God" is Hosea's terse exposé of the calf-worship. It is the difference, as Isaiah graphically describes it, between Jehovah, who carried Israel like a nursing father, and Bel and Nebo, who have to be loaded on the backs of weary beasts that they may go into captivity with a people they are impotent to save (Isa. xlvi.1-4). And it leads up to the very emphatic question: "To whom will ye liken me, and make me equal, and compare me, that we may be like?"[48] This is the challenge of these ancient experts on comparative religion. For them there was only one answer; and that answer is to be commended to the careful consideration of the students of that far different school of comparative religion which is so popular today. A comparative study to be just and adequate must show the same readiness to recognize differences as to stress resemblances, especially when the differences are great and fundamental and the resemblances relatively insignificant.

## II. The Sacrificial System as Viewed by the Prophets

It is an obvious fact that, while sacrifice is referred to as being performed very soon after the fall of man (Gen. iv.), little is said about it until the time of the Exodus.[49] It is in the so-called priestly legislation that the details of sacrifice and its *rationale* are given; and it is the claim of the critics that this legislation is post-Mosaic. The earlier critics had assigned it to the period of the United Kingdom (Saul to Solomon) and consequently regarded it as pre-prophetic. The later critics (since Graf) have regarded it as exilic or post-exilic. This raises two important questions: (1) What have the prophets to say about Mosaic sacrifices? and (2) What is their attitude toward sacrifice in general?

### 1. The Prophets and Mosaic Sacrifices

We have seen that the rise of the Development or Historical school of criticism whose great achievement was the late dating of P is usually traced from the publication of Graf's *Untersuchungen* in 1865. It is therefore both interesting and important to note that Graf had already in his Commentary on Jeremiah (1862) prepared the way for the revolutionary position advocated in the *Untersuchungen*. For in the Commentary Graf declared emphatically, in discussing Jer. vii.22f., that this passage makes it unmistakably plain that in the time of Jeremiah no one knew anything about God's having given a law regarding sacrifice at Sinai, and that consequently "the ceremonial laws in the middle part of the Pentateuch" could not have been in existence in Jeremiah's day but belong to the latest portion of the Pentateuch and date from the post-exilic period.[50] From that day to the present time it has been customary to point to this passage especially, as proving that the prophets of the 8th and 7th centuries B.C. knew nothing of a ritual of sacrifice imposed upon Israel at Sinai.[51]

### a. Jeremiah vii.22ff.

In view of the seriousness of this claim and the fact that it is based primarily on Jer. vii.22f., the passage in question must be carefully examined. It reads as follows:

"Thus saith Jehovah of hosts, the God of Israel: Add your burnt-offerings unto your sacrifices, and eat ye flesh. For I spake not unto your fathers nor commanded them in the day that I brought them out of the land of Egypt, concerning burnt-offerings or sacrifices: but this thing I commanded them, saying, Hearken unto my voice, and I will be your God, and ye shall be my people."

The words with which this prophetic utterance begins are especially noteworthy, "Add your burnt-offerings unto your sacrifices, and eat ye flesh." The burnt-offerings (*oloth*) were offerings of which the offerer was not permitted to eat any part. The sacrifices (*zebachim*) are often called peace-offerings and of these the offerer was permitted to eat the greater part in a sacrificial meal of which the members of his family and others might partake. The words quoted seem clearly to imply that many Israelites of Jeremiah's day resented the fact that they were required to offer the whole of the burnt-offering and could eat no part of it. What appealed to them about the sacrificial ritual was not reconciliation with God through atoning blood, nor the privilege of making an offering of thanksgiving to Him and having communion with Him by partaking of the gift, but the fact that in the case of some of their offerings they could eat most of it themselves, and make of it a feast of good things; and they resented the fact that they could not do this with all of them. This shows an extremely low and carnal conception of the meaning of the whole sacrificial system, and one which readily accounts for the denunciatory tenor of this great temple address in which the people are accused of making God's house a "den of robbers," a place of escape, not from sin but merely from the consequences of sin. It is to such a people that Jehovah says: "Add your burnt-offerings unto your sacrifices, and eat ye flesh." It is the same thought as we find in Ps. 1.8-14, where God indignantly repudiates the idea that He is "hungry." He does not need to have His people share their food with Him. The beasts of the forest are His and the cattle upon a thousand hills. Men who grudge Him that part of their offerings which He has claimed as His own are welcome to keep the whole for themselves. The very spirit in which they offer it makes the offering meaningless and valueless, an offense in His sight.

The reason for the startling words we have just considered is given in words almost equally surprising: "For I spake not unto your fathers nor commanded them in the day that I brought them out of the land of Egypt, concerning [AV, ARV] burnt-offerings or sacrifices." These words seem at first glance to bear out fully the claim of the critics that Jeremiah knew nothing about a sacrificial system introduced by Moses at the time of the Exodus. But such a conclusion rests upon the failure of the English translation to do justice to the ambiguity of the Hebrew words rendered "concerning"; and particularly to the fact that, as is made clear by a study of the usage, they may also be rendered by "because of" or "for the sake of."

(1) A literal rendering of the Hebrew would be "upon the matters of." This expression (with the plural of the noun)

is rare, occurring only five times, and may have several shades of meaning. In Jer. xiv.1, "concerning the drought" may be an adequate rendering, and the same may be true of the heading of Ps. vii., "concerning the words of Cush." But in Deut. iv.21, "concerning you" would be quite inadequate. "For your sakes," "because of you," or "on your account," is the natural rendering. It was because the people tried his patience beyond endurance that Moses sinned as he did: "Jehovah was angry with me for your sakes (because of you)." This indicates quite clearly that this expression may be stronger than "concerning." "Because of," "for the sake of," "on account of," would be equally appropriate in all of the passages where this expression occurs: it is clearly required in Deut. iv.21.[52]

(2) The same variety of meaning appears in the five instances where the noun is in the singular (literally, "upon the matter of"). In Ex. viii.12, "concerning the frogs" may be adequate, but "because of," "on acount of," might be better under the circumstances. In Gen. xii.17, xx.18, "because of Sarai" is the natural rendering; in xx.11, "for my wife's sake" is better. In neither case would "concerning" be adequate. "Because of truth" is the appropriate rendering in Ps. xlv.4.[53]

(3) Finally it is to be noted that the preposition "upon" (without the noun following), which is of frequent occurrence, is also used with the same variety of meaning. In Gen. xxvi.7, "for Rebekah" is equivalent to "for the sake of" (cf. xx.11). In 1 Kgs. ii.18, "I will speak for thee unto the king" (AV and ARV), may be intentionally ambiguous. Bathsheba may mean that she will speak about Adonijah and his desire for Abishag to Solomon, but that she will do this without any active advocacy of his suit. If such is the meaning, "concerning" would be a good rendering. But it seems certain that Adonijah understood it to imply such advocacy and took her words in the sense of "on account of," "on behalf of." This latter meaning is still clearer in 2 Kgs. x.3 where Jehu challenges the rulers of Jezreel to choose a son of Ahab "and set him on his father's throne, and fight for [AV, ARV] your master's house." "Concerning your master's house" would be weak. "For," "for the sake of," "in behalf of," is clearly the

meaning. A careful examination of these and other passages makes it clear that in a number of cases "concerning" is, we may say, a too objective and non-committal rendering. The expression may be used where an active interest involving either the speaker or the one addressed is clearly present, and then "because of," "on account of," "for the sake of," is a better and certainly in some cases the only adequate rendering.[54]

It is obvious that if in Jer. vii.22 we employ the stronger rendering "because of" or "for the sake of," this verse not merely ceases to support the inference which the critics base upon it, but it becomes exceedingly appropriate in the context. The Lord does not say to Israel that He gave no commands to their fathers *concerning* sacrifice. At first the people listening to Jeremiah might think that was his meaning. But a moment's reflection would convince them that such could not be the true purport of his words. What Jehovah meant was that He did not speak to their fathers *for the sake* of sacrifices, as if He needed them and would suffer hunger unless He were fed by these grudging offerings of sinful men who had no conception of the real relation in which they stood to Him.[55] The language appears to be intentionally ambiguous, even startlingly so. But the words, "Put your burnt-offerings unto your sacrifices and eat ye flesh" are intended to give the clue to their meaning. Then after pointing out in this striking way that God has no need of the sacrifices of His creatures, the prophet goes on to declare that obedience was the real aim and requirement of the Sinaitic legislation.

*b*. The other passage which Graf appealed to in his commentary as proving that the prophets knew nothing of a law of sacrifice as introduced or expressly sanctioned by Moses is Amos v.25 which teaches, Graf maintained, that "even during the forty years of wandering through the wilderness, when Israel stood under the especial protection and leading of his God, no animal or meal offerings were brought to Him." The weakness of this argument is obvious. The narrative in Num. xiv.-xxvi. makes it quite plain that during the years of wandering Israel, instead of standing under the especial protection and leading of Jehovah, was suffering His displeasure in a signal and even unique degree. The whole generation of wrath was to perish in the wilderness because of disobedience (Num. xiv.21-36). The words of Amos indicate that this time of punishment was also a time of apostasy, which was quite natural; and this is clearly the view of it taken by Stephen (Acts vii.). The Mosaic ritual of sacrifice was intended for an obedient people. The generation of wrath was suffering for disobedience. To it this ritual of sacrifice could mean little or nothing. So it added apostasy to disobedience. Amos' words have consequently no bearing upon the question whether a ritual of sacrifice was ordained for Israel through Moses.

## 2. The Attitude of the Prophets to Sacrifice in General

This brings us to the larger question, What was the attitude of the prophets to sacrifice in general? It is claimed that the prophets of the 8th and 7th centuries not merely denied that the God of Israel had commanded sacrifices at Sinai, but even held that sacrifices of any kind were repugnant to Him. In other words we are told that the great prophets of Israel did not regard the sacrificial system as divinely imposed through Moses, but simply looked upon it as part of the ancestral or primitive religion which their fathers had practiced as the heathen did, and which they had now come to regard as not merely unnecessary, but even as contrary to the true genius of the religion of Israel.[56] There are several objections to this view.

*a.* It makes the attitude of the prophets themselves inconsistent and even contradictory. Jeremiah, who, according to the interpretation of vii.22, which we have been considering, denies flatly that sacrifices had any ancient and divine authorization, most emphatically approves sacrifice in xvii.24-26, xxvii.19-22, xxxiii.10, 11, 18. Either we must say that Jeremiah was very inconsistent or else deny that these other passages are from his pen. This same contradiction would appear with equal plainness in Deuteronomy which, whether it be regarded as "prophetic" or "priestly," the critics assign to the golden age of prophecy. The summary of the first table of the Decalogue, or what Jesus called, "the first and great commandment" is this, "Hear O Israel: Jehovah our God is one Jehovah: and thou shalt love Jehovah thy God with all thy heart and with all thy soul and with all thy might." It may be regarded as a classic statement of the theology of "prophetic religion." But chap. xii. expressly requires the offering of various kinds of sacrifices at the place which Jehovah shall choose for His worship (vss. 6, 11, 27). The same contradiction would appear on this theory within the limits of a single psalm. In Ps. li. we read in vs. 16, "For thou desirest not sacrifice," while in vs. 19 we are told that God will "be pleased with burnt-offerings and whole burnt-offerings." This is explained by saying that the last verses of this psalm are a later addition by one who did not share the prophetic conception of the worthlessness of sacrifice. But such an interpretation overlooks the fact that it is "a broken spirit, a broken and a contrite heart" which makes the sacrifices of the law acceptable to God. An editor, who believed in the efficacy of sacrifice, would certainly have been more likely to cut out the verses in this psalm to which he objected than simply to add an appendix contradicting them.

*b.* The classic utterance on this subject is of much earlier date than that of the 8th century prophets. In rebuking Saul for his failure to carry out the will of Jehovah concerning Amalek, Samuel said to the king: "Hath Jehovah as great delight in burnt-offerings and sacrifices, as in obeying the voice of Jehovah? Behold to obey is better than sacrifice and to hearken than the fat of rams" (1 Sam. xv.22).[57] And as the utterly pagan notion of sacrifice as a means of buying off the deity, of escaping the consequences of sin without repentance or obedience, became more and more dominant in the nation, it was natural that obedience and sacrifice should be represented by the prophets at times as if they were mutually exclusive or stood in sharp contrast with one another, instead of as being most vitally connected. This is brought out very clearly by Isaiah in the Great Arraignment which stands at the beginning of his prophecies. After describing the abundance of the offerings of the people and their devoted attendance upon the worship of the temple he cries out: "I cannot away with iniquity and solemn meeting" (i.13). The coupling of the two words "iniquity and solemn meeting" is the great indictment brought by this prophet against his people. They brought together iniquity and worship in an unholy alliance. They did not seek by true worship to atone for and be rid of iniquity, but by a merely formal worship they sought to escape, as they believed, the consequences of their sins while continuing to live in them. They even "drew sin as with a cart rope" (v.18) as if it were a desirable acquisition. Isaiah's Great Arraignment and Jeremiah's Temple Address deal with the same perversion of the meaning of sacrifice. To say that these prophets reject sacrifice as such is an utterly mistaken position.

c. Micah vi.6-8 is frequently referred to as the expression of what has been called the "quintessence" of prophetic religion, as a religion which is purely inward and spiritual, requiring neither sacrifice nor any other external rites. But this is a misinterpretation of the passage. For it is to be noted first of all that the sacrifices which the prophet rejects are not those required by the Mosaic law, but sacrifices offered in a pagan spirit. This is made clear by the words, "thousands of rams," "ten thousand rivers of oil." The law did not require vast offerings and gifts: the efficacy of the offering did not depend on its amount.[58] It is made still clearer by the words, "Shall I give my first-born for my transgression, the fruit of my body for the sin of my soul?" The law of Moses nowhere enjoined human sacrifice, but this was a prominent feature of the religion of Israel's Semitic neighbors. Consequently it is pagan sacrifice which is here so emphatically rejected. Then the prophet states the ideal of true religion: "to do justly, and to love mercy, and to walk humbly with thy God." We might regard this as a very brief summary of the two tables of the Decalogue, as stating the whole duty of man. But it is to be noted that while the ideal of godly living is stated here, nothing is said about the consequences of failure to measure up to the ideal or as to how these consequences can be avoided. Micah might have said to the men of his day as Jesus said to the young lawyer, "This do and thou shalt live." The whole subject of expiation for sins against this law, this moral ideal, is not touched upon. It would be better to say, is not touched upon directly, for apparently the concluding words do refer to it, since "to walk humbly" with God clearly implies the keeping of all His laws and commandments, as well the ceremonial as the moral.[59]

*d.* By the post-exilic prophets and during the entire period which preceded the earthly ministry of Christ, sacrifice was given an important place. Indeed, according to the critics the elaborate cultus of the Priest Code was formulated and completed during or shortly after the Captivity and introduced by Ezra as of divine authority. According to this view, the expression, "the law and the prophets," which occurs in the New Testament, represents a sequence which is incorrect and should be changed to "the prophets and the law," since the great bulk of the law is placed by the critics in the exilic or post-exilic period which followed the golden age of prophecy. This means according to the critics that the most detailed laws regarding sacrifice date from the period after its emphatic repudiation by the Great Prophets of Israel. Consequently if the 8th century prophets attained to the conception of a spir-

itual religion which required no sacrifices, and if this conception is the true one, then for centuries the history of
Israel represents a terrible apostasy from the teachings of
these great religious leaders. Those who are prepared to
insist that the laws of Moses could not have been given to
Israel at Sinai because they were not observed by later generations, should remember that the same argument can be
used against their theory of prophetic religion. For they
must admit that this conception of religion, supposing it
ever to have existed, was emphatically repudiated by the
authoritative teachers of the centuries which followed.

*e.* Still more important is the New Testament application of this theory. If Prophetic Religion repudiated sacrifice and stood in sharp contrast to Priestly Religion which
magnified the importance of sacrifice, declaring that without the shedding of blood there is no remission, and if the
religion of the New Testament, of Jesus in particular, was
"prophetic" in this sense and finds classic and adequate
expression in the parable of the Prodigal Son, then sacrifice
is unnecessary and the Cross loses its meaning as signifying
atonement for sin and becomes simply the supreme illustration of a love which is faithful even unto death. This
is the logical result of the attempt to make the great prophets of Israel, who denounced so vigorously that abuse of
sacrifice which made the temple a den of thieves, the enemies of sacrifice as such. Nothing could be more serious
than this.

## III. The Reform of Josiah and the Centralization of Worship

It is the contention of the critics that the centralization
of the worship at the one sanctuary at Jerusalem was first
introduced by Josiah (622 B.C.) and that this is conclusive
proof of the late date of Deuteronomy. This claim involves two points: (1) that a multiplicity of altars was

legitimate up to that time, (2) that centralization was first introduced at that time.

1. It is claimed that the laws of JE allow many altars. This is based primarily on the words: "in every place where I record my name" (Ex. xx.24, E). This means, we are told, that an altar could be erected anywhere for the offering of sacrifices to God, and it is alleged that the practice of the people prior to Josiah's reform favors such an interpretation. There are a number of objections to this view:

a. The meaning of the words "in every place" is not perfectly clear. The most natural rendering would be "in all of the place"; and this might mean, in the entire land of Canaan.[60] But even if we adopt the rendering "in every (or, any) place," the statement is still qualified by the important words, "where I cause my name to be remembered" or "recorded." This apparently refers to a theophany, or some other special manifestation of God's presence. Consequently it would only be at special places, hallowed by the presence of God, that altars to His name could be erected.[61]

b. The establishment of the central sanctuary was, according to Deut. xii., to take place after the Lord had given Israel rest from all her enemies round about (vs. 10). Apparently this time did not arrive until the days of David (2 Sam. vii.); and David was not permitted to build the temple because he had been a man of war and had shed blood. Consequently it cannot be maintained that the law given in Deuteronomy contemplated the immediate erection of a central sanctuary. The law might have been in existence centuries before the time came for carrying it into effect. Israel's failure to take full possession of the land and expel all of the Canaanites at once was responsible for the long delay; that and the frequent apostasies which were the direct result of close and constant contact with the heathen that were left in the land.

c. For the intervening period, assuming Deuteronomy

to be Mosaic as it claims to be, the practices which we find may be accounted for in two ways:

(1) It may be due to that principle of sanity and humanity which is a marked feature of the law of Moses. Of this we have several notable examples.

(a) The requirement that the passover be kept was absolute the penalty for failure to keep it was very severe (Num. ix.13). Yet the law provided a second opportunity, one month later, for the observance of the passover by those who for good reasons could not observe it at the proper time (vs. 6). (b) While the necessity of blood-atonement is stressed (e.g., Lev. xvii.11), the very poor might offer a bloodless offering (Lev. v.11f.) which apparently was validated by being offered on the altar of burnt offering. (c) Furthermore, we find that the good intention might be accepted even if the technical requirement was violated. Hezekiah's great passover was celebrated in the second month, and a multitude of people from the Northern Kingdom who were not "sanctified" were allowed to participate. The first irregularity was provided for by the law. The second was not. But Hezekiah prayed that this irregularity might be forgiven. And the Chronicler who was a stickler for the letter of the law not merely has no word of censure but tells us that the Lord did as Hezekiah asked (xxx.18f.).

(2) The many altars may also be explained by the terrible dislocation of the divinely established order which was due to apostasy. After the Schism the Levites (and priests, 2 Chron. xiii.9) who were living in the Northern Kingdom went to Judah. Jeroboam discouraged and probably largely prevented any participation by the people in the feasts at Jerusalem. Consequently the words of Elijah, "thine altars" (1 Kgs. xix.10, 14), and the expression, "the altar of Jehovah" (xviii.30), should be explained in accordance with the above mentioned principles. The times were out of joint!

2. It is further claimed that the reform of Josiah first

introduced this centralization of worship as a new and un-heard-of thing. As to this several important matters are to be noted:

*a.* The occasion of the reform of Josiah was the dis-covery of "the book of the law" in the temple. It must be admitted that this expression might be adequately rendered by the words, "a law book." But the importance attached to the book would favor the view that a definite, well-known book was referred to. While it cannot be demon-strated that this book contained the entire Pentateuch, the only conclusive argument against so natural an inference would be definite proof that the Pentateuch was not then in existence. It is this which the critics have to establish.

*b.* The reform of Josiah was primarily directed against idolatry (2 Kgs. xxii.17, xxiii.4-7, cf. xxi.21f.). Centrali-zation of worship was only a minor part of it (xxiii.8, 9).

*c.* Jeremiah, who prophesied at the time of this great reform and apparently refers to it in demanding the keep-ing of the "covenant," does not regard centralization as the aim, certainly not the primary aim, of the covenant (Jer. xi.10, 12, 13). He speaks of "this place which is called by my name" (vii.10, 11, 14, 30). He never uses the words of Deuteronomy "shall choose," or refers to Jerusalem as the "chosen" place. On the contrary he speaks of Shiloh as the place where Jehovah set His name at the first (vii.12, 14; xxvi.6, 9) and threatens Jerusalem with a like fate.

*d.* The reform of Josiah was not the first reform. It was preceded by that of Hezekiah which was about a cen-tury earlier. This earlier reform is described as being definitely in the interest of the central sanctuary (2 Kgs. xviii.22; cf. 2 Chr. xxxii.12, Isa. xxxvi.7).

*e.* Solomon's prayer (1 Kgs. viii.) makes the temple the pre-eminent and permanent place of worship for all Israel. It is natural to regard his use of the words "choose," "name," "place," "put name there," as reflecting the very phraseology of Deut. Hence the critics must treat the prayer as "Deuteronomic," which means to them, either that it is not Solomonic at all, or that it has at least been drastically edited by D.

*f.* The nine-and-a-half tribes so resented the erection of what they mistakenly supposed to be intended as a rival altar by the two-and-a-half tribes that they were prepared to go to war with them over it (Josh. xxii.). This was before the death of Joshua.

*g.* The Book of Deuteronomy commands the erection of a special altar for a special purpose on Mt. Ebal (xxvii.5f.), as being quite consistent with the law of the central altar already established (xii.5f.).

*h.* Since the keeping of the passover was the most important event connected with the central sanctuary, it is to be noted that the attempt to place D before P leads to a striking contradiction. According to D the passover is to be kept at the central sanctuary (xvi.5-12);[62] according to P the people are to eat it in their houses (Ex. xii.7, 46). If the law of P be regarded as applicable to the time when all the tribes were living in tents pitched within a camp which had the tabernacle as the centre, and the law of D be considered as a modification of this law to make it apply to the time when the Israelites would live in towns and cities, many of which would be quite remote from the central sanctuary, there is no contradiction or difficulty of any kind. But considered as a permanent law introduced centuries after Israel had been settled in the land and the law of the central sanctuary established, this law of P would be an anomaly. Similarly the permission given in Deut. xii.15 to "kill (or, sacrifice) in all thy gates," the only proviso being, that the meat be not eaten with the blood, is perfectly intelligible as a piece of permanent legislation intended for the period after Israel is settled in the land. Otherwise the Israelites could eat flesh only at the time of the annual feasts unless they made a special journey to the sanctuary. Obviously Lev. xvii.3, 4 was intended to be a temporary law, applicable to the period before Israel was settled in the land. Here again the only proper order is P followed by D, not D followed by P.[63]

*i.* In the Book of the Covenant which is assigned to E, it is required (Ex. xxiii.14, 17) that the males appear three times in a year "before the Lord Jehovah." While this does not expressly refer to the existence of a single, central sanctuary, it is entirely in accord with such a view.

*j.* Finally it is to be remembered that the idea of a central sanctuary was, according to Scripture, held up before Israel from the times of the Exodus by the construction of the tabernacle at Mt. Sinai to be a centre of worship for all Israel. The ark was the symbol of God's presence; and its proper place was in the tabernacle. Ex. xxxix.-xl. tells us again and again that the elaborate tabernacle so fully described in this book was erected "as Jehovah commanded Moses." Even in the troublous times of the Judges, pious Israelites recognized it as a duty and privilege to worship annually at the house of the Lord at Shiloh (1 Sam. i.3). It is only when the account of this tabernacle is assigned to a post-exilic date and treated as merely a "reflection backward" of Solomon's temple, a kind of imaginary portable temple, that this situation is altered. Nevertheless it cannot be denied that P describes the tabernacle as "Mosaic" and as belonging to the period of the Exodus.

The treatment by the critics of two of the points in the evidence cited above is especially illuminating:

(1) The dedication of the temple in the days of Solomon is given considerable space in 1 Kgs. viii. More than half of this long chapter of 66 verses is devoted to Solomon's words of dedication and prayer (vss. 12-53). Apparently the historian considered the occasion an epoch-marking one and Solomon's words of especial importance. They are full of the thought that this house which was being dedicated was to be the centre of Israel's worship and that this was the fulfilment of David's earnest desire. The words of Solomon point to Deut. xii. and other passages in that book. It is perfectly proper to describe the prayer as "Deuteronomic." And this

"coloring" is to be expected if Deuteronomy is Mosaic and if the command that the king have "a copy of the law" and "read therein all the days of his life" (Deut. xvii.18) was obeyed by Solomon. But what the critics mean when they say of this prayer that it is "markedly Deuteronomic" is that since Deuteronomy dates from the time of Josiah, Solomon could not possibly have uttered it.[64] Its Deuteronomic flavor, instead of being a proof that Solomon obeyed the command contained in Deut. xvii.18, is regarded by the critics as proof positive that this prayer cannot be regarded as authentic.[65]

(2) The same treatment is accorded the account of Hezekiah's reform recorded in 2 Kgs. xviii.22. We are told that "most critics regard this reference to Hezekiah's reform as an interpolation."[66] This is supported by the statement that "On none of the historical books has the influence of Deut. been so pervasive as on Kings."[67] The serious import of such a statement is clear when we remind ourselves that Kings is regarded by the critics as our most reliable source for the period which it covers.[68] If it must be regarded as written or edited by supporters of Josiah's reform for the express purpose of proving that Josiah's innovation was not really an innovation but a return to the practice of the days of Hezekiah, and of Solomon, where are we to turn for a true account of this important event? It is only when the statements we have been considering are rejected as unreliable that it can be affirmed that "the actual course of history" supports this major doctrine of the critics, that Deuteronomy belongs to the time of Josiah. And then few if any facts are left to determine what that actual course was, since nearly all the pertinent evidence has been rejected as unreliable.

In the light of the above evidence, it is obvious that the claim that the Deuteronomic code was first introduced in the days of Josiah and that its requirement of centralization of worship was unknown before that time cannot be admitted to be in accord with the *actual course of history, in so far as that is known,"* unless the documents upon which we are dependent for that history are regarded as unreliable and as "colored" by the theology of a later age.[69]

# CHAPTER III

# PRIESTLY RELIGION IN THE POST-EXILIC PERIOD

IT IS ARGUED in support of the view that the three codes of the Pentateuch reflect three distinct periods in the course of the actual history of Israel, that (1) the sharp distinction which is drawn between priests and Levites in the Priest Code does not appear in the pre-exilic period and that the office of the high priest is post-exilic, and (2) that the Priest Code as a whole fits the post-exilic period but is quite out of harmony with the two which preceded it.

## I. THE DISTINCTION BETWEEN PRIESTS AND LEVITES

The claim of the critics regarding the distinction between priests and Levites may be summarized as follows: (1) The JE legislation (Ex. xx.-xxiii., xxxiv.) does not even restrict priesthood to Levites; (2) D gives all Levites equal rights, considering "every Levite a potential priest"; (3) Ezekiel gives inferior status to all Levites except the family of Zadok, from which all priests are to come (xliv.7-16); (4) P presupposes the difference between priests and Levites, and recognizes the office of high priest, limiting it to Aaron and his descendants.

### 1. The JE Legislation

The statement that the JE legislation does not even restrict priesthood to the Levites is of interest for several reasons:

*a.* We have seen that J is almost entirely history and that E has only a brief legal code. Since priests and Levites are referred to especially in connection with the observance of the ceremonial law we would expect to find most of the references to them in the more elaborate legal passages of the Pentateuch. Such is the case.

(a) Priests are not mentioned in the legal portions of J and E: the so-called Decalogue of J (Ex. xxxiv.), the Decalogue of E (Ex. xx.), or the Book of the Covenant. In the narrative portions J refers to Egyptian priests (Gen. xlvii.22, 26), to Jethro the priest of Midian (Ex. ii.16). E refers to Egyptian priests (Gen. xli.45, 50) and to Jethro (Ex. iii.1, xviii.1). Ex. xix.6 declares that Israel shall be "a kingdom of priests" and vss. 22, 24 describe certain Israelites as "priests" before the giving of the law and consequently before the distinctive requirements for priesthood in Israel were established.[70]

(b) As regards Levites the only passage in J or E is Ex. iv.16 (J), where the expression "Aaron the Levite" may mean no more than that Aaron, like Moses, belonged to the tribe of Levi. This is all the J and E narratives in the Pentateuch have to say about priests and Levites in Israel.

b. Especially noteworthy is the passage in Joshua which describes the entrance into the Promised Land and the capture of Jericho (chaps. iii.-vi.). It is assigned in the main to JE.[71] The "priests" are referred to 24 times in these four chapters. In iii.3, where they are first mentioned, they are called "the priests the Levites," and after that simply "the priests." It would be natural to infer that the fuller title is given at the beginning for the sake of accuracy and that in the 23 references which follow they are called "priests" for the sake of brevity and because it is obvious that the same priests are referred to throughout this section and that "the priests the Levites" is their full and proper designation. But the critics insist that the restriction of the priests to the tribe of Levi was unknown before the time of Josiah. Consequently the one verse (iii.3) which uses this "Deuteronomic" expression must be cut out of its context and assigned to D. When this has been done, it can be asserted that this passage refers only to "priests" and knows nothing of Levitical priests. This may seem very simple since it affects only one verse. But the elimination of this one verse permits the critics to assign a meaning to the word "priest" in all of its other occurrences in these chapters which is contradicted by the clear sense of the narrative as it stands in the Book of Joshua. Had the full expression "the priests the Levites" been used in all the 24 occurrences it would be somewhat harder to get rid of. But that would have been clumsy and monotonous, and the usage which is followed is natural and has been followed by hosts of writers. The only difficulty is that it lends itself more readily to "critical" manipulation.[72]

## 2. The Usage of Deuteronomy

a. The Levites are mentioned 14 times in Deuteronomy. In ten of these, his dependence upon gifts and tithes is stressed: he dwells "in the gates" of others and has no "inheritance" (xii.12); he is classed with the stranger, the widow and the fatherless (xvi.11, 14); and is not to be forgotten (xii. 19, xiv.27). Three passages are specially noteworthy. (1) xviii.6, 7 allows a Levite, who wishes to do so, to minister at "the place which Jehovah shall choose." It is alleged that the Levites here referred to are priests of the high places, whose shrines were abolished and declared unlawful by the reform of Josiah. But there is nothing in the narrative itself to support this claim. And such an interpretation is rendered improbable by the statement in 2 Kings xxiii.9 that "the priests of the high places came not up to the altar of Jehovah in Jerusalem, but they did eat of the unleavened bread among their brethren." Those who insist that Deut. xviii.6 refers to these priests of the high places must admit that this "humane" provision regarding the dispossessed priests was not actually enforced, perhaps, because it could not be. (2) xxvii.14 assigns them the rôle of pronouncing the blessings and cursings at Mt. Ebal. But since the tribe of Levi is expressly mentioned as one of those that stand on Mt. Gerizim to bless, it would be natural to infer that the Levites here referred to are "the priests the Levites" mentioned in vs. 9. (3) This is favored by the fact that xxxi.25 describes the Levites as "the bearers of the ark of the covenant of Jehovah," which was a great honor and often performed by the priests.

*b.* Priests are referred to 14 times in Deuteronomy. In half of these occurrences they are called "the priests the Levites" (xvii.9, 18, xviii.1, xxiv.8, xxvii.9) or "the priests the sons of Levi" (xxi.5, xxxi.9). In the remaining seven they are simply called "priests" or "the priest." That no difference is involved is shown by the fact that the same duties are assigned to both; they are compared with the judges in authority, and in such passages as xvii.12 and xviii.3 the context makes it clear that the priests are the same as "the priests the Levites" just referred to. The reference to "the priest" in xx.2 and xxvi.3, 4 suggests a special individual who would naturally be the high priest.

A comparison of these passages in Deuteronomy in which Levites and priests are referred to gives no definite support to the claim that "every Levite was a potential priest." The Levites and priests were alike in having no inheritance and in being set apart to the service of God. But in general the contrast is so great that we would naturally expect the priests to be a separate and superior class within the body of the Levites. The passages mentioned above which give prominence to the Levite do not alter the picture materially. The fact that the Levites were given the duty of bearing the ark has its explanation in the simple fact that when Israel was at Sinai there were only two priests and one high priest. The ark was heavy. Aaron was then a man 84 years of age. His two sons could not have carried it on long journeyings without assistance. This was naturally made a duty and a privilege of the Levites, despite the fact that on certain occasions, as for example the crossing of the Jordan, this duty was performed by the priests to add to the solemnity of the occasion.

That a distinction was made between the priests and the Levites long before the time of Josiah is indicated by

the description given to us in Kings of an epoch-making
event in the history of Israel, the dedication of Solomon's
temple. In connection with this event we are told: "And
all the elders of Israel came and the priests bare the ark"
(viii.3). This is the general statement. Then, as is often
done, it is elaborated and we read: "And they brought up
the ark of Jehovah and the tent of meeting and all the holy
vessels which were in the tent; and the priests and the
Levites brought them up." This may mean either that the
priests carried the ark and the Levites carried the tent and
all the rest of the vessels. Or it may mean that on this occasion the Levites were permitted to share with the priests
in the honor of bearing the ark to its resting place in the
temple. One thing is clear, however, that a distinction is
here made *between* the priests *and* the Levites, and that this
is done with reference to an event of Solomon's reign. The
explanation of this statement given by the critics, the only
one which can be given, is stated by Kuenen thus: "The
distinction between priests and Levites—emphatically enforced by P . . . —only appears once in the whole pre-
exilian and exilian literature. It is in 1 Kings 8:4, and the
passage, both on this and other accounts, lies under suspicion."[73] But the reason there are in the early literature
so very few references of any kind to priests or Levites is
simply because nearly all the references to them are assigned to P and treated as late. In the books of Samuel-
Kings the Levites are mentioned only three times. Consequently this statement in 1 Kings viii.3f. because it is
definite and precise and made regarding an event of great
importance should not be waved aside, but given the attention which it deserves.

### 3. Ezekiel and the Priesthood

It is the claim of the critics that the first evidence of a
separation between priests and Levites is to be found in
Ezek. xliv.4-16, where it is declared that the house of Israel

have given the service of God into the hands of strangers who have polluted it, that the Levites who "have gone away far from me" and practised idolatry shall "bear their iniquity" and shall be assigned to the menial tasks, and that only "the priests the Levites, the sons of Zadok" who have been faithful shall be permitted to perform the priest's office in the future. This assignment of the Levites to an inferior position which is instituted by Ezekiel is then, we are told, presupposed by P as a recognized distinction. Several objections weigh heavily against such an interpretation of this admittedly difficult passage:

*a.* If Ezekiel was thirty years old in the fifth year of Jehoiachin's captivity, his birth occurred just about the time of Josiah's reform. Even if he was considerable under twenty-five when carried captive, the fact that he was of priestly family would make it highly probable that he was in a position to know what the reform of Josiah involved and how fully it was carried out. His prophecies indicate familiarity with many of the sayings of Jeremiah and he may often have heard him preach. He probably knew that Jeremiah had approved Josiah's covenant and reform.

*b.* We have seen that Deut. xviii.6f. refers, according to the critics, to the priests of the high places who were thrown out of office by the centralization of worship, although the passage itself has nothing to say about this. But, if it be admitted that such an interpretation is possible, one thing is clear: no stigma of any kind and no degradation is implied in this passage. Any Levite who wishes to may serve at the central sanctuary. The situation described in 2 Kings xxiii.4f. is different. The thing which is especially denounced in the worship of the high places is that it is idolatrous; and we are told that "the priests of the high places came not up to the altar of Jehovah in Jerusalem, but they did eat of the unleavened bread among their brethren." The implication seems to be that they did not care, did not dare, or were not permitted, to exercise a right which Deuteronomy expressly secured to them. This would be remarkable, because Kings is supposed to reflect clearly the Deuteronomic viewpoint, and Kings tells us expressly that the covenant of the king was obeyed.

*c.* Now we are told that Ezekiel, a younger contemporary of Josiah and Jeremiah, a prophet living in exile but familiar with the history of the great reform, gives an account of it quite different from that of the Deuteronomic reformers themselves. He stigmatizes the conduct of all Levites except the priests of the line of Zadok as highly reprehensible and degrades them, assigning them the menial service of the sanctuary. Yet he gives them, or allows them to continue to bear, the name Levite, which prior to that time had been a name of honor and distinction. To say with Wellhausen that "Ezekiel merely throws a moral mantle over the logic of facts" does not meet the situation as the critics envisage it at all. For the moral mantle is, if the critics are to be believed, a scandalous and libellous one. If worship at the high places was perfectly lawful until the reform of Josiah, and especially if idolatrous rites were at least tolerated up to that time, then these priests were innocent of any real wrong-doing. If the critics are right, Ezekiel was as unjust to them, as was the writer or editor of Kings in denouncing that outstanding "religious conservative" king Jeroboam the son of Nebat as one "who made Israel to sin." These men certainly deserved fair treatment at the hand of one who claimed to be a prophet of Jehovah.

*d.* Finally it is to be remembered that Ezekiel's prophecy all refers to a time then future, a time when the land will be redistributed according to a totally new plan and when the temple will have been rebuilt, not at Jerusalem but at a place separated from the city by some miles. The Jews after the exile made no effort to carry out any of these requirements. Yet we are told that they made Ezekiel's words regarding the priests and Levites the basis for a drastic, unjust, and libellous distinction between them. The ex-

planation of Ezek. xliv. is not easy. But this one adds to
the difficulty instead of decreasing it.

### 4. The Priestly Legislation

It is claimed that (a) the Priest Code recognized and
enforced the distinction between priests and Levites as "a
statute forever," and that (b) it introduced the office of
the high priest and assigned great prominence to Aaron
and his descendants.

### a. Priests and Levites

As to the first of these points little need be said. That
the portions of the Pentateuch assigned to P draw a sharp
distinction between priests and Levites is quite obvious.
The assumption which we reject is that this difference was
first made definite and final in post-exilic times and not
already in the days of Moses. The distinction was an important one. It was also one which was likely to cause
jealousy and arouse opposition. Numbers xvi. tells us very
plainly of an attempt on the part of Levites to usurp the
functions of the priests. This incident is described in the
narrative itself as having taken place in the period of the
wilderness-wanderings. It implies that the distinction between priest and Levite was challenged already at that time.
But this passage is assigned to P "in the main"[74] and regarded by the critics as illustrating the difficulty which the
attempt to enforce this new distinction encountered nearly
a thousand years after the time of Moses. Yet it is Moses
and Aaron who are represented as the prominent figures in
this controversy which had such grievous consequences for
those who challenged their personal authority.

It is also worthy of note that P, unlike Ezekiel, represents the position of the Levites as an honorable and worthy
one (Num. xviii.25f., cf. xvi.8-10). Does this mean that
the "moral mantle" was no longer needed? It is also argued

that the noticeably small number of Levites who returned from captivity is an indication of the inferior position which the Levites had acquired. But if this view which we are considering is correct it is remarkable that any Levites returned. Disgraced and degraded, they might well have felt that they were better off where they were.[75]

A further point which should not be overlooked is the striking anomaly which this theory brings about between the conditions which existed after the Exile and the history which the priestly writers give of the early period. According to Num. iv.48 (P) at the time of the Exodus the Levites numbered 8,580 males of 30 years old and upward. According to that document there were at that time only four men ordained as priests and two of them perished almost immediately for disobedience. This left only two priests (Eleazer and Ithamar) and the high priest (Aaron). According to Ezra ii. the number of priests who returned was 4,289. The number of Levites is given as 74, to which are added singers 128, porters 139, Nethinim and Solomon's servants 392. If we include the singers and porters with the Levites the total is only 341 which is less than a tenth of the figure for the priests. Regarded as true history these figures are remarkable but by no means questionable. The descendants of Aaron might easily reach or exceed the total stated in the course of nearly a millennium; and the high importance given to the priest by the Law of Moses would be an inducement to faithful priests to return and reestablish the worship of the Lord. The Levites had far less reason for doing so. But considered as fabricated or fictitious history the figures given in Num. iv. seem incredible. The extreme fewness of the priests and the vast number of Levites as given in P is hard to account for in a "late" document and stands in most startling contrast with the actual conditions of the *late* period as described in the Book of Ezra.[76]

### *b*. The High Priesthood and Aaron

Ezekiel in his legislation does not mention the high priest. Consequently it has been argued that the office was unknown in his day and was first introduced by P. Such an inference is not necessary. Ezekiel might have known of the office without expressly naming it. But if the centralization of the worship first began at the time of Josiah, the office of high priest would be the natural consequence of the elevation of Jerusalem to a position of unique and exclusive importance. Unfortunately for the advocates of this theory "the actual course of history" does not support it. It is true that the laws of J and E do not mention a high priest. This is not remarkable, since, as we have seen, they have so little to say about priests of any kind. D does not explicitly mention the "high priest." But the statements regarding "the priest" in xx.2 and xxvi.3, 4 certainly seem to refer to a pre-eminent priest who would properly be the high priest. Such an inference is warranted by the statements of Kings, where we find Jehoiada (xii.10), and Hilkiah (xxii.4, 8, xxiii.4) described as "high [i.e., 'great'] priest," and Seraiah (xxv.18) called "chief priest" which apparently designates the same office. This closely parallels the statements of the Chronicler who refers to Hilkiah as "high priest" and gives the title "chief priest" to Amariah, Jehoiada, Azariah. This must mean either that the Chronicler agrees with Kings as to the antiquity of the office of the high priest or that the priestly writer has edited the Books of Kings to make them agree with the attempt of the post-exilic historians to represent the office of high priest as ancient, i.e., Mosaic. The general position of the critics is that while the Deuteronomic school edited the Books of Kings in order to make the history there recorded correspond with the reforms introduced by Josiah, the post-exilic writers of the Priestly school instead of still further editing Kings wrote a history of their own, the Books of

Chronicles which give the history of the pre-exilic period viewed in the light of the theories and practices of post-exilic Judaism. But if the office of high priest is post-exilic, then we must admit that the priestly writers were not content with writing their own history (Chronicles), but went still further and at crucial points edited the earlier histories as well. It is the claim of the critics that Kings is far more reliable than Chronicles. But if Kings has been worked over, first by the Deuteronomist in the interest of Josiah's reform, and then by the Priestly writer in the interest of post-exilic theories, it is hard to see where really trustworthy history of the pre-exilic period is to be found.

According to the Old Testament itself Aaron was the first high priest and he was inducted into that office by Moses. According to the theory we are examining, not only is the office of high priest of post-exilic origin, but Aaron himself and an Aaronic priesthood also are largely if not entirely a fabrication of this late period. This, as we have seen, is the natural result of assigning the vast bulk of the priestly legislation to the post-exilic period. But aside from this there are certain points which are noteworthy.

(1) Aaron is referred to 13 times in J passages in Ex. iv.-xii. and xxiv. All of these references have been since Wellhausen regarded as suspicious and the critics are accustomed to say "Aaron is missing from J."[77] But this is the case only when these 13 references are eliminated as later additions to the text. In other words, the document must be edited in the interest of the conclusion, before the conclusion which is desired can be reached.

(2) Joshua xxi. is largely devoted to the account of the assigning of cities to the priests the sons of Aaron. According to the narrative itself this was done by Joshua as provided by Moses. This whole section has to be regarded as reflecting post-exilic conditions and therefore as late. We have already seen that, by assigning the reference to "the priests the Levites" in iii.3 to D², it becomes possible for the critics to assert

that the J document from which it is eliminated knows nothing of a distinction between priests and Levites. Now, by assigning the bulk of chapter xxi. to P, it becomes possible to say that the pre-exilic period knows nothing of an Aaronic priesthood despite the fact that this chapter expressly recognizes such a class as existing in the days of Joshua.

## II. The Priest Code and Post-Exilic History

In concluding his chapter on "The Priests and the Levites" Wellhausen remarks:

"To any one who knows anything about history it is not necessary to prove that the so-called Mosaic theocracy, which nowhere suits the circumstances of the earlier periods, and of which the prophets, even in their most ideal delineations of the Israelite state as it ought to be, have not the faintest shadow of an idea, is, so to speak, a perfect fit for post-exilian Judaism, and had its actuality only there."[78]

This is a very dogmatic statement, both in what it denies and in what it affirms. The claim that the priestly legislation does not "fit" the early periods and that the prophets had not "the faintest shadow of an idea of it" has been already discussed. We must now examine the claim that the priestly legislation is "a perfect fit for post-exilian Judaism and had its actuality only there." The only way to test this statement is by examining it in the light of the history of the post-exilic period as this is recorded in the books of Ezra, Nehemiah, Esther, Haggai, Zechariah, and Malachi, all of which profess to deal with the period in question.[79] It should not be difficult to determine whether they support the view that the Priest Code is a perfect fit for post-exilic Judaism. We note the following:

### 1. Features Peculiar to P which Are Not Referred to in the Post-Exilic Period

a. The entire legislation of P centers around the "tent" or "tabernacle" which it declares was made, set up, and dedicated at Sinai, "as Jehovah commanded Moses." Such a tabernacle was never constructed in post-exilic times.

(1) The description is elaborate and detailed. Yet these Jews of the post-exilic period not merely made no effort to build a tabernacle instead of a temple: they seem to have ignored features of P which they might well have respected, if P was a perfect fit for this period. Thus, P tells us that the tabernacle was set up on the first day of the first month (Ex. xl.2). The Second Temple was nearly five years in building and was completed on the 3rd day of Adar (Ezra vi.15) which was the twelfth month. Apparently it was dedicated at once. Why did not the Jews wait a few weeks and dedicate it "as Jehovah commanded Moses" on the first day of the first month?

(2) The most sacred vessel in the tabernacle was the ark (Ex. xxv.10-22, xxxvii.1-9, xl.3, 20f., in which were the two tables containing the testimony. The Second Temple had no ark and no mention is made of the Ten Commandments.

(3) An important function of the high priest was to divine by Urim and Thummim (Ex. xxviii.30, Num. xxvii.21). This was a memory and a pious hope in the days of the Second Temple (Ezra ii.63, Neh. vii.65). No mention is made of the ephod.

b. P contains an elaborate account of the ritual for the day of atonement (Lev. xvi. and xxiii.27f.). It was to be observed on the 10th day of the seventh month. In Ezra iii.1-6 we read of the setting up of the altar in the seventh month and of the keeping of the feast of tabernacles which began on the 14th day of that month. But the day of atonement is not mentioned. This is especially noteworthy because the day of atonement is the only fast day prescribed in the Pentateuch. Fasting is referred to occasionally in the post-exilic books. But the word used in them (tsum) never occurs in P; and conversely, they do not use P's expression "afflict the soul" (Lev. xvi.29, cf. Ps. xxxv.13), although a similar expression does occur in Ezra viii.21 and Dan. x.12.

c. Other laws regarded by the critics as peculiar to P which are ignored by the post-exilic writers are the laws regarding the cities of refuge (Num. xxxv., Josh. xx. and xxi.), the jealousy ordeal (Num. v.), the wave offering (Ex., Lev., Num.). The word "qorban" (offering or oblation) which occurs frequently in P is used only of the "wood-offering" (Neh. x.34, xiii.31) which is not mentioned in P.

## 2. Features of P Not Mentioned in the Post-Exilic Period which Are Mentioned in the Records Dealing with Pre-Exilic Times

*a.* Such are the whole burnt offering *(kalil)*, offering made with fire *(ishsheh)*, peace offering *(shelem)*, trespass-offering *(asham)*, drink offering *(nesek)*.

*b.* No mention is made of the ritual significance of blood or of the prohibition of eating with the blood (but cf. Zech. ix.11).

*c.* No mention is made of leprosy (Lev. xiii), of Nazirites (Num. vi.).

*d.* According to the critics circumcision of infants on the 8th day is a requirement of P (Gen. xvii. and xxi.). It is the sign of the covenant. Yet the post-exilic books make no mention of it at all. On the other hand the books of Joshua and 1st and 2nd Samuel attach great importance to the distinction between circumcision and uncircumcision. That the rite there referred to was a different rite, performed on adults not infants, cannot be proved from Scripture. Yet the great issue for the returned exiles was apparently not circumcision (of infants) but marriage with non-Israelite women. This evil is dealt with at length in Ezra ix.-x.; and its suppression is based on D (Deut. vii.3) not on P. Since this intercourse with heathen must have involved intimate dealings with those who were uncircumcised, the failure of Ezra and Nehemiah to mention circumcision is remarkable. It would be especially remarkable if the rigid requirement of P had only recently been imposed.

## 3. Features of P which Are Found in Both the Pre-Exilic and Post-Exilic Periods

*a.* Many of the institutions which are referred to in the post-exilic books and required in P are also required in the earlier codes or mentioned in the histories of the earlier (pre-exilic) period. These are the sabbath, the passover, the feast of unleavened bread, the feast of tabernacles (Ezra iii., Neh. viii.), which is referred to the time of Joshua. In the case of the sacrifices and offerings this is true of the burnt offering *(olah)*, the peace offering *(zebach)*, heave offering *(terumah)*, the continual burnt offering (cf. 1 Chr. xvi.40, 2 Chr. ii.4, also 1 Kgs. xviii.36), the meal offering *(minchah)*, the sin offering (Hos. iv.8, cf. Mic. vi.7), freewill offerings (2 Chr. xxxi.14), first fruits *(bikkur*, 2 Kgs. iv.42), firstlings, first-born *(bekor*, cf. Ex. xxxiv.20, J), the first fruits *(reshith)*, tithes, shewbread, incense *qetoreth)*, frankincense *(lebonah)*.

*b.* It may also be noted in this connection that the camel, described as unclean in P (Lev. xi.4) is referred to in Genesis in J and E. Chronicles agrees with Samuel that camels were widely used in the time of David. Judges agrees with J that the Ishmaelites (Midianites) of patriarchal times had camels.

## 4. We Find Innovations in the Post-Exilic Period

Institutions not mentioned in P are referred to in the post-exilic books.

*a.* Singers and singing are not mentioned in P in connection with the worship of the tabernacle. But in Ezra and Neh. the singers constitute an important part of the community; and Chron. gives an elaborate account of the organization of the service of song for the worship of the sanctuary and attributes it to David. Both of these facts would be significant if P were late: a recognized institution of post-exilic times would not be mentioned at all in this elaborate code, and the historians of the period would attribute it not to Moses but to David.

*b.* Scribes are not mentioned in the Pentateuch, nor the use of sackcloth (Neh. ix.1), offering of the one-third shekel (Neh. x.32) and of a wood-offering (x.34). The many sacrifices offered at the dedication of the temple (Ezra. vi.17) have no basis in P, but rather remind us of the dedication of Solomon's temple.

*c.* The failure of the divine name, "Jehovah of hosts," to occur even once in the Pentateuch is in marked contrast to its frequent occurrence (86 times) in Hag., Zech., Mal.

*d.* The central sanctuary is never called the "temple" *(hekal)* in the Pentateuch, though this word occurs frequently in the historical and prophetical books of the exilic and post-exilic periods. The "nethinim" and the "porters," likewise mentioned in Ezra-Neh., are not referred to in the Pentateuch.

e. The representation of Jerusalem as a Benjamite city in Josh. xv.8, xviii.28, and the failure of the Pentateuch to mention it at all (save as Salem, Gen. xiv.18) is also remarkable if P is late.

It is also to be noted that the post-exilic books contain comparatively few allusions to the early history of Israel. Abraham is mentioned only once (Neh. ix.7), Isaac never, Jacob once (Mal. i.2, cf. Ezra viii.18). The expression, "God of Abraham, Isaac, and Jacob (Israel)," found in P (Ex. vi.3) and in the early literature, is never used. Esau is mentioned once (Mal. i.2). No mention is made of the Abrahamic covenant, which is stressed in P (Gen. xvii., Ex. vi.4). But Malachi refers to the covenant with Levi. Joshua is mentioned in connection with the keeping of the feast of tabernacles (Neh. viii.17). The two who are mentioned most frequently are Moses, whose law is referred to 11 times, and David who is referred to a like number of times. In view of the claim that the prophets of the pre-exilic period show little knowledge of the history and institutions of the early times, it may be noted that the allusions to it in these post-exilic books are also both meagre and casual. This is especially noteworthy because the critics make use of the meagreness of allusion in the prophets and other pre-exilic books to the Pentateuch and the Mosaic Law as proof of non-existence.

The public confession of sin recorded in Neh. ix. is the fullest résumé of Israel's history anywhere to be found in the post-exilic books. This résumé of the history is especially interesting because an examination of it clearly shows that it does not confine itself to the history as recorded in P but includes data from J, E and D. This may be regarded as confirming the view that the "book" of the law of Moses (cf. Ezra vi.18, Neh. viii.1, xiii.1) was the entire Pentateuch.

The failure of P to mention singers (see above) is especially noteworthy. According to *The Westminster Study Edition of the Holy Bible,* "The regulations for the Levites and singers do not go back to the times in which he [the Chronicler] sets them. It is, for instance, noteworthy that they do not appear in the Pentateuch, which was finally edited about 400 B.C. But by working them into the context of the story of Israel's past he succeeds in making them stand out vividly and dramatically before his readers' eyes" (p. 522). This means that the failure of the Pentateuch, which restricts itself to laws which it represents as *Mosaic,* to mention regulations which the Chronicler describes as *Davidic,* must be attributed to the untrustworthiness of the Chronicler who was prepared to manufacture his facts in the interest of vivid narration and, writing a century or more later than P, attributed to David regulations unknown to P or not regarded by him as Davidic. However the critics may explain this anomalous situation which results from the late dating of P, we have here a striking example of the failure of P to agree with the history of pre-exilic, exilic, and post-exilic times as recorded in Chronicles, Ezra, and Nehemiah.

Such data as the above justify two conclusions. The claim that the Priest Code fits the post-exilic period like a glove is as little justified as the claim that it does not fit the pre-exilic period. It is as clear from a study of the books dealing with the post-exilic period as it is from those dealing with the pre-exilic period that "it is impossible to find records of practice in regard to innumerable details of the laws."[80] If ignorance of a law proves its non-existence, many of the laws of P did not exist in the time of Ezra.[81] If the critics were to expurgate the post-exilic history as thoroughly as they do the pre-exilic they could easily prove that P is later than Ezra. On the other hand if they would accept the occasional references to these laws in the books which deal with the pre-exilic praxis and if they would accept at its face value the oft-repeated claim of the Old Testament that Israel's failure to keep the law of Moses was due to an evil heart of unbelief, the elaborate hypothesis erected by the critics would be seen to be devoid of any adequate foundation in fact.

Finally, it is to be kept carefully in mind in judging the Development Hypothesis as a whole, that the point at issue between its advocates and those who hold that the Law was given by Moses is not as to whether the Law was disobeyed and ignored. The constant complaint of the Old Testament prophets and historians is that Israel's record is one of shameful disregard of the oracles of God, the custody of which gave her a unique position among the races of mankind. The question at issue is whether this non-observance and neglect proves that this Law was non-existent in pre-exilic times. This the critics have not succeeded in proving and cannot prove from the Old Testament. For the *"actual course of history,* so far as that is known" quite clearly indicates the contrary, and the verdict pronounced upon that course of history by the historians and prophets is thoroughly consistent with it. When the critics reject those statements in the record which indicate that the law was ancient, they are not only guilty of tampering with the evidence, but they also make the denunciations uttered by Israel's historians and prophets of her failure to keep the law both farcical and cruel. For these teachers of Israel insisted that all of Israel's sufferings were due to the failure of the people to keep a law which, if the critics are correct, was unknown to them and so could not have been to them that "law of life and knowledge," the observance of which was to bring blessedness and the breach of which was to make them an outcast among the nations. If the critics are to make good their claim that the Law of Moses did not exist in pre-exilic times, it must be because they can show that there is convincing evidence outside the Bible which refutes the consistent claim of the Bible that the Law was given by Moses. Are they in a position to do this?

# PART III

# THE PRESENT STATE OF THE PROBLEM

". . . the word of our God shall stand forever"
(ISAIAH xl.8)

# THE PRESENT STATE OF THE PROBLEM

AS TO the present state of the problem of the Pentateuch, it may be said in general that the critics were never more sure that their reconstruction of the Old Testament is demonstrably correct. They regard the question of the Mosaic authorship of the Pentateuch as now no longer matter for serious debate. It is only as to the extent, date, authorship, and provenance of these *"post*-Mosaic" documents that they are prepared to permit a certain amount of difference of opinion.

Thus, Canon Richardson does not hesitate to say: "One thing is certain. There can be no going back on the positions gained by the discoveries of biblical research. There may be modifications here and there, but the broad general conclusions are beyond cavil."[1] While this is a substantially correct statement of the attitude of the higher critics today, this author has found it necessary to make a significant admission: "It is true that although the knowledge is there, clear and accessible, there still remains the problem of distribution; large masses of the population unfortunately know nothing at all about the Bible and how it was written, and the door is still open for all kinds of superstition and misuse."[2] As an example of what he would apparently regard as superstition and misuse, Richardson instances the question of the Second Isaiah. After stating this modern interpretation very briefly, he goes on to say: "And, moreover, these things are not in doubt; they are not hypothetical reconstructions or tentative suggestions, but truth as assured as anything can be in the sphere of literary research."[3] So, according to this writer, it is only ignorance, superstition, misuse, on the part of large masses of the population, which prevents the universal acceptance of the conclusions of the critics. Such an attitude, for Richardson is simply repeating a claim which has become a well-worn *cliché*, ignores completely the fact that in the case of many Christians failure to accept the conclusions which the critics declare to be so assured, is not due to ignorance of the Bible, but to the intelligent and sincere conviction that these conclusions must be false because at so many points they flatly contradict the definite statements of the Bible, as to what it is, what it says, how it was written, and the authority with which it speaks.[4] And the fact that "large masses of the population" still refuse to accept them might well lead the critics to reconsider their conclusions instead of blaming the lack of success in securing their general acceptance on the stupidity or obstinacy of their opponents. But our special reason for quoting these statements is that they serve to bring out so clearly the fact that the critics hold that their main task has been accomplished, that their reconstruction of the Old Testament is practically complete, and that only "certain modifications" in it are to be expected, or to put it somewhat more strongly, will be tolerated by them. We have been examining these main conclusions. We shall now proceed to consider some of the "modifications" which have been proposed in recent years. Then we shall pass on to consider several other important subjects, prominent among which is the bearing of archaeological research on the problem of the Pentateuch.

# CHAPTER I

# NEGATIVE AND POSITIVE DEVELOPMENTS

## I. FURTHER DISINTEGRATION OF DOCUMENTS

DESPITE the confidence with which the critics refer to their "assured results," it is always to be remembered that the basic principle of the higher criticism, the one which they have used most effectively, is an utterly lawless one and cannot be kept within any fixed or definite bounds. The progressive disintegration of documents cannot be halted by any authoritative or arbitrary Thus-far-and-no-farther! And while many of the results of its application in recent years may be regarded as permissible "modifications," there have been others which, if generally accepted, would have completely undermined some of the foundations of the critical structure which have been regarded as most secure.

The developments of the last two or three decades furnish numerous examples of this process of disintegration. We have seen that Eissfeldt has endeavored to divide J into two continuous documents (L and J), which run through the Pentateuch and on into the Historical Books; that Mowinckel has sought to carry E back of Gen. xv. or xx. by assigning to it the second J source, thus making E begin in Gen. ii.; that Pfeiffer has discovered two fragmentary sources in the early part of J which he has called S¹ and S², the sundering of which from J makes J begin as abruptly as E; that Von Rad has divided the narrative portions of P between two sources which he calls A and B; that Morgenstern has claimed the "Decalogue of J" (Ex. xxxiv.) as part of an ancient Kenite document, which he regards as the oldest code in the Pentateuch (written before

899 B.C.!) and makes the basis of Asa's reform. Such proposals are indicative of the incessant activity of the critics and of the "modifications" which they are prepared to regard as permissible. On the other hand, Volz and Rudolph have attacked the view, generally accepted since Hupfeld, that E represents a distinct source, insisting that what is called E merely represents editorial additions to J (a virtual return to the Supplementary Hypothesis). Volz threw a second bombshell by asserting that P was not a narrative-writer *(kein Erzähler)* and therefore could not have been the author of Gen. xxiii. He also asserted that there never was a separate P account of the Flood, and that the splitting up of such passages as Gen. xxix.31-xxx.20 and xxxiv. is not warranted. Needless to say, such modifications as these last have not been welcomed by the critics. They represent a backward step which is not acceptable to them.

But there have been other "modifications" proposed in recent years that are much more drastic than those mentioned above and which must have caused not a little concern to those who regard the "broad general conclusions" of the critics as beyond cavil. In commencing his *Geschichte der israelitischen Religion,* Hölscher remarked that it would be delightful if "the basic outlines" which had been established by the end of the 19th century could be regarded as "assured results" *(anerkannte Ergebnisse).* But he described the state of scientific study of the Old Testament at the time of writing (1922) as one of "uncertain groping and searching" *(Tasten und Suchen).* Then, having expressed his regret at the lack of agreement among scholars, he proceeded to attack the Critical Hypothesis at two points as to which there had been, generally speaking, the maximum of agreement. The first of these, as we have already seen, was Ezekiel. This book he declared to be post-exilic and he finally rejected about six-sevenths of it as consisting of editorial additions.[5]

More important than Hölscher's dismemberment of

Ezekiel was his attack on Deuteronomy. We have seen that the claim of De Wette, that Deut. is the book which was discovered in the temple in the 18th year of Josiah and made the basis of his reform, has been the official view in critical circles for more than a century, despite the fact that there has been much difference of opinion as to the extent of the book which was discovered. Driver assigned the bulk of Deut. (v.1-xxvi.19) to D. In opposition to this almost "traditional" view Hölscher came out with the bold assertion that the so-called Deuteronomic Law has nothing to do with the law book of king Josiah which was found in the year 620, but belongs in the early Persian period (*cir.* 500 B.C.). Having stated this position rather briefly in the *Geschichte,* Hölscher proceeded a few months later to defend it in detail.[6] This involved a sharp distinction between the "original Deuteronomy" *(Urdeuteronomium)* and later additions of which he recognized many. Following the lead of Steuernagel and others, he accepted the view that the oldest parts of the code are to be found in the passages which use the Second Person Singular, what we may call the "thou sections."[7] Applied to the vitally important chapter xii., this means that vss. 1-12, 16 are not original. But Hölscher rejected several other verses also, with the result that only 12 are to be regarded as original (vss. 13-14, 17-19, 21-22, 26-27, 29-31). Since verses 1-7 are the ones which refer most clearly to the centralization of worship, it is easy to see that by making such an analysis Hölscher could arrive at the conclusion that Deut., meaning of course Deut. in its original form, has nothing to say about centralization of worship and consequently could have no direct bearing on Josiah's reform. This leads at once to the question whether 2 Kgs. xxii-xxiii. refers to Deut. By a critical analysis of these chapters which makes the relevant passages post-exilic, Hölscher is able to maintain that in their original form these chapters do not refer to Deut.[8] Passing on to Jeremiah and Ezekiel he assures us that the "genuine" Jeremiah and the "genuine" Ezekiel—he admits that these books in the form in which we know them do "undoubtedly" refer to Deut.—make no reference to Deut. He declares further that the references to Deut. in Haggai and Zechariah are due to later "Deuteronomic" editing. It is by such a process of discrediting and silencing the relevant witnesses that the desired conclusion is arrived at that Deut. is post-exilic and may have appeared about 500 B.C.

This radical conclusion at which Hölscher arrived— hardly more radical than that of some other critics—was promptly challenged by Welch of Edinburgh. Welch maintained that there is only one passage in Deut. which demands centralization of worship at the one central sanctuary, the "you" section, xii.1-7. In the words, "But unto the place which the LORD your God shall choose out of all your tribes to put his name there" (vs. 5), Welch recognized a definite requirement of worship at the one central sanctuary; and he regarded this command as furnishing the basis for the centralization of worship at Jerusalem required by Josiah's reform.[9] But Welch also insisted that none of the other references (about twenty) to the "place" which the Lord will "choose" were originally intended to have this precise meaning. He declared that most of them merely required that worship be performed at a shrine or altar dedicated to the worship of Jehovah, thus merely excluding worship at pagan shrines. He also maintained that the words, "in one of thy tribes" (vs. 14), merely restricted the lawful worship of Jehovah to a Jehovah-shrine in the tribe to which the worshipper belonged and did not require worship by all the tribes at the one central sanctuary. Consequently, having established, as he believed, that vss. 1-7 of this chapter are the only ones which refer to centralization of worship, he proceeded like Hölscher to reject this passage as a later addition, but for a different reason which led to a quite different result. For, by eliminating vss. 1-7 as a later addition to a code which in even its most rigorous requirements restricted worship only within tribal lines, he found support for the conclusion that the original Deut. code was much earlier than the time of Josiah, that it originated in the Northern Kingdom, and that it was only the later insertion of the centralization law (vss. 1-7) into this older North Israelite code which made it of use in bringing about Josiah's reform. Thus Hölscher and Welch, though using the same critical method, the partitioning of Deuteronomy, arrived at strikingly different results. The one has been called a radical, the other a conservative, critic. But the only difference between them is that one applied the disintegrative method of dealing with the evidence in one way, the other in another.

Welch's treatment of Deut. xii.1-7 is a striking illustration of the dangers inherent in the "critical" method of dealing with the Bible. Verse 5 of this chapter contains the *first* mention of the "place" which the Lord will "choose." About twenty other times in this and the following chapters, notably xiv. and xvi., we find similar expressions. If we look upon the Book of Deut. as a self-consistent whole, we will naturally suppose that the first mention of this "place" which is to be so important for the worship of Israel in the future will give the fullest and the most precise description of it and that those which follow are to be understood in terms of the first reference. If the first mention specifies a place which is to be chosen "out of all your tribes," it would be only natural and proper to infer that the other passages, even if they do not describe it as precisely and fully as does the one where it is first mentioned, will all, unless there is definite indication to the contrary, refer as it does to the one central sanctuary. This is the reason that commentators have been so generally agreed that the centralization of worship at the one central sanctuary is one of the important themes of this book. But if this first, most precise, and therefore most important reference to this subject is cut away and treated as a later addition, then it becomes possible to place a somewhat different meaning on the less precisely worded statements which follow, with the result that, as we have seen, Welch could argue with some measure of plausibility that the original Code made no reference at all to such a concentration of worship (at Jerusalem) as the reformers of Josiah's day are supposed by the critics to have inaugurated.[10]

Another scholar who has given special attention to the problem of Deuteronomy is Von Rad. His "conjecture" is that the original code originated in the later period of the Monarchy and in the circle of the national Yahweh prophets, and that much of it is based on old, even very old sources. From the standpoint of the critics, this is quite conservative. In this connection we are interested in only a single point. In discussing the relation between Deuteronomy and Jeremiah, Von Rad asserts that Jer. vii.21-23 cannot be an attack on Deut., because "Nowhere in Deut. are burnt offering and sacrifice commanded."[11] Such a statement sounds startling, since the concordance shows that they are definitely commanded in xii.6, 11, 13, 14, 27 and xxvii.6 (cf. xvi.2, 21, xvii.1, xviii.1, 3, xxi.3-9, xxxiii.10). But Von Rad has already stated that the "original" Deut. *(Urdeuteronomium)* is to be found in the "thou" passages, as claimed by Steuernagel and others. So when we examine the above listed thirteen passages, we find to our surprise that nine of them are "thou" passages. Consequently, they must all be eliminated on one ground or another from the "original Deut." before the statement that Deut. has nothing to say about the priestly cultus can be accepted as correct. For it can only be said of a Deut. code, from which all mention of this cultus has been carefully eliminated that "Nowhere in Deut. are burnt offering and sacrifice commanded." So the ambiguity in the use of the word "Deuteronomy" must be carefully

noted or the reader may accept a meaning and draw inferences which are quite out of accord with the actual facts.[12]

For another example of disintegrative analysis we turn
to Josh. xxiv. This chapter has been generally assigned
practically as a whole to E, and consequently regarded as
much later than the time of Joshua. How much if any of
the address attributed to him is really his, will therefore on
critical principles be decidedly problematical, despite the
fact that vss. 1f. declare that "Joshua gathered all the tribes
of Israel to Shechem" and said "unto all the people. Thus
saith Jehovah, the God of Israel, Your fathers dwelt of old
times beyond the river, even Terah, the father of Abraham,
and the father of Nahor: and they served other gods" (cf.
vss. 6, 14, 15, 17). But the address is not merely historical,
it does not simply concern the "fathers," it is intensely
personal; and Joshua frequently addresses the people as
"you" (e.g., vss. 8, 9, 10, etc.), as he applies this history to
them, exhorts them to obedience, and warns them against
apostasy. Then in conclusion and by way of contrast and
final appeal he declares: "but as for me and my house we
will serve the Lord" (vs. 15b). It is only natural to suppose
as we read this address, that by the "you" Joshua means
all Israel including his own family, and that when he speaks
of "me and my house," he is simply referring to that one
family in all Israel for which he was peculiarly responsible
and pledging them to loyalty to the Lord, even though all
the rest of Israel should turn away from serving the God
of their fathers. But we find that Noth takes a quite different view of this impressive incident.[13] Adopting the theory
that the Joseph tribes to which Joshua belonged were the
only ones which sojourned in Egypt, he identifies "your
fathers" with the Leah tribes which according to this
theory had come from the East, perhaps in several migra-
tions, and had never been in Egypt; and in the "me and my
house" he finds the Joseph tribes referred to which had
sojourned in Egypt before entering the land. Such an

interpretation is, of course, definitely opposed by vss. 4*b*-7, which clearly state that all the tribes had sojourned in Egypt. So Noth eliminates this passage as editorial *("ein Fremdkörper")*. Having done this he is able to find support in this chapter for the theory that there were two distinct covenants: one of the Joseph tribes at Sinai, the other of both the Joseph and the Leah tribes at Shechem. But it is only when the evidence is altered to suit the theory, that the theory can be regarded as proved by the evidence.

These examples show, as do many others already given, how by dextrous manipulation of his sources a critic can prove to be possible or even probable something which the passage when taken as a whole and in its obvious sense emphatically denies. They also show how numerous, endless indeed, are the "modifications" which disintegrative analysis can gradually bring about in the "assured results" of the higher criticism, that imposing modern structure which the critics have so long been engaged in building out of, and to take the place of, that "jerry-built" structure which they call the Old Testament.[14]

## II. FORM CRITICISM

One of the objections often raised against the theories of the higher critics regarding the Pentateuch and the Old Testament as a whole is that they are negative and destructive in their results. J, E, D, H, P, not to mention others, are merely symbols; and they represent unknown individuals or equally unknown "schools." Their dates and places of origin are problematical. As a result of the application of critical processes, the Old Testament has become increasingly a collection of anonymous or pseudonymous writings, the authorship, date, and provenance of which is largely a matter of conjecture. The general trend has been in the direction of a later and later dating of these documents. Consequently, the critics have been somewhat concerned to find some way of obtaining positive results from their negative method, and if possible to trace to an earlier date some at least of the material which their method has brought down to a date later than that assigned to it by tradition. A method of attaining this result which has become quite popular in recent years is called Form Criticism *(Gattungsgeschichte)*. It is the attempt to trace back into the *pre*-literary period the forms and patterns which are found embedded in the literature that has been preserved for us in the Old Testament.

While the name form criticism has only come into common use in comparatively recent years, it is in fact simply the application of a principle and method which has long been employed by the critics. In his *Lectures on Old Testament Prophecy* which were published in 1902 shortly after his death, A. B. Davidson[15] stated it as a general canon, "That a prophetical writer always makes the basis of his prophecies the historical situation in which he himself is placed." He pointed out that this principle had already been formulated by Bleek in 1869. Davidson found in this what he regarded as the clearest proof that the Second Part of Isaiah must be assigned to a writer living near the end of the Babylonian Captivity. This was equivalent to saying that the date of a document is to be determined by the situation which it presupposes.[16] In his Commentary on Genesis (1901), Gunkel directed his attention especially to the different literary forms or patterns *(Gattungen)* which appear in it. In 1906 he published an elaborate study of the nature and origin of these forms, such as proverbs, triumph songs, love songs, royal odes, dirges, sagas, myths, fables, etc., with a view to tracing their history in the light of Biblical and secular literature. Repeatedly in this study he used the expression *"Sitz im Leben,"* which has been anglicized as "situation in life."[17] In 1917 and again in 1926 he applied this historico-literary *(literaturgeschichtliche)* method to the Psalms. So Gunkel has been properly called the father of Form Criticism;[18] a fact which indicates

quite clearly that form criticism is the child of the higher
or source criticism of Wellhausen and the heir to its principles, methods, and results.[19]

This study of forms or patterns has been taken up by
many other scholars, notably Eissfeldt, who has devoted
more than a hundred pages of his *Einleitung* (1934) to the
pre-literary stage, i.e., to the tracing back of short sayings
*(Redeformeln)* to their origin in pre-literary times and the
determining of their "situation in life." Eissfeldt agrees
with Gunkel that these sayings must usually have been very
short: "a single story, a proverb, a short song," as appropriate to the capacity of a pre-literary people.[20] For example, the words of blessing with which we are told
Rebekah was dismissed from her father's house would
represent such a brief saying:[21]

"Thou art our sister. Be thou the mother of thousands of
  myriads;
And let thy seed possess the gate of those that hate thee."

This would represent a very ancient "form" of the blessing bestowed on a bride when she left her father's house.
Even if J be dated in the 9th century a thousand years
after the time of Abraham and the question whether the
story contained in Gen. xxiv. is historically true be regarded as doubtful or answered in the negative, nevertheless according to the principles of form criticism, since
marrying and giving in marriage must be regarded as a
prominent feature in the pre-literary period, this literary
pattern *(Gattung)* may be regarded as very ancient, as
reflecting a "situation in life" as ancient as or even far more
remote than the time when Abraham is supposed to have
lived.

For another example we turn to Von Rad, who has
written a valuable monograph on the subject of form
criticism.[22] We have seen that as a source critic Von Rad
is disposed to disintegrate Deuteronomy rather drastically.

Consequently, it is interesting to find that Von Rad has discovered in Deut. xxvi.5b-9 what he describes as a short historical Credo or confession of faith. Its phrasing may be "Deuteronomic" (i.e., late), but the credo itself he regards as pre-Deuteronomic. He tells us: "men prayed in this way and certainly not first in the time of the Deuteronomist," which makes this credo a definite literary "form."[23] Von Rad proceeds to analyze it. He notes carefully its inclusions and its omissions. It includes the descent into Egypt, the oppression, the exodus, and the conquest; it omits the covenant at Sinai and the giving of the Law. He stresses two points particularly: the mention of the conquest, the failure to mention Sinai. He points out that the same pattern appears in Deut. vi.20-24 and Josh. xxiv.2b-13. All three mention the conquest and ignore Sinai. From this he draws the inference that these passages represent a distinct pattern which he calls the conquest-form *(Landnahmegattung)*, and which appears in a number of other places in the Old Testament. These he regards as examples of redemptive history *(Heilsgeschichte)*. On the other hand he holds that the Sinai pattern represents Law; and he finds examples of it in Deut. xxxiii.2, 4, Ps. l, and lxxxi. Thus, he distinguishes two credo-forms or patterns. He connects the Sinai-form with the observance of the feast of tabernacles and with Shechem, the conquest-form with the feast of weeks and, with some hesitation, with Gilgal.[24] He argues that the tradition contained in the conquest-credo goes back to the patriarchal period while the pattern containing the Sinai legend he regards as much later. He thinks that it was worked into the J document by the writer of J himself and did not become popular until the time of the exile. In this way the form critic endeavors to find in books and documents which he considers late, forms or patterns which may go back to an ancient and pre-literary period.

While the methods of the form criticism were first applied to other and quite different literary patterns, their application to the legal codes of the Pentateuch has brought this type of criticism prominently before Biblical scholars. This has been due especially to the work of Albrecht Alt whose *Die Ursprünge des israelitischen Rechts* appeared in 1934. Starting out with the remark that the account which the Old Testament gives of the origin of its legal codes—that they were given to Israel through Moses—is "seemingly quite simple and unambiguous," he declares at once that this unity is only apparent; and he proceeds to establish this thesis by an examination of the Book of the Covenant (Ex. xxi.-xxiii.), which he describes as the "oldest corpus" of laws. His contention is that this corpus contained two distinct classes or "forms" of laws: the Casuistic and the Apodictic, the former of which he holds to be of Canaanite origin, the latter of Israelite.

The casuistic pattern[25] is according to Alt distinctly marked by the "if style" and the use of the third person. The first example given is xxi.18-19, "And if men strive together," etc. The phrasing is completely objective. The "I" of the lawgiver and the "thou" of the person addressed are foreign to it. It does not mention judges or priests and is concerned only with secular matters; with what Alt calls the *"Betätigungsbereich der normalen Gerechtsbarkeit,"* a phrase which we render with some hesitation by "the sphere of ordinary judicial procedure." Such laws come according to Alt under the general caption of "judgments" *(mishpatim).*

On the other hand, the apodictic style[26] in its simplest form is found in xxi.12, "He that smiteth a man, so that he die, shall surely be put to death." In the Hebrew, this law begins with a participle and consists of only five words *(makkeh 'ish wameth moth tumath).* The form of expression is rather striking. Other examples, even if slightly expanded, are found in vss. 15, 16, and 17. A special feature of these laws lies in the fact that they may form a "series"; and our attention is directed to the series of twelve curses in Deut. xxvii.15-26 all of which likewise have as the subject of the sentence a participle, although the order of words is reversed, the "cursed" appearing at the beginning, instead of, like the words "shall surely die," at the end.

It is to be noted that the two examples which have been cited have this in common: both are entirely objective and use the third person exclusively. This is important because the first example which Alt gives of a non-casuistical and therefore Israelite addition to a casuistical law is xxi.23*b*, "then thou shalt give life for life." Here, he tells us, an apodictic conclusion has been added to a casuistic premise, the if-clause. This represents, according to Alt, a change in the original Canaanite law, which was, he thinks, probably milder and contented itself with compensation. Similarly we are told that in vss. 13, 14, the order of which Alt reverses, we have only the premise or if-clause of the original laws, the main clause which states the "verdict" being apodictic and therefore Israelite; this being indicated by the "I" and the "thou." Thus, on the one hand, the "I" is Jehovah and indicates that the law is of Israelite origin, while on the other the word "God" may according to Alt refer to any god, e.g., a Canaanite deity, and is therefore not Israelite but Canaanite. How characteristic of the Israelite pattern Alt regards the use of the second person to be is indicated by the fact that he refers the reader to a whole series of "thou" commandments in Lev. xviii.7-17. These being found in the Holiness Code (H) would of course be regarded as definitely Israelite. Then he points out that similar clauses of prohibition (thou shalt not) are found in the Book of the Covenant, e.g., xxiii.1-3, 6-9. This prepares the way for the discussion of the Decalogue.[27]

According to Alt, the Decalogue, when reduced "to simple form," belongs to the apodictic pattern. Since four of the last six commands are "shalt nots," we are to assume that all ten originally were of the same form and that the positive form of the fourth and fifth is due to later reconstruction. The commandments are of various lengths; and Alt is of the opinion that they probably did not have a metrical form, like the five-word pattern referred to above. He is inclined to regard this as a departure from the metrical norm, rather than as representing a stage before that metrical norm was established.

As to the origin of the apodictic pattern which he finds in the Decalogue, Alt tells us that it consists of a short sequence of short sentences which show uniformity of style and always agree in this, that they are categorical prohibitions. He declares that they arise out of a different situation from the casuistical laws, not the local community (*die einzelne Gemeinde*) but the whole people (*ganze Volkgemeinschaft*) and its God speaking through it to the individual. He thinks that the Decalogue, of course in its original form, is the oldest example of apodictic laws. For proof of this he appeals to the Preface (Ex. xx.1) and to Ps. lxxxi. But he admits that the proof is inconclusive. He holds that apodictic law must go back to the desert period. In Palestine it came into contact with the Canaanite system, which Alt describes as secular and passive or static, in marked contrast with the Israelite law which is expansive and aggressive, claiming for Yahweh every department of life and recognizing no profane or neutral zone. Conflict between the two was, he tells us, inevitable and he concludes with the statement that one of the tasks of Criticism must be to trace out this "original Dualism" in the history of the Old Testament.

As an example of form criticism Alt's treatment of this subject is very interesting; and it is not surprising that it has attracted wide attention. Alt has put his case strongly but there are weaknesses in his argument. (1) The distinctions which are drawn are arbitrary and inconsistent. E.g., if the use of the third person is to be regarded as a characteristic of the casuistical style, then the pattern found in xxi.12, 15, 16, 17 certainly has more in common with the casuistic pattern, in its simplest form, than with the apodictic. And vs. 16 shows that this pattern can be amplified and modified quite as easily as the casuistic. (2) If "thou" is characteristically apodictic, then we have two kinds of apodictic sentences, one of which embodies this characteristic feature, while the other does not. (3) The fact that fusion must be recognized in many of these laws is an indication that there is no such fundamental difference between them as is alleged. (4) The claim that the casuist- ical laws are Canaanite is greatly weakened by the admis- sion that we have no first-hand knowledge of what the Canaanite laws actually were.[28] The casuistical pattern is characteristic of the Code of Hammurabi. It is a very natural way to state and deal with hypothetical cases. If human analogies are to be sought for, this Code may have been known to Moses and its phraseology followed to some extent. (5) Some of the distinctions drawn are clearly based on inadequate information or on no information at all. We are told that the Canaanite casuistic law is secular; and knows nothing of priest or judge. But priest and judge (the usual word) are *never* mentioned in Ex. xx.-xxiii. It is true that the word "gods" is apparently used in xxi.6, xxii.8, 9, 28 of judges. But three of the four occurrences are in passages which are characteristically casuistical. Similarly it is characteristic of the Book of the Covenant as distinguished from the Decalogue that the Deity is only rarely mentioned, the divine sanction and authority under- lying them all is assumed rather than stated. Yet one of these occurs in a casuistic law (xxii.10f.) and another in an apodictic (vs. 20). (6) It is pure assumption that distinct patterns of laws are to be recognized here, that these pat- terns must be traced to different sources, and that this proves the laws to be of different origin. When we study the Book of the Covenant, for example, and compare it with the Code of Hammurabi, we are struck at once with the difference in style. Practically all the laws of Hammurabi have the same stereotyped form. They are all casuistical. They begin with "if" (*shumma*, "assuming that"). Nearly 300 times in the Code this word is used to introduce a law. It is monotonous and wearisome. The pattern of the Book of the Covenant is different. There is variety in it, despite the fact that the casuistical "if" occurs frequently. And this variety is due in part to the subject-matter. Such commands as these: "Three times thou shalt keep a feast unto me in the year," "He that curseth his father or his mother, shall surely be put to death," "If a man shall steal an ox, or a sheep, and kill it, or sell it; he shall restore five oxen for an ox, and four sheep for a sheep," are so different in content that it is only natural that different forms of expression should be used. What is the objection to the positive form of the Fourth Commandment? Ought it to read, "Thou shalt not desecrate the sabbath day"? Is it necessary that all the commands of the Decalogue should be negative or all positive? Is it necessary that they should all be the same length? Because some of the laws of the Book of the Covenant in their simplest form have a five-word structure, must we assume that this pattern is the oldest or one of the oldest Israelitish patterns, and that departures from it must be regarded as either dating from the time before the pattern was established or as being departures from a norm already established? The whole theory bristles with assumptions which cannot be proved; and it consists of inferences which are based on data which are to say the least too meagre to warrant the conclusions drawn from them.

Most serious of all both in itself and in its implications, this theory involves the assumption that the Israelites derived or adapted a large part of their basic legislation from the Canaanites and that the part of it which was originally Israelite was modified to a greater or lesser degree through contact and in conflict with them. That the Israelites were influenced, often and gravely, by the cults and customs of the surrounding nations is a lamentable fact which is writ large on the pages of the Old Testament. No less emphatic is the declaration that this represented apostasy from the law of their God, which he himself had given them through Moses. But according to this view, the "Mosaic" Law which they were commanded to keep was itself strongly influenced by the laws and practices of the Canaanites, which Israel was so earnestly exhorted to shun and abhor.

The assumption that the variety which appears in the literary forms contained in the Old Testament is indicative of diversity of origin and authorship and that the critic is in a position to trace them to different forms or patterns which have been derived from quite distinct sources, is one which cannot be proved. It rests on the fallacy that such diversity is unnatural and artificial and must go back to certain uniform patterns and represent a combination of them. For an illustration we turn to Prov. x.1-xxii.16. Here we have 375 verses, which in general show a marked similarity in form. The most frequent pattern is the contrasted couplet or distich. E.g., "The wise in heart will receive commandments: but a prating fool shall fall" (x.8). Usually the two parts of the couplet are joined by "and" which, in view of the implied contrast, is properly rendered by "but." Thus, in chap. x., the "and" is usually rendered "but" in AV and ARV. But in vss. 18 and 22, both versions render by "and"; ARV by "and" also in vss. 23 and 24. There is no conjunction in vss. 5, 15, 16, 20. AV and ARV insert "but" (in italics) at vs. 5, but not in the three other verses. Verse 26 has a form which is unique as far as this chapter and this group of chapters is concerned, and which appears only rarely elsewhere in the entire Book of Proverbs: "As vinegar to the teeth, and as smoke to the eyes, so *is* the sluggard to them that sent him." Thus, we have in this chapter the following patterns, which we list according to frequency of occurrence: (1) Antithetic couplets joined by "and" in the sense of "but"; (2) Synonymous or climactic couplets joined by "and" in the sense of "and"; (3) Paratactic couplets (not joined by a conjunction) which are or may be strongly antithetic; (4) Correlative sentences which may be regarded as climactic. According to the principles of form criticism, we have here at least four different patterns each one of which is to be regarded as distinct and as having a different origin and history. And the aim of the critic would be to break up this chapter and this group of chapters according to its patterns and if possible to assign each to a different *pre*-literary source. The objections to such a treatment are quite obvious. It assumes that these differences in form must or at least may all have had a different origin and history. This means that back of the variety which characterizes this collection of proverbs we are to seek for uniformity of pattern as a characteristic of a given race, religion, environment, or "situation in life." It also assumes that we have in the Old Testament or outside of it sufficient data to make such a demonstration possible. We believe these assumptions to be mistaken. And we feel justified in drawing the same inference regarding the elaborate attempt we have been considering to apply form criticism to the Decalogue and the Book of the Covenant.

It may be noted in this connection that form criticism as applied to the Pentateuchal Codes has not been confined to critical circles. In 1920 M. G. Kyle published a book entitled, *The Problem of the Pentateuch: A New Solution by Archaeological Methods.* This was a study of the literary forms of the legal portions of the Pentateuch. After a detailed investigation, Kyle arrived at the following conclusion: "These varied investigations and the striking comparison with the Documentary Theory which they provide tend to establish the trustworthiness of the Pentateuchal records at their face value. They are not to be broken up into fragments, as from different authors at widely separated dates, and so made to present to us an entirely reconstructed national and ecclesiastical history of Israel, but are to be read as they stand, and their peculiarities of style and vocabulary and arrangement to be accounted for by the *kinds* and *uses* of laws presented and the journalistic manner of composition" (p. 284). This volume has received little or no comment from the form critics. Of it and of Kyle's other volume, *Moses and the Monuments,* published in the same year, G. A. Barton has said: "These volumes were acute and learned, but revealed a mind incapable of appreciating the evidence on which the modern conception of the Pentateuch rests."[29] The modern conception to which Barton has referred is clearly that the Pentateuchal records are not to be taken at their "face value" as trustworthy records of fact.

How much of theory and how little of certainty there is in this approach to the problem of the Old Testament is illustrated by the case of Ps. lxviii. This psalm belongs to the pattern known as the triumph ode. According to the form critics we may regard the pattern as very ancient. So Buttenwieser, while accepting the view that most of the Psalms are post-exilic, finds in the second part of this psalm (vss. 6-28 in their *original* form) an ode which appears to him so old that he assigns it to "the time of Deborah," claiming that it is "the only survivor of the songs of the Wars of Yahweh."[30] On the other hand Gunkel, while also regarding the triumph ode as a very ancient form of poetry, insists that this psalm must belong to a very late period and that all the descriptions in it which point to historical events (these he regards as post-exilic or Maccabean) are to be disregarded and the psalm to be treated as "eschatological."[31] A third view is that of Barnes, who describes the psalm as a *Te Deum* and says of it: "A *Te Deum* may owe something to the occasion of a particularly

striking deliverance, but in its essence it is timeless." So
he assures the reader that it would be "an idle task to try
to fix it to one and thence to adduce its date."[32] Thus, we
have three different views: the psalm is very early, the
psalm is very late, the date of the psalm cannot be determined! According to the heading the psalm is *Davidic*.
But this fact has no significance in the eyes of any one of
these scholars.

### III. BARTHIANISM

Another movement which has become increasingly influential in recent years is the Theology of Crisis or Dialec-
tic Theology of which Karl Barth is the most prominent advocate. It had its beginning with the publication of Barth's
*Commentary on Romans* about thirty years ago. Consequently, it is even younger than the movement we have
just been considering.[33] But it is now much the more important. Barthianism is such a large subject that anything
approaching an adequate treatment would require a
volume. What we are concerned with is simply the relation
of Barthianism to the Higher Critical Movement.

It may be said in general that the Barthians, like the
form critics, accept and build upon the conclusions of the
higher criticism as to the literary and historical problems
presented by the Old Testament. Such a statement as this
may seem surprising or even amazing to some. It is amazing
because fundamentally higher criticism and Barthianism
would seem to be poles apart. In defining "classical Well-
hausenism," Coppens lists as the last of three "easily
discernible postulates" regarding Biblical history the following: "Finally, they postulate the law of immanence in
order to explain this history and consequently they reject,
*a priori,* any appeal to supernatural intervention."[34] This
statement may seem extreme. But no one can read much of
the literature of criticism without observing an attitude of
reluctance to accept the supernatural in the Biblical

record, which easily passes over into open hostility and denial—a denial which would often be far more obvious than it is but for its use or rather misuse of the familiar language of orthodoxy. A thoroughgoing critic, W. F. Bade, made this significant statement some years ago:

"The change from transcendence to immanence in our thought of God has involved the corresponding transition from an objective to a subjective theory of revelation. Hence for our time and for our purposes the word 'revelation' is used to describe a process almost the reverse of what is commonly understood by it. Not through the medium of external agencies, but in and through personality does God reveal himself to men. The divine Reason within man 'is the candle of the Lord.' Conscience and intellect are God's prophets to the soul."[35]

It sounds startling, but it is true that to the consistent higher critic "revelation" comes to mean exactly the opposite of what it used to mean. Jeremiah described the false prophets as men who spoke a message "out of their own hearts" (xiv.14, xxiii.16-26) in contrast to the true prophet who had received a message *ab extra*, a "word of the Lord" which he regarded as coming to him from God and not as the fruit of his own meditation or cogitation. So Bade's definition of revelation would exactly fit Jeremiah's definition of a false prophet. This is immanentism.

In contrast to this naturalistic immanentism, Barth and his followers have stressed the doctrine of transcendence. To the question, "Who by searching can find out God?", they answer emphatically, "No man! God must reveal Himself. God must Himself break through the darkness, bridge the chasm, which hides and separates Him from sinful man. God must speak to man directly, if man is to know Him and serve Him aright." This sounds like transcendentalism or supernaturalism, and a vigorous form of it.[36] Were we simply to go on and say that this revelation of God's will, this authentic Word of God, is the Holy Bible, we would be stating in general terms the historic faith of evangelical Christendom. But we cannot stop there.

Despite the fact that higher criticism and Barthianism

may seem to be poles apart in their fundamental position, in their attitude to the trustworthiness of Scripture, which is the point that chiefly concerns us, they are not sworn enemies but virtual allies. For while they have not arrived at it by the same road—Barthianism undoubtedly owes far more to Kant, Hegel, and Kierkegaard than it does to Eichhorn, Hupfeld, and Wellhausen—both deny the trustworthiness of the Bible as a record of historical facts and events. According to the Barthian, redemptive history does not take place in the sphere of history regarded as the sequence of time-space events. All such events belong in the domain of the superhistorical or primal history *(Urgeschichte)*. Van Til, a vigorous critic of this movement, describes it as follows, using quotations all of which are from Barth's *Romans*.

> "In primal history, the history of pure negation and pure affirmation, we become 'the partners of Abraham.' Faith opens our eyes to the fact that 'historical Abraham does not really concern us' and at the same time 'it opens the road to the understanding of the non-historical Abraham of the Genesis story.' In primal history we are no longer confronted with a 'chaos of faces' that have no meaning. In primal history the past is relieved of its dumbness and the present of its deafness. 'The Genesis narrative opens its mouth and utters the non-historical truth that to Abraham his faith was reckoned as righteousness. . . . But Abraham cannot be our contemporary; he can say nothing to us that we are competent to hear, apart from the radiance of the non-historical.' In primal history our intercourse with Christ becomes contemporary intercourse, intercourse 'which lies beyond the scope of our sight and hearing.' "[37]

From this Van Til draws the following apparently quite logical and necessary conclusion: "Orthodox theologians need not exercise themselves in defending the historicity of the gospel narrative, and critics accomplish nothing by destroying it; by faith we are always face to face with Christ and all the faithful."

Such being the conception of history, of Biblical history, advocated by the Barthians, it is quite obvious that the higher critic has nothing to fear from this movement. The critic might conceivably carry his work of disintegration so far as to undermine the entire factual basis of Christianity; and the Barthian would still declare that for him the Bible is just as much the Word of God as it ever was. Its essential truths belong to the superhistorical; and the domain of the superhistorical is beyond the reach of the higher critic! The Barthian declares that the Bible is the Word of God in the sense that it is only in and through the Bible that God speaks to men. But he also holds that the Bible contains much that is human and faulty and that, as the "Word of God written," it is a lifeless thing, which has no saving meaning for the reader. It is only God Himself speaking through this Word who can make it live in the hearts of men, who can make the believer of today the contemporary of Adam, of Abraham, of David, of Paul, and of the Lord Jesus Christ. And the faith by which man obtains this life-giving contemporaneity is, he declares, quite independent of what in ordinary parlance is called the *historicity* of the gospel narrative or of the Pentateuch or of the Bible as a whole.

Such a conception of Scripture fits like a glove the "broad general conclusions" of the higher critics. Whether the Barthian actively aids and abets the higher critic in his assault upon the historical trustworthiness of the Biblical record or not, he has no valid reason for opposing him, since the radical conclusions of the one cannot disturb the faith of the other. On the contrary, the Barthian may even rejoice in these conclusions as proving his contention that the old conception of Christianity as a "historical" religion is completely discredited.

This resort to the superhistorical may seem to many to offer the solution of the great problem raised by the higher criticism as to the trustworthiness of the Bible. It may seem reassuring in view of the radical and destructive conclusions of the critics, conclusions which the critics themselves declare to be so assured. But it raises nonetheless, and in acute form, the inevitable question as to what the message of the Bible is and what is the authority of that message. Let us take two simple examples, one from the Old Testament, the other from the New.

The Bible represents the Decalogue as being in an eminent sense a Word of God. Its Ten Commandments are called the "ten words." It is affirmed to have been uttered by the voice of God at Mount Sinai. It contains what Jesus described as "the first and great commandment" and "the second which is like unto it." Probably very few if any of the higher critics would admit that these words were uttered by the voice of God at Sinai in the days of Moses. Many or most would assign them to the document E (8th century) and some would claim that in their present form they are a later addition to E. They regard them as the product of a long and gradual development of religion and morals in Israel. What authority, then, has the Decalogue for us today? If its "situation in life" is the time of Ahab, if as some suppose the last of the Commandments, "Thou shalt not covet," owed its inclusion to popular indignation over the judicial murder of Naboth, what reason have we for holding that this ancient code is any more authoritative for us today than the laws of Hammurabi, of Solon, or of Justinian? Must they not all be placed in the crucible of human experience and tested as to their ability to meet the present "situation in life" which is conceivably quite different from that of hundreds or thousands of years ago? And to what can the critic appeal save to his conscience and intellect as the voice of God in deciding this terribly urgent question?

What answer, then, has the Barthian to this question? If the real "situation in life," if we may still call it that, of the Decalogue, is the superhistorical, and if it is only the Spirit of God which can make this lifeless code real for the man of today and give it that contemporaneity which will make it living and meaningful to him, the answer would seem to be that the Decalogue can have no meaning for him and no authority over him, unless and until the Spirit of God makes it to him a Word of God. Otherwise, it would seem, he may ignore, neglect, or defy the Decalogue with impunity, because it has not so accredited itself to him. Consequently, the witness of the Holy Spirit to the Bible becomes to the Barthian a matter of supreme importance.

The proposition that "the Supreme Judge" in all matters of faith and practice "can be no other but the Holy Spirit speaking in the Scripture,"[38] would seem therefore to be one to which all Barthians would subscribe and upon which they would insist. Probably most if not all of them do subscribe to it. But the difficulty at once arises, What is it in Scripture upon which the Holy Spirit passes judgment and which He declares to be the Word of God for the Christian believer? It cannot be the Biblical "situation in life" of the Decalogue as an actual historical setting. For the Barthian is quite willing to accept the conclusions of the higher criticism which give it an utterly different (non-Mosaic) setting from that stated in Exodus and Deuteronomy. Consequently, the Holy Spirit, as the Spirit of truth, cannot testify to the correctness of the historical setting of the Decalogue. The setting cannot be accepted as factual, as historical. So this Word of God which appears in the Bible in a very definite historical setting must be taken out of that setting and treated as superhistorical (allegorical, mythical?) before it can become the Word of God to which the Spirit testifies.

We turn to our New Testament example. In John i.29 we read: "The next day John seeth Jesus coming unto him, and saith, Behold the Lamb of God, which taketh away the sin of the world." Here also, the "situation in life" seems perfectly clear. The time was the ministry of John the Baptist. The "next day" was the day after the Jews had sent priests and Levites to question John as to his authority for the ministry in which he was engaged. Verses 31-34 indicate clearly that this was subsequent to the bap-

tism of Jesus, and probably shortly after the temptation by
Satan. The speaker was John the Baptist and the words,
"Behold the Lamb of God," were his words. Yet a recent
writer speaks of it on this wise: "That John the Baptist
uttered the particular saying, 'Behold the Lamb of God,'
at that particular moment is improbable; but that it is a
true unfolding of the meaning of the life of Jesus for all
Christians is undeniable."[39] In other words, the Christian,
if a Barthian, may question or reject the historical setting
of these wonderful words. He may deny that the Baptist
ever uttered them. Yet he may be perfectly sure that they
are true. The setting may be *un*historical, we may call it
*super*historical, but the jewel which it contains is a gem
of flawless beauty and of inestimable worth.

These two examples illustrate sufficiently clearly we believe the fatal weakness of Barthianism as a cure for the
negative conclusions of the higher critics. Christians have
always believed, and they have regarded it as a distinguishing and distinctive feature of their religion, that it is a
religion of fact and history, that the things most surely
believed by them are well-accredited facts. The higher
critics have been engaged for many years in discrediting the
historical setting and framework of the Bible. For them it is
largely *un*historical. The Barthian discards the historical
setting and translates the picture it contains to the superhistorical world, where the laws of fact and history, at least
as ordinarily understood, do not operate. In this respect
Barthianism is an even more serious enemy of Historical
Christianity than is the higher criticism. For it obscures
the issue raised by the higher criticism as to the trustworthiness of the Bible by teaching that the facts of history can
be at one and the same time historically untrue and un-
historically true. Such a teaching may appeal to the esoteric
philosopher, it may interest the Modern Athenian, but
it will never satisfy the "large masses of the population"
which Canon Richardson would fain interest in the new ap-

proach to Bible study. By faith "a Christian believeth to be true, whatsoever is revealed in the Word, for the authority of God speaketh therein."[40] But the Christian cannot believe that what the Bible records as historical fact can be discredited as true in the historical sense by the critics and then accredited as true in an unhistorical sense by the authority of God speaking through a discredited Scripture. He can believe, where he cannot prove. That is faith. He cannot believe to be true what he knows to be false. He cannot believe that the God of truth will accredit to him as true what he is convinced the critic has proved to be false. To ask him to do this is to ask the impossible.

# Chapter II

# THE PENTATEUCH AND ARCHAEOLOGY

ARCHAEOLOGY, broadly defined as the study of ancient times, is by no means a modern or recent science. Nabunaid the last king of Babylon might be called an archaeologist; and the Renaissance was profoundly influenced by the rediscovery of the Greek Classics. But archaeology as the science based on the excavation, decipherment and critical study of ancient records is comparatively recent. Napoleon's expedition to Egypt in 1798 opened up its treasures. The bringing of the Parthenon marbles to England by Lord Elgin about the year 1800 marked the beginning of Greek archaeological research. The excavations of Botta, Layard and Rassam about the middle of the century opened up the treasures of Assyria and Babylonia. Schliemann, excavating at Troy and Mycene in the Seventies, discovered the pre-hellenic age and prepared the way for the discoveries of Evans at Knossos. Many of the most notable discoveries have been made within the fifty years of the present century. We mention only the Code of Hammurabi (1901), the Assouan and Elephantine Papyri (1904+), the Hittite discoveries at Boghazkeui (1906+), the tomb of Tutankhamun (1922), the sarcophagus of Ahiram (1923), the Ras Shamra alphabet texts (1929+), the Chester Beatty papyri (1930). Important discoveries have been made more recently at Jericho, Lachish, Gaza, Mari, Byblus, Alalakh, Ras Shamra (Ugarit), Ezion-geber, Transjordania and numerous other sites. All of these discoveries, some of them quite unexpected and even accidental, others the result of careful study and planned research, have thrown very welcome light upon places and periods, peoples and persons, in the remote past; and some of them have necessitated drastic revision of opinions confidently and plausibly asserted until the new facts disproved them. Archaeology is now one of the major fields of modern scientific research, and the progressive and forward-looking twentieth century in which we live is perhaps the most backward-looking age of all.

In view of the wonderful discoveries which have been made within a century and a half, it is important to observe at the outset, that the field of exploration is so vast that archaeological research may be said to be in many respects still in its beginnings. Many of its results must still be regarded as tentative.[41] One of the most revolutionary of the discoveries mentioned above, that at Ras Shamra, was made like the El Amarna Letters, by accident. That it will be followed by others at least as remarkable is not only possible but, judging by the record of the last fifty or one hundred years, so probable as to be almost certain. Consequently, caution and reserve should be exercised in speaking of the results of archaeological research. While much light has been thrown upon many dark corners of the past, there is much that is still dark; and some of the things which seem to be very clear may assume a quite different shape when the light becomes still clearer. We shall consider very briefly the most certain of the results of archaeological research and their bearing upon the date of the Pentateuch.

## 1. The Great Antiquity of the Ancient Civilizations

It is a well-known fact that at the time when the higher criticism had its beginning, the traditional date of Moses (died 1451 B.C. acc. to Ussher's chronology) gave to the Pentateuch as a Mosaic document a very exceptional, if not quite unparalleled antiquity. In 1795 Wolf published his *Prolegomena* to Homer in which as Grote points out in his *History of Greece* (1846-56) the absence of easy and convenient writing "was one of the points against the primitive integrity of the *Iliad* and *Odyssey*."[42] Grote himself regarded the traditional date (1200 B.C.)[43] for the Trojan War as quite unprovable. He connected the beginnings of "real history"[44] with the first recorded Olympiad (776 B.C.) and regarded somewhere between 850 B.C. and 776 B.C. as the probable date of the Iliad and Odyssey.[45]

At a time when the history of the ancient world was still being gleaned largely from the Classics of Greece and Rome, the traditional date of Moses and his authorship of the Pentateuch may well have appeared remarkable and difficult of acceptance. It is true, as we have seen, that Astruc and Eichhorn did not deny that the Pentateuch could have been written at this early date. But students imbued with the opinions of Wolf and Grote could not but regard the traditional date of the Pentateuch with a scepticism which would lead readily to positive denial.

Such being the case the following statement in the article "Greece" in the *Encyclopaedia Britannica* (14th ed., 1929) acquires no little significance:

"When does Greek history begin? Whatever may be the answer that is given to this question, it will be widely different from any that could have been proposed half a century ago. Then the question was, How late does Greek history begin? Today the question is, How early does it begin? Grote suggested that the first Olympiad (776 B.C.) should be taken as the starting-point of the history of Greece, in the proper sense of the term 'history.' At the present moment the tendency would seem to be to go back as far as the 3rd or 4th millenium B.C. in order to reach a starting point."[46]

When Grote published his *History* he expected to be faced with the charge that he was "striking off one thousand years from the scroll of history."[47] He met it with the claim that the thousand years in question had no right to the name history. Today that thousand years has been restored and another thousand, perhaps much more, added to it.[48] The parallel with the Pentateuchal problem is striking. The critics are agreed today that to determine its date scientifically as much as a thousand years is to be deducted from the traditional date. For more than a century the critics have been asking the question, How late are the sources of the Pentateuch? They are certain that they must be much later than 1400 B.C. How late, they are not sure. If P is exilic or post-exilic and the book read by Ezra was the then recently completed Pentateuch, a thousand years have been "struck off" from the age of the Pentateuch.

In very marked contrast with the tendency of the higher criticism to lower Old Testament dates, to shorten the perspective of Biblical history in such a way as to relegate the Abrahamic age and even the Mosaic to the realm of myth and legend, the tendency of archaeological research has been to extend the historical period far back of the earliest dates assigned to Moses or Abraham. The discovery of the Code of Hammurabi in 1901 and of great numbers of letters and business documents from the time of the First Dynasty of Babylon has made it clear that, whether Hammurabi be the Amraphel of Genesis xiv. or not, the beginning of the Second Millennium B.C. was an era which enjoyed a stable and advanced civilization. If Ur of the Chaldees is correctly located in Southern Babylonia (*Mugheir*), we know that city was a centre of culture and wealth a thousand years before Abram was born. And when he journeyed to Haran, among the many cities which he passed was probably the recently rediscovered Mari whose palace of 300 rooms may have given him temporary shelter. If on the other hand Ur is to be located in Mesopotamia, it is interesting to note that the recent excavations at Brak (25 miles South of Nisibis) have unearthed a palace of Naramsin, which was at least 500 years old when Abram came to Haran, less than 100 miles away. Whether the dynastic period in Egypt begins about 3000 B.C. (Breasted) or more than a thousand years earlier (Petrie), Egyptian civilization was ancient in the time when Moses become "learned in all the wisdom of Egypt." Whatever may apply to certain periods or localities—for culture may have been as varied then as now—the beginning of the Second Millennium B.C. can no longer be thought of as belonging to the domain of myth and legend, a period enveloped in the mists of the pre-historic. Mighty empires had arisen and passed away, great kings had lived and died, centuries before Abraham departed from Ur of the Chaldees. The critics have been inclined to dissolve the patriarchs Abraham, Isaac and Jacob into mythical or legendary figures. But archaeology has shown conclusively that the Bible assigns them to a period which was historical in the fullest sense of the word and which had centuries of history behind it.

This is a matter of great importance. We have only to consider how difficult the position of the defenders of the traditional view of the Pentateuch would be today if it had been proved that "striking off a millennium" or more from ancient dates in general is required by first hand archaeological evidence, to realize the significance of the verdict it has actually rendered. Whatever may be said as to the specific question of the date of the Pentateuch, the fact is too obvious to be denied that speaking generally the conclusions of the critics and the findings of the archaeologists have pointed in diametrically opposite directions. While the one have been engaged in striking off a millennium or more from the history of Israel, the other have been engaged in deepening and broadening the historical perspective and giving back more than the critics have taken away.[49]

At this point, however, the defender of the Mosaic tradition is met with the claim that the new discoveries of archaeology as to the duration of man's existence on the earth have proved too much and so overthrown the chronology of the Old Testament. The date 4004 B.C. for the starting point of human history is declared to be a preposterous one and is cited as conclusive evidence that Old Testament chronology is hopelessly unscientific. It is to be noted, therefore, that this date which still appears in some editions of the Authorized Version was calculated by Archbishop Ussher about 1650 A.D. and was first placed in the margin of that version in 1701. It is no part of the text. It rests in the main upon the assumption that the genealogies in Gen. v. and xi. are intended to supply the reader with the materials for an exact chronology of the entire extent of human history from creation to the birth of Abram. Against this assumption is the fact that no such use of these genealogies is ever made in the Bible, Old Testament or New Testament. And it has long been recognized by conservative scholars that there are other serious objections in the Bible itself to this widely accepted view. The chronology of Genesis is quite in accord with the view that man had lived on the earth many centuries before 4004 B.C.[50]

## 2. The Antiquity of Writing

Since doubt as to the antiquity of writing was a factor in Wolf's denial of the genuineness of the Homeric poems, it is important to note that the findings of archaeology have shown this argument to be entirely baseless. The story of the deciphering of the records which the excavator has discovered is almost as thrilling as is the story of their discovery. The deciphering of the Old Persian by Grotefend (1802), of the Egyptian hieroglyphs by Young and Champollion (1822) and of the Old Babylonian by Rawlinson (1846) unlocked vast and varied documentary treasuries of the ancient world. They made it clear that two great systems of writing, the Egyptian hieroglyphic and the Babylonian cuneiform, were in existence centuries before the time of Moses. Both of these systems of writing were very complicated and cumbersome. Babylonian, for example, has more than 300 signs, practically all of which may have more than one meaning. Consequently, the discovery of many private letters and other documents dating from the time of Hammurabi and the First Dynasty of Babylon which indicated that a by no means negligible portion of the people in that ancient world were able to read and write was of great importance. This gave significance to the statement that Moses was "learned in all the wisdom of the Egyptians." It implied that he might well have been able to read and write Egyptian and perhaps also the Babylonian cuneiform. The command to Moses to "write in a book" is, therefore, perfectly in accord with our knowledge of this period.

Not only does the Pentateuch indicate that writing was well known in the days of Moses, it also contains several statements which are of great interest. Five times in Ex. v. allusion is made to the "officers" (*shoterim*) of the Israelites. This word is almost certainly derived from the same root as the Babylonian word "write" (*shataru*) and would mean "writers." These "writers" were clearly the men who kept the tally lists of the Israelite workmen who were working for Pharaoh. Such lists have been discovered both in Babylonia and in Egypt.[51] Two other statements are of interest. Gen. xxxviii.18 refers to Judah's signet. It is probable, but not certain that this signet had writing on it. Thousands of signets from the Abrahamic age and much earlier have been discovered in Babylonia. The mention of a "book" in Gen. v.1 is of interest. By the word book we may probably understand a "tablet," in the sense of a record. Genealogical tablets and lists were known in Babylonia centuries before Abraham; and it is probable or at least possible that he carried cuneiform tablets containing such records with him from Haran to Canaan.

### 3. The Antiquity of Alphabetic Writing

Especially interesting in this connection are the discoveries which have been made quite recently, with regard to the antiquity of alphabetic writing. At the beginning of the present century when Hastings' *Dictionary of the Bible* was being published, the Moabite Stone (9th century B.C.) was regarded as the oldest inscription in existence written in a Semitic alphabetic script; and it was argued that the use of the cuneiform script in the Amarna letters indicated that an alphabet was not used in Palestine as early as the 15th century B.C.[52] Recent discoveries at Serabit, Gezer, Ugarit (Ras Shamra), Beth Shemesh, Byblus, Lachish, etc., have proved conclusively that both to the north and the south of Palestine and even in Palestine itself several simple alphabet scripts were in use at the time of the Conquest and earlier.[53] The origin and interrelation of these alphabets raises many interesting problems. It is possible that the Ras Shamra alphabet is derived from the cuneiform or the hieroglyphs. It is also possible that it was worked out more or less *de novo* by someone who was familiar with the alphabetic principle. In any case its simplicity would favor the view that it was widely used. Consequently, since it is now impossible to deny that simple alphabetic writing was known as early as the time of Moses and perhaps much earlier,[54] the presumption is now strongly in favor of the view not only that Moses could have himself made careful record of the events of his own time and of the laws revealed to him by God for the people to keep during their generations, but also that for the earlier times he may have had access to records which even then were of great antiquity.

An interesting point in this connection is the writing of numbers. In the Hebrew text of the Old Testament, the numbers are always spelled out (cf. AV and ARV); figures are never used. This has raised the question whether this method of writing was the original one. Since the Egyptians, Babylonians, and Aramaeans used numerical signs, it is natural to conclude that the Israelites did the same; and the ostraca found at Samaria prove that such signs were used by them at least as early as the 9th century. The use of the letters of the alphabet by the Greeks to denote numbers has led to the claim that this practice goes back to Old

Testament times; and the attempt has often been made to explain difficulties in numbers and dates by saying that letters were confused which closely resembled one another.[55] This is of course possible. But there is no direct evidence to show that this numerical use of the alphabet was known to the Israelites. Consequently the fact that on the Ras Shamra tablets numbers are spelled out just as in the present text of our Hebrew Bibles is significant. Writing out the numbers would contribute greatly to the accuracy of the text.[56]

### 4. The Antiquity of the Hebrew Language

The discovery of the Mesha Stone in 1868 was epoch-making not only because it was for many years the earliest of the North Semitic inscriptions in alphabet script but also because it was written in a language almost identical with Biblical Hebrew.[57] During the last few years additional light has been thrown on the question of the Hebrew language. The letters recently discovered at Lachish (1935) dating from the very close of the monarchial period show a remarkable correspondence with the Hebrew of the Book of Jeremiah. More important for our problem was the discovery of several pottery vessels at Lachish and bronze plaques at Byblus containing brief inscriptions in alphabetic script and in a language which scholars have pronounced to be Hebrew.[58] These are dated in the 13th and 12th centuries. But they are too brief and fragmentary to be of great linguistic value. Most important of all are the Ras Shamra alphabetic tablets, which consist of mythological and other texts from about the 15th century B.C. These are written in a language which has been variously described as proto-Phoenician, North Canaanite, proto-Hebrew, etc. The language is as yet only imperfectly studied. But its syntax has been found to be similar to that of Biblical Hebrew.[59] And it is significant that not only is this very largely true of its vocabulary, but that even the characteristic peculiarities of some of the common words in Hebrew appear in these tablets.[60]

It is also to be noted that words which the critics have been accustomed to speak of as "late" are found in these tablets. The word "trespass-offering" (asham), which was assigned by Wellhausen to the secondary portions of P, is mentioned in these early tablets. And such words as "come" (athah), "divide" (baqa), "footstool" (hadom), two rarely mentioned measures (log, Lev. xiv.10ff., lethek, Hos. iii.2), "cry" (tsawach from which "crying," Isa. xlii.11), are found in these tablets.

Of especial interest is the fact that features which have been regarded as characteristic of Aramaic are more marked in these texts than in the Biblical Hebrew of any period.[61] This is significant because it has long been asserted by the critics that "Aramaisms," i.e., Aramaic roots, forms, or expressions in Biblical Hebrew, are a proof of late date. Such a conclusion is not supported by the Bible. According to Dt. xxvi.5 the pious Israelite was instructed to testify to the significance of the ritual of the first fruits by saying, "A Syrian [Aramaean] ready to perish was my father," etc. This clearly refers to Jacob; and the name "Aramaean" was quite appropriate to Jacob in view of his long sojourn with Bethuel and Laban who are repeatedly called "Aramaeans" (Gen. xxv.20, xxviii.5, xxxi.20, 24). They are described as his kinsmen; and it is probable that Abram was not a Babylonian, but belonged to the Aramaic branch of the West Semitic peoples.[62] This would lead us to expect to find Aramaisms in the Pentateuch if this document belongs to the date traditionally assigned to it. And it is noteworthy that according to the analysis adopted by the critics Aramaisms appear in all of the documents, even in the oldest (J). The Ras Shamra tablets make it now abundantly evident that the presence of Aramaisms may be an indication of early date.[63] The material for a history of the Hebrew language is still very meagre and inadequate. But the confident assertions that have been made by the critics must clearly be modified. The Ras Shamra inscriptions have brought so many surprises that careful scholars should refrain from dogmatic assertions as to what could or could not have been the exact form of the language spoken by the Israelites during the course of the Second Millennium B.C. Since it is now clear that the occurrence of Aramaisms in the Pentateuch is no proof of late date, it is important to observe that Persian and Greek words which would be indicative of late date are conspicuous by their absence. That Babylonian and Egyptian words should and do occur is only to be expected if the account which the Pentateuch gives of itself is correct.

### 5. Other Evidence Bearing on Credibility and Early Date of Pentateuch

While such evidence as the above is of great apologetic value, it must be admitted that direct confirmations of the Pentateuch are not as numerous as could be wished, or as many have hoped for. As compared with excavations in Egypt, Babylonia, Assyria, the results of research in Palestine have been relatively meagre. It is to be noted, therefore, that this is what a careful reading of the Old Testament would lead us to expect. The land of promise was a battle ground from early times. Ten nations are mentioned as in possession of it in Abraham's time. The conquest under Joshua was intended to make a clean sweep of the idolatry-pervaded culture of its inhabitants. To some extent it did this. But, despite the most solemn warnings, the Israelites made friends of these nations, adopted their culture and beliefs, and because of disobedience and apostasy were allowed to become a prey to their enemies. Neighboring peoples, the Amorites, Philistines, Midianites. Moabites, Ammonites, Syrians, and the great world powers, Assyria, Babylon, Greece and Rome, swept over the land in succession, subdued and despoiled it, taking away its wealth and enslaving its people. If the archaeologist has found little treasure in Palestine, this is only what the Biblical record should lead us to expect. In excavating the Royal Tombs of Egypt the archaeologist has often found that robbers, whose interest was not antiquarian, had been there first and taken away the best. The ruined heaps of many ancient cities in Palestine show how many despoilers went before the modern archaeologist in the search for its treasures.

How thorough was this spoilation of Palestine is illustrated by the fact that in determining the chronology of Palestine the despised potsherd has acquired an almost unique importance. Since Petrie conducted excavations at *Tel-el-Hesi* fifty years ago the chronology of Palestinian archaeology has been very largely "sequence dating" or "pot-sherd" chronology. This means that the various types of pottery occurring in the many strata of the excavated sites have been the means of determining the relative order and age of the various strata that have been discovered. This is very helpful. But in many ways it is inadequate. And the results it can give, unless supported by additional evidence, are only approximate.

In 1935 the excavators at Lachish made what has been called the "most important discovery of modern times in respect to Biblical criticism."[64] It was a very ordinary looking ewer of earthenware, about 18 inches high, and it could be only incompletely pieced together out of 40 fragments. What made it so important was the fact that it has on it an inscription of 11 letters in alphabet script in a language "strikingly similar to Biblical Hebrew." A red pottery bowl and the fragment of another bowl containing brief inscriptions were also found. The fact that such great importance should be attached to such very meagre evidence is a clear indication of the thoroughness with which the land of Israel was plundered and despoiled as the Old Testament records plainly declare.[65]

Furthermore it is to be remembered that such evidence as the spade may be able to recover for us is very likely to exhibit the dark side of Israel's religious history rather than that true and ideal Israel which followed the teachings of "Moses and the prophets." Some years ago a book was published bearing the striking title *The Earthy Smell of Palestine in Israel's Religion*.[66] The aim of the author was to point out that there is much that smells of the earth in Israel's religion and also to connect with the earth much to which the Bible assigns a heavenly (miraculous) origin. There is a sense in which the title is highly suggestive. For the earthly and base elements in the actual worship of many, perhaps most Israelites, its idolatries, immoralities and obscenities, are far more likely to come to light than its spiritual things, the true spiritual worship of Israel. The spade can prove the existence of an idolatrous religion by unearthing the idols of silver and gold, of brass and iron, wood and stone. And it has done so.[67] It has proved that as the Bible declares idolatry flourished in Palestine both before and after the Conquest. It has not revealed that spiritual religion which was of the heart, which was founded on revelations the early records of which were perhaps destroyed or carried away, and which apparently only rarely exerted any great influence on the life and conduct of Israel as a whole. Can we expect it to do so? The ark and the sacred vessels of Solomon's temple were carried away by Nebuchadnezzar and those which were restored by Cyrus and remained to the days of the Romans were destroyed or carried away by Titus. The words with which Jesus described that final tragedy—"There shall not be left here one stone upon another, that shall not be thrown down"—account for the failure of the spade to unearth rich treasure in the land of Israel.

It is also to be noted that there is comparatively little in the lives of the Patriarchs and the history of their descendants as recorded in the Pentateuch of which we might expect to find direct confirmation from archaeology. Abraham, Isaac and Jacob were sojouners in a land not their own. They did not take it into possession. They built a few altars and digged some wells. The greatest events in their lives were in a sense intimate and personal. The supreme test of Abraham's faith was when he and Isaac were alone on the Mount which God told him of. His victory over the four kings was for him and Lot of great importance, but Chedorlaomer and Amraphel would hardly record it. Kings have never been eager to record their defeats. The most prominent of the patriarchs was Joseph. But, despite his exalted position and great achievements, he was only a creature of Pharaoh. Kings have always been prone to claim for themselves the credit for the achievements of their underlings. The vastness of the building operations of the kings of Egypt supports the statements of the Book of Exodus regarding the oppression of the Israelites. An immense *corvée* was needed for such ambitious projects. And the proud Pharaoh would be quite unlikely to record the disasters of the Exodus.[68] If the contemporary historians of Rome scarcely mentioned the name of Him whose life on earth has divided history into two great epochs—before Christ, after Christ—we may well ask ourselves how much of Pentateuchal history we may expect the fragmentary records of a distant past to confirm directly or amplify in detail. The great service which archaeology is rendering is by showing that the picture of events recorded in the Pentateuch is correctly drawn. For if the setting and background can be shown to be correct, the presumption is in favor of the trustworthiness of the narrative and of its early date.

Abraham built no cities. But the fact that all or nearly all the cities in which he lived or which he visited are now known to have been in existence in his day is a matter of importance. The contract which probably recorded his purchase of Macpelah may never be found. But the fact that thousands of contract tablets have been discovered in Babylonia and elsewhere dating from centuries before the time of Abraham indicates that the possession of the field and the cave was "made sure" to Abraham by a legal transaction. Ephron the Hittite is unknown to us. But the extended influence of the Hittites and their presence in Palestine by 2000 B.C. is now an established fact. The sum mentioned, "400 shekels of silver," is a quite considerable one, which may account both for the fact that the amount is stated and that Ephron tried to represent it as a trifling sum which a "mighty prince" should not haggle over.

The xivth chapter of Genesis has long been a problem to the critics. They have never assigned it to any one of the main sources recognized by them. Many of them have treated it as late and quite unreliable. Nelson Glueck as a result of extensive explorations in Transjordania has declared that "The archaeological facts agree completely with this literary tradition. There was at about ±1900 B.C. such a thoroughgoing destruction visited upon all the great fortresses and settlements of the land within the limits we have examined, that the particular civilization they represented never again recovered."[69] This indicates that the expedition of the four kings against the five was a military undertaking of very considerable magnitude, in which the Lot episode, while of supreme interest to Abram, was a very minor detail.

Among the important discoveries of quite recent times has been the prominent rôle played by the Hurrians in the Second Millennium B.C. and earlier. That the Hurrians are the same race as the Biblical Horites (Gen. xiv.6) appears to be very generally recognized. Thus, the archaeological discoveries of the modern scientist confirm the "archaeology" of the Pentateuch (Deut. ii.12).

The problem of the Philistines has not yet been satisfactorily solved. Most scholars will probably admit that the allusions to the Philistines in Genesis are quite in accord with our present knowledge. Abimelech's words to Isaac, "Go from us; for thou art much mightier than we," imply that the Philistines were far from numerous in his day. The great increase in their numbers in later times is probably to be connected with the overthrow of the Minoan civilization in Crete several centuries later. Just when this took place is uncertain. It is claimed that the allusions to the Philistines in Exodus and Joshua would be anachronisms if the Exodus took place about 1450 B.C. But fuller light may prove these later statements regarding the Philistines to be as accurate as the earlier ones appear to be. Too little is known about the Philistines to justify definite assertions.[70]

The evidence which has gradually accumulated as to the use of iron is an instructive illustration of the danger of drawing definite conclusions from meagre evidence or from the lack of it. Nearly fifty years ago in his article on iron in Hastings' *Dictionary,* Petrie wrote: "The use of iron was comparatively late . . . No clearly dated example of it is known in Egypt before about B.C. 700 . . . Iron is mentioned under Tiglath-pileser I (c. 1100) . . . It appears, then, that iron began to spread about B.C. 1000 . . ." A recent statement from this same authority indicates the great increase in our knowledge on this subject. Petrie points out that iron weapons were known in Egypt about 1350 B.C. and as a result of his excavations at Gerar and Bethpelet he declares that "The abundant use of iron was well established a century later, by 1200 B.C."[71] It may be premature to assert that the allusions to iron in the Pentateuch are now proved to be quite compatible with its Mosaic authorship. But the trend of the evidence is very definitely in that direction. It is easy to assert that a statement in a document is an anachronism. But the substantiating of the assertion requires a definite knowledge which we do not at present possess.

We have seen that the great anachronism which the Wellhausen School claims to have discovered in the Pentateuch is the "Mosaic Law." They assert that it is an anachronism for the pre-exilic period. We have seen that this claim cannot be made good as far as the Old Testament itself is concerned, unless the Biblical history is expurgated and its own account of the failure of Israel to keep the Law of Moses is rejected as untrue. The question which now confronts us is whether archaeology confirms the claim of the critics.

It is quite true that the spade of the archaeologist has not discovered for us a *Mosaic copy* of the Law. Much as the opponents of the Wellhausen theory would welcome such a discovery, it is very unlikely to take place. But archaeology has made it increasingly clear that such a law might well have been given to Israel in the days of Moses. For the clearer it becomes as a result of excavations in and around Palestine that the nations with which Abraham and his descendants came in contact were mature and had long established social, cultural, literary, and religious backgrounds, the more difficult does it become to deny that the theocracy established by Moses might have been of such a character as the Pentateuch represents. The elaborate Code of Hammurabi had been in existence since patriarchal times. Many of the laws given to Moses resemble the statutes of Hammurabi. Why should not Moses have given Israel a code of laws such as Hammurabi had given to Babylon centuries before?[72]

The Egyptian Pyramid Texts and the Sumero-Babylonian hymns show that religious hymns such as are found in the Pentateuch (Ex. xv., Deut. xxxii., xxxiii.) were written long before Moses' day. We know that there were great temples and elaborate worship in Egypt and Babylonia centuries before Moses. This makes it probable that the Israelites who were as religious as the neighboring peoples would have such a worship as is described in the Pentateuch. David and Solomon wished to make the temple a worthy dwelling place for Jehovah. Why should not Moses have had the same aim in regard to the tabernacle? At Ras Shamra there were many temples. There was a "chief of the priests"; and the names of some of the Mosaic sacrifices assigned by the critics to P and regarded as post-exilic occur on Ugaritic tablets of the 14th or 15th centuries B.C. Why then must the high priestly office be a late development in Israel, and Aaron the high priest an invention of the exilic or post-exilic age? The fact that the religious institutions enacted by Moses differed from those of Egypt, Babylon and Canaan is due according to the Bible to their distinctive character as a direct revelation from God. But it is becoming increasingly clear that the elaborate requirements of the Mosaic law—civil, moral, religious, ceremonial—were no anachronism for the Mosaic age, but just what the theocracy founded by Moses the man of God required.

## 6. Conflicting and Shifting Views of Archaeologists

Finally, it is to be noted that the present status of archaeology does not entitle the friends or foes of the Mosaic tradition to speak with too great assurance on many points. This is indicated by the wide differences of opinion between eminent archaeologists as to even quite important matters. Some thirty years ago Hammurabi's accession was placed as early as 2350 B.C. Only a few years ago 2067 B.C. was accepted by many as very probably correct. Today as a result of the recent discoveries at Mari it is being placed as late as 1730 B.C.—a difference of about 600 years! The date of the fall of Jericho is also vigorously debated. Garstang has contended that its destruction occurred about 1400 B.C. Other scholars insist that it took place a century or two later.[73] Such differences of opinion show that there is still much that is uncertain and suggest the degree to which theories as to what must have been the course of actual history may influence the conclusions even of archaeologists whose aim is to be rigidly scientific.

## 7. *Oral Tradition* versus *Written Documents*

In view of the evidence which has come to light in recent years to prove that in the Mosaic and even the Patriarchal periods writing was relatively simple and widely used, it is somewhat significant that many writers on the Old Testament and archaeology are so loath to admit that as a written document the Pentateuch or even any considerable part of it is of early date. It is being insisted, even by men who fully recognize the revolutionary character of recent discoveries, that the historical accuracy of the narratives of Genesis, for example, is due at least in the main to the accuracy of "oral tradition," and that the late dating of the documents advocated by the Wellhausen School is substantially correct. This is in one respect a great gain. Formerly the wildest theories, which regarded the patriarchal narratives as mythology and folklore, were defended on the ground that they represented "oral tradition"; and it was asserted that oral tradition was exceedingly unreliable. Now we are being assured that the archaeological accuracies of the Pentateuch are due to the great accuracy of oral tradition. This is stressed in the recent writings of such prominent archaeologists as Albright and Woolley.[74] Both of these scholars are clearly much more willing to revise the estimate of the value of oral tradition held by the critics than to attribute the accuracy of the documents of the Pentateuch to the likelihood that these documents are much older than the critics have been willing to admit. This attitude seems inconsistent in view of the importance which they attach to the discoveries which have been made as to the prevalence of writing in the patriarchal period.

The reason for this seeming inconsistency is not far to seek. It is to be found in the fact that the archaeologists referred to as representative of this position, do not regard the Pentateuch as being entirely trustworthy in its historical statements; and consequently, while according it as oral tradition much greater reliability than formerly, they are not willing to assign to it the degree of trustworthiness which they would attribute to contemporary written documents. This places them in an advantageous position in criticizing the statements of the Pentateuch. Woolley, for example, finds the statement that Abraham lived 175 years highly questionable. So he calls attention to the fact that in ancient times as today a child might be named for his grandfather and he tells us that if we assume that "Abram-Abraham represents not less than *three* human generations, then the difficulty of the Old Testament chronology disappears and the unusual virility of the centenarian ceases to be a stumbling block."[75] In other words, if the figure of Abraham is a conflate or composite representing three or even five generations (Abraham, a grandson named Abraham, and even a great-great-grandson of the same name) blended together by oral tradition, the figure 175 ceases to occasion difficulty. On this view oral tradition has made one man out of two or three men.

Similarly Albright tells us in dealing with the subject of "Moses and Monotheism" that: "We are handicapped in dealing with this subject by the fact that all our sources are relatively late, as we have seen, and that we must therefore depend upon a tradition which was long transmitted orally."[76] But if oral tradition is accurate, the handicap should not be serious! It is not surprising then that Woolley remarks: "It might look as if by insisting on the oral basis of the narrative portion of Genesis I was abandoning all the advantage that might have been gained from the discovery of the early date of writing in Syria; we seem to be back in the position in which it was held reasonable to doubt the very existence of the patriarch. . . . I would emphasize the fact that the oral tradition in itself is a very much more reliable authority than certain critics have allowed."[77]

These statements make it quite clear that even according to the advocates of the accuracy of oral tradition, this accuracy is only relative and falls short of the reliability of a well preserved and authenticated written document. These statements further indicate that the fact of the untrustworthiness of oral tradition would have made the necessity that matters of importance be put down "in black and white" quite as obvious in the time of Moses and of Abraham as it is today.

Is it probable, if writing was in common use in the days of Moses and had been so for centuries, that a record of such great authority and importance as that contained in the Pentateuch would be left to the vicissitudes of oral tradition? We read in Ex. xxiv. that "Moses wrote all the words of Jehovah" (vs. 4) and that "he took the book of the covenant and read it in the audience of the people" (vs. 7). This was only proper and right. The people who were expected to say, "All that Jehovah hath said will we do and be obedient," had a right to have recorded "in black and white" what their God had commanded and what they had promised to do. When Hammurabi centuries before Moses codified the laws of his kingdom, he did not trust them to oral tradition. He had them carved on a great block (perhaps on several blocks) of diorite; he invited the "oppressed man" to come and have the words written on this monument read to him that he might know his rights; and he called on all the mighty gods whom he worshipped to curse the man who defaced or covered up or removed this massive stele with its elaborate legal code. Yet Albright would have us believe that the Israelites who believed that their laws were given to them by God Himself at Sinai and who could have had them in writing and according to Ex. xxiv.4f., Deut. xxvii.8, Josh. viii.32, did have many of them in writing, were willing for hundreds of years to depend upon oral tradition. It is difficult to reconcile two such seemingly contradictory attitudes, the Hammurabi attitude which is so modern in its insistence on the letter, the written word, and the attitude of the neo-higher critic who prefers oral tradition, while forced to admit that a written code was quite possible. If the Code of Hammurabi could have been written and actually was written in the cumbersome Babylonian cuneiform, there is no reason why the laws of Moses could not have been written down some centuries later in a simple alphabet script, if they were actually given to Moses as the record expressly declares, especially if they were as they claimed to be a direct and uniquely authoritative revelation from God. The account of the writing of the Law of Moses on the stones of the altar at Mt. Ebal (Josh. viii.30f.) will seem unhistorical only to those who deny that a Mosaic law could have been in existence at the time of the Conquest.

What applies to legal codes is also true of the narratives of the Pentateuch. Woolley declares quite emphatically that "to suppose that the story of Abraham in the form in which we have it in the Old Testament could have been written in his own time or for many centuries after his own time is to betray a complete ignorance of what men anciently wrote."[78] The warrant for this statement is by no means clear. We know that from early times prominent officials in Egypt left behind them biographical narratives, e.g., that of Methen, of the time of Cheops and Snefru. We also know that the romantic story of Sinuhe, a nobleman of the time of Amenemhet I., was current in Egypt in written form in the Middle Kingdom, perhaps as early as the time of Abraham or earlier. If as Woolley tells us, "Possibly Abraham may have put down in writing for the benefit of his household so much of the familiar laws of Sumer—familiar to him, but liable to be forgotten by his descendants—as he thought applicable to their nomad life,"[79] is it not highly probable that he, or his son Isaac, or his grandson Jacob, or certainly Moses "put down in writing" those important transactions of the life of the father of the faithful "which were liable to be forgotten by his descendants?" To deny this would amount to asserting that Abraham or his immediate descendants or Moses did not consider these events sufficiently important to make them a matter of careful written record.[80]

It appears then that the only valid objection to the early committing to writing of these and other narratives or codes in the Pentateuch must be found in clear evidence that these records are out of harmony with the actual history of the times with which they purport to deal. That there are many problems and difficulties still to be solved we have already admitted. But we have also pointed out that the verdict of archaeology has been increasingly corroborative of the accuracy of these records; and the more it does this the stronger is the argument for the early date of the Pentateuch.

Since it is clear then that the attitude of the student of the Pentateuch today toward the question of the Mosaic authorship will be influenced if not determined by his general estimate of the credibility of the Biblical record, it is to be carefully noted that this estimate will be determined very largely by his attitude toward the supernatural. If he rejects as absurd the declaration that Moses received the Law directly from God, if he considers its miracles incredible, if he discounts the claims of the Old Testament regarding God's unique dealings with the Patriarchs as simply the expression of national pride and prejudice, he will be disposed to treat the documents which record them as late and unreliable, however accurately they may in other respects reflect the historical situation of the age which they purport to describe and from which they purport to come. Consequently the final question, as it is also the basic question for the student of the Old Testament, of the Bible as a whole, is his attitude toward the supernatural.[81]

## THE ISAIAH SCROLL

The statement made above, that it is "so probable as to be almost certain" that other discoveries as remarkable as the Ras Shamra may be made at any time, has recently received striking confirmation. In a cave in the Judean hills near the northern end of the Dead Sea, some Arabs discovered a broken jar containing a number of scrolls. The largest is about 24 feet long and contains the entire Book of Isaiah in 54 columns. The manuscript is undated. But it is written in an early form of the "square letter," which places it according to Albright not later than 100 B.C. If this dating be correct, the discovery carries our knowledge of manuscripts of the Old Testament about a thousand years back of the oldest previously known. Burrows has made the following statement regarding it:

"The text of Isaiah in this manuscript is practically complete. With the exception of a few words lost where the edge of the column has been torn off and the relatively unimportant omissions to be noted below, the whole book is here, and it is substantially the book preserved in the Masoretic text. Differing notably in orthography and somewhat in morphology, it agrees with the Masoretic text to a remarkable degree in wording. Herein lies its chief importance, supporting the fidelity of the Masoretic tradition."[82]

Those who like the writer believe in the one Isaiah will be encouraged by the fact that the manuscript not only contains the entire Book of Isaiah but that chap. xl. follows immediately on chap. xxxix. without the slightest break. In fact, chap. xl. begins with the last line of the column which contains xxxviii.9-xxxix.8. Unfortunately it must also be noted, lest the age of the manuscript should dispose us to attach too much weight to its readings, that it shows at times clear indications of careless copying. It apparently contains too many mistakes and inconsistencies to justify us in regarding it as a thoroughly reliable witness to the original text of Isaiah. Its variations from the Masoretic text[83] and its agreements and disagreements with the ancient versions will doubtless be debated by scholars for years to come.

Of the other scrolls regarding which we have information, the most important is a rather fragmentary text of Habakkuk, which is supplied with a commentary. The significant thing about this commentary is that it is in Hebrew, not as might have been expected in Aramaic. A third roll contains a "Sectarian Document" which is also in Hebrew. Should all or most of the other rolls—there appear to have been about a dozen in all—prove to be in Hebrew, this may have some bearing on the question as to the extent to which Hebrew was still the literary language of Palestine in Maccabean times.[84]

# Chapter III

# THE PENTATEUCH AND NATURALISTIC EVOLUTION

WE HAVE PREFERRED to call the theory which we have been examining the Development Hypothesis, rather than to use the name "historical" which many of its advocates prefer. The aim of the historian should be to present actual facts in such a way that they will appear in true perspective and correct relation to other facts. That it is the aim of the advocates of the Graf-Wellhausen hypothesis to do this, need not be called in question. But, as we have endeavored to show, their treatment of the available facts is so dominated by a theory the correctness of which they hold to be proved and the acceptance of which they consider to be the badge of true scholarship and a truly scientific spirit, that this tendency or bias must be taken account of in appraising their methods and conclusions. It is significant that the rise of this new and revolutionary theory followed closely upon the publication of Darwin's *Origin of Species* (1859), which gave such encouragement and impetus to all theories of development. But its roots are to be traced farther back, to the Hegelian philosophy and the positivism of Comte, to a theory of development which whether idealistic or materialistic is "naturalistic" because it tends directly to the denial of that supernaturalism which is so prominent and distinctive a feature of the Bible. Even a cursory examination of the literature of the higher criticism makes it clear that it has been increasingly dominated by three great principles of evolutionary theory: (1) that development is the explanation of all phenomena, (2) that this development results from forces latent in man without any supernatural assistance, and (3) that the "comparative" method, which uses a naturalistic yardstick, must determine the nature and rate of this development.

It is only necessary to state these principles to observe how prominently they have figured in that reconstruction of Biblical history which we have been discussing, and in what sharp conflict they stand to the things which the Bible so clearly teaches. It is all but impossible for scholars who have been trained in this evolutionary school of thought which teaches that man has developed from the lowest forms of life and that progress is natural and inevitable, to do justice to a history the great aim of which is clearly to declare that, unlike the animals, man was created by God in His own image, that man fell from that high estate by sinning against God, that the record of man's life upon earth is deeply marked by sin, and that stagnation and degeneracy, failure to live up to the standard set for him by his own conscience, by the noblest teachings and attainments of his ablest leaders, and by divine revelation, is a prominent, in fact the most prominent feature of human history. It is impossible for those who accept the teaching that man has risen and must rise by virtue of the exercise of his inherent powers and that education is the solution of all man's problems, to do justice to the claim of the Bible that supernatural power alone can save man from a course which is downward, that education, culture, science is not enough, that the individual man must be regenerated if society as a whole is to be raised, that the Cross is the supreme exhibition of man's hatred of God, and that it is only in the Cross that the justice and mercy of God meet and are fully reconciled. It is impossible for those who find in the history of the culture and religion of all the nations of antiquity the standard with which the history of Israel is to be compared and by which the truth of the Biblical account of it is to be judged, to do anything like justice to the insistent claim of the Old Testament that God hath not dealt with any other people as He did with Israel, that the call of Abram marked the beginning of God's unique dealings with a peculiar people, and that it was this very particularism which prepared the way for the universalism of the Gospel.

Study of the higher critical reconstruction of the Old Testament—the history of the formation of the Pentateuch is made to cover practically the whole Old Testament period—makes it clear that the great objective of the critics is to reconcile the redemptive supernaturalism of the Bible with that naturalistic evolution which dominates our thinking to so great an extent today by restating the one in terms of the other. A more radical transformation could hardly be attempted. Yet it cannot be denied that many of the "reinterpretations" of the statements of the Old Testament adopted by the critics would be regarded as too far-fetched and improbable to deserve mention, not to say serious consideration at the hands of intelligent men and women, were it not for the fact that some such interpretation is demanded if the Old Testament is to be made over after this modern pattern. And the very extremes to which the critics are obliged to go to apply their theory to the facts of the Old Testament show how stubborn are these facts and how completely redemptive supernaturalism enters into the warp and woof of Old Testament history. Little wonder that the Bible has become increasingly a battleground. For it is the great protest against a theory which has become so entrenched that it is regarded by many as invincible.

The issue of which we are speaking was ably stated by Abraham Kuyper in his Lectures on *Calvinism* (1898) in terms of the "abnormalist" and the "normalist" viewpoints. The difference is this. The abnormalist holds that man is abnormal, that a *disturbance* has taken place in him which has affected his inmost being and the whole of his conduct and relationships, and that this disturbing abnormality can only be overcome by a regenerating force from without. In other words, the Bible teaches that man is a sinner, a fallen being, and that only the grace of God can save him. The normalist, the consistent evolutionist, believes that man is not abnormal, but merely immature, that he has come a long way and may have a long way to go, that he is able to cope with all the difficulties that confront him, that the set of his face is onward, that *human* progress is inevitable. Consequently the abnormalist and the normalist have "two absolutely different starting-points,"[85] and their estimates of human history are no less distinct. The great question is, Which of these conflicting viewpoints is correct? We observe, therefore, that the abnormalist view of human history which is set forth in Scripture finds support along several different lines.

## *1. The Origin of Man*

There are two accounts of the origin of man which are widely accepted today. The one is that man is a special creation distinct from the lower animals. This is the Biblical account. The other regards him as related to them genetically and developed from them by means of natural and inherent forces. The great argument for a distinct origin for man, aside from the statements of Scripture, is the obvious and undeniable difference between man and the lower animals. This has been well stated by Bavinck as follows:

"For greater far than the undeniable points of similarity is the far-reaching difference between man and animal indicated by the vertical position, formation of hand, skull, and brains, and still more by the reason and self-consciousness, by thought and language, by religion and morality, by science and art."[86]

The case for the evolutionist was stated some years ago with equal clearness by Sir Arthur Thomson in the following striking words:

"Immense gaps in our knowledge are immediately apparent when we inquire into the origin of living organisms upon the earth, the beginnings of intelligent behaviour, the origin of Vertebrates, the emergence of Man, and so on. We know very little as yet in regard to the way in which any of the 'big lifts' in evolution have come about, and yet we believe in the continuity of the process. That is implied in our ideal conception of evolution, which we accept as a working hypothesis. It is not very easy to say what it is that is continuous, but we mean in part that there is at no stage any intrusion of extraneous factors."[87]

The fact that there are "immense gaps" in the evidence in support of the evolutionary theory of the origin of man will appear clearly to anyone who will examine the evidence. The "missing link" between man and the lower orders still eludes the evolutionist.[88] It is his "working hypothesis," that the evolutionary process must be "continuous" and that this continuity must exclude all "extraneous factors," which if accepted gives the theory of the evolutionist that appearance of demonstrable fact which is largely responsible for its wide acceptance today. The consistent evolutionist is restricted to one explanation, continuity. Consequently the continuity must be assumed to be established theoretically even though there are "immense gaps" in it actually.

## 2. The Antiquity of Man

It has been pointed out above that the Ussher Chronology which dates the creation of man at 4004 B.C. is not required by the statements of the Bible. That there are long intervals which are passed over in silence is not only possible, but highly probable. It is to be noted, however, that while the findings of archaeology indicate that human history covers a period much greater than 6,000 years, it gives no support to the immense figures demanded by the evolutionary anthropologist for the development of man from the lower animals. Few if any careful students of history would place the beginnings of history as determined by contemporary documentary evidence earlier than 10,-

ooo years ago.[89] How long the pre-historic period may have been must be largely a matter of conjecture. That Neanderthal man goes back as far as 50,000 B.C. may be possible. But when the scientist demands 100,000 years for the Piltdown skull, 150,000 more for the Heidelberg jaw, and yet a further 250,000 for Java "man" (*pithecanthropus erectus*) he is putting on the seven league boots of theory and travelling faster than the facts of the case at all justify, far less require.[90]

### 3. The Fall of Man

It is obvious that there is nothing in the Bible which is more in conflict with the "continuity" of the evolutionary process than the doctrine of the fall of man. The evolutionist may be willing to speak of a "fall upward," but that is a contradiction in terms. He may admit that man tripped or stumbled on the threshold of the world which he was to conquer, and that a "continuous abnormality" has marked the course of his progress *ad astra*. But he cannot admit that this abnormality should do more than hamper or delay man's progress. It cannot be allowed to seriously affect or defeat that progress. According to the Bible the fall was not a fall upward; it was not a trip; it was a catastrophe of the first magnitude. By it sin entered into the world and death by sin. Sin entered man's world from without and became his master. And with sin came degradation, degeneracy, death. On the basis of the Biblical doctrine of the fall of man it is quite as natural to account for "primitive" man as representing the depth to which man fell, as it is from the standpoint of evolution to see in him the depth from which man has climbed.[91] And it is only on the basis of the acceptance or rejection of this Biblical doctrine that the interpretation of human history set forth in the Bible can be correctly understood and evaluated. The doctrine of the fall of man is either the key to the understanding of human history, both sacred and pro-

fane; or it is the proof that the Bible is written from a point
of view and on the basis of assumptions which must today
be regarded as entirely mistaken and erroneous. There is
no *via media* between these two positions.

### 4. The History of Man as Set Forth in the Bible Is Abnormalist and Catastrophic

Biblical history is the most amazing record in existence.
There is no other book which so combines optimism and
pessimism, which is so complimentary to man and so condemnatory. It is complimentary because it assigns man the
highest origin and sets before him the most splendid
destiny as rightly his. It is condemnatory because it shows
with the utmost candor how sadly man has failed to prove
himself worthy of the one or capable of attaining the other.
The frankness of the Bible is astonishing. The man who
is created in the image of God and placed in a garden where
he enjoys communion with God, almost immediately it
would seem disobeys God, and is driven from the garden.
His oldest son becomes a murderer, a fratricide; and one of
that son's descendants composes a "hymn of hate" which
aptly expresses the law of the jungle. A new beginning is
made with another son Seth. Among his descendants there
is one who walks with God. But in the course of time man
becomes so corrupt that universal destruction is necessary
and only one righteous man and his family are saved. This
great and catastrophic judgment is followed by another,
the confusion of tongues. Then a new start is made with
Abraham, the "friend" of God. And again history repeats itself. The record of the "seed of Abraham" is a
tragic story of good and evil, with the evil largely in the
ascendant. The magnanimity of Joseph stands out against
a dark background, nine brothers who were worthy to be
descended from Cain, who slew his brother Abel. At Sinai
the Law is given. Israel heard the voice of God. Then
while Moses was in the Mount they turned aside to worship

a golden calf. The period of the Judges was one when "every man did that which was right in his own eyes." David, the man after God's own heart, the sweet singer of Israel, the type of the Messianic king, was guilty of adultery and murder. His son built the temple of Jehovah and then married many wives and built temples for their idol gods and worshipped them. Good king Jehoshaphat married crown prince Jehoram to the daughter of Ahab. Good king Hezekiah was succeeded by Manasseh. Even after the impressive lesson of the Babylonian Captivity, the Jews oppressed the poor, broke the sabbath, married strange women, caused Ezra and Nehemiah to weep and almost despair. And finally, when their long promised King appeared and did among them works which none other had ever done, works of love, of mercy, of compassion, so great was their enmity that the yoke of the hated Roman seemed preferable and they cried out, "Crucify him"; "We have no king but Caesar." They were willing that His blood should be upon them and their children; and so it has been for centuries and is today. Israel passed on the torch to the Christian Church and the history of the Christian Church as recorded in the New Testament and in the course of nineteen "Christian" centuries resembles in many ways that of the Jewish. It has had its triumphs and its defeats, its martyrs and its apostates. The church at Ephesus grew so mightily that all the province of Asia heard the Word. The church at Corinth tolerated gross sin and caused the apostle the greatest anxiety for a time. Stephen died as a martyr. Demas forsook Paul having loved this present world. The history of the Christian Church has been a strange commingling of light and darkness.

## 5. Extra-Biblical History Confirms Biblical History

Abnormalist history is not found only in the Bible. One of the best known historical works of modern times bears the significant title, *The Decline and Fall of the Roman Empire* (1776-1788). In the Preface to this elaborate work, Gibbon defined its scope as the tracing of "the memorable series of revolutions, which, in the course of about thirteen centuries, gradually undermined, and at length destroyed, the solid fabric of human greatness"; and in his Conclusion, he referred to the decline and fall of the Roman empire as "the greatest, perhaps, and most awful scene in the history of mankind." Yet Gibbon was an optimist, a believer in human progress. He believed that civilized man had risen from the "human savage" and that he might make indefinite progress towards perfection. But he said, "His progress in the improvement and exercise of his mental and corporeal faculties has been irregular and various; infinitely slow in the beginning and increasing by degrees with redoubled velocity: ages of laborious ascent have been followed by a moment of rapid decline."[92]

The theme upon which Gibbon wrote in such detail was the decline and fall of the *Roman Empire*. But it might easily have been expanded to cover the history of the great empires of which Rome was the successor. Egypt, Babylon, Assyria, Persia, Greece! Each had its times of prosperity and its "decline and fall." And at the present time, when the energies of "civilized" man are largely devoted to the inventing and forging of new and deadlier weapons of destruction, anxious voices are asking whether "decline and fall" is to be written large over the culture and civilization of Europe and the world in this twentieth "Christian" century. Such being the case there is no good reason in the nature of things why the higher critic should look with suspicion upon the Book of Judges which represents the social, moral and religious lawlessness of the period which it covers as a series of lapses from a better state and standard to which Israel had already attained, or rather, to speak accurately, from a standard which had been imposed from Above and accepted by Israel at Mt. Sinai. The almost total destruction of the tribe of Benjamin, considered in the light of its occasion, is a melancholy illustration of those moments of "rapid decline" of which Gibbon speaks. And it might as well be asserted that the New Testament could not have been already in existence for more than a thousand years because the "wicked popes" of the 15th century so flagrantly violated every principle and precept of the Gospel of Christ, as to assert that the Mosaic age, which was itself deeply marked by apostasy, could not have been followed by just such an age as the Book of Judges pictures to us, an age of "darkness and light." It may seem to the evolutionary higher critic a very simple solution of that tragic decline in faith and morals, to say that the conditions which the Book of Judges pictures to us are the "actual course of history," but that the very definite statement that these conditions represented a tragic apostasy from a higher and better standard is a misrepresentation, a pious attempt of later writers to idealize the past history of Israel. But were these same critics to attempt to rewrite the history of the Dark Ages after a similar fashion or to assert that the shocking state of Christendom in the 15th century proves that Luther and the other Reformers did not call Christendom back to a forgotten Gospel, but were themselves the discoverers or inventors of the Gospel, the absurdity of their contention as to the Book of Judges would be apparent to all. Hamlet was not the first to say, "The time is out of joint."

The evidences of degeneracy, of the tragic facility with which man can deteriorate, with which one generation or one individual can squander and abuse the cultural treasures slowly and laboriously accumulated by many that have gone before, are so numerous and so startling that it is only by taking very long views and fixing his eyes on the bright side that the devotee of progress can convince himself that it is inevitable or attempt to put together a timetable according to which it is to proceed.[93] It is customary to regard the lowest savage of today as the nearest to primitive man. But while scientists have not succeeded in developing a brute into a man, it is easy to find many examples of men who have sunk to or below the level of beasts.

Stagnation as well as decline and fall has marked the history of mankind upon the earth. In writing of the Byzantine Empire, Gibbon has told us: "In the revolution of ten centuries not a single discovery was made to exalt the dignity or promote the happiness of mankind."[94] The expression "the unchanging East" is proverbial. China has often been compared to a slumbering giant. Breasted who was a great advocate of the idea of human progress has said of the Egyptians: "Had the Egyptian been less a creature of habit, he might have discarded his syllabic signs 3,500 years before Christ, and have written with an alphabet of twenty-four letters." Progress has often been very slow and again and again it has been quite invisible except to the eye of the theorist who proceeds upon the assumption that progress is inevitable.

The writing of history requires the objective and unbiased temper of the true scientist. It has often been vitiated, especially since Hegel, by the attempt to philosophize history. It is of course true that the bare facts of history need to be correlated and interpreted if their true significance is to be fully appreciated. But there is a real danger lest in explaining the facts we manipulate them in the interest of a pre-conceived theory. The evolutionist as a historian can be singularly blind to the most obvious facts of history. And the most glaring illustration of this is his attempt to impose the theory of natural development upon the facts of Biblical history.

## Chapter IV

# THE FUNDAMENTAL AND ABIDING ISSUE IN THE PROBLEM OF THE PENTATEUCH

WE HAVE SEEN that the higher critical study of the Pentateuch has been dominated, especially since the appearance of Wellhausen, by the theory of natural development and by the attempt to treat the religion of Israel as originally identical, or practically so, with the religions of other Semitic peoples, and to account for the distinctive features of the religion of Israel as due to the genius of the Jew for religion. The strength of this theoretical reconstruction lies in its simplicity. The history of man's existence on the earth is to be viewed as a process of development, the continuity of which cannot be interrupted by the intrusion of any extraneous factors. Naturalistic evolution is to explain all phenomena. If this theory is accepted, all relevant facts must be made to accord with it and where evidence is wanting the gaps must be bridged or filled up in a way which is in accord with the theory. A partial and incomplete explanation which is in harmony with the theory will be regarded as probable; a very dubious conjecture will acquire weight and cogency if the exigency of the theory requires its acceptance; evidence which otherwise would be accepted without question will be ignored or summarily rejected if it does not accord with the theory because the theory has been accepted as proved.

We quote again from Sir Arthur Thomson:

"It gives us pause to think of the origin of Vertebrates, of Birds, of Mammals, of Man. We cannot speak with much confidence of the operative factors. In spite of this unsatisfactory ignorance, however, the scientific mind recoils with a jerk from the assumption of 'spiritual influxes' or mystical powers of any sort interpolated from outside to help the evolving organism over the stiles of difficulty. The scientific task is certainly unfulfilled; it may be beyond human attainment to accomplish it; but we must not try to speak two languages at once."[95]

With direct reference to the Genesis account he tells us:

"The idea of a Divine inbreathing which made a mammal man, or an animate body, in St. Paul's phrase, a spiritual body, seems to us to be counter to the idea of continuity in evolution, as if there were two worlds and not only one."[96]

This is certainly a weak defense of evolution as a solution of the problem of the origin of Man. It tells us that the scientist can and should speak only one language, the language of natural development. The "mystical," the "spiritual," what the philosopher has for centuries called the "meta-physical," is a language which he does not know and does not want to learn. To recognize the "intrusion" of the supernatural into the processes of nature would amount to speaking two languages at once; and that the scientist must not try to do. This amounts to saying that if Christianity, if the religion of the Bible, is to commend itself to the "scientific" mind and to receive a bill of health from the evolutionist, the supernatural element must be eliminated. Uniformitarianism is the distinguishing characteristic of this New Christianity.[97] We have endeavored to show that the great objective of the Wellhausen hypothesis has been to restate the redemptive supernaturalism of the Bible in terms of naturalistic evolution. A careful study of the application of this hypothesis to the Pentateuch should convince the reader that the question of the supernatural is fundamental to the whole problem of Biblical criticism. For if the supernaturalism of the Bible is denied, the historical trustworthiness of the Book cannot be maintained.

It is not necessary to add to the evidence that has already been given to establish the fact that it is their hesitation to accept the supernatural or positive rejection of it, which is mainly responsible for the attitude of the critics toward the question of the Mosaic authorship of the Pentateuch. But an example which illustrates this fact with especial plainness will be appropriate in this connection. We have seen that Albright declares emphatically that alphabetic writing was "common" in Palestine in patriarchal times and that he points out many examples of the historical accuracy of the Old Testament. He even declares that the Wellhausen hypothesis must be considerably modified. Yet we find that he accepts in general the documentary analysis of the critics and assigns the *written* documents to much the same dates as did Wellhausen.[98] This seems inconsistent. But it is not really so, as is shown, for example, by the evidence to which Albright appeals as proof that P in its present form can hardly be pre-exilic. He finds this evidence in the censuses in Num. i.-ii. and xxvi. These, he tells us, "have been proved to be recensional doublets with a long manuscript tradition behind them"; and he goes on to say, "Since the original census must have belonged to the United Monarchy and probably to the time of David (2 Sam. xxiv.), we must allow considerable time for the differences in manuscript transmission to have arisen."

These statements bring the issue clearly before us. According to the Book of Numbers two censuses were taken during the exodus period. The first (Num. i. and ii.) was taken at Mt. Sinai, early in the second year after the Exodus; the second (chap. xxvi.) was taken in the 40th year, just before Israel entered Canaan. Both censuses were commanded by Moses. The one represents the total of the adult male Israelites (not counting Levites) that had come out of Egypt. The other represents the total of the new generation which had grown up during the forty years of wandering to replace the generation of wrath that had perished in the wilderness because of disobedience. Albright tells us that these two censuses "must" represent variant accounts of a census taken in the time of the United Monarchy and he is inclined to identify that census with the one ordered by David, which had such unhappy consequences. Obviously were this explanation correct it would be absurd to appeal except in a most general way to any documents written by Moses or in his time. The most that could be said would be that the writer (or writers) of P in endeavoring to glorify the Mosaic age made use of a vague (oral?) tradition regarding a Mosaic census for the purpose of utilizing for his (their) idealized history of the Mosaic age two variant accounts of an actual Davidic census.

Why is it necessary to take this view of two carefully prepared censuses expressly assigned by the Book of Numbers to the Mosaic period? In other words, what is the warrant for Dr. Albright's "must"? There is nothing inherently absurd or even unlikely in Moses' ordering a census, or two censuses with a long interval of time between them. The obvious difficulty—it is so obvious that Albright does not even mention it—is that the figures given in these censuses are regarded by the critics as absurdly large, far too large for the time of Moses, but as perhaps reasonably possible for David's time (2 Sam. xxiv. gives still larger figures!).[99] Consequently it is assumed that P is here using data which cannot be earlier than the time of David and are probably very considerably later. Two things especially are to be noted with regard to these figures:

(1) There are no statistical data in the entire Bible that are more carefully given, and, we may say, safeguarded than those of the first census at Sinai. (a) In chap. i. the sum of the males of 20 years old and upward is given for *each* of the tribes (vss. 20-43); and it ends with the total for the twelve tribes (vs. 45). (b) Chap. ii. gives the grouping of the twelve tribes under the four standards, three tribes to a standard. Here we have first the total for each of the tribes of the standard, then the total for the standard, then the grand total for the four standards of the twelve

tribes. (c) These figures are checked by the circumstance recorded in Ex. xxxviii. There we are told that every male of 20 years old and upward was required to pay a half-shekel of silver as ransom-money, to be used in the construction of the tabernacle. At half a shekel for 603,550 persons, this amounted to 100 talents and 1775 shekels. The 100 talents were used to make the 100 sockets of the sanctuary and the vail; and the 1775 shekels were used to make hooks for the pillars, etc. This meant that every Israelite who was numbered at Sinai had contributed a part to the very structure of the tabernacle at which he was to worship the God of his fathers.[100] Beautifully appropriate and suggestive if the census was taken by Moses and the tabernacle was constructed at Mt. Sinai! But what an ingenious romancer P must have been, if he used a *Davidic* census and worked its statistics into the construction of a *Mosaic* tabernacle which never really existed but was, as Wellhausen calls it, a "reflection backward" of *Solomon's* temple. (d) The same figure for the adult males is given in round numbers in Ex. xii.37b(J) and in Num. xi.21 (JE). This carries us back to the earliest sources recognized by the critics, and shows that the "priestly" writer P was in strict accord with the "prophetic" writers J and E.[101]

(2) Not only are these statistical figures given with the utmost care and carefully checked by their use in the construction of the tabernacle; they find support in the character of the narrative itself. The supernaturalism of the narrative is in accord with them and justifies them; we may even say, is required by them.[102] The problem of nourishing this vast multitude has caused commentators much difficulty. The Bible recognizes the difficulty and its solution is that God fed Israel for forty years with manna. This is not a mere figure of speech. We are told when this feeding began (Ex. xvi.) and when it ended (Josh. v.12), what the manna looked like, what it tasted like, and how it was to be gathered and prepared. We are told expressly

that it was given to them on six days only, with a double portion on the sixth day to provide food for the seventh. This was no common bread. It was "bread from heaven." They thirsted also (chap. xvii.) and God gave them water in a miraculous way out of the flinty rock. These were God's ways of sustaining the people which He had brought out of Egypt by mighty power, by signs and wonders and a strong hand.

Moses in the first of his farewell addresses to Israel refers to the wonders of God's dealings with Israel in part as follows:

"For ask now of the days that are past, which were before thee, since the day that God created man upon the earth, and *ask* from the one side of heaven unto the other, whether there hath been *any such thing* as this great thing is, or hath been heard like it?

"Did *ever* people hear the voice of God speaking out of the midst of the fire, as thou hast heard, and live?

"Or hath God assayed to go *and* take him a nation from the midst of *another* nation, by temptations, by signs, and by wonders, and by war, and by a mighty hand, and by a stretched out arm, and by great terrors, according to all that Jehovah your God did for you in Egypt before your eyes?"

Moses here casts his argument that God had not dealt with any people as He had with Israel, into the form of a rhetorical question which to his way of thinking could have but one answer. If we answer it as Moses expected Israel to do and as he would have us do, Albright's "must" loses its cogency. It is only when men seek to eliminate the mighty acts of God from the history of the Exodus period and accept the view that the Israelites who were enslaved in Egypt must have been relatively few in number, that they did not differ to any extent from other nomads who had sojourned there, that their customs and beliefs differed little from those of other Semitic tribes, and that their escape from Egypt took place under conditions and circumstances which may have seemed to them remarkable but admit of quite simple (i.e., natural) explanation—in short it is only to those who are prepared to desupernaturalize the whole narrative that the "must" seems either convincing or compelling. And of course, if the censuses recorded in Num. i., ii. and xxvi. as taken in the days of Moses, must actually represent a census taken first by David, the fact that Moses could have written the account of such a census or such censuses ceases to be relevant.

Many other examples of this rejection of the supernatural might easily be given. The one just referred to—the Mosaic censuses—has to do with history as involving the supernatural. Equally significant, in some respects even more significant, are the instances in the field of prophecy. For example, Deut. xxviii. purports to be a prophetic utterance by Moses in which he lays down the conditions under which Israel is to occupy and retain the land promised to the fathers. The blessings described are to be the reward of obedience; the curses enumerated will be the inevitable consequence of disobedience. The whole chapter speaks of the future, of things to come. But it is understood quite differently by many of the critics. According to Pfeiffer, the chapter is composite, about one half being post-exilic; and he says of vss. 47-57, "the siege and destruction of Jerusalem in 586 and the ensuing woes are clearly depicted."[103] And Pfeiffer refers in support of this view to an article by W. A. Irwin entitled "An Objective Criterion for the Dating of Deuteronomy."[104] This objective criterion is the correspondence between this passage in Deut. viewed as history and the destruction of Jerusalem by Nebuchadnezzar. On the other hand Welch is equally positive that most of Deut. xxviii. is pre-exilic, because he finds in it a vivid picture of the destruction of Samaria by Sargon: "How tremendous the blow appeared and what an agony it brought to the men who endured it can still be measured in the sections of chap. xxviii. which can be dated in that time."[105]

Such statements are significant because they so completely ignore the predictive element as such. They simply assume, as a sound and established principle of interpretation, that these hortatory and minatory exhortations of Moses, which relate to things to come, are to be dated by their *fulfilment*. Pfeiffer, Puukko and others find this *date* in the fall of Jerusalem; Welch more than a century earlier in the fall of Samaria. But all are agreed in ignoring the predictive element completely.

The reason for this attitude has been ably stated by Pfeiffer in his discussion of the date of the Book of Daniel.[106] He lays down the principle that "historical research" can deal "only with authenticated facts which are within the sphere of natural possibilities and must refrain from vouching for the truth of supernatural events." The latter must, he insists be "an article of faith." And he declares that, "In a historical study of the Bible, convictions based on faith must be deemed irrelevant, as belonging to subjective rather than objective knowledge." Thus, the sharpest kind of an antithesis is drawn between Biblical or redemptive history *(Heilsgeschichte)* and secular or scientific history. So when Pfeiffer tells us that the Book of Daniel is Maccabean, he is simply relegating all of its miracles and prophecies as such to the sphere of subjective knowledge. In other words, to the man of science Daniel is Maccabean, its miracles incredible stories, its prophecies history cast in prophetic mold (apocalypse); to the man of faith the book is to be taken at its "face value." How these two attitudes are to be reconciled would be the problem of problems for these critics were it not for the fact that in practice they simply ignore the "traditional" or "face value" view in the interest of the so-called "scientific" one.

As applied to Deut. xxviii. this means that when this

chapter is treated "scientifically," it is to be interpreted exactly like 2 Kgs. xvii., if with Welch we regard it as having been "fulfilled" in the siege of Samaria, or like 2 Kgs. xxv., 2 Chr. xxxvi., Jer. lii., if as Pfeiffer argues with equal positiveness we find its "fulfilment" in the days of Nebuchadnezzar. According to either view the *prophetic* form of Deut. xxviii. is to be disregarded utterly and the chapter is to be read as *history*.

All such interpretations illustrate the fundamental difference between the Biblical and the so-called "scientific" position. Whether Moses actually wrote and recorded the words contained in this chapter or they are to be regarded as pseudo-prophecy written to describe the actual fall of Samaria or of Jerusalem, is or should be for the truly objective and scientific historian primarily a question of the reliability of the report of a historical fact recorded in a historical record. The record vouches for the fact. Those who believe the record to be true find in it conclusive proof that Moses was able to foretell and actually foretold a future event with a definiteness which reads like history. The negative critic proceeding on the assumption, either definitely stated or tacitly assumed, that predictive prophecy is impossible, insists on reading this prophecy as history written after the event it foretells, a treatment which changes its character completely. Indeed, it would be far more logical simply to reject the prediction entirely, than to try to transform it into something quite different, by making the fulfilment in history of the prediction the key to the date when it was uttered.

Consequently, while we may rejoice that critics and archaeologists of high rank are now prepared to admit that Moses was able to read and write and could have recorded the events of his time, exactly as, on the testimony of the Bible, Old Testament and New, the Christian Church has for centuries believed that he did, we cannot expect them to admit that Moses wrote the Pentateuch and that it is trustworthy history unless or until they are prepared to accept as trustworthy the account which it gives of God's wonders of old. If these wonders are incredible, the Pentateuch cannot be regarded as trustworthy history. The redemptive supernaturalism that pervades it is a stumbling-block to the rationalist. When the critics praise the historical accuracy of the Pentateuch and at the same time summarily reject its statements where the supernatural is clearly involved, they make it unmistakably plain that they regard as impossible the very things which it represents as supremely important, those things which make it uniquely precious to the Christian believer, the record it gives of God's wonders of old.

# CHAPTER V

## THE FINAL QUESTION, "WHAT THINK YE OF CHRIST?"

WHILE THE QUESTION of the reality of the supernatural is basic to the study of the Pentateuch and of the Bible as a whole, it assumes its most urgent expression in the pages of the New Testament. Naturalistic evolution may figure prominently, as we have seen that it does, in the question which we have been considering, the problem of the date and authorship of the Pentateuch. But the greatest question of all for the evolutionary critics is this, "What think ye of Christ? Whose Son is He?" If the supernatural appears in the Pentateuch, it appears with equal plainness in the Gospels. The Jesus of the New Testament is a supernatural Person. He is God made manifest in the flesh. If the supernatural is to be regarded as an "intrusion" in Israel's history, then Jesus Christ becomes the supreme *intrusion*. How shall the evolutionary critic deal with Him? Jesus said of Moses, "He wrote of me"; and He went on to say, "If ye believe not his writings, how can ye believe my words?" This means that, if we believe Moses, we will believe Christ, and, if we do not believe Moses, we will not believe Christ. Why is this? It is simply because the redemptive supernaturalism of the Books of Moses is essentially the same as the redemptive supernaturalism of the New Testament, is preparatory to it, and has its fulfilment in the Messiah of whom Moses spoke. Deny this redemptive supernaturalism in the Pentateuch and logically there is no place for the supernatural Christ of the New Testament.

Since the viewpoint of the Bible is consistently theistic

and involves the acceptance of belief in a righteous and gracious God who has revealed Himself supernaturally in word and deed to man, the only consistent and logical position is to accept or reject this viewpoint as a whole: to accept the supernaturalism of the Pentateuch and the supernaturalism of the Gospels or to reject both. To attempt to halt the desupernaturalizing of the Bible with the Pentateuch or with the Old Testament is logically inconsistent and practically impossible. Yet there are many who seem to believe that they can hold on to the precious truths of the Gospel whatever may be the fate of the Old Testament at the hands of its critics. Such a position is insecure and precarious to say the least, and cannot satisfy the consistent and thoughtful Christian.

The seriousness of the attack upon Biblical theism which results from the wide acceptance of the destructive conclusions of the critics regarding the Old Testament is shown by the means by which many Christians today are seeking to combat it. We have seen that the Theology of Crisis, of which Barth and Brunner are the most widely known representatives, has given us the word "suprahistorical." Accepting more or less fully the results of the desupernaturalizing process to which the critics have subjected the Bible as a whole and especially the Old Testament, they endeavor to save those supernatural facts which the thoroughgoing evolutionist rejects as unhistorical, by saying that they are suprahistorical. It is difficult to understand how any event which actually occurred on this earth and directly concerned or affected man could be anything but historical. We may of course distinguish between known and verifiable facts and unknown or doubtful ones. But history deals with phenomena which are so to speak "matter of record," the existence or occurrence of which is established by evidence. The siege of Troy and the destruction of the Spanish Armada, the Colossus of Rhodes and the Colosseum at Rome, the birth and the assassination of Julius Caesar, Virgil's *Aeneid* and Milton's *Paradise Lost*, are all historical phenomena, however widely they may differ in character. As such they are all amenable to the laws of evidence; and our information regarding them will require scrutiny as to its reliability, a scrutiny which will vary in its intensity in proportion to the importance of the phenomenon itself and the amount and character of the evidence available regarding it. But as natural phenomena they are all amenable to this law. If they fail to pass the test, we question or reject their reality. As to this all thoughtful persons are agreed, at least in principle. How then are we to deal with supernatural phenomena? Are they amenable to the laws of evidence or are they not?

It may help us to answer this question, if we turn again to a book which has already been referred to more than once. In *From the Stone Age to Christianity,* Professor Albright states it to be his aim "to show how man's idea of God developed from prehistoric antiquity to the time of Christ and to place this development in its historical context." This is a subject which has often been treated by evolutionary critics. Dr. Albright is a distinguished archaeologist and his volume is a historical study. He is a convinced evolutionist, and states his viewpoint to be that of "rational empiricism in dealing with historical problems."[107] He begins with Java-, Ghassulian-, Mt. Carmelman; he discusses artifacts, cave-drawings, primitive utensils, burial mounds, cult objects, monumental and documentary evidence of the most varied kinds. The wealth of information which he pours out may well amaze and appal the reader; and it is all designed as an attempt to trace man's development historically from the Stone Age to Christianity.

What makes this book especially significant for our study of the Pentateuch is this. It begins with the Stone Age; it includes the Mosaic Age; it ends with the Gospel Age. The bulk of the volume deals with the pre-Christian period. In his treatment of it, Dr. Albright makes it clear, as we have learned from his treatment of the censuses in the Book of Numbers, that he regards the supernaturalism of the Pentateuch as an obstacle to its acceptance as historical. When he comes to the New Testament he states his position more plainly. In dealing with the miracles of the New Testament he tells us: "Here the historian has no right to deny what he cannot disprove. He has a perfect right to unveil clear examples of charlatanry, of credulity, or of folklore, but in the presence of authentic mysteries his duty is to stop and not attempt to cross the threshold into a world where he has no right of citizenship."[108] Professor Albright does not use the word "suprahistorical." But if we understand him correctly, his viewpoint is essentially the same as that of the Barthian School. It is that the supernatural events of the New Testament record do not lie in the plane of human history and can neither be proved nor disproved by the student of history. The historian, as a historian, must take an agnostic position regarding the New Testament miracles. He has no right to deny them, but he cannot prove them. They belong in a world where he has no right of citizenship!

The issues raised by the statement just quoted are of the utmost importance. The first question which suggests itself is this. How can the historian unveil spurious miracles, if the whole domain of the supernatural lies outside of his province? How can he discriminate between true and false in a world in which he has no right of citizenship? If he can eliminate the false, is it not proper to assume that he must be able to recognize and verify the true? It would certainly seem so, unless the very fact that a mystery involves the supernatural is to be regarded as proving that it is not authentic.

The inconsistency of this position is shown also by the preposterous rôle which it assigns the historian. The historian may study the cusps in the molar teeth of the gorilla and compare them with the teeth of *pithecanthropus erectus* with a view to bridging the gap between man and the lower animals. He may scrutinize artifacts and cave-drawings to prove that man evolved slowly from a primitive state. These lie within the sphere of the historical. But "the historian cannot control the details of Jesus' birth and resurrection and has thus no right to pass judgment on their historicity.[109] What could be more tragically pathetic, if it were true? The meagre remains of Java-man are historical evidence. They prove that he lived and died; and the evolutionist tells us that he died 500,000 years ago. But the empty tomb and the angels and the resurrection appearances and the ascension from Olivet, which establish the truth of those wonderful words of Jesus which were uttered at the tomb of Lazarus, "I am the resurrection and the life," are not historical. The historian cannot deal with them. What, we repeat, could be more pathetic? What greater fiasco can we think of than this? The greatest and most momentous events in human history, if true, are declared to be non-historical. The historian may discuss the question whether Sargon was the son of Tiglathpileser. But he may not discuss the question whether Jesus was born of a virgin. He may investigate the legend of the Seven Sleepers of Ephesus; he may investigate the question whether Frederick Barbarossa is slumbering in some cavern in the mountains and will yet awake to deliver the Germans in their hour of peril. But the far weightier question whether Jesus of Nazareth was declared to be the Son of God with power by the resurrection from the dead,—that question he must leave unanswered. What a humiliating rôle this assigns to the historian! The supreme facts of history are not historical!

In view of this tragic fiasco, it is to be noted that it is the inevitable result of the acceptance of that principle of uniformitarianism of which we have been speaking. If no "intrusion from without" can interrupt or affect the *con-*

*tinuum* of naturalistic development, then the redemptive supernaturalism of the Bible must either be rejected *in toto* or be relegated to a domain of which the scientific historian cannot take cognizance. It is called the suprahistorical. But it looks very much like the old familiar territory of myth, legend, and folklore, only with a new and more imposing name. But whatever name may be given to it, the word "historical" cannot apply. This claim that the supernaturalism of the Bible is suprahistorical is an attempt to combine naturalism and supernaturalism. It seeks to recognize and conserve the great redemptive facts of supernatural religion while accepting a theory which makes their occurrence in human history an intrusion which must be resented and denied. To make oil and water mix were a far simpler matter.

Aside from its inherent weakness the greatest objection to the claim that the miracles of Scripture are not historical, in the commonly accepted meaning of that word, is the fact that this doctrine is so manifestly contrary to the teachings of Scripture. This is illustrated by the two supernatural events which have been most frequently attacked and to which Dr. Albright especially refers as events which "because of their highly intimate character" are "set forever beyond the reach of the critical historian." Whatever else may be said about them, this much is unmistakably plain: these great miracles are recorded in the New Testament as fully accredited and authenticated facts. We have two accounts of the Virgin Birth. One is in Matthew's Gospel and gives facts known only to Joseph; the other is in Luke's and gives facts known only to Mary. Joseph and Mary were the two human witnesses to the great mystery of the Incarnation. They were the two and the only two human witnesses qualified to testify. And their testimony is recorded, that out of the mouth of two witnesses every word might be established. If their testimony as to the parentage of Jesus cannot, if true, be regarded as establishing a historical fact, then the parentage of no child born since the days of Adam and Eve can be regarded as a matter of history, despite the fact that momentous issues have often depended on this very question.

What is true of the Virgin Birth is equally true of the Resurrection, except that the words "personal and intimate" cannot be regarded as applicable to it. This transcendent event is recorded in all four of the Gospels, each of which also records several of the post-resurrection appearances of Jesus to His disciples. The historian Luke declares expressly that Jesus "showed himself alive after his passion by many proofs, appearing unto them by the space of forty days, and speaking the things concerning the kingdom of God." Paul in writing to the church at Corinth declares that Jesus "was seen of Cephas, then of the twelve; after that he was seen of above five hundred brethren at once; of whom the greater part remain unto this present, but some are fallen asleep." With these words, Paul definitely asserted that, twenty-five years or more after the death of Christ, there were several hundred persons still living who had seen with their own eyes their risen Lord. In his defense before king Agrippa, Paul asked this question, "Why should it be thought a thing incredible with you, that God should raise the dead?" And after briefly rehearsing the evidence, he appealed to Agrippa's own knowledge of the facts: "For the king knoweth of these things . . . for this thing was not done in a corner." In short, Paul declared the resurrection of Christ to be a fact of history. He appealed to evidence to prove it a fact and his conclusion was this: "But now is Christ risen from the dead and become the first fruits of them that slept." And Christian apologetes and historians have with Paul declared the resurrection of Christ not only a fully authenticated fact of human history but one the acceptance of which as a fact is of the utmost importance to man.

How then can it be asserted that the resurrection is not a "historical" event, that it is "set forever beyond the reach of the critical historian"? The only warrant for such a position must be found in that contention which Paul sought so earnestly to refute, that it is "incredible that one should raise the dead." If, as David Hume asserted two centuries ago, no amount of evidence could suffice to establish the occurrence of a miracle, if in more modern parlance no intrusion from without into the sequence of the natural development of man upon earth can be tolerated, then Paul was mistaken and the other New Testament writers were mistaken in representing the resurrection as a historical fact the occurrence of which was established by abundant and conclusive evidence.

It has been the bold and confident assertion of Christians throughout the centuries that Christianity, the religion of the Bible, Old Testament and New, is historical in the fullest sense of the word, that its great doctrines are based on well-authenticated historical facts. It has been their boast that they have not followed cunningly devised fables but that the evidences of the truth of Christianity will stand the closest scrutiny. They have invited the doubting Thomases of every age to satisfy themselves that this is so.

A Christianity whose supernaturalism is *un*historical or *supra*historical is not the Christianity of the Bible nor of that Christian Church which derives the content of its faith from the Bible; and one of the most serious indictments of the theory of evolution is that it forces those who are not content with a bare and empty naturalism to take refuge in a mysticism which is not based on, nor prepared to regard, the redemptive supernaturalism of the Bible as consisting of historically demonstrable facts. Whether men will believe these facts is a different matter, as is also the question whether these facts will have any meaning to them. The soldiers that guarded the tomb were witnesses of a mighty act of God, yet took money to deny it. Spiritual things are spiritually discerned. But facts are facts whether men believe them or not. And the great concern of the thoughtful Christian today should be to know whether the things which the Bible records as facts of history actually took place as it tells us that they did. It is our duty to test them and prove them. And if we reach the conclusion, as a multitude of believers in every age have done, that they are true facts of history, then it is our duty to reject as false a naturalistic philosophy which cannot acept as historically true the things which are most surely believed among us, but rejects them or relegates them to a domain to which the laws of historical evidence cannot apply.

"If ye believe not his writings, how shall ye believe my words?" This is the searching question which has troubled the Christian Church ever since the denial of the Mosaicity of the Pentateuch came to be regarded as one of the "assured results" of modern Biblical criticism. It has troubled the Christian Church because it takes what many would fain regard as an Old Testament question, a problem of ancient Jewish history, a topic of remote and antiquarian interest, and makes it a question of vital concern to every thoughtful, logically-minded Christian. If our attitude toward the problem of the Pentateuch will determine our attitude toward Jesus Christ, then the question whether Moses wrote the Pentateuch cannot be an academic question to any one for whom the words of Jesus, words which are "spirit and life," are precious. This is the reason that, despite the most confident denials of a rationalistically controlled literary and historical criticism, the majority of Christians throughout the world continue and will continue to believe and maintain that the Pentateuch is not a late, anonymous, untrustworthy composite, but is correctly described as "The Five Books of Moses," the man of God. And those who hold this time-honored and thoroughly Biblical view may well rejoice that they are today in a far better position to give a reason for believing that Moses wrote the Pentateuch, than was the case a century or even a generation ago.

# APPENDICES AND NOTES

# DRIVER'S ANALYSIS OF THE PENTATEUCH

The analysis given below is that of the revised edition (1909) of the *Introduction*. Comparison with the first edition (1891) shows relatively few changes. The following points are of interest: (1) In Genesis the changes are negligible; (2) in Exodus the Code of the Covenant (xx.20-xxiii.33) is transferred from J to E, and there are a number of other changes affecting the JE analysis; (3) in Leviticus, Numbers, and Joshua, the changes are few: (4) a second Deuteronomist (D²) is recognized in parts of Deuteronomy and in Joshua.[1]

## THE DOCUMENT P

Genesis i.1-ii.4*a*; v.1-28, 30-32; vi.9-22; vii.6, 11, 13-16*a*, 17*a* (except *forty days*), 18-21, 24; viii.1-2*a*, 3*b*-5, 13*a*, 14-19; ix.1-17, 28-29; x.1-7, 20, 22f., 31f.; xi. 10-27, 31-32; xii.4*b*, 5; xiii.6, 11*b*-12*a*; xvi.1*a*, 3, 15, 16; xvii.; xix.29; xxi.1*b*, 2*b*-5; xxiii; xxv.7-11*a*, 12-17, 19-20, 26*b*; xxvi.34-35; xxvii.46-xxviii.9; xxix.24, 29 (with perhaps fragments in xxx.1*a*, 4*a*, 9*b*, 22*a*); xxxi.18*b*; xxxiii.18*a*; xxxiv.1-2*a*, 4, 6, 8-10, 13-18, 20-24, 25 (partly), 27-29; xxxv.9-13, 15, 22*b*-29; xxxvi. (in the main); xxxvii.1, 2*a*; xli.46; xlvi.6-27; xlvii.5-6*a* (LXX), 7-11, 27*b*-28; xlviii.3-6, 7; xlix.1*a*, 28*b*-33; l.12-13.

Exodus i.1-5, 7, 13, 14; ii.23*b*-25; vi.2-vii.13, 19, 20*a*, 21*b*-22; viii.5-7, 15*b*-19; ix.8-12; xi.9, 10; xii.1-20, 28, 37*a*, 40, 41, 43-51; xiii.1, 2, 20; xiv.1-4, 8-9, 15-18, 21*a*, 21*c*-23, 26, 27*a*, 28*a*, 29; (xv.19) xvi.1-3, 6-24, 31-36; xvii.1*a*; xix.1-2*a*; xxiv.15-18*a*; xxv.1-xxxi.18*a*; xxxiv.29-35; xxxv.-xl.

Leviticus i.-xvi. (xvii.-xxvi. largely H), xxvii.

Numbers i.1-x.28, 34; xiii.1-17*a*, 21, 25, 26*a* (to *Paran*), 32*a*; xiv. (1, 2) 5-7, 10, 26-30, 34-38; xv.; xvi.1*a*, 2*b*-7*a*, (7*b*-11), (16, 17), 18-24, 27*a*, 32*b*, 35, (36-40), 41-50; xvii.-xix.; xx.1*a* (to *month*), 2, 3*b*-4, 6-13, 22-29; xxi.4*a* (to *Hor*), 10, 11; xxii.1;

xxv.6-18; xxvi.-xxxi., xxxii.18, 19, 28-32 (with traces in xxxii.1-17, 20-27); xxxiii.-xxxvi.

Deuteronomy i.3; xxxii.48-52; xxxiv.1a (in the main, 5b, 7-9.

Joshua iv.13, 15-17, 19; v.10-12; vii.1; ix.15b, 17-21; xiii.15-32; xiv.1-5; xv.1-13, 20-44, (45-47) 48-62; xvi.4-8; xvii.1a, 3, 4, 7, 9a, 9c-10a; xviii.1, 11-28; xix.1-8, 10-46, 48, 51; xx.1-3 (except "and unawares"), 6a (from *until* to *judgment*), 7-9 [cf. LXX]; xxi.1-42 (xxii.9-34).

## THE DOCUMENT J

Genesis ii.4b-iv.26; v.29; vi.1-4, 5-8; vii.1-5, 7-10 (in the main), 12, 16b, 17b, 22-23; viii. 2b-3a, 6-12, 13b, 20-22; ix.18-27; x.8-19, 21, 24-30; xi.1-9, 28-30; xii.1-4a, 6-20; xiii.1-5, 7-11a (to *east*), 12b (from *and moved*), 13-18; xv. (analysis uncertain); xvi.1b-2, 4-14; xviii.1-xix,28, 30-38; xxi.1a, 2a, 33; xxii.15-18, 20-24; xxiv.1-67; xxv.1-6, 11b, 18, 21-26a, 27-34; xxvi.1-14 (15), 16-17 (18), 19-33; xxvii.1-45; xxviii.10, 13-16, 19; xxix.2-14, 31-35; xxx.3b-5, 7, 9-16, 20b (*now . . . sons*), 22b β, 24-xxxi.1, 3, 46, 48-50; xxxii.3-13a, 22, 24-32; xxxiii.1-17; xxxiv.2b-3, 5, 7, 11-12, 19, 25 (partly), 26, 30-31; xxxv.14, 21-22a; xxxvii.12-18, 21, 25-27, 28b (to *silver*), 31-35; xxxviii.1-30; xxxix.1-23; xlii.38-xliv.34 (with traces of E), xlvi.28-xlvii.4, 6b, 13-26, 27a (to *Goshen*), 29-31; xlix.1b-28a; l.1-11, 14.

Exodus i.6, 8-12, 20b; ii.15-23a (to *died*); iii.2-4a (to *see*), 5, 7-8, 16-18; iv.1-16, 19-20a, 22-26, 29-31; v.3, 5-23; vi.1; vii.14-15a, 16, 17 (partly), 18, 20c-21a (to *from the river*), 23-25; viii.1-4 (numbered as in *English* version), 8-15a, 20-ix.7, 13-21, 23b, 24b, 25b-34; x.1-11, 13b, 14b-15a (to *darkened*), 15c-19, 24-26, 28-29; xi.4-8; xii.29f.; xiii.21f.; xiv.5-7, 10a (to *afraid*), 11-14, 19b-20, 21b (to *dry land*), 24-25, 27b, 30-31; xvi.4-5, 25-30; xvii.1b-2, 7; xix.3b-9, 11b-13, 18, 20-25; xxiv.1-2, 9-11; xxxii.25-34; xxxiii.1-4 (mainly), 12-23; xxxiv.1-4 (mainly), 5-28 (mainly).

## THE DOCUMENT E

Genesis xv. (analysis uncertain); xx.1-17, (18); xxi.6-21, 22-32a, (32b), (34); xxii.1-14, 19; xxviii.11-12, 17-18, 20-22; xxix.1, 15-23, 25-28, 30; xxx.1-3a (to *knees*), 6, 8, 17-20a, 20c-22bα,

23; xxxi.2, 4-18a, 19-45, 47, 51; xxxii.2, 13b-21, 23; xxxiii.18b-20; xxxv.1-8, 16-20; xxxvii.2b (from *Joseph*), 3-11, 19-20, 22-24, 28a (to *pit*), 28c-30, 36; xl. (with traces of J); xli.1-45 (with traces of J), 47-57; xlii.1-37; xlv.1-xlvi.5 (with traces of J); xlvii.12; xlviii.1-2, 8-22 (in the main, probably); l.15-26.

Exodus i.15-20a, 21-22; ii.1-14; iii.1, 4b, 6, 9-15, 19-22; iv.17-18, 20b-21, 27-28; v.1-2, 4; vii.15b (partly), 17 (partly), 20b; ix.22-23a, 24a, 25a, 35; x.12-13a, 14a, 15b, 20, 21-23, 27; xi.1-3; xii.31-36, 37b-39, 42a; xiii.17-19; xiv.10b, 19a; xv.1-18, 20-21; xvii.3-6, 8-16; xviii.1-27; xix.2b, 3a, 10-11a, 14-17, 19; xx.1-21, 22-xxiii.33; xxiv.3-8, 12-14, 18b; xxxi.18b; xxxii.1-8, 15-24, 35; xxxiii.5-6 (in the main); xxxiii.7-11.

## The Document JE

This consists of all passages in which J and E cannot be distinguished sufficiently clearly to permit of a detailed analysis. While describing such passages as JE, Driver often gives a tentative analysis or refers to the opinions of other scholars. As indicated above, there is only one chapter in Genesis which is treated as JE, and only a few chapters in Exodus. In the case of Numbers and Deuteronomy, on the other hand, all such passages are listed as JE.

Genesis xv. (2a, 3b, 4, 6-11, 17-18, probably J; 1, 3a, 2b, 5, 16, probably E; the rest consist of later additions).

Exodus xii.21-27; xiii.3-16; xv.22-27; xxxii.9-14.

Numbers x.29-33, 35-36; xi.1-xii.16; xiii.17b-20, 22-24, 26b-31, 32b-33; xiv.3-4, 8-9, 11-25, 31-33, 39-45; xvi.1b-2a, 12-15, 25-26, 27b-34; xx.1b, 3a, 5, 14-21; xxi.1-3, 4b-9, 12-35; xxii.2-xxiv.25; xxxii.1-17 (in the main), 20-27 (in the main), 34-42.

Deuteronomy xxvii.5-7a; xxxi.14-15, 23; xxxiii. (from independent source); xxxiv.1b-5a, 6, 10.

## The Document D

Few if any traces of D are found by the critics in Genesis—Numbers. The bulk of Deuteronomy is D. Certain passages, usually short, which "connect imperfectly with the context or present difficulties of representation" are assigned to a later writer (D²). The P and JE passages in Deuteronomy are listed above.

## THE BOOK OF JOSHUA

In Joshua, Driver recognized the sources, P, JE and D². He made no attempt to distinguish between J and E except that he assigned nearly all of chap. xxiv. to E. For the details the reader is referred to the *Introduction* (pp. 103-116).

APPENDIX II

## THE ANTIQUITY OF MAN (Gen. v. and xi.)

With regard to the genealogies in Genesis v. and xi. there are a number of important points to be noted.

1. It is significant that neither chapter v. nor xi. ends with a total for the period covered and that the data supplied by these chapters are never used elsewhere in Scripture as the basis for chronological calculations. Several long dates are given (e.g., Gen. xv.13, Ex. xii.40, 1 Kgs. vi.1, cf. Acts vii.6, xiii.20); and a statement as to the length of time between the Creation and the Flood, and between the Flood and the Call of Abram would be very interesting. But such statements occur nowhere in the Bible, though found for example in Josephus.

2. These genealogies have a symmetrical form which suggests that links may have been omitted. Gen. v. gives the names of ten men, the last of whom has three sons (Shem, Ham and Japheth). In Gen. xi. there are also ten names (if following Lk. iii.36 and the LXX of Gen. xi. we insert a Cainan after Arphaxad) and the last has likewise three sons (Abram, Nahor and Haran). Since we are expressly told that all of these patriarchs had more than one son ("and begat sons and daughters" is used of them all), the mention of three sons of Noah and three of Terah is in a sense arbitrary and suggests that the lists are constructed with a view to giving only such information as may be needed by the reader and that they are cast in a form which would make it easy to remember them. A notable instance of this is the genealogy in Matt. i. which is arranged in three groups of 14. That the arrangement there is arbitrary is shown by the fact that, in order to make three groups of 14 and have the divisions come with David and the Captivity, 4 kings are omitted in the second group and Jechonias is counted twice. Since these facts are quite obvious, the words "so all the generations were" are clearly to be understood to mean "all the generations" *given in these lists.*

3. The statement in Gen. xi.26, "and Terah lived seventy years and begat Abram, Nahor, and Haran" does not accord with the theory that we are dealing with an exact chronology. The words apparently mean that at the age of 70 Terah became a father. That all three of these sons were born at the same time or in the same year seems improbable. And comparing Gen. xii.4 which tells us that Abram was 75 when he departed out of Haran with Acts vii.4 which declares that this took place "after his father was dead" we are forced to the conclusion that Abram was not Terah's oldest son but was born 60 years later. That Abram should be mentioned first is natural if the only object of the genealogy is to point out that Terah had three sons, the most famous of whom was Abram. But xi.26 would be an absurd ending of a genealogical table intended to give an exact chronology of the post-diluvian period.

4. That many of the genealogies in the Old Testament are abridged is a well-known fact. Jehu is usually called the son of Nimshi. But he was the son of Jehoshaphat, the son of Nimshi. Ezra vii. describes Ezra the priest as a descendant of Aaron in the 16th generation. But 1 Chron. vi. makes it evident that a number of names are omitted in Ezra. "Son" often means descendant." The genealogy in Matt. i. tells us that Joram "begat" Ozias (Uzziah) who was his great, great grandson; and this genealogy of 42 generations is reduced to three in the summary statement, "The book of the generation of Jesus Christ, the son of David, the son of Abraham" (vs. 1).

5. The only objection which can be raised against the view that, as in many other instances so in the genealogies of Gen. v. and xi., links may be omitted, is the fact that the age of each patriarch on attaining fatherhood is expressly stated. This is thought to justify or require the conclusion that the total for the entire period can be ascertained (in round numbers) by adding up the total ages of these worthies when they became fathers. But this argument is not convincing. The general scheme of Gen. v. is this: "$x$ lived—years and begat $y$: and $x$ lived after he begat $y$—years and begat sons and daughters, and all the years of $x$ were—years and he died." The great aim of the statement seems to be to stress two things, the re-

markable longevity of each patriarch both as regards the time of attaining parenthood and as to total age, and also the melancholy fact that despite the great age attained the curse pronounced in Gen. ii.17 was finally fulfilled, "and he died." The statement "and begat sons and daughters" points out that the command of Gen. i.28 was obeyed by them. In the case of the post-diluvians this formula is reduced to, "and $x$ lived— years and begat $y$, and $x$ lived after his begetting $y$—years, and begat sons and daughters." Here the omission of the words "and all the years of $x$ were—years" seems to be due to the fact that the longevity of the post-diluvians is not so remarkable as in the case of the pre-diluvians. And the omission of the words "and he died" makes the record end in terms of the command of ix.1, which was so vitally important in view of the Flood. In the case of both genealogies the statement of age at parenthood does not stand alone but is connected with other data which have no place in a chronology in a strict sense. Consequently we are not justified in inferring that these genealogies are meant to give an exact chronology from the fact that this one item which would be essential to a chronology is given. If the formula "$x$ begat $y$" can, in the statement "Joram begat Ozias," mean "Joram begat (the ancestor of) Ozias," there is no reason why adding the statement of age "Joram lived— years and begat Ozias" could not mean exactly the same thing.

6. The view that these tables are not intended to give a strict chronology is favored by certain phenomena which appear in them. If Gen. v. is regarded as chronological, Methuselah's death very nearly synchronized with the date of the Flood, since Noah's 600th year apparently equals Methuselah's 969th. This has led to very startling conjectures. It has been asserted that Methuselah's death must have immediately preceded the flood and that his name was a prophetic declaration of this (the interpretation of Methuselah as meaning "he died and a sending," i.e., "when he [Methuselah] is dead, it [the flood] will come" is extremely improbable). It has even been asserted that since Methuselah lived 969 (full) years, he must have swum about for most of a year before he was drowned by the flood. If the genealogy of the post-diluvians is strictly chronological, the first three of them (Shem, Arphaxad, and

Salah) were all alive when Abram was born, while all the others (Eber, Peleg, Reu, Serug, and Nahor) except Terah had passed way. The Jewish commentator Rashi tells us that the feast at Isaac's weaning was called "a great feast," because "the great men of that generation were present at it—Shem, Eber, and Abimelech." The fact that such highly improbable inferences can be drawn from the figures given in Gen. v. and xi. seems to indicate clearly that the data supplied in these chapters were not intended to serve as the basis for a system of chronology covering the period between Adam and Abraham.[2]

Since archaeology indicates so convincingly that man has been on the earth much more than 6,000 years, the defender of the trustworthiness of the Genesis record should be thankful that a careful study of the Biblical data does not lead to the conclusion that the Ussher chronology must be accepted as taught in Scripture; and he should therefore recognize that to insist on the acceptance of that chronology is to place a stumblingblock in the way of those who sincerely desire to accept the Book of Genesis as historically reliable.

## PROPER NAMES AND THEIR MEANINGS

For the archaeologist proper names, both of places and persons, are of great interest. Much valuable information may be contained in a name. The old saying, "What's in a name?" has for him a special meaning. But the interpretation of names is often very difficult and tantalizing; and there are few subjects connected with the Bible on which more nonsense has been written than on the subject of proper names. Archaeology has been making this painfully apparent, by calling attention to the mistakes which it is so easy to make in regard to them. On the other hand, archaeology has done much to show that proper names are used with remarkable accuracy in the Pentateuch.

1. The fact that a name occurs in the Old Testament is of course no proof in itself that the name is Hebrew and should be derived from a Hebrew root. There never was any excuse for deriving the name Pharaoh from the Hebrew root *para*. It has long been recognized that it is Egyptian and means "great house" (cf. "Sublime Porte" as used of the Sultan of Turkey); and it is now becoming increasingly clear that its use in the Pentateuch is correct for the period which it represents. On the other hand, it may be regarded as doubtful whether any of the names of the five principal cities of the Philistines are really Semitic names. Gath ([wine, or oil?] press) and Gaza (strong place?) have that appearance. But whether these are the true meanings is not certain. Ashdod, Ashkelon, and Ekron have been given most fantastic meanings. Whether Delilah is a Hebrew name is still uncertain. If she was a Philistine, the name may be Philistine (a language of which we still know little or nothing): it may be a Hebraized form of a Philistine name which does not represent it any more accurately than Gibraltar represents the Arabic *Jebel-Tariq*: it may be a Hebrew rendering of the Philistine, just as Dorcas

is the Greek for the Aramaic *Tabitha*. To try to find Hebrew
meanings for the names of Achish of Gath, of Ephron the Hittite and of many others is hazardous to say the very least.

2. Failure to recognize that homonyms occur among proper
names as in other words has led to much confusion. *Rimmon*
is the word for pomegranate in Hebrew. But to how many of
the half dozen persons or places mentioned in the Old Testament as having this name, this meaning would apply is far
from certain. That the Syrian god Rimmon was a nature god
probably identical with Hadad (Assyrian, Adad) seems clear.
He was the god of the storm, the thunderbolt. That he had
any connection with the pomegranate seems decidedly improbable. Similarity or even identity in sound does not necessarily
prove identity in origin or meaning.

3. The fact that many of the names in the Old Testament
are significant and are explained as such, has led to much confusion and to many unwarranted statements regarding them.
Two points are especially to be noted:

*a.* It has been alleged that because some names in the Old
Testament are declared to be significant, meanings and even
significant meanings should be found for all of them. This
has led to many forced and fantastic interpretations, which
have threatened to make the whole subject ridiculous.

*b.* In the case of names which are treated as significant in
the Old Testament and explained as such, it is to be noted
carefully that the explanation may be of two kinds: it may be
in the nature of an exact etymology, or it may involve a word-
play or pun, based on similarity in sound or meaning.

(1) Examples of exact or approximate etymology are:
Ishmael (God will hear), Isaac (he will laugh), Ephraim (fruit-
ful), Manasseh (forgetting), Benjamin (son of right hand),
Ichabod (Where is glory?, or, There is no glory). To these may
be added the symbolic names Jerubbaal, Lo-ammi, Ruhama,
Beulah, Aholibah, etc.

(2) Examples of names based on association of ideas
are also easily found. The appropriateness of the name Noah
is stated thus: "And he called his name Noah, saying this one
shall comfort us." Noah comes apparently from a root *nuach*
meaning "rest"; "comfort" is from a root *nacham*. The roots

are similar in sound and also in meaning. But the explanation involves a word play; it is not an etymology, strictly speaking. Cain (*qayin*) and "I have gotten" (*qanah*) likewise have two consonants in common and there may be a similar approximation in meaning. Exactly what it is, we do not know for certain. Japheth is explained as follows: "Let Elohim enlarge (*japht*) Japheth. Since *japht* and Japheth are practically identical this might be regarded as an exact etymology. But Japheth may come from a root meaning "to be fair" or perhaps from some other. The words, "because I asked him of the Lord" (1 Sam. i.20), indicate the general appropriateness of the name Samuel. The exact meaning is unknown. "God hath appointed him" would be appropriate.

The name Joseph has, as we have seen, a double appropriateness. Joseph means "may he add." Rachel wanted another son. But her first thought was gratitude that God had removed (*asaph*) her reproach of barrenness. So we have in "Joseph" both an exact etymology and a word play. Similarly, in naming Zebulun, Leah said, "Elohim has given (*zabad*) me a good gift (*zebed*). Now will my husband honor (*zabal*) me because I have borne (*yalad*) him six sons." The verbs *zabad* and *zabal* have two root letters in common; and the honor would be the proper reward of the gift. It is perhaps proper to note also that the consonants which differ, the "l" and the "d" are both found in the verb "to bear" (*yalad*), which states the nature of the gift and the reason for the honoring. Such an ingenious subtlety would be quite appropriate under the circumstances.

It is very important to give due regard to this difference which may appear in the explanations of proper names. For it has often been asserted that the interpretations of names such as those just cited are "folk-etymologies" which are quite inaccurate and serve to prove these early records to be unreliable and utterly unscientific. This is due to the attempt to treat as exact etymologies, explanations which involve a word-play or pun. For example, if the Babel of Gen. xi. is the same as the Babylon (*Babel*) referred to elsewhere in the Old Testament, the name is Babylonian and means "gate of God" (*Bab-ili*). It was called Babel because the gate of a city was the place where important acts were performed (business transacted, justice executed, etc.) and in this case the act of God was "confounding" (*balal*) the tongues. The record does not say that Babel means "confusion" but that the city was called Babel (gate of God) because there God confounded the tongues, which is something quite different. So interpreted the statement is quite correct philologically.

Whether the explanation of the name Gershom, "I was a sojourner (*ger*) there (*sham*)," should be regarded as giving the meaning of the name, or as simply a word play on the meaning "exile" (from *garash* "drive out") is not certain. Either explanation is possible.

A word of especial interest is the word "woman." In Gen. ii.23 we read, "to this one shall it be called woman (*ishshah*) for from man (*ish*) was taken this one." It would be easy to infer that the Hebrew word for woman is simply the feminine of the word for man, as if we were to say, "She shall be called man-ess because taken from man." But the root from which the word woman is formed is not the same as the root of the word man. This appears clearly in the Aramaic and Arabic. Consequently we may infer that the nexus lies in the meaning rather than in the etymology. If the one root means "to be delicate," the other "to be strong," the difficulty would be removed. It is not necessary to assume that here or in any other cases we are dealing with crude folk-etymologies which must be regarded as utterly unscientific.

The name "Moses" illustrates the difficulty of interpreting Biblical names. It was given by the daughter of Pharaoh. We would expect it to be Egyptian. The princess knew Moses' parentage, but she would hardly have given "her son" a name which would stigmatize him as belonging to a slave people. The meaning of the name Moses is uncertain. The most widely accepted etymology is from the Egyptian word *mes* meaning "child." The explanation of the name perhaps favors this: because "I drew him out" of the water. The verb rendered "drew out" may be the Egyptian word "to bear (a child)"; and the princess may have meant to represent the taking of the babe from the Nile as equivalent to a birth and so to suggest that the Nile god was his father. The verb occurs only here, where such an interpretation is perhaps favored by the LXX, and in Ps. xviii.16 (= 2 Sam. xxii.17). As an Egyptian word its preservation in Old Testament Hebrew would be accounted for by the popularity of the story of Moses' birth and naming. It is also possible that the verb used is a Hebrew verb which was sufficiently close in meaning to the Egyptian to bring out the idea the princess had in mind; and she may have known enough Hebrew to have enjoyed a rather subtle word play. At least no one is in a position to prove that the account of the name given in Exodus is not strictly accurate when correctly interpreted.[3]

The same applies to the other Egyptian proper names (e.g., Asenath, Potiphar, etc.) which appear in the Pentateuch. It has often been asserted that these names are clear evidence of late date. But until far greater certainty has been reached as to the meaning of these names, it is highly arbitrary and dogmatic to assert that they cannot be as old as the events described. The remarkable accuracy with which foreign names are recorded in the Old Testament should prevent the careful scholar from making hasty assertions to their discredit.[4]

A name of especial interest is Israel. The interpretation given in Gen. xxxii.28 and Hos. xii.4 suggests the meaning "He will persist (or prevail) with (literally, as to) God." But the more natural meaning would be "God persists" (making *El* subject). Such a double meaning is suggested by the circumstance under which the name was given. The power of Jacob's Adversary was shown by the fact that He had only to touch Jacob's thigh to render him helpless. Yet He said, "Let me go" and in reply to Jacob's words, "I will not let thee go, except thou bless me," the new name was given, which suggests that feeble Jacob may prevail with the omnipotent God. It is interesting to compare, in this connection, the significant name "Jehovah our Righteousness." It occurs in Jer. xxiii.6 and xxxiii.16 and is written in exactly the same way in both places. But the context makes it clear that the meaning is not the same in both. In xxiii.6 it is the name which will be given to the Messiah, the righteous Branch, and it is to be read: "Jehovah, our Righteousness." Here the Messiah is declared to be Jehovah Himself who is the righteousness of His people.

In xxxiii.16 it is the name of Israel and is clearly to be understood to mean, "Jehovah (is) our Righteousness," a name appropriate to Israel whose righteousness is derived from Jehovah.

Finally we observe that what seems to be the obvious meaning of a name is sometimes open to serious objection: "swine" for Hezir, "brother of folly" for Ahitophel, "forsaken" for Azubah (1 Kgs. xxii.42), "dove" for Jonah, "fool" for Nabal, Amon and Mordecai explained as containing the *names* of heathen gods, are all more or less dubious etymologies.[5] A modern example may serve to illustrate this. To one to whom "taffy" means only a kind of hard candy (toffee), the word sounds strange as applied to the Welshman in the Mother Goose rhyme, "Taffy was a Welshman, Taffy was a thief." Does it describe the Welshman as a kind of "candy kid"? The idea seems absurd even for such a collection of amusing nonsense as this book of nursery jingles. But the absurdity lies wholly in the explanation. For the name "Taffy" has nothing to do with candy. It is the anglicizing of the Welsh form of the name David. And since David is the name of the patron saint of Wales, it is typically Welsh and quite appropriate, except for the fact that a David ought not to be a thief.

It is clear that archaeology has proved the absurdity of many of the meanings assigned to proper names in the past. It is no less clear that it has done much to confirm the correctness of Bible names when properly understood. We may expect it to throw much more light on this difficult but fascinating subject.

# NOTES TO PREFACE AND INTRODUCTION
## (Pp. v-x, 1-18)

[1] This expression is used by Albright in *From the Stone Age to Christianity*, p. 1.

[2] *Encyclopaedia Britannica* (14th ed.), article "Shakespeare," p. 447.

[3] *Against Apion*, I, 8.

[4] Used about 20 times in Ex. xxxix.-xl.

[5] W. H. Green, *Higher Criticism of the Pentateuch*, p. 38.

[6] That Josephus regarded Moses as the author of Genesis is shown by the sentence which follows the one just quoted: "This interval of time was little short of three thousand years." (*Against Apion*, I, 6)

[7] The use of the divine name, "Most High" (xxxii.8) is reminiscent of Gen. xiv. (cf. Num. xxiv.16), just as "Rock" (xxxii.4, 18, etc.) is connected with Ex. xvii. (cf. Gen. xlix.24, "the stone of Israel"). The word "separate" (*id.*) suggests Gen. x.5, 32 (P) and xxv.23 (J). The reference to Sodom and Gomorrah (xxxii.32) recalls Gen. xviii.-xix. (J). The remark of the Jewish commentator Rashi on the Blessing is worthy of notice: "Thou wilt find in the case of all the tribes, that the blessing of Moses is drawn from the fountain of the blessing of Jacob" (cf. Waller in Ellicott's *Bible Commentary*).

[8] The fact that, except in Deuteronomy, Moses is regularly spoken of as "Moses" or in the third person is not a strong argument against the Mosaic authorship. Historians both ancient and modern in writing of events in which they figured prominently have employed the same objective style of writing. Julius Caesar and Josephus are two notable examples from the past. Furthermore, whatever be the force of the argument the critics are in no position to use it. For the book in the Pentateuch which they have been most emphatic in denying to Moses is Deuteronomy; and this is the very one in which he constantly uses the first person. The old argument that Moses could not have spoken of himself as the meekest of men (Num. xii.3) overlooks the force of the word "suddenly" (vs. 4). It was because Moses' meekness prevented him from dealing severely with so serious a situation as the challenging of his God-given authority by his own sister and by his elder brother who was high priest that Jehovah "spake suddenly" and dealt severely. It is also to be noted that the Hebrew word rendered "meek" has also the meaning "afflicted." In view of the situation described in chap. xi., especially vss. 10-15, the latter rendering would be very suitable here. The attitude taken toward him by his nearest relations may well have seemed to Moses the "last straw."

[9] This is not only admitted but positively asserted by the critics. Pfeiffer tells us: "No Hebrew law, whether oral or written, was regarded as binding unless of Mosaic origin, and the ritual prescriptions of Ez. xl.-

305

xlviii. were never enforced as such, even though they had a profound in-fluence on the practices of the Second Temple" *(Introduction,* p. 210). Yet, like all Wellhausians, Pfeiffer does not hesitate to disregard this tra-dition completely. This leaves the critics with a strange anomaly to ac-count for. The laws laid down in Ezekiel are, as Pfeiffer points out, nu-merous and precise. But we never read of the "Law of Ezekiel." The name of Ezekiel appears only twice in the book which bears his name, and nowhere else in the Bible. The name of Moses occurs about 800 times! How is this anomaly to be explained, if little or nothing in the Pentateuch can confidently be assigned to Moses?

10 For a summary account of objections and objectors to the Mosaic tradition, cf. W. H. Green, *Higher Criticism,* pp. 47-52; Holzinger, *Hexa-teuch,* pp. 25-40.

11 Ecclus. xlv.5. The first reference to the canon of the Old Testament as consisting of "the Law and the Prophets, and the other books of our fathers" is found in the Prologue of Ecclesiasticus written perhaps 50 years later by the grandson of the author.

12 Cf. A. Westphal, *Les Sources,* p. 25, who refers to the Talmudic tract *Sanhedrin.*

13 Cf. R. D. Wilson, *Studies in the Book of Daniel,* Series II, pp. 12-41.

14 Both Philo and Josephus believed that Moses wrote the account of his death. Josephus tells us this was out of fear "lest they should venture to say that, because of his extraordinary virtue he went to God" *(Antiq.* IV, viii.48). The Talmudic tractate, Baba Bathra (14b) assigned the last eight verses of Deut. to Joshua.

15 According to Dr. R. D. Wilson the "conservative position" regarding the Pentateuch is as follows: "That the Pentateuch as it stands is historical and from the time of Moses; and that Moses was its real author, though it may have been revised and edited by later redactors, the additions being just as much inspired and as true as the rest" *(A Scientific Investigation of the OT,* p. 11, cf. p. 174).

16 W. H. Green, *Higher Criticism,* p. 47f. The fact that scholars have differed and still differ as to these alleged anachronisms is an indication that the case against Mosaic authorship of these passages is not proved. Gen. xxxvi. is an illustration of this. The words "before there reigned any king over the children of Israel" (vs. 31) undoubtedly suggest the time of the monarchy. But Gen. xvii.16 contains the promise of kings in Israel (cf. Deut. xvii.14f. also xxviii. 36), a promise which Israel's bondage in Egypt and wanderings in the wilderness might seem to contradict, and these words of Gen. xxxvi.31 would then indicate that Moses was not unmindful of the seeming failure of the promise. Furthermore it is difficult to see any sufficiently compelling reason for inserting a long list of Edomite duke-kings into the text of Genesis. That Chronicles should include it in the genealogical material which it took over from Genesis would be natural. But it is highly unlikely that such a list would be inserted in Genesis from Chronicles in the post-exilic period.—It is by no means certain that the Dan of Gen. xiv.14 is the same as the Dan of Jgs. xviii.29. Garstang has recently accepted Petrie's argument that the former lay south of Jerusalem

and may be the Dannah of Josh. xv.49. See the discussion of "The Pentateuch and Archaeology" in Part III, Chapter II of this volume.

17 For a fuller discussion of the history of the higher criticism, cf. W. H. Green, *The Higher Criticism of the Pentateuch* (1895), J. Orr, *The Problem of the Old Testament* (1909), H. Holzinger, *Hexateuch* (1893), A. Westphal, *Les Sources du Pentateuque* (1888-1892), Cornill, *Introduction* (1907). For details of analysis and dating compare the works on *Introduction* by Driver, Cornill, Gray, Creelman, Eissfeldt, Oesterley and Robinson, Pfeiffer, and also the discussions in Brightman's handy volume, *The Sources of the Hexateuch*. [Green and Orr wrote in opposition to the higher criticism, Green's opposition being more thoroughgoing than Orr's. The other books are by its advocates.]

18 Jean Astruc, *Conjectures sur les Memoires origineaux Dont il paroit que Moyse s'est servi pour composer le Livre de la Genese.*

19 The Mosaic authorship had been denied by Alex. Geddes in 1792 who held that the Pentateuch dated from the time of Solomon, but was compiled from ancient documents "some of which were coeval with Moses, and some even anterior to Moses" (*The Holy Bible*, Vol. I, p. xix.).

20 Cf. his *Einleitung* (4th ed.). But Eichhorn still maintained the substantial Mosaicity of the Pentateuch, as composed from documents dating from the Mosaic age.

21 The analysis proposed by Astruc and Eichhorn was comparatively simple. Astruc assigned about 760 of the 1,534 verses of Genesis to the Elohistic document and about 630 verses to the Jehovist. Eichhorn gave about 800 verses to the Elohist, and about 650 to the Jehovist. Astruc called the Elohistic and Jehovist documents A and B respectively. He recognized a third source (C) in vii.20, 23, 24, and designated three chapters (xiv., xxxiv. and xxxvi.) and parts of six others (xix., xxii., xxv., xxvi., xxviii., xxxv.) by a symbol D which he thought might represent several different sources, i.e., a total of 129 verses which did not belong to A or B. Eichhorn described 180 verses as "insertions" (ii.4-iii.24, xiv., xxxiii.18-20, xxxiv.1-31, xxxvi.1-43, xlix.1-27 [?]). Especially noteworthy is it that both Astruc and Eichhorn assigned the bulk of chapters xl.-l. to the Elohist.

22 *Die Quellen der Genesis und die Art ihrer Zusammensetzung.* The idea that the Elohistic source was composite had already been proposed by Ilgen in 1798, and Hupfeld referred to both Ilgen and De Wette as preparing the way for his own theory.

23 *Die Quellen*, pp. 195-203. The former rôle had been stressed by Eichhorn who regarded the editor as extremely conscientious (*Einleitung*, 1823, Vol. III, p. 101).

24 The symbol H is frequently used to designate the Holiness Code (Lev. xvii.-xxvi.) which is held to be an early stratum of P.

# NOTES TO PART I (Pp. 21-126)

1 This work by the Regius Professor of Hebrew in Oxford University was published in 1891, and has passed through a number of editions. The high esteem in which it is still held in critical circles is indicated by the

fact that when Leonard Woolley in his *Abraham* (1936) summarized for his readers "the generally accepted conclusions of Biblical criticism" (p. 15f.), he referred them to Driver's *Introduction* for the details. A summary of Driver's analysis of the Hexateuch is given in Appendix I. An informing survey of the progress and present state of Old Testament criticism, as it is viewed by an ardent advocate, is given in the paper "The Present State of Old Testament Studies" by George A. Barton in *The Haverford Symposium on Archaeology and the Bible* (1938), edited by Elihu Grant, pp. 47-78. See also the survey by H. H. Rowley in *A Companion to the Bible* (1939), edited by T. W. Manson, pp. 31-77. These are both by Protestant scholars holding the critical position. In *The Old Testament and the Critics* (1942), J. Coppens, professor at Louvain gives an informing survey and discussion of the development of the critical movement up to the time of writing. The sketch is objective. But the last 30 pages are especially addressed to Roman Catholics, the aim being to show just what are the limits set to "criticism" by the Biblical Commission of 1906. Here the writer shows himself to be an expert casuist; and he makes it quite plain that his own sympathies lie in the direction of the acceptance of some at least of the conclusions of the critics. The most recent *Introduction* to the Old Testament, in English and written from the critical viewpoint, is that of R. H. Pfeiffer (Harper, 1941). The position of the author is briefly stated as follows: "Broadly speaking, the Graf-Wellhausen hypothesis is adopted as fundamentally sound in the following analysis of the Pentateuch. In some points, however, the views presented here differ from all others, particularly in beginning the J document with the call of Abraham in Gen. xii. and in postulating the existence of a non-Israelite source in Genesis (indicated by S: South or Seir)" (p. 141). Where he differs from Driver, Pfeiffer seems to take on the whole a more radical position.

2 We are justified in speaking of Hupfeld's hypothesis as a three-document theory because, while Astruc and Eichhorn recognized only two main documents in Genesis and did not carry their analysis beyond the early chapters of Exodus, Hupfeld distinguished three sources in the first four books of the Pentateuch (Genesis-Numbers). A fourth source (D), makes up the bulk of Deuteronomy. But this source appears only very rarely, if at all, in the first four books. Consequently it is only in Deuteronomy, which contains some material from J and E and a few verses from P, and in Joshua where J, E, D, and P, are all recognized as occurring, that we can speak of a four-document analysis of the Hexateuch. It should be noted, however, that many scholars distinguish various strata in these four documents. They divide J into J¹ and J² (called L and J by Eissfeldt), and recognize several E's, D's and P's. Only exceptionally can such minutiae be dealt with in such a discussion of the theory as is undertaken in this volume.

3 The Jehovistic and Elohistic groups of psalms in the Psalter are in some respects analogous. The reason for the variation is by no means clear. But in the Psalms as in Genesis the preference is not exclusive but preponderating.

4 This was recognized by Astruc who found a third source already in the Flood Narrative and considerable additional material which he regarded as non-Hebraic, since the name of God did not occur in it.

5 Chaps. xxxiv., xxxvi., xxxvii., xlvii.

6 Three in chap. xxxviii. and eight in chap. xxxix.

7 *Elohim* does not occur in chaps. x.-xvi., xviii., xxix., xxxiv., xxxvi.-xxxviii., xlvii., xlix.; and only once in chaps. iv., xxiii., xxv., xxvi., xxxix., xl., xliv.

8 Driver assigned Gen. xxx.22a to E (*Introd.*, p. 16; *Commentary on Genesis*, p. 276); but he admitted it might be P (*Introd.*, p. 12; *Commentary*, p. v.). It is to be noted that the total of 85 includes 15 cases where the definite article is used with *Elohim* (the *Elohim*). These are nearly all assigned to E (xxii.1, 3, 9, xxxi.11, xxxv.8, xli.25, 28, 32*bis*, xlii.18, xlv.8, xlviii.15*bis*); J receives xxvii.28, xliv.16; none are P. In the first 20 chapters of Genesis, "the *Elohim*" occurs five times in P (v.22, 24, vi.9, 11, xvii.18), twice in J (vi.2, 4), twice in E (xx.6, 17).

9 The LXX varies considerably from the Hebrew in its rendering of the divine names in these chapters. But the consistent usage of the Massoretic Text favors its originality.

10 Comp. Gen. vii.16 and Ex. iii.4 where this identity is made especially clear. Observe how "Spirit of Jehovah" and "Spirit of God" are equated in 1 Sam. x.6, 10; cf. xi.6, xvi.14.

11 But cf. xxii.9, xxxiii.20, xxxv.1, 3, 7, where this is not the case.

12 Some critics assign them to a second Jehovist source (J²). But a Jehovist should use the name Jehovah.

13 We meet it first in v. 13 and more than 50 times in the rest of the book.

14 That the emphasis is not on the mere name but on the meaning of the name is favored by the fact that the name *El Shaddai* occurs only 5 times in Genesis. It was as an Almighty God that Deity revealed Himself to Abraham (xvii.1). But if the meaning of Ex. vi.3 is that *El Shaddai* was the special name of *Elohim* in the days of the Patriarchs it would be remarkable that it is used so rarely.

15 Payne Smith's statement that "In the history of Joseph there is the greatest possible precision in the use of the divine names" cannot be accepted without qualification. For if the historian always used the word *Jehovah* we should expect to find it in xlvi.2 instead of *Elohim*. But the distinction which he draws between narrative and dialogue appears to be a valid one in general.

16 It is also to be noted that in Hebrew a question can be expressed without the use of an interrogative. As spoken this would be indicated merely by the inflection of the voice. There are many examples of this in the Old Testament; and since the rhetorical question is frequently employed for the sake of emphatic assertion, "and by the name of Jehovah was I not known unto them?" might be equivalent to saying that the name Jehovah was quite as well known to the fathers as any other. For a fuller discussion of this passage see "Critical Note on Exodus vi.3" by R. D. Wilson in *Princeton Theological Review*, XXII, 108-119.

17 The only warrant for cutting a single verse (vs. 29) out of Gen. v. (P) and assigning it to J must be found in the claim that P could not have used the word Jehovah before Ex. vi.3. Otherwise, since Gen. v.29*b* is clearly based on iii.17, it would be perfectly natural for the writer of chap. v. to follow the phraseology of chap. iii., using the words "toil," "ground" (*adamah*), "Jehovah," and "cursed," all of which occur in it.

18 The words of vs. 14, "I am that I am" (or, "I will be what I will be"—several renderings are possible), and the command to tell the people "I am" (*Ehyeh*) has sent Moses unto them, indicate clearly that the emphasis is on the meaning of the name. For "I am" occurs nowhere else in the Old Testament as a name of Deity but Jehovah (i.e., Yahweh, meaning "He is" or "He will be") is here declared to be the name of the God of the patriarchs, with the clear implications that He was known to them by that name.

19 Astruc, *Conjectures*, pp. 301ff., Eichhorn, *Einleitung*, 2nd ed. (1787), Vol. II., pp. 327f., 4th ed. (1823), Vol. III, pp. 145f. Eichhorn was very positive that the documentary analysis could not be carried beyond Ex. iii. He was apparently unwilling to admit any direct contradictions between the sources of Genesis (*ibid.* p. 98). De Wette on the other hand did not hesitate to list Gen. iv.26 under "Errors in respect to historical truth," as an illustration that "Later manners, customs, institutions, and opinions are referred back to ancient times" (cf. *Crit. & Hist. Introd.*, Eng. Transl. by Parker, II., pp. 51, 55, 69).

20 McNeile, *Commentary on Exodus, in loco.*

21 Cf. also the *Critici Sacri* (1660) and La Haye's *Biblia Maxima* (1660).

22 A third word for "God" (*El*), which is comparatively rare in the Pentateuch, is also used 7 times in these chapters.

23 The same applies to Ex. xiii.17-22, xiv.18f., xix.3, 18f., xx.1f., 19-26, xx.21f., xxiv.11f., xxxi.1f., Num. xxi.5f., Dt. i.17f. Cf. also 1 Sam. x.

24 Similar variations appear in the Koran (cf. R. D. Wilson, " 'God' and 'Lord' in the Koran" in *Princeton Theological Review*, XVII. 644f.).

25 In the case of the name Joshua, the critical analysis is more consistent. The change of name from Hoshea to Joshua is announced in Num. xiii.16. The critics assign this to P and give all the references to Joshua which occur up to that point to E or JE.

26 Note: "Jerubbaal who is Gideon" (vii.1); and especially viii.28-35 where we find the following: "Gideon" (vs. 28), "Jerubbaal, the son of Joash" (vs. 29), "Gideon" (vs. 30), "Gideon, the son of Joash" (vs. 32), "Gideon" (vs. 33), "Jerubbaal-Gideon" (vs. 35). On critical principles we might expect the document (E) which announces the new name to use it regularly thereafter and the other document (J) to use only Gideon. But the critical analysis does not seem to work out that way.

27 Two names, Horeb and Sinai, are given to the "Mount of God." If Horeb is regarded as characteristic of E (Ex. iii.1, xvii.6, xxxiii.6), the mention of Sinai six times in Ex. xix. constitutes a serious difficulty, since all critics apparently find a considerable E element in this chapter. According to Driver the verses which mention Sinai are either P (vss. 1, 2*a*) or J (vss. 11, 18, 20, 23), while vss. 2*b*, 3*a*, 10-11*a*, 14-17, 19 are given to E.

The name of Moses' father-in-law is given as Reuel (Ex. ii.18 [J], Num. x.29 [JE]), as Jethro (iii.1, iv.18*bis*, xviii. [7 times], all E) and perhaps as Hobab (Num. x.29 [JE], cf. Jgs. iv.11). But this analysis destroys the continuity of both E and J. E.g., E skips from Ex. ii.14 (or 10) to iii.1 and then to iii.4*b*.

28 Delitzsch, *Commentary on the Psalms (in loco)*. Variety is especially noticeable in poetry owing to the parallelism. Cf. for example, Pss. xlvii.5, lv.16, lvi.10f, lviii.6, lxix.13, lxx.1, 6. Ps. xxv. uses Jehovah 9 times and ends with the words, "Redeem Israel, O *Elohim*, out of all his troubles." Similarly in the New Testament we find in Rev. xii. the names satan, devil, accuser, dragon and serpent, all applied to the same malevolent being.

29 The title "Jehovah of hosts" occurs frequently in Haggai, Zechariah and Malachi. Zechariah uses it 50 times. It occurs three times in a single verse (i.3) and twice in each of five other verses. In chap. viii. it is found 17 times. These books use "Jehovah" more frequently than the fuller form. But there seems to be little if any effort in them to avoid the monotony of an identical repetition which may be intended to be emphatic.

30 This may also be due to the further aim to show that *Jehovah* and *Elohim* are identical, and that while *Elohim* demands the sacrifice it is *Jehovah* who provides it. For a discussion of the theological significance of these two expressions comp. Oehler, *Theology of Old Testament*, pp. 129, 131ff.

31 Cf., the Gesenius Hebrew-Dictionary, edited by Francis Brown, p. 219a.

32 Similarly the name "Israel" in Gen. xlviii.8, 11, 21, is assigned to the redactor because E is not supposed to be aware of the change of name, the two mentions of which are assigned to J and P. (Cf. Part II, note 77.)

33 The claim that the sequence of events in the second account cannot be harmonized with that of the first cannot be made good. See below, note 80; also Green, *Unity of Genesis*, pp. 20-28.

34 In Num. xvi.15 it is assigned to JE because it cannot have this technical meaning.

35 The expression in iv.1, 17, is "conceive and bear." This occurs elsewhere in Pent. in J (9 times), E (4 times). In Gen. xxi.2 it is kept from being P by splitting the verse.

36 If *anoki* is the older form of expression, the fact that Abraham uses it in speaking with the children of Heth (Gen. xxiii.4) is an argument for the accuracy with which this chapter reflects, even in its phraseology, the patriarchal age. Yet the critics are almost unanimous in assigning this chapter as a whole to P.

37 There are some critics, e.g., Procksch, who regard the headings as not original in P, but as the work of an editor or redactor. P. J. Wiseman (*New Discoveries in Babylonia about Genesis*, 1946) argues forcefully that these headings are really colophons such as are found at the end of Babylonian tablets (e.g., the Creation Tablets). The theory is an attractive one, but it does not accord readily with the facts. E.g., Gen. xxv.12, "Now these are the generations of Ishmael, Abraham's son" is clearly the heading of vss. 12-18.

**38** Astruc assigned xii.4, xvi.16, xvii.1, xxv.20, 26, to J. Eichhorn gave vii.6, xii.4, xvi.16, xxv.26, to J. Hupfeld claimed all for P except xxxvii.2, xli.46, l.26.

**39** The determination of the critics to make this phrase distinctive of P is shown by the fact that Driver suggested that in Num. xxxii.11 it is an isolated P phrase in JE, while Dt. xxxiv.7 where it also appears is one of the very few verses in Deuteronomy (ten according to Driver) which are assigned by the critics to P.

**40** Similarly the technical term (*yabam*) used of the obligation of a man to marry the wife of a brother who had died childless and "raise up seed" to the said brother occurs in J (Gen. xxxviii.8). The only other occurrences of this verb are in Deut. xxv.5, 7, which gives the law of levirate marriage.

**41** *Documents of the Hexateuch*, Vol. II, p. 221.

**42** Note also that "were born" is used in xxxv.26. This expression is regarded as a mark of J in Gen. iv.26, vi.1, x.21, 25. Here it occurs in a verse which the critics want to regard as P.

**43** That P's style is not nearly as distinctive and unmistakable as is alleged is indicated by the fact that, while Driver assigns the bulk (about 2/3) of Gen. xxxiv. to P, most critics apparently have followed Hupfeld in assigning these verses to E. Oesterley and Robinson (*Introd.*, p. 35) partition vs. 3 and assign the second half to E. This gives both "love" and "speak kindly" to what Driver regarded as P. If P's style were really unmistakable, such difference of opinion would be impossible.

**44** *Introduction*, p. 160. It remains to be seen whether Pfeiffer's theory, which he announced more than a decade ago, will gain general acceptance among the critics. Pfeiffer adds an interesting footnote (p. 172) to his discussion of the document E: "The most conspicuous differences in vocabulary [between J and E] are the two words for 'handmaid' (*shiphchah*, J; *amah*, E) and the two for 'small' (*tsair*, J; *qaton*, E)." The words for "handmaid" have, it is true, long been regarded as distinctive of J and E respectively, despite the fact that according to Pfeiffer's analysis J's word occurs also in E (Gen. xx.14; xxx.18), in JE (xxx.43) and in P (5 times). But that Pfeiffer should speak of the two words for small as "conspicuous" examples of the difference in vocabulary between J and E is a remarkable confession of the *similarity* in vocabulary which characterizes them and of the difficulty which the critics encounter in the attempt to distinguish between them. According to Pfeiffer *tsair* occurs in Genesis in the following places: S (4 times), J (5 times); *qaton*, in S (once), J (7 times), E (5 times), P (once). This indicates that *qaton* is even more characteristic of J than it is of E.

**45** Ex. iv.9 has to be assigned to J, because the name *Jehovah* is used 8 times in vss. 1-11. The *verb* from which P's noun (*yabbashah*) is derived occurs in both P (Ex. viii.7) and J (viii.14). The *verb* from which J's noun (*charabah*) is derived occurs twice in Gen. viii.13. This verse is divided between P and J, with the result that the verb "be dry" occurs once in each. It is also to be noted that both *nouns* are used in Josh. iii.-iv. P's word occurs in iv.22 and is assigned to D². J's word occurs in iii.17, iv.18, and is assigned to JE. The only conclusion to be reached is that P's word is not distinctive of P and that J's word may have been used by either E or P.

46 Mowinckel holds, as many others have done, that in the early chapters of Genesis J is composite. But it is significant that he "discovers in the supposed Deutero-Yahwistic sections the presence of the Elohist" (Coppens, *The O. T. and the Critics*, p. 39). This is welcome confirmatory evidence that J and E are far more similar than most critics have been willing to admit. It is also to be noted that Von Rad has proposed an analysis of P which begins in Gen. i. (*Die Priesterschrift im Hexateuch,* 1934).

47 Other examples are: (1) Two words for "tribe" (*matteh* and *shebet*) occur frequently in the Hexateuch. *Matteh* is the usual word in P. But *shebet* also occurs: e.g., *matteh* occurs 35 times in Num. i.-x. (P), but *shebet* is used in iv.18; *matteh* occurs 25 times in Josh. xxi.1-42, but *shebet* appears in vs. 16. In Num. xviii.2, xxxvi.3, Josh. xiii.29 (all P), both words appear in the same verse. (2) Two words for "possession" or "inheritance" (*achuzzah* and *nachalah*) are of frequent occurrence. The former is regarded as especially characteristic of P. But in the long P sections in Num. xxv.-xxxvi. and in Gen. xlviii.3-6 (P) both words are used. (3) Two words (*ohel* and *mishkan*) are used many times in the Pentateuch to describe the Mosaic tabernacle. There are indications of a difference in meaning, *mishkan* (ARV "tabernacle") designating the solid structure of boards covered over with gold and *ohel* (ARV "tent") the tent which covered it (cf. Num. iii.25, 36). But both words are also used apparently in a broad sense to describe the whole structure, i.e., as synonyms (cf. Num. ii.2 with iii.23, 29, 35; in iii.38 they are equated). Yet both the broad and narrow usage of "tabernacle" appears in these chapters which the critics assign to P (cf. Orr, *Problem*, p. 170). (4) In the case of the two words for "generation" (*toledoth* and *dor*), the critics are disposed to regard both as characteristic of P.

48 Driver, *Introd.*, p. 14. This significant confession is made in a brief footnote.

49 Some critics assigns this verse to D. It has even been declared to be the only clear example of Deuteronomic editing in Genesis.

50 The AV renders about 40 different Hebrew and Aramaic words and expressions by "destroy."

51 The four words in order of frequency are: *shachath, saphah, haphak* and *muth* (in *hiphil,* "cause to die").

52 This is noteworthy because the verb for "destroy" (*shachath*) which occurs most frequently in this J passage is in the Flood Narrative assigned to P (5 times).

53 A fourth expression, "was turned," occurs only once (xiv.5J).

54 It is to be noted however that *anoki* occurs repeatedly in Isaiah (in passages regarded by the critics as late), Jer., Zech., and once each in Dan. and Mal.

55 Pp. 16f.

56 In "A Critical Dissertation Concerning the Murder of King Henry," which is appended to the *History*, Robertson in the first paragraph as in

the heading refers to Darnly as "King Henry," a designation never used in pp. 126-160 of the *History* itself.

⁵⁷ E.g., in the chapter entitled "The Execution of Mary Stuart" (vol. xii., pp. 99-259), Froude refers to her (aside from quotations) about 60 times as "Mary Stuart" and about 90 times as the "Queen of Scots." Sometimes one or the other is used in the course of a number of pages; at other times we find both on the same page. On the other hand, Froude uses the expressions "Scotch Queen" and "Scottish Queen" so rarely (aside from quotations) that we might infer that he deliberately avoided them, and a higher critic might challenge the authenticity of the passages in which they occur (Vol. xi.556; vi.328, viii.87, ix.256). Variation in the use of proper names is very marked in the style of Charlotte Brontë. See *Shirley* and *Villette*.

⁵⁸ The occurrence of these two words and their renderings in the versions are striking in 1 Sam. xxv. and 2 Sam. xiv. (*a*) In 1 Sam. xxv. *amah* occurs 6 times (vss. 24^bis, 25, 28, 31, 41), *shiphchah* twice (vss. 27, 41). The only one of our 8 versions which follows the usage of the original by using two words, one for each Hebrew word, is the ARV. (*b*) In 2 Sam. xiv. *amah* occurs twice (vss. 15, 16), *shiphchah* six times (vss. 6, 7, 12, 15, 17, 19). As in 1 Sam. xxv., ARV uses two English words, one for each Hebrew word. But none of the other versions observe the distinction consistently, if at all. Thus AV, which is marked as a rule by variety of diction, uses here only one word ("handmaid") for both Hebrew words.

⁵⁹ In the AV five synonyms render the Hebrew word for journey, viz., removed, departed, took their journey, journeyed, went from. Two synonyms render the word for encamp, viz., encamp and pitch. No reason for the variations is apparent except the desire to secure variety. E.g., in the case of pitch and encamp, the sequence is: pitch (5 times), encamp (5 times), pitch (twice), encamp (once), pitch (6 times), encamp (once), pitch (once), encamp (once), pitch (3 times), etc., etc. It would be absurd to argue that the AV rendering of Num. xxxiii. is a combination of a "pitched" version and an "encamped" version, put together by a redactor. But may it not be equally absurd to attribute the variations in Neh. iii. where "next" is used in vss. 2-12 and "after" in vss. 16-31 (except vss. 17, 19, where "next" is used) to anything but the same desire for variety? It is quite arbitrary to say of Neh. iii. as Batten does: "This proves that we have a composite production, as a single writer would either have used the same term throughout or mixed the words indiscriminately." How are we to know what a "single writer" would do? In Ps. cxxi., the AV uses the word "keep" three times in vss. 3-5 and "preserve" three times in vss. 7-8, to render one and the same Hebrew word. Would variety have been better secured by mixing them up?

⁶⁰ The use of the word "boy" as the rendering of *yeled* in Joel iii.3, Zech. viii.5, is probably due to the presence of the word "girl," the expression "boy and girl" being a natural one. But why is "boy" used once only in the Pentateuch (Gen. xxv.27) and there as the rendering of *naar*? Exactly similar questions arise in the case of the Hebrew. In Gen. xxix.1 "went on his journey" is the rendering of "lifted up his

feet" (ARV marg.). This expression occurs nowhere else in the Old Testament. "Children of the east" occurs nowhere else in the Hexateuch. Why they are used here no one knows. Yet this verse is arbitrarily assigned to E.

61 Cf. Montgomery and Harris, *The Ras Shamra Mythological Texts*, pp. 88f., 98. Cf. also Job xiii.2 and xxxiii.9 where both forms also occur in the same verse.

62 The subject-matter is sometimes responsible for an analysis for which the diction furnishes no basis whatsoever. The only warrant for cutting the words "and Miriam died there and was buried there" (Num. xx.1*b*) out of a P verse and assigning them to JE lies in the fact that if Ex. ii.1-9, xv.20f., and Num. xii.1-15 are assigned to E or JE, P knows so little of Miriam (Num. xxvi.59) that we should not expect her death to be mentioned in it. But "died and was buried" would be quite as appropriate to P as to JE.

63 The Amalekite's account of the death of Saul is given of course only as his own version. It is not necessary to suppose that the writer or compiler of the Books of Samuel was any less conscious than is the reader of today, that the two accounts of Saul's death do not agree.

64 Since Skinner assigns xii.10f. and xxvi.6f. to J, we must either hold that we have here a duplicate account in J or else regard J itself as composite which Skinner and not a few others are quite prepared to do.

65 The brief genealogy in Gen. iv.16-24 (J) is regarded as a doublet of the genealogy in Gen. v. (P). But the one is expressly declared to trace the line of Cain, the eldest son of Adam, while the other gives the descendants of Seth who was born after Cain slew Abel (cf. iv.25f.). That the genealogies are distinct is not rendered questionable by the fact that two names which seem to be the same appear in both lists and that there is a superficial resemblance between a couple of others.—On this theory it is quite natural to assume that Israel murmured for water only once and that Marah (Ex. xv.), Massah (Ex. xvii.) and Meribah (Num. xx.) are parallel accounts which are to be assigned to J, E, or JE, and P respectively. But there is no cogency in the argument that there was only one murmuring; and the three events are so different that the attempt to identify them by ignoring the differences makes it necessary to disregard all those details which give meaning and verisimilitude to each. All that remains is that the people murmured for water and somehow their need was supplied.

66 Skinner, *Genesis*, p. vi. Petrie has recently pointed out that "A curious prejudice exists among critics that no kind of event can occur twice, that each kind of circumstance is unique, and bars repetition" (*Palestine and Israel*, p. 44). The explanation of this "curious prejudice" is to be found, as stated above, in the necessity of finding a way of partitioning JE and of distinguishing J from E when it is admitted that diction and style are insufficient for that purpose.

67 Hupfeld, *Die Quellen*, p. 40.

68 Can it be affirmed in the face of history that God could make only one covenant with Abram and could not repeat, reaffirm, or amplify it, and that therefore Gen. xv. (JE) and xvii. (P) must give two accounts

of one and the same incident? Or that Isaac could not have digged or redigged wells at Beersheba (xxvi.33 J) and used the name his father had used (xxi.31 E)? If Jesus fed the 5000, could He not also feed the 4000? If the temple needed cleansing at the beginning of His earthly ministry, did it not stand in still greater need of it at its close?

69 Similarly in Judg. vii. an attempt has been made to discover two versions of Gideon's victory over the Midianites, a "pitcher-torch" version (J) and a "trumpet" version (E). This leads to a hairsplitting analysis (cf. G. F. Moore, *Judges*).—In Gen. xxxi.45-55 the "heap" and the "pillar" are coupled together *three* times. Yet the attempt is made to assign the former to J and the latter to E (Skinner, *Genesis*, pp. 399f.).

70 Driver assigned vss. 1-2a, 4, 6, 8-10, 13-18, 20-24, 25 [partly], 27-29 to P. The majority of critics assign these verses, with some variations, to E, but admit a "priestly redaction" (cf. Brightman, *Sources*, p. 134). To eliminate Shechem's personal advocacy of his suit for Dinah from the Hamor story, the references to Shechem in vss. 13, 18, 20, 24 must be attributed to the redactor. Furthermore, if the Hamor story is to represent Shechem as innocent of all wrong-doing the statements to the contrary in vss. 13 and 27 must also be R.

71 Skinner, *Genesis*, p. 443. Cf. Hupfeld, *Quellen*, p. 67. To distinguish a "Reuben" story (E) from the "Judah" story (J), many critics regard the "Reuben" of vs.21 as representing an original "Judah." Rudolph rejects the critical analysis of this chapter (*Die Josephgeschichte*, 1933). But his solution of the difficulty (that the Midianites drew Joseph out of the pit and sold him to the Ishmaelites, while the brothers were eating their meal at a distance) seems far-fetched and does not accord with vs.36b. The simplest explanation is that the names Ishmaelite and Midianite were so nearly synonymous as to be used interchangeably or that the caravan was composed of representatives of both. The confusing way in which these words are used, together with the ambiguity of the "they"s, suggests that the narrative in its present form goes back to a time when the story was so fresh and familiar in the minds of all that there could be no uncertainty as to its meaning.

72 The order of the tribes as given in B and C (it begins with Judah) appears elsewhere only in Num. vii. (P). The usual order as given in P begins with Reuben (Gen. xxxv., xlvi., Ex. i., Num. xiii., cf. Ex. vi.). Comp. 1 Chr. ii.1-2. This notable variation does not seem to figure in the critical analysis at all.

73 When we compare these three verses we notice the following facts: (1) There are 11 different nouns (incl. adjectives and participles) in vs. 21 (P) and 17 in vss. 22-23 (J), also one verb in the former and three in the latter. (2) Of the nouns 5 occur in both passages: viz., "all" or "every," "man," "bird," "earth," "cattle"; "that moved" (vs. 21, *romes*) and "creeping things" (vs. 23, *remes*) are from the same root (*ramas*). (3) Of the nouns found only in vs. 21 (P), "flesh" occurs in J (Gen. ii.21, 23, 24, vi.3), "creeping thing" (*sherets*) occurs in Gen. only in i.20 (P, rendered "swarm," also in Lev. and Dt.), but "creep" (the verb) is found in Ex. viii.3 (J, rendered "swarm"), "beast" is frequent in both P (Gen.

i.) and J (Gen. ii.-iv.). (4) Of the nouns found only in vss. 22-23 (J), "spirit" occurs in Gen. i.2 (P) and "spirit of life" in vi.17 (P), "ground" (*adamah*) in i.25 (P), "creeping thing" (*remes*) in i.24, 25, 26 (P); "face" and "heaven" occur in both J and P. Noah is mentioned both in J and P. (5) The verb "die" (*gawa*) which occurs in vii.21 (P) is rare. It occurs only six times in Gen. (all P). (6) Of the 3 verbs in vss. 22-23 (J), "die" (*muth*) occurs 8 times in Gen. v. (P), "blot out" is P in Num. v. 23, "left" (*shaar*) is rare in the Pent., usually P, but in Ex. viii.9, 11 it is J. (7) This leaves only a few words in vss. 22-23 (J) for special consideration: "breath" (*neshamah*), elsewhere in Pent. only Gen. ii.7 (J) and Deut. xx.16; "nostrils" (*aph*) occurs in ii.7 (J) and in this sense is rare in Gen. (iii.19, xix.1, xxiv.27, in J; xlii.6, xlviii.12, in E, also Ex. xv.8); "dry land" (*charabah*), elsewhere in Pent. only Ex. xiv. 21b (J), but cf. Gen. viii.13 where the verb "be dry" occurs in vs. 13a in P and 13b in J; "living thing" (*yequm*), elsewhere only Gen. vii.4 (J) and Deut. xi.6; "only" (*ak*) occurs in P in Gen. ix.4, 5 and Ex. xii.15, 16. Consequently while this brief passage is characterized by the use of an unusually varied vocabulary, which is clearly intended to emphasize the extent of the destruction, there is no sufficient reason for assigning vs. 21 to a different source from vss. 22-23.

74 A bird is sent out *three* times. This narrative might be regarded as repetitious and be divided between P, J and E. But Astruc, Eichhorn and Hupfeld gave it to the Jehovist as do more recent critics.

75 Astruc was consistent in assigning vii.18-20 to three sources (vs. 18 to the Jehovist, vs. 19 to the Elohist, vs. 20 to a third source [C]). But the generally accepted view among critics is that all three verses belong to P. In dealing with vss. 21-23, Astruc assigned vs. 21 to the Jehovist, vs. 22 and vs. 23 to the same source as vs. 20 (C). But Eichhorn's view that vs. 21 belongs to the Elohist has been generally accepted. Vs. 22 was assigned by Eichhorn, DeWette and Hupfeld to the Elohist (P); Wellhausen, Driver and others give it to J. Vs. 23 was given by Eichhorn, DeWette, Hupfield, Wellhausen and Driver to J. Cornill thinks vs. 23b may be P. This indicates that the critics do not regard the repetitions as requiring a three-fold analysis. It also shows that the diction is not clearly indicative of source. Von Rad, of course, finds both of his P sources present in these chapters.

76 Somewhat similar is the record of the sending out of the spies (Num. xiii.). The command to Moses (vss. 1-2) is followed by the summary statement that Moses carried out the command (vs. 3a), and the status and names of the men sent out (vss. 3b-15) is given, ending with an attestation and a statement regarding Joshua (vs. 16). Then in view of the lengthy digression, it is again stated that Moses sent them out (17a), his instructions are given (vss. 17b-20) and vss. 21-25 tell of their execution of the command. There is no sufficient warrant for dividing up this narrative. Yet the critics assign vss. 1-17a to P and most of the rest to JE.

77 For a fuller discussion of the Plagues, see the article by the present writer, "Old Testament Emphases and Modern Thought" (*Princeton Theol. Review*, Oct. 1925, pp. 606-36).

78 A unique expression in the Pent. (cf. vs. 4). Its presence here leads Skinner to suspect Deuteronomic influence, despite the fact that the hand of D is not supposed to appear to any marked degree, if at all, in Genesis.

79 Skinner, *Genesis*, p. 339. Pfeiffer pays an enthusiastic tribute to the excellence of J's literary style (*Introd.*, pp. 156f.). Eissfeldt regards this chapter as composite, listing it under both J and E, but makes no attempt to partition it between them (*Einleitung*, pp. 223f.).

80 Compare Josh. ii.15f. where we are told that Rahab let the spies down by a cord through the window, and then of the instructions she gave them for their escape, etc. Clearly vss. 16-21 are intended to supply further details regarding what took place *before* Rahab let them down. In 1 Kgs. xviii.30f. we have first the summary statement, "And he (Elijah) repaired the altar." Then we are told how he did it. In Num. x.11-12 we have a brief statement that the Israelites left Sinai and journeyed to the wilderness of Paran. This is followed in vss. 13-36 by a list of particulars all of which enlarge upon this important statement. The critics assign at least vss. 11-28 to P.

81 Cf. Gen. xii.4f. where the statement that "Abram went and Lot went with him" is almost immediately followed by the words "And Abram took Sarai his wife and Lot his brother's son . . . and they went forth to go . . ." Here the critics cut vss. 4*b*-5 out of a J context and give it to P. Somewhat similar is the account of Jacob's death. It is briefly referred to in xlvii.28, because his living 17 years in Egypt indicated that he died at 147 (vs. 9). Then vss. 29-31 narrate a request regarding his burial which he made of Joseph in anticipation of his death and perhaps a considerable time before it. Then we read of his last illness (xlviii.1), of the blessing which he bestowed on Joseph's sons (vss.2-22), of his blessing of all his sons (chap. xlix.1-28), of a charge to all his sons regarding his burial at Macpelah (vss. 29-32), of his death and burial (xlix.33-l.14). Any one familiar with Hebrew narrative style will hesitate to find three documents here and assign xlvii.28 to P, vss. 29-31 to J and xlviii.1-2*a* to E, and to divide the rest mainly between J and E. The main reason for assigning xlvii.29-31, which records Jacob's *request of Joseph* regarding his burial to J and the *command* he gave to his *sons* to the same effect in xlix.29-32 to P, lies in the fact that the one passage refers to the oath described in Gen. xxiv.2 which the critics assign to J, while the other refers to matters recorded in chap. xxiii. which they assign to P. That Jacob could only give instructions once is preposterous. The fact that he first exacted a solemn promise from Joseph and then instructed all his sons to the same effect merely shows how deeply concerned he was that his wishes be carried out.

82 Outside of Genesis both words occur in other sources: "run" is E in Num. xi.27, P in Num. xvi.47; "dungeon" is J in Ex. xii.29, D in Deut. vi.11, P in Lev. xi.36.

83 Not only do nearly all the allusions to "shaving" occur in P, but P uses *two* expressions, "shave" and "cause a razor to pass over the flesh." Both expressions are used in the "law of the Nazirite" (Num. vi): the one in vss. 9, 18, 19, the other in vs. 5 (cf. viii.7). Observe (1) the

elaborate detail in vss. 3-5; (2) the expression "all the days," etc., which occurs three times (vss. 4, 5, 6), each phrased slightly different from the other two; (3) the expression "this is the law of the Nazirite" which occurs twice (vss. 13, 21), vs. 21 being a concluding summary, which emphasizes the whole (compare the concluding summaries in Lev. vii.37f., xi.46f., xiii.59, xiv.54-57, xxvi.46, Num. v.29f.).

84 "Make peace" occurs nowhere else in the Pentateuch. "Make (literally, cut) a covenant" occurs in J, E and D (also in 2 Chron., Ezra, Neh.). "Cause to live" is found in J, E, D and P. "Princes of (or, in) the congregation" is rare in the Pentateuch, and cannot easily be assigned to P in all passages (note Num. xvi.2b P, xxxii.2 JE). Nor can "prince" or "congregation" be regarded as exclusively P. "Prince" occurs in E (Ex. xxii.28), "congregation" in JE (Num. xiii.26b, xvi.26, xxxii.4). "Swear to" occurs in all four documents, especially often in D.

85 Had this sentence been cast in some such form as the following, "And Joshua together with the princes of the congregation having made peace with them, and spared their lives with a solemn oath, entered into a covenant with them," the source analysis would have been much more difficult. It is the fact that the three parts of the verse are loosely connected by "and" which makes partition of it a simple matter. To say that it justifies it is something quite different!

86 Other examples of compound sentences which certain of the critics partition between two or three sources are: Gen. xxx.22 "And *Elohim* remembered Rachel [P], and *Elohim* hearkened unto her [E], and he opened her womb [J]." So Cornill; Driver assigns both the first and second to E.—Num. xiii.17, "And Moses sent them to spy out the land of Canaan [P]; and he said unto them, Get you up this way by the south [J]; and go up into the hill-country [E]." Driver does not try to separate J and E.—Num. xiv.1, "And all the congregation lifted up their voice [P], and they cried [E]; and the people wept that night [J]." Driver says of this verse "mainly P."—Observe how the emphatic elaboration in Num. xxv. 1-5 makes it easy to divide it into a J account (vss. 1b, 2, 4) and an E account (1a, 3, 5). [The analysis in the three passages in Numbers is that given by Brightman.] In none of the above verses is there any sufficient basis for the analysis. All three could easily be given to one source. But analysis helps to establish the continuity of the documents and to support the doublet theory. So each verse is treated as composite.—A striking illustration of the extremes to which the search for duplicates can be carried is Ex. xv. Most critics, apparently, assign the song of Moses (vss. 1-18) and that of Miriam (vss. 20-21) to the same source (Driver, to E). But McNeile (*Com. on Exodus*) assigns the former to J, the latter to E and remarks: "The description would lose its force if Miriam merely repeated a song composed by Moses. It is E's account of the song which J in vs. 1 ascribes to Moses." The inference seems to be that the redactor has combined two accounts of the song, a J account which attributed it to Moses and an E account which regarded it as Miriam's, and to avoid needless repetition, simply gave one verse of the Miriam version. Yet the narrative makes it quite clear that Miriam simply took the opening

sentences of Moses' song and made them into a chant or response for the women to sing. What is there in this which is unnatural or lacking in "force"?

87 See, for example, the *Biblia Hebraica* edited by Rudolf Kittel from which the following examples in Genesis are taken. Procksch in his Commentary on Genesis makes considerable use of metrics.

88 Vs. 5-13 of this chapter are a good specimen of repetition and elaboration. Vs. 7 might be regarded as stating sufficiently the general principle of which the case of Zelophehad's daughters is a specific instance. But vs. 8 goes on to state this general rule expressly and then vs. 9 repeats vs. 7 almost word for word.

89 Compare Gen. xv.2-3 which has been already discussed.

90 "Do" is one of the most frequently occurring verbs in the Old Testament and "speak" is as little characteristic of P as "say" is of J. "Set time" (*moed*) is P in Gen. i.14, xvii.21, xxi.2, but J or E in Gen. xviii.14, Ex. ix.5, xiii.10, xxiii.15.

91 Except for certain verses in Gen. xv. which are assigned by Driver and others to E.

92 The unanimity with which these three entire chapters (i., xvii., xxiii.) are assigned to P is rather singular since the methods which are employed by the critics to break up other chapters seem to be no less applicable to them. Chapter i., as we have seen, could be divided into a fiat and a fulfilment narrative much more easily than the account of the plagues; and one of them could be given to P, the other to E. Chap. xvii. would yield two accounts of the covenant of circumcision, the one referring to circumcision at puberty as illustrated by the case of Ishmael (E), the other to the circumcision of infants on the 8th day, as illustrated by Isaac, yet unborn (P). Chap. xxiii. would yield two accounts of Abraham's acquisition of Macpelah, a gift version and a purchase version.

93 As has been already pointed out while Driver assigns these verses to P, most critics assign them to E.

94 The division of the Psalter into five books goes back to ancient times. Delitzsch, for example, traces it back to the Old Testament period. The tradition that this was intended to make the Psalter correspond to the Law seems inherently probable.

95 All critics are agreed that sections from J, E, JE, D, and P are found in Joshua, or at least passages which resemble these Pentateuchal sources. There are some who find the "prophetic" sources (J and E) even in Judges, Samuel and Kings. This resemblance is readily explicable as due to the fact that the Pentateuch, owing to its great authority as Mosaic, early became a standard of literary style, which subsequent writers followed either consciously or unconsciously.

96 Cornill, *Introduction*, p. 155.

97 According to Gray, "not only does the Pentateuch stand apart, but the books of Joshua, Judges, Samuel, Kings, in spite of certain connecting links, attained substantially their present form by different editorial processes (*Critical Introduction*, p. 52). On the other hand Pfeiffer regards the Pentateuch as "only the first part of a work in nine volumes

(Gen.-Kings)." Of this work he says: "The first five volumes, comprising the history to the death of Moses and the Mosaic legislation, were separated from the last four and canonized as the Law of Moses about 400 B.C.; the four historical books that followed (Josh., Judg., Sam., Kings) were not recognized as sacred scripture until two centuries later" (*Introd.*, pp. 129f.). This is a very positive statement. But the only evidence in support of it is that, by applying the same methods to the analysis of the four books as to the five, similar results can be obtained, as was to be expected. But where is there the slightest evidence of the existence of a nine-volume collection which was subsequently divided into two collections, collections of such diverse intrinsic value that it took the second 200 years longer than the first to attain "canonicity"?

[98] Skinner, *Genesis*, p. xxxix.

[99] Skinner, *Genesis*, p. lvii. Yet Volz has ventured to assert that Gen. xxiii. is J and not P and to reject the splitting-up of xxix.31-xxx.24 and of chap. xxxiv.

[100] Rollin H. Walker, *A Study of Genesis and Exodus*, p. 24. Such is the necessary result of the claim that the redactor combined sources which were mutually contradictory. It must be admitted that the task of harmonizing passages may seem at times difficult or even impossible, and the attempts to harmonize them may seem far-fetched. But it is certainly more natural to suppose that the writer or compiler regarded them as compatible than to hold that they are contradictory and that he knew this to be the case.

[101] Skinner, *Genesis*, p. viii.

[102] J. E. McFadyen, *Old Testament Scenes and Characters*, p. 21.

[103] Walker goes on to say, in the paragraph quoted above: "To stand for the necessary accuracy of all the details would force us to the absurdity of believing at the same time the account which says that God caused a strong east wind to drive all the waters of the Red Sea to the west so that the children of Israel could pass over, and the contradictory account which says that, instead of being driven out of the way by a wind, Moses stretched forth his rod and the waters parted in both directions and stood up like a wall on either side." Here the "absurdity" is of the critic's own making. The narrative tells us quite plainly that it was when Moses stretched out his rod that the Lord caused the wind to blow (Ex. xiv. 21).

[104] If it is so clear from E's account of the expulsion of Hagar (Gen. xxi. 8-21) that Ishmael must have been a small child, little more than a baby, is it not remarkable that the redactor who fitted JE into the framework of P should have so plainly represented him as a youth some 16 years of age (xvi.15, xxi.5), when he could easily have avoided the difficulty by a slight change in his dates? Is it not far simpler to suppose that the editor saw no such contradiction as is alleged? It is not necessary to hold that Abram placed both the bottle *and* the lad on Hagar's shoulder (xxi.14). The words "and the lad" may connect simply with the words "and gave." Similarly the words, "and she cast the child," may mean that when Ishmael was in a fainting condition, she staggered along with this child, who was as large as herself, in her arms till she reached the

shade of a bush and "dumped" him down there (let him fall from her nerveless arms), so exhausted that she could not carry him a step further or hold him a moment longer (cf., e.g., Payne Smith in Ellicott's *Commentary*). The fact that many artists have represented Ishmael as a small child does not justify the critics in using such an interpretation to make P contradict E.

105 *The Book of the Prophet Ezekiel*, p. xiv. That the "Westminster" series in which this commentary appeared represented the "critical" viewpoint is sufficiently indicated by the fact that the volume on Genesis was prepared by Driver. As to Ezekiel Driver was quite as emphatic as Redpath: "No critical question arises in connection with the authorship of the book, the whole from beginning to end bearing unmistakably the stamp of a single mind" (*Introd.*, p. 279). Pfeiffer distinguishes "three sides of Ezekiel's teaching" and points out (*Introd.*, p. 544) that I. G. Matthews in his *An American Commentary to the O.T.* (1939) tears them apart and attributes them to "three or more distinct individuals." This is a striking illustration of the subjectivity of the higher critical method and the inconclusiveness of the conclusions which result from it. It is quite possible for the critic to become so intent on the detection of variations and differences as to be incapable of recognizing those evidences of unity and coherence which he would otherwise regard as proof that the document which he is seeking to partition is a self-consistent whole.

## NOTES TO PART II (Pp. 127-202)

1 The philosophy of Hegel (died 1831) gave a great impetus to the study of history. But Hegel's interest was not in history *per se*, but in the *philosophy* of history. Both Hegel, the idealist, and Comte, the positivist (died 1857), used history to prove their respective theories regarding the *development* of human history. They regarded Mosaic monotheism as a development from lower forms, magic or fetichism.

2 Graf had as a young man attended the lectures of Reuss at Strassburg (1833). Reuss then announced, but did not publish until many years later, the theory of the late date of P. Wellhausen in his *Prolegomena* declares that he had "learnt most and best" from Vatke who had introduced Hegelian principles into his History of the Old Testament (1835). Westphal has summarized the development briefly as follows: "We shall call, once for all, *Historical School*—without pronouncing any judgment whatsoever by the term—the school whose founders have placed in honor the *historical* method, and who through the expression of views sharply opposed to those of tradition, have provoked the debate of which the *historical* value of the Pentateuch is the subject. This school, the precursors of which were De Wette, Reuss, George and Vatke, had Henri Graf for its founder, and bears today the name of Wellhausen" (Westphal, *Les Sources du Pentateuque*, II, xix.). Among the most influential of its early advocates were Kuenen, Budde and Stade on the Continent, Robertson Smith and Driver in Great Britain, Briggs and W. R. Harper in America.

³ Cf. Green, *Higher Criticism*, p. 140; De Wette, in agreement with Stähelin, Bleek and Tuch, assigned the Elohistic document to the time of Samuel or Saul (*Introd.*, 5th ed., 1840, cf. Parker Trans. II, pp. 105ff., 146).

⁴ Driver, in the first edition of his *Introduction* (1891), assigned the Book of the Covenant to J, but later (1897) adopted the view that it belonged to E.

⁵ Regarding the Book of Esther as "a brilliant hoax," Pfeiffer defends this view of it by saying: "Nor was such a successful deception unprecedented among the Jews. From the modern point of view, three of the most influential writings in the Old Testament—the Deuteronomic Code, the Priestly Code, and Daniel—were technically fraudulent—although their authors were sincere men, free from guile, and inspired by noble religious ideals" (*Introduction*, p. 745). Albright has recently taken vigorous issue with this view from the standpoint of archeology: "Nearly every book and passage of the Old Testament has been stigmatized as a literary forgery by at least one scholar. Now it cannot be emphasized too strongly that there is hardly any evidence at all in the ancient Near East for documentary or literary fabrications" (*Stone Age*, p. 45; cf. p. 244).

⁶ Gray, *Critical Introduction*, p. 33.

⁷ E.g., Joshua, Samuel and the prophets in the Old Testament, Stephen and Paul in the New Testament, state this fact very definitely. In the woe which He pronounced on Jerusalem (Matt. xxiii.), Jesus pointed out that the Jews were rejecting Him as their fathers had rejected the prophets; and He declared that if they were true followers of Moses, they would accept His teachings (Jn. v.46f.).

⁸ Comp., e.g., the brief summary of opinion given by Brightman (*Sources*, pp. 96f.). According to Morgenstern (*The Oldest Document in the Hexateuch*, 1927), this so-called Decalogue of J originally formed part of an ancient Kenite document (K) which began he thinks with the birth of Moses and traces of which are to be found in J and E. He dates it before 899 B. C. and believes it to have formed the basis of Asa's reform (1 Kgs. xv.). Barton has hailed it as "the most noteworthy addition to our knowledge of the literary origins of the Pentateuch made during the last twenty years" (*Haverford Symposium*, p. 50). Eissfeldt (*Einleitung*, p. 147) and Pfeiffer (*Introd.*, p. 224) are much more cautious in discussing it. Oesterley and Robinson dismiss it as of little importance (p. 40) and Rowley (in Manson's *Companion*) does not mention it.

⁹ The parenthetical way in which the first and most important of the commands is introduced—"for thou shalt worship no other god"—is sufficient proof of this.

¹⁰ "Appear before" might be rendered "see the face of." "Besought" might be rendered "mollify, or sweeten, the face of."

¹¹ The stealing of Laban's "gods" (xxxi.30), also called *teraphim* (vss. 19, 34, 35), is appealed to as proof of idolatrous worship in patriarchal times. This narrative is assigned to E. But it does not state that Jacob knew of or connived in Rachel's action. And even if he did, xxxv.1-8 (also E) would indicate that he later realized that such use of images was sinful. In Judg. xvii.-xviii., such worship is clearly idolatrous, and Samuel

links idolatry with "iniquity" and "nothingness" (1 Sam. xv.23). *Teraphim* were used by Michael to deceive Saul's messengers when David's life was in peril. This incident resembles Rachel's in some respects. That the Israelites often lapsed into idolatry or near-idolatry is repeatedly stated and deplored in the Bible. The important point is that nowhere is idolatry spoken of with approval in the Old Testament, neither in Genesis nor elsewhere.

12 The fact that Elijah exterminated the Baal worship of Jezebel, but as far as is known made no attempt to destroy the worship at the shrines of the calves at Dan and Bethel, does not prove that he approved or tolerated it. His attitude is clearly shown by the fearful woe he pronounced on Ahab in the garden of Naboth, which he likens to that visited on Jeroboam for his "provocation" (1 Kgs. xxi.19ff.). The task given to Elijah was great enough as it was. Humanly speaking it almost cost him his life. The task of rebuking the priest at Bethel might well in the patience of God wait for another Elijah-like prophet, Amos the herdsman of Tekoa. Furthermore it seems clear that it was the purpose of God to allow the worship of the calves to continue in the Northern Kingdom that it might be a test of obedience and a stumbling block to every one of the kings of that kingdom and might in the final overthrow of the Ten Tribes give to all Israel a terrible object-lesson as to the consequences of the breaking of the first two commandments of the Decalogue (2 Kgs. xvii.).

13 Orr, *Problem*, p. 144.

14 Oesterley and Robinson, *Hebrew Religion*, pp. 131f.

15 Barton, *Religion of Israel*, pp. 61f. It is widely held by the critics that Yahweh was originally a Kenite deity, that the Kenites were metal workers who worshipped a fire-god, the god of the smoking mountain (a volcano), and that the story of Moses' sojourn with Jethro, properly understood, tells how Moses became a devotee of this god of the Kenites. (cf. Lods, *La Religion*, pp. 52f.) But according to the Biblical narrative this Deity revealed Himself to Moses as the God of the patriarchs, Abraham, Isaac and Jacob (Ex. ii.24, iii.6, 15, 16, iv.5, vi.3, 8) and Jethro himself acknowledged Jehovah's preeminence (Ex. xviii.11). Albright asserts that Moses was a monotheist. His definition of monotheist is this: "If . . . the term 'monotheist' means one who teaches the existence of only one God, the creator of everything, the source of justice, who is equally powerful in Egypt, in the desert, and in Palestine, who has no sexuality and no mythology, who is human in form but cannot be seen by human eye and cannot be represented in any form—then the founder of Yahwism was certainly a monotheist" (p. 207). In this definition the words "who is human in form" are especially to be noted.

16 For a historical and critical study of these theories, cf. W. Schmidt, *The Origin and Growth of Religion* (1931). The following points are of especial interest. Comte in his Positivistic Philosophy (cir. 1840) had found in fetishism the origin of man's religious beliefs; and this theory was developed by Lubbock (*The Origin of Civilization*, 1870). In 1856 Max Müller had published his *Essay on Comparative Mythology*, and he came

to be regarded as "the Founder of Comparative Religion." J. F. McLennan's *Primitive Marriage* (1866) and the article "On the Worship of Animals and Plants" (1869-70) brought totemism "into close connection with religion"; and it became "an integral part of all succeeding evolutionary theories, as those of Lubbock, Tylor, Spencer and others," notably Robertson Smith and J. G. Frazer. In 1892, J. H. King (*The Supernatural, its Origin, Nature and Evolution*) sought in magic (impersonal 'power') an older form of religion than animism.

17 The Hebrew says "the place," but this definiteness does not define the location of the place but merely describes it as the place where Jacob spent the night. "A certain place" is a good rendering, since the word "lighted upon" (i.e., "encountered") suggests the casualness of the event, as indicated by the words "for the sun had set" or "was about to set."

18 The language is intentionally indefinite. Any suitable stone would do.

19 Cf. Skinner, *Genesis*, p. 376; Oesterley and Robinson, *Hebrew Religion*, p. 42; Lods, *La Religion d'Israel*, p. 18.

20 In *The Old Testament: An American Translation* (1927), the rendering is, "reaching a certain place." In *The Short Bible: An American Translation* (1933), the Old Testament passages of which were translated by the same four men (Powis Smith, Meek, Waterman, Gordon), the rendering is changed to "reaching a certain sanctuary."

21 *Great Men and Movements in Israel*, pp. 314f. This law contains two provisions: the use of unhewn stone and the prohibition of steps. The reason for the second is expressly stated. It says nothing about the "feelings" of the stone, but is to safeguard the *purity* of the worship by preventing any indelicate acts. No explanation of the first requirement is given. One which naturally suggests itself is, that the hewing of the stone would show its fragility and man's power over it, while the altar was intended to represent God's permanent provisions for the expiation of man's sinful and wilful acts.

22 Even today there are people calling themselves Christians who regard the finding of a horseshoe or the carrying of a rabbit's foot as "lucky." Some years ago a book was published which dealt elaborately with the subject of *Kentucky Superstitions*. The author (D. L. Thomas) had collected almost 4000 of them. Such or similar superstitions can be duplicated in ancient Babylonian magical texts. They are just as modern as they are ancient, and as ancient as they are modern.

23 Skinner (*Genesis*, p. 246) so characterizes Budde's view.

24 "Oak of the early rain," "archer oak," are equally possible or probable meanings. Furthermore the fact that the Israelites retained many pagan names does not prove that they themselves were pagan. We use the word Wednesday. That does not mean that we are (still) worshippers of Woden.

25 The expression "fear of Isaac" (Gen. xxxi.42) as a designation of the God of the patriarchs is a striking one. As the writer has shown elsewhere (*Princeton Theological Review*, XVI., pp. 299f.), it throws light in a remarkable way upon Isaac's attitude toward the God who had caused

him to pass through the fearful experience recorded in Gen. xxii. The word occurs about 50 times; and the rendering "fear" is strongly supported by the ancient versions and has been generally accepted by scholars. Yet Albright speaks of it as having caused "much difficulty" and proposes a meaning "kinsman" (based on the meaning "thigh," Job xl.17), for which there is little basis (*op. cit.*, p. 189). The only reason the meaning "fear" is difficult is because it stands in the way of an interpretation which supports the view that the patriarchs like their Semitic ancestors claimed (physical) kinship with their god or gods.

26 Peake's *Commentary*, p. 207. Peake refers in support of this interpretation to Frazer's *Golden Bough*. For it is such "comparative" study which enables the critic to remember something which the Old Testament legislator forgot many centuries ago! Frazer tells us: "The instrument for the detection of savagery under civilization is the comparative method, which, applied to the human mind, enables us to trace man's intellectual and moral evolution, just as, applied to the human body, it enables us to trace his physical evolution from lower forms of animal life" (*Folk-Lore in the Old Testament*, p. ix.f.).

27 Wellhausen, *Prolegomena*, p. 88. Cf. Barton, *Religion of Israel*, p. 12; Oesterley and Robinson, *Hebrew Religion*, pp. 96f.; Lods, *La Religion d'Israel*, p. 28.

28 *Problem of the Old Testament*, p. 320.

29 Oesterley and Robinson, *Hebrew Religion*, p. 143.

30 Barton, *Religion of Israel*, p. 86. According to Albright, "Jeroboam may well have been harking back to early Israelite traditional practice when he made the 'golden calves' " (*Stone Age*, p. 230; cf. Peake's *Commentary*, p. 301). Barton, in quoting this verse has construed the plural verb as singular. But the fact that the verb is plural is significant. For it indicates clearly that this worship of the two calves was not only idolatrous but polytheistic.

31 *Op. cit.*, p. 203.

32 "The worship of animals formed an integral part of the religions of the Egyptians in every period of their history" (Budge, *From Fetichism to God*, p. 67). The Apis cult goes back to very early times and at Alexandria the Serapis worship continued until the Serapeum was destroyed by Constantine (*id.*, p. 73). "Bull worship is a very common phenomenon throughout the history of the human race" (Mond and Myers, *The Bucheum*, 1934, Vol. I, p.1).

33 Lods describes the Canaanite religion as well calculated to "appeal strongly to the senses by the orgiastic character of certain of its manifestations: lamentations for the dead, sacred prostitution, ecstatic prophecy" (*La Religion*, p. 82). Speaking of the conquest and the extermination of the Canaanites, Albright says: "Thus the Canaanites, with their orgiastic nature-worship, their cult of fertility in the form of serpent symbols and sensuous nudity, and their gross mythology, were replaced by Israel, with its nomadic simplicity and purity of life, its lofty monotheism, and its severe code of ethics" (*op. cit.*, p. 214). He also refers to "the gross Phoenician mythology which we know from Ugarit and Philo Byb-

lius" (p. 214, cf. p. 178). That the same element of sensuality was a marked feature of Egyptian religion is pointed out by Budge (*From Fetichism,* pp. 62f., 431).

34 According to Albright, "Goddesses of fertility play a much greater rôle among the Canaanites than they do among any other ancient people. . . . These Canaanite goddesses were nearly always represented in iconography as naked, as we know both from the many hundreds of 'astarte' plaques from the period 1700-1100 B.C. which have been discovered by excavators and from the fact that the Canaanite goddesses Astarte and Qudshu (or Qadesh) always appear naked in Egyptian portrayals of this age, in striking contrast to the modestly garbed native Egyptian goddesses. Another dominant characteristic of the Canaanite goddesses in question was their savagery . . ." (*op. cit.,* p. 177).

35 Despite his claim that the worship of Israel was aniconic, Albright speaks of the calf worship as "a dangerous revival since the taurine associations of Baal, lord of heaven [he connects it as we have seen with Canaan rather than Egypt], were too closely bound up with the fertility cult in its most insidious aspects to be safe" (*op. cit.,* p. 230).

36 As expressed, for example, in Hosea's denunciation: "They sacrifice with harlots [i.e., sacred prostitutes]" (iv. 14).

37 Cf. Driver, *Introd.,* pp. 185, 199. To the same effect Cornill, ". . . it [the Deuteronomic revision] completely dominates the representation in Joshua, Judges and Kings" (*Introd.,* p. 224).

38 We are told by the critics that the fact that the word rendered "harlot" in Hos. iv.14 (*qedeshah*) means "holy" or "consecrated" (woman), i.e., hierodule, "shows that in its origin there was no thought of immorality" (Oesterley & Robinson, *Hebrew Religion,* p. 126). This may be more or less true of pagan religions in general. But if it is taken as applying to the religion of Israel, it implies that the attitude of the prophets (and of Deut. considered as Mosaic) was extreme and constituted a radical departure from established custom. It is not to be wondered at, therefore, that these writers denounce the doctrine of the prophets that retribution must follow Israel's sin and tell us: "At the worst, Israel was no worse than other nations, and had neither merited the exile nor its degradation as a subject nation ever since" (p. 331). This is understandable and quite logical. If the religion of Israel did not differ essentially from that of other nations, the vehement denunciations of the prophets were severe and unjust. But it is difficult to understand how these writers can go on to say, ". . . indeed, it was better than the other nations, for it alone of all nations acknowledged the One and Only God." Did the unique status of Israel as a "holy nation" which worshipped "the One and Only God" permit them for centuries to practice the abominations of the heathen as a legitimate part of His worship? Or were the prophets, as the expounders and defenders of the Mosaic Law (Mal. iv.4), justified in their utter repudiation of such *abominations?* That is the question at issue between the Critical and the Biblical views of Old Testament history. And the answer of the critics is one which should be abhorrent and repulsive to every worshipper of the "One and Only God."

39 Cf. Canon Harford in Peake's *Commentary*, p. 187; also H. P. Smith, *The Religion of Israel*, p. 112. Gen. xxii. which is divided between J and E is treated as a "prophetic" protest against the practice of human sacrifice. This would imply that pre-prophetic religion had considered it lawful and right.

40 In support of this view it is pointed out that Elijah went to Horeb, the mount of God. The weakness of this argument is shown by three things: (1) Elijah's prayer at Carmel to the God of Israel was answered immediately by fire, while the priests of the Canaanite Baal received no answer to their protracted intercessions; (2) Elijah was fleeing from Jezebel; (3) The words, "What doest thou here Elijah?", sound like a rebuke and suggest that the prophet whose God had shown His Almighty presence at Carmel should not have fled away at the threat of Ahab's bloodthirsty queen.

41 "Except that he [Yahweh] was more powerful, he did not differ essentially from Chemosh of Moab . . ." (H. P. Smith, *Religion of Israel*, p. 61). "Externally and to a superficial observer it may well have seemed that, even in the times of the Monarchy, the religion of Israel was distinguishable only in certain minor points from the religion of the neighboring tribes" (Principal Joyce, in Peake's *Commentary*, p. 428).

42 E.g., Loisy, *The Religion of Israel* (1910), pp. 95-140, especially pp. 102ff.; J. M. P. Smith, *The Moral Life of the Hebrews* (1923); Oesterley and Robinson, *Hebrew Religion* (1930); Lods, *La Religion d'Israel* (1939).

43 Cf. Wm. Schmidt, *Origin and Growth of Religion*, pp. 167-218. After pointing out the difficulties which Lang encountered in securing a hearing for his view, Schmidt traces the subsequent history and, after referring to the writings of a number of scholars, he expresses himself confidently as follows: "No one who has read the long list of eminent researchers given in the preceding sections can fail to realize that the question of 'high gods of low races' has passed beyond the first stage, in which it fought for existence or was tacitly neglected, and has at last reached a certain degree of quiet security" (p. 217).

44 Lewis Browne, *This Believing World*, p. 236. This is in line with the statement of Wellhausen, "The prophets have been the spiritual destroyers of the old Israel" (*Prolegomena*, p. 491). According to A. Eustace Haydon, "Yahweh was rescued from this drift into oblivion by the great prophets of the eighth and seventh centuries" (*Biography of the Gods*, p. 230).

45 Barton, *Religion of Israel*, p. 101; Oesterley and Robinson, *Hebrew Religion*, p. 207.

46 What the critics do in effect is to substitute the miracle of the discovery of this high conception of Deity by the prophets for the miracle of God's revelation of Himself to Abraham, Moses, and the prophets. According to Powis Smith, "The eighth century in Israel stands out from all the centuries by reason of the fact that it produced four great Hebrew prophets, Amos, Hosea, Isaiah, and Micah. The appearance of these men marked a new era in the religious life of Israel and in the history of mankind" (*The Moral Life of the Hebrews*, p. 73). "The eighth century . . . produced"! How it came to produce these great men, we are not

told. Perhaps like Topsy they just grew! Loisy recognized the difficulty to some extent at least, when he said: "One of the most singular characteristics of Jahvism is assuredly the evolution which out of the seer, diviner, and sorcerer, out of the raving enthusiast, produced the prophet of the last period of the monarchy; the judge of kings, the defender of the poor, the preacher of righteousness, always preoccupied with a future by the traditions of his office, but subordinating his predictions to his moral teaching" (*The Religion of Israel*, p. 143). This is a "most singular" characteristic, one which makes the prophets stand out conspicuously among the religious leaders of mankind. How is it to be explained? Were the prophets the "freak" product of naturalistic evolution? or, Were they the channels of a supernatural revelation? Did they discover new truths about God? or, Did they call Israel back to the worship of the God who had called Abraham and who had delivered their fathers from the bondage of Egypt and made known to them His holy law amid the thunders of Sinai?

47 The attribute of love in the God of Israel is clearly set forth in the Book of Deuteronomy which purports to be Mosaic. The same is true of many of the Psalms which are assigned by the headings to David.

48 This question has already been asked in xl.18, 25. Here it is repeated with a four-fold emphasis of iteration which makes it especially impressive.

49 The most impressive account of sacrifice in Genesis is in chap. xxii. But the only thing that is stressed in it is the obedience of Abraham to the command of God.

50 *Der Prophet Jeremia*, p. 123.

51 B. S. Easton begins his statement and defense of the Wellhausen Hypothesis in the *Internat. Stand. Bible Encyc.* (p. 754) by appealing to this passage.

52 This expression is rendered by AV and ARV in 2 Kgs. xxii.13, 2 Chron. xxxiv.21 by "concerning the words of this (the) book." In view of the context, which tells us that the king rent his clothes when he heard the words of the book, "concerning" seems decidedly weak. "On account of" or "because of" would be better.

53 In Num. xvi.49 (AV, "about the matter of") and xxv.18 (AV, "for Peor's sake") might well be rendered, "because of" or "on account of." The words "upon the matter that" in Dt. xxiii.4 and 2 Sam. xiii.22 are rendered by AV and ARV "because that."

54 Since "upon the matters of" is the fullest form, we might expect it to be the strongest and most emphatic of the three, and therefore the most likely to have such a meaning.

55 One of the most striking differences between the Babylonian Deluge Story and the account given in Genesis appears in the attitude to sacrifice. The Babylonian account declares that after the flood, when Ut-Napishtim offered sacrifice, "the gods gathered like flies above the offerer of sacrifice." Plainly they were hungry, even starving, because they had not been fed by sacrifice for several weeks. Such a suggestion is quite foreign to the Biblical account. Comp. Acts xvii.25.

56 "Sacrifice and many of the forms of religion Israel shared with the

nations, and it is not the *institution*, but the *repudiation*, of sacrifice that distinguishes the religion of Israel" (G. B. Gray, *Com. on Isaiah*, p. 17).

57 The circumstances under which this great utterance was made are noteworthy. Saul had tried to substitute sacrifice for obedience, or at least had read into the command to "slay [lit., cause to die] . . . ox and sheep, camel and ass" a meaning which was not there, viz., the permission to use them (the oxen and sheep) in a sacrificial meal. This would have given Samuel a good opportunity to declare the "prophetic" doctrine that Jehovah had never commanded sacrifice nor did He desire it. Instead Samuel stated what was the true doctrine of both Moses and of the prophets, that sacrifice is not a substitute for obedience, that obedience is the basic requirement and that to make sacrifice a means of escaping the consequences of disobedience is "rebellion" and "stubbornness." Samuel as a true prophet denounced the abuse of sacrifice, not sacrifice itself, as is shown by the fact that he himself offered sacrifices. This great utterance has been described by the critics as "a summary of later Jewish theology" (H. P. Smith, *Com. on Samuel*). The reason for describing it as "Jewish" is that it does not breathe the spirit of "prophetic" religion.

58 The sacrifices required by the Law served admirably to stress this fact. The "continual" burnt offering of *one* lamb in the morning and *one* lamb in the evening for all Israel (Ex. xxix.38f.) was a constant reminder that the God of Israel was not like the heathen gods who required holocausts to satisfy their hunger.

59 "To walk humbly [*tsana*] with thy God" occurs only here. In Prov. xi.2 the "lowly" (or humble) is contrasted with "pride." And in Deut. xvii.12 the man is censured who acts "presumptuously" or proudly and does not obey the priest and the judge. Consequently "to walk humbly" with God means to observe all those rules and respect all those agencies which He has appointed by which man is to approach Him and as a sinner obtain His pardon and favor. He is to obey the priest, who is God's representative in religious matters, and the judge, who is in charge of civil affairs. So Micah vi.8 expressly teaches the loftiest ideal of prophetic religion and implies the necessity of the office of the priest that those who fall short of this ideal may secure forgiveness and grace to help in time of need.

60 H. M. Wiener so understood it (*Internat. Stand. Bible Encyc.*, p. 108). Wiener regarded this law as referring to the building of altars by laymen, not as intended for the priests.

61 The practice of the patriarchs lends support to this interpretation. It seems to have been their custom to build altars where God appeared to them.

62 The expression, "and thou shalt turn in the morning and go unto thy tents" (vs. 7), is a striking one. "Tent" is used in Deut. more rarely of the abodes of the Israelites than "house." In fact this is the only place in Deut. where "tent" is used in the legislation. It is an illustration of the Mosaic atmosphere of Deuteronomy.

63 In contrasting Deut. xvi.1f. with Ex. xii. (P), Orr says, "This implies the earlier family observance, while it is inconceivable that a law ordain-

ing the home observance should arise *after* Deuteronomy" (*Problem*, p. 314).

64 G. B. Gray, *Critical Introd.*, p. 81. Cornill calls it "purely Deuteronomic" (*Introd.*, p. 208).

65 A striking illustration of the way in which the assigning of one book or passage to a late date tends to drag others after it is Ps. xc. Delitzsch said of it: "There is hardly a literary monument of antiquity, which can so brilliantly justify the traditional testimony to its origin as this Psalm." As one of the proofs that it is "a prayer of Moses the man of God," he pointed out that it has "a great many points of contact with . . . the discourses in Deuteronomy . . ." But if Deuteronomy is denied to Moses, then the close connection of Ps. xc. with Deuteronomy ceases to be proof that Moses wrote it and becomes instead convincing evidence that he could not possibly have written it.

66 Foakes Jackson in Peake's *Commentary*, p. 310.

67 J. E. McFadyen, *Introduction*, p. 97.

68 It is one of the established principles of the higher criticism that Chronicles is quite unreliable as history. It is "priestly" history, written from the standpoint of P, and designed to give the authority of Moses and David to institutions introduced centuries later.

69 The argument against the late date of Deuteronomy has been ably presented by W. Möller in *Are the Critics Right?* [1899]. Cf. esp. pp. 1-55.

70 These passages in Ex. xix. are regarded as belonging to E or J.

71 Of the 82 verses in this passage Driver assigned 7 to P, 18 and a half to D2, the rest to JE. As a result, the "priests" are mentioned twice in P, and 4 times in D2 (including iii.3, "the priests the Levites") which leaves 18 to JE. It is to be noted that Driver assigned viii.30-35 to D2, vs. 33 being the only verse in Joshua besides iii.3 in which the words "the priests the Levites" occur. The passages in chaps. xiv., xviii., xxi., which refer to the Levites and priests are all assigned to P. On this wise the Book of Joshua is analyzed according to the theory held by the critics and so made to support it.

72 The importance which may attach to a *single* phrase, a *single* word, a *single* letter, finds many striking illustrations. Elsewhere in this volume a quotation appears from C. J. Elliott's Commentary on Numbers which forms part of the *Bible Commentary* edited by Bishop C. J. Ellicott. A careful proof-reader queried the Elliott thinking it should be Ellicott, a very natural error on his part. In the Preface to the first part of Volume V. of *The History of the Christian Church*, Dr. David S. Schaff makes this statement: "The further treatment of the Middle Ages, Dr. Schaff left to his son, the author of this volume." Delete the words "his son," and there would be nothing in the Prefaces to either of the parts of Volume V. to indicate the relationship if any between these two distinguished historians. And a higher critic, living some centuries hence and unacquainted with *The Life of Philip Schaff* by his son, David S. Schaff, or with other data which are now known or accessible to all, might very plausibly argue, that the words "his son" were inserted by an editor who was struck by the similarity in name, and that had David S. really been the son of

Philip, he would not have referred to this interesting and important fact so briefly.

73 *The Hexateuch,* p. 203.

74 The source analysis of Num. xvi.-xvii. is very complicated. A JE account is distinguished which has nothing to say about priests and Levites. The P narrative is divided into two, the shorter of which deals with this difference.

75 In Ezra's company there were at first priests but no Levites (viii.15). Finally some Levites were secured. For a fuller discussion of this subject, cf., Möller, *Are the Critics Right?* pp. 124ff. and his article, "Ezekiel," in *Internat. Stand. Bible Encyc.;* also Orr, *Problem,* pp. 315ff.

76 Aaron who was 83 years old at the time of the Exodus (Ex. vii.7, P) might well have had by that time many sons, and numerous descendants. Yet P, although mentioning Eleazer's son Phineas, tells us definitely that four sons were consecrated to the priesthood and that two of them were slain for disobedience. Four priests reduced to two! Two priests to conduct the service of the tabernacle! Large families were highly prized among the Israelites. The service of the tabernacle, which was according to P the centre of worship and especially of sacrifice for a congregation of 600,000 adult males, would seem to require at the very beginning a numerous priesthood. Yet P tells us expressly that there were only two! The account in P does not agree with post-exilic conditions. Nor does it seem to be at all what we should expect priests of the post-exilic age to have invented. The only natural explanation is that, remarkable as it seems to be, it simply represents "the actual course of history" in the days of Moses and Aaron.

77 Brightman (*Sources of the Hexateuch*) in discussing the Priestly Code tells us in a footnote (p. 208): "Aaron is missing from J; and is only incidental in E; in Dt. ix.20, x.6, xxxii.50." In order to make this statement he has already in his text of J written the word "Aaron" in small print 13 times to indicate that its presence is due to the redactor.

78 *Prolegomena,* p. 151.

79 The critics regard the Books of Chronicles as "reflecting" post-exilic usage. They also regard as post-exilic most of the Psalms, parts of Isaiah, Joel, Jonah, etc. But to appeal to such documents involves an argument in a circle. They describe late praxis and ideas only if they themselves are late.

80 That, according to the critics themselves, the Priest Code does not exactly fit the times of the Restoration (Ezra and Nehemiah) is shown by the fact that Lods refers to the one-third shekel levy (Neh. x.32), the tithe on cattle (Lev. xxvii.32), the day of atonement (Lev. xvi.) and the morning *and evening* perpetual burnt offering (Ex. xxix.38f., Num. xxviii. 3f.) as proof that certain elements in the P legislation were still unknown at that time (*La Religion,* p. 189). He holds that the redaction of the Pentateuch took place "during the 4th century, before the end of the Persian domination (332)."

81 How serious was the dislocation produced by the Exile and the dis-

asters which preceded it is shown by the fact that while David had constituted 24 courses of priests, only four appear to have been represented
among those who returned with Zerubbabel (Ezra ii.36-39).

## NOTES TO PART III (Pp. 203-288)

[1] *A Preface to Bible Study* (1946), p. 30.

[2] *Idem*, p. 29. This complaint has a familiar sound. Writing in the
*British Weekly* (July 13, 1922), Professor George Jackson of Manchester
declared that as far as England was concerned "the battle is over," the
leading scholars of all evangelical denominations being numbered among
the critics. But he made this striking confession: "We are afraid it is no
exaggeration to say that probably five-sixths of the Old Testament teaching given in the Sunday-schools of this country [England] last Sunday was
based on the presuppositions of fifty or a hundred years ago," by which
he meant, upon the supposition, among others, that Moses wrote the
Pentateuch (cf. *Princeton Theol. Review*, Vol. xxi., p. 79).

[3] This is not a correct statement of the case as to the alleged Deutero-
Isaiah. Here, as in so many other cases, the problem is not primarily or
basically literary, but theological. The theory of a Second Isaiah is proved
only for those who hold to be proved the theory regarding prophecy
which makes it necessary. For those who believe that Isaiah could both
have foreseen the Babylonian Captivity and prophesied from the standpoint of that Captivity, the critical theory is both unconvincing and
unnecessary.

[4] *The Westminster Study Edition of the Holy Bible* (1948) provides many
illustrations of the seriousness of this *difficulty*. The text used is that of
the King James Version. But the introductory material, both general and
special, and the footnotes set forth what Richardson calls "the broad
general conclusions" of the critics. Thus the Biblical text of Gen. xlix.
contains a prophecy which is introduced by the words: "And Jacob called
unto his sons, and said, Gather yourselves together, that I may tell you
that which shall befall you in the last days." The footnote reads in part
as follows: "v. 1. Jacob summons his sons in order that he may tell them
about their future . . . The allusions in the poem are to conditions in
the period of the Judges, Samuel, and David. The date of the composition, therefore, is probably the 10th century B.C." This means that statements which the Biblical text represents as having been uttered by Jacob
are to be regarded as *composed* some 500 years later, because they refer
to events or situations lying that far beyond the time of Jacob's death.
In other words, what the Biblical text clearly represents as prophecy, *prediction*, is explained in the footnote as largely if not entirely history, or
"prophecy after the event" (*vaticinium ex eventu*). Is Canon Richardson
prepared to stigmatize it as "superstition" or "misuse" for the reader of
the Holy Bible to believe that this *holy* book says what it means and
means what it says? However he may describe it, the fact is too obvious
to ignore, that the interpretations of the critics often stand in glaring

contradiction to the Biblical text which they profess to interpret. This is the insuperable obstacle to the acceptance of their conclusions by "the great mass of the population." It is a difficult task, as the critics have been learning to their sorrow, to interest people in studying a book by telling them they must not believe what it says.

5 See his *Hesechiel der Dichter* (1924). Writing about twenty years later W. A. Irwin (*The Problem of Ezekiel*, 1943), describes the "certain and solid" progress in the study of this book as "most meagre" and declares that it "is in an uncertainty that merits castigation as utter and unrelieved chaos." Irwin's conclusions are apparently nearly if not quite as radical as Hölscher's. He regards about a fifth of the book as genuine. Perhaps the most interesting thing about Irwin's treatment is that while he accuses Hölscher of *subjectivism*, he insists that he has himself followed a severely inductive method. This inductive method leads him to reject or question every date given in the book.

6 *Komposition und Ursprung des Deuteronomiums*, in *Zeitschrift für alttestamentliche Wissenschaft* (1922), pp. 161-255.

7 This view is not generally accepted by the critics. Thus, Oesterley and Robinson hold that "a satisfactory analysis on this basis is nearly impossible" (*Introd.*, p. 46).

8 *Komposition*, pp. 189f., 201, 231. Cf. Hölscher, *Das Buch der Könige, seine Quellen und seine Redaktion* (1923).

9 *The Code of Deuteronomy* (1924), pp. 57f., 193ff.; also *Deuteronomy, the Framework of the Code* (1932).

10 We have seen that the priests are mentioned 24 times in Josh. iii.-vi. and that only where they are first mentioned (iii.3) are they called "the priests the Levites." Consequently, if the words "the Levites" are cut out of this one verse, it can be argued that this entire group of chapters knows nothing of the "Deuteronomic" title, "the priest the Levites." But conversely when it is allowed to remain it clearly gives the full meaning of all the other 23.

11 *Das Gottesvolk in Deuteronomium* (1929), pp. 73f., 95.

12 The attacks on the Josian dating of Deut. have been so numerous and the discussions so elaborate, that a volume could easily be written on this one subject. Eissfeldt expressed the opinion (1934) that the "accepted" critical dating, i.e., the Josian, is more firmly established than ever (*Einleitung*, pp. 190f.). This seems to be the view of Oesterley and Robinson, who are disposed to place D before H and to admit that D originated in the Northern Kingdom (*Introd.*, pp. 58, 64-66). Yet a connection with Bethel would seem to be out of the question in view of the calf worship which Hosea and Amos so severely denounced.

13 *Das System der Zwölf Stämme Israels* (1930), pp. 69ff.

14 According to Gunkel, "The Old Testament resembles a *Notbau*, which has been erected upon the ruins and out of the materials (*Werkstücke*) of an earlier, much more beautiful structure. Hence it has naturally been the principal task of Research since the awakening of the modern spirit, to take the different fragments (*einzelne Stücke*) out of their present context and to determine their age and their character: in other

words, the main problems of Research have been literary (*literarkritisch*)" (*Die Israelitische Literatur* in *Kultur der Gegenwart* [1906], p. 99). ("Make shift" might perhaps bring out the meaning of *Notbau* better than "jerry-built." But either rendering will serve to make it clear that to Gunkel as to many other critics the Old Testament is a badly put together, patchwork edifice or hovel, the seams and patchings of which are so clearly marked that the discerning critic can easily identify the fragments out of which it has been constructed.)

15 *Old Testament Prophecy*, p. 245.

16 See above footnote 3.

17 *Die Israelitische Literatur* (1906). This fifty page sketch is of basic importance to the student of form criticism. Gunkel professes to build on Wellhausen, affirming that form criticism takes over where source criticism leaves off.

18 Cf. A. Alt, *Die Ursprünge des israelitischen Rechts* (1934), p. 11; L. J. McGinley, *Form-Criticism of the Synoptic Healing Narratives* (1944), traces this method to Wellhausen's studies in the New Testament and Gunkel's in the Old (pp. 1-3).

19 Thus Cadbury, a N.T. scholar, says of it: "At the outset it should be observed that this newer criticism is not destructive of the source criticism of the older generation since it concerns itself with the pre-literary rather than with the written stage of the history of the gospel materials" (*Haverford Symposium*, p. 94), a statement which applies equally to form criticism of the Old Testament. Form criticism does not reject but rather builds upon the destructive conclusions of the source criticism. That is its fatal weakness.

20 *Einleitung*, p. 9. The title of this section of his work is, *"Die Vorliterarische Stufe: die kleinsten Redeformen und ihr Sitz im Leben"* (pp. 8-141).

21 *Idem*, p. 71.

22 *Das Formgeschichtliche Problem des Hexateuchs* (1938).

23 *Idem*, p. 3.

24 *Idem*, pp. 31ff., 37ff.

25 *Ursprünge*, pp. 12-33.

26 *Idem*, pp. 33ff.

27 *Idem*, pp. 52ff.

28 *Idem*, p. 26.

29 *Haverford Symposium*, p. 56.

30 *The Psalms Chronologically Treated*, p. 35.

31 Gunkel, *Die Psalmen* (1926), pp. 286f.

32 W. E. Barnes, *The Psalms* (1931), vol. ii., p. 316.

33 The names of Barth and Brunner do not appear in the index of the 14th edition of the *Encyclopaedia Britannica* (1929).

34 *The Old Testament and the Critics*, p. 25.

35 *The Old Testament in the Light of Today* (1915), pp. 12f.

36 This is the warrant for the use of the term "crisis theology." God must break through to man, if man is to know God. This break-through is the crisis. But Van Til points out in his *The New Modernism* (1946)

that these words are not used by Barthians in their usual sense. Immanence does not mean that God is present in the world which He has created: rather is it a pantheistic conception which tends to make immanence spell "meaningless identification." On the other hand, the transcendent God or the "wholly other" of Barth and Brunner is "not wholly other at all, in as much as he is correlative to his complete identification with man" (p. 367f.).

37 *The New Modernism*, pp. 95f.

38 *Westminster Confession of Faith*, Chap. I, Sec. 10.

39 R. V. G. Tasker, *The Nature and Purpose of the Gospels*, p. 94.

40 *Westminster Confession*, Chap. XIV, Sec. 2.

41 Leonard Woolley, in writing recently (1936) of the excavations at Ur where sensational discoveries have been made, utters this word of caution, "We have, it is true, found thousands of inscribed tablets, and the greater part of them date from about the time of Abraham, but we have excavated the merest fraction of the city's area and within that area the tablets which survive are not the hundredth part of what were written there during the quarter of a century or so that Abraham may have passed at Ur" (*Abraham*, p. 9).

42 Vol. II., p. 77.

43 For the chronology he refers especially (Vol. I., pp. 470f.) to Ffynnes Clinton's *Fasta Hellenica*.

44 Preface, p. vii.

45 Vol. II., p. 70.

46 Vol. X., p. 762. Cf. J. W. Jack's section on the "Antiquity of Civilization" in his survey of Biblical Archaeology in Manson's *Companion to the Bible*, pp. 182f.

47 Grote's defense of his position is well worth quoting: "To such as are accustomed to the habits once universal, and still not uncommon, in investigating the ancient world, I may appear to be striking off one thousand years from the scroll of history: but to those whose canon of evidence is derived from Mr. Hallam, M. Sismondi, or any other eminent historian of modern events, I am well-assured that I shall appear lax and credulous rather than exigent or sceptical."

48 Schliemann, who was the first to use the spade successfully to solve the Homeric problem, in his first excavations dug down to bed rock expecting to find the Troy of Homer at the lowest level, only to discover that the city he sought was near the top. The lowest strata are now known to belong to a period older by centuries than the time of the Trojan war.

49 While cautioning his readers against the unqualified acceptance of the claim of the "champions of the Bible" that archaeology has proved to be their "potent ally," Burrows makes the following judicious statement: "To be sure, archaeological discoveries are not always reassuring. As a matter of fact, they have raised some very perplexing questions. On the whole, however, archaeological work has unquestionably strengthened confidence in the reliability of the Scriptural record. More than one archaeologist has found his respect for the Bible increased by the experience of excavation in Palestine." (*What Mean These Stones?* [1941], p. 1).

Coming from a professor of Biblical Theology who accepts the "critical" viewpoint, this statement is especially valuable.

50 See Appendix II.

51 This word is only used in a technical sense and the more usual word for "scribe" is *sopher*. But, according to 2 Chr. xxvi.11, xxxiv.13, the two offices were distinguished at least as late as the reign of Josiah. It is noteworthy that the LXX usually renders *shoter* by "scribe" (*grammateus*).

52 De Rogué's theory that this alphabet was derived from an early form of the Egyptian Hieratic script favored the assigning of it to an early date (perhaps as early as 2300 B.C.). But there was no documentary proof of this.

53 In his *Palestine and Israel* (1934) Petrie writes: "It was then in a documentary age in Palestine that the Abramic period began, hedged in east and west by documentary civilizations already rich with the experience of a couple of thousand years" (p. 28), and he declares that "to regard this as an illiterate age is only a token of our limitation of the past by our own ignorance" (p. 29).

54 How epoch-making are these discoveries is illustrated by the fact that in his *Bible in the Light of Archaeology* (1932), Albright gave as a reason for dating Deut. not earlier than the 10th cty., "the frequent references to writing" and added, "writing was certainly not employed in such cases as divorce contracts (xxiv.1-4) before the monarchy" (p. 155). Less than a decade later he declares in *From the Stone Age to Christianity* (1940) that alphabetic writing was used in Palestine "from the Patriarchal Age on, and that the rapidity with which forms of letters changed is clear evidence of common use" (pp. 192f. cf. pp. 42f.).

55 For example by Petrie, *Palestine and Israel*, p. 35.

56 In this connection it is to be noted that the Ras Shamra tablets prove that a talent of 3000 shekels was in use in the vicinity of Palestine in the 15th cty. Since the total for the half-shekel levy taken at Mt. Sinai (Ex. xxxviii.25, P) is in terms of a talent of 3000 shekels, this evidence for the early use of such a talent is interesting.

57 It and the Siloam Inscription (discovered in 1880) remained for a number of years the only inscriptions dating from pre-exilic times which could be called Hebrew. G. Cooke (*Textbook of North Semitic Inscriptions*, 1903), classifies only the latter as Hebrew.

58 Albright has recently declared that four lines on a recently discovered Byblus plaque are in "perfect Biblical Hebrew so far as the consonantal structure goes" ("A Hebrew Letter from the 12th Century, B.C." in *Bulletin of Amer. Schools for Oriental Research*, No. 73 [Feb., 1939] pp. 9ff.). And he holds that the language of the Mari tablets while Accadian indicates that the West Semitic nomads spoke a tongue which was "virtually identical" with the ancient Hebrew spoken in the Abrahamic age (*Stone Age*, p. 112).

59 Montgomery and Harris, "The Ras Shamra Mythological Texts."

60 E.g., the verbs "go" (*halak*), "take" (*laqach*), "bow down to" (*shachah* in *hithpalel* stem).

61 E.g., the Hebrew consonants *"sh"* and *"z"* sometimes appear as *"t"*

and "*d*" respectively in the Ras Shamra tablets, and the Aramaic relative (*d*) is used instead of Hebrew *asher*.

62 This is favored by his name. If the second part of the name Abram means "exalted" and comes from the root *rum* (to be high), the name is not Babylonian but West Semitic (Aramaic or Hebrew), since the verb *rum* is not used in this sense in Babylonian (cf. Clay, *Amurru*, p. 171).

63 Prof. R. D. Wilson was a vigorous opponent of the claim of the critics that Aramaisms are an indication of late date. His article, "Aramaisms in the Old Testament" (*Princeton Theol. Review*, Vol. XXIII., [1923] pp. 234-266) was based on the evidence then available to scholars. The more recent discoveries have strikingly confirmed his position.

64 This statement was made by Prof. Langdon of Oxford in the *Times* (London) and is quoted by Marston, *The Bible Becomes Alive*, pp. 173f.

65 The evidence that simple alphabets were in use and that writing was fairly common in Palestine from patriarchal times lends support to the theory that the scantiness of literary remains is due to a considerable extent to the use of perishable writing materials, such as papyrus (cf. Burrows, *What Mean These Stones?*, pp. 20, 185). Conquerors and plunderers would hardly carry away clay tablets dealing with the everyday life of the people; and if such documents had been broken up the fragments would in many cases be quite as imperishable as the potsherds which have rendered such signal service in determining questions of relative chronology.

66 H. Gressmann, *Palastina's Erdgeruch in der israelitischen Religion* (1909).

67 "Terra Cotta figures of an undraped female deity are a feature of every excavation" (Garrow Duncan, *Digging Up Biblical History*, Vol. II., p. 80).

68 Ever since the discovery more than fifty years ago on the El Amarna tablets of references to the *Habiru* as trouble makers in Palestine, the question has been debated whether these were the Hebrews who invaded the country under Joshua. Subsequent discoveries, of which those at Mari are the most recent, indicate that *Habiru* was a broad term which might apply to the Hebrews, but was not restricted to them. This would be quite natural if the word means "nomad" or something similar. The same may be true of the word *Apiru* which occurs on Egyptian records of approximately the time of the Exodus. Both of these words might be used of the Hebrews, even if all three words are etymologically unrelated. —If the claim that the names of several of the sons of Jacob occur on the Ras Shamra tablets should prove to be correct, it would indicate that these names belong to the early period of Israel's history.

69 *The Other Side of the Jordan*, p. 114. Petrie has described Gen. xiv. as "a leaf of the Canaanite record." He holds that "No writer after Joshua would ever have described in vague terms places so well known to Israel" (*Palestine and Israel*, p. 28). In Pilter's *The Pentateuch: A Historical Record*, the greater part of the book is devoted to Gen. xiv.

70 The allusions to the Philistines in Ex. and Josh. are regarded as anachronisms by Petrie unless the date of the entry of Israel into Palestine is placed at about 1180 B.C. (*Palestine and Israel*, pp. 56ff.). But J. Garrow

Duncan (*New Light on Hebrew Origins*, p. 114) and J. W. Jack (in his sketch of "Biblical Archaeology" in Manson's *Companion to the Bible*, pp. 196f.) advocate a much earlier date for the presence of Philistines in Palestine. According to Jack, "we now know that, although the main body entered Canaan about 1190 B.C., there was probably an earlier settlement of them along the coast in the thirteenth and fourteenth centuries, just as there was of the Danaua in Syria." We have still much to learn from archaeology about the Philistines.

71 *Palestine and Israel*, p. 72. In *Seventy Years in Archaeology*, Petrie says: "The iron furnaces and great tools [at Gerar] proved that iron was commonly used at 1150 B.C., and iron knives started as early as 1350 B.C." (p. 276). The discovery of a 14th century axe head at Ras Shamra is noteworthy as indicating the wide diffusion of iron implements. The recently discovered Ashnunnak dagger is more than a thousand years older (28th cty.). Objects made of meteoric iron have been found that are of a still earlier date.—It is claimed that the mention of camels is an anachronism for the patriarchal age. But since camels "were certainly known in the Predynastic Period in Egypt" (*Guide to the Egyptian Collections of the British Museum*, 1909, p. 95) and had probably been domesticated by the Arabs for centuries, the fact that Abraham, like the Ishmaelite traders, should be said to have had camels is certainly not surprising. The fact that nothing is said about horses before Jacob went down into Egypt may with equal or greater probability be taken as an indication that the writer of Genesis was well acquainted with the actual conditions of patriarchal life.

72 "Scholars have sometimes supposed that the social and moral level of the laws attributed to Moses was too high for such an early age. . . . Here again, the archaeological evidence does not prove that the Hebrew laws were actually given by Moses; it merely proves that they may have been given as early as the time of Moses" (Burrows, *What Mean These Stones?*, pp. 57f.). Such a statement as this indicates that the critics are by no means as confident as they were some decades ago that the late date of the bulk of the Mosaic law can be regarded as axiomatic.

73 If Garstang's date for the fall of Jericho is correct, the Pharaoh of the Oppression may well have been Thothmes III, which is the view most in accord with the chronology of the Bible. But many scholars still hold to the view of Lepsius that Rameses II was the Oppressor. The claim that only the Joseph tribes were in Egypt and that the Israelite clans entered Palestine at several different times, from different directions, and under different leadership, is irreconcilable with the express statements of the Bible.

74 Cf. Albright, *From the Stone Age*, pp. 33-43; Woolley, *Abraham*, pp. 27ff.

75 *Abraham*, p. 281.

76 *Stone Age*, p. 196, cf. p. 201. Yet Albright is very positive that Moses taught monotheism (p. 309).

77 *Abraham*, p. 38.

78 *Op. cit.*, p. 27.

79 *Id.,* p. 32.

80 The same disappointing attitude is to be found in Jack's, in many respects highly encouraging, survey of the results of archaeological research, in Manson's *Companion to the Bible* (1939), pp. 172-203. He emphasizes the antiquity of ancient cultures of Bible lands, the antiquity of writing, even of alphabetic writing, the accuracy of the cultural and geographical background of the O.T., etc., yet apparently he was still unable to break away from the critical theories regarding the late date of the Pentateuchal documents, which he had previously held.

81 Cf. James Orr, *Problem of the Pentateuch,* pp. 10ff.

82 *Bulletin of the American Schools of Oriental Research* (October 1948), p. 16.

83 In view of these references to the Masoretic Text, it is to be noted that it is of course only the consonantal text that is referred. These scrolls are unpointed. They have neither vowel-points, accents, or punctuation. They use vowel-letters oftener, however, than the MT and somewhat differently.

84 The above statements are based largely on the issue of the *Bulletin* mentioned above, and especially on the photographs of the Isaiah manuscript contained in it and in the September issue of *The Biblical Archaeologist.*

85 P. 177 (Revell edition), p. 204 (Eerdmans edition).

86 "Creation or Development?" in *Methodist Review,* Nov. 1901. According to Sir Arthur Keith, "A full analysis of the structural details of man's body shows that about 30% of them are peculiar to him" (article "Man," p. 761a, in *Encycl. Brit.,* 1929).

87 *The Wonder of Life,* p. 639. Sir Arthur Keith has told us: "There remain great blanks in the line of evidence which links the origin of modern man to an extinct form of anthropoid ape. Between the highest kind of anthropoid and the lowest type of man, represented at present by Pithecanthropus, there still exists a great gap; the transitional forms which fill this gap still remain to be discovered. Yet the evidence as it stands, imperfect as it is, points to man's departure from an anthropoid status early in the Miocene period, certainly 1,000,000 years ago, perhaps more . . ." (article "Man" in *Encycl. Brit.,* 1929). Cf. also Bateson's address "Evolutionary Faith and Modern Doubts," delivered before the American Association for the Advancement of Science, in 1921, in which while admitting that "We cannot see how the differentiation into species came about. Variation of many kinds, often considerable, we daily witness, but no origin of species," he yet concluded with the words, "Let us then proclaim in precise and unmistakable language that our faith in evolution is unshaken" (Quoted from L. T. More, *The Dogma of Evolution,* p. 28). "The popular attitude among scientists of the present day toward evolution is expressed in the words of Vernon Kellogg as being that of certainty as to the *fact* of evolution having occurred but of ignorance as to the *causes* which have brought it about" (article, "The Evolutionary Hypothesis in the Light of Modern Science" by Floyd E. Hamilton, *Princeton*

*Theol. Review*, Vol. XXII [1924], p. 420). [The article by Kellogg appeared in *The New Republic* (April 11, 1923, pp. 180f.).]

88 The startling claim that the discoveries of the past few years have "reduced the gap between man and the anthropoids to a very narrow interval, which is practically bridged by a number of evolutionary series, the most striking of which is dentition" (Albright, *Stone Age*, p. 4) is based largely on the "proceedings of the Symposium on Early Man" held in Philadelphia about ten years ago (cf. G. G. MacCurdy, *Early Man*, 1937). While the new discoveries are interesting it is safe to say that only one already convinced of the truth of this hypothesis would see in them conclusive proof of its correctness.

89 Apparently Albright does not place the use of writing in Babylonia or Egypt earlier than about 4000 B.C. (*Stone Age*, pp. 9, 17).

90 "To reckon with millions of years, in the past or in the present, is child's play and unworthy of mature minds, and is at best of no greater value than the gigantic numbers of Indian mythology" (Bavinck, as cited).

91 The determination of evolutionists to insist that early man must have been "primitive" is shown by their readiness to ignore "Galley Hill" man. These remains were found in "Chellean" deposits near the Thames and should have, according to geologists, a great antiquity. They differ as Sir Arthur Keith admits "in no important respect" from modern man. The only reason they are ignored is because they do not fit into the evolutionary theory. This is practically admitted by Sir Arthur (as cited).

92 Vol. IV., p. 494. The fact that Gibbon was a classicist who saw in the Greco-Roman civilization "the solid fabric of human greatness," and that his attitude toward Christianity was one of ill-concealed hostility, made it impossible for him to appreciate fully the basic reasons for the "decline and fall" which are set forth so clearly by the apostle Paul in the Epistle to the Romans, and led him to blame Christianity for its downfall. Had he lived in the 20th century Gibbon would have written as an outspoken evolutionist, despite the fact that his theme would have accorded ill with that superficial optimism which is characteristic of the evolutionist's writing of history.

93 How completely history can refute the wisdom of would be sages and prophets is illustrated by the following: "It has been said that 'if nature does not take leaps, she at times makes very long strides.' Human nature is making one now. Before we are much older war will have become impossible. The growing moral consciousness, one might say even the growing sense of humour will bring it to an end. It will soon be as absurd for a man to walk in Regent St. in uniform, behelmeted and besworded, as to walk there in chain armour. In the best thinking the soldier is already obsolete; and it is thought that kills and makes alive. The nations are rushing into fellowship" (J. Brierly, *Life and the Ideal*, p. 149). Since Brierly penned these words (1910) the world has felt the scourge of war as never before.

94 *Decline and Fall*, vol. vii., p. 46.

95 *Introduction to Science*, p. 212.

96 *What is Man?*, p. 33.

97 Declaring that "The New Christianity is due to a new attitude," President Patton has accounted for this new attitude by pointing out that, "Philosophy and science have led men to take a uniformitarian view of the world. This may show itself in a spiritual or a materialistic way. Whether you consider the world as mind and the world-process as the gradual unfolding of a system of thought-relations, or whether you regard it as matter and the world-process as the gradual change from simple to complex relations, in either case the process is a gradual one, proceeding without break of continuity and leaving no room for miracle and supernatural intervention." And his conclusion is: "Of course, if either form of uniformitarianism is true—either pantheism or materialism—Christianity must be false . . ." (*Fundamental Christianity*, pp. 177ff.).

98 *Stone Age*, pp. 189ff.

99 Gray, in attacking the credibility of the figures given in Numbers, declares that "it is the great merit of Colenso to have demonstrated the absolute impossibility of the numbers" (*Commentary on Numbers*, in *Internat. Crit.* Series, p. 13). Lods, in arguing that the traditions of the exodus period were long handed down by oral tradition and received as is usually the case "many enrichments and numerous modifications" before being committed to writing, cites the invention of the manna as proof of this contention: "They did not any longer take account of the conditions of the life of nomads: hence the stories of the manna. They represented the tribes not as scattered over vast areas in order to find the pasture required by their flocks, but as a people already as numerous as Israel of the period of the monarchy, travelling in a body (*se déplacant en bloc*) across steppes that had neither vegetation nor water" (*La Religion*, p. 48). In other words a late record which was dependent on oral tradition changed a natural account which truly reflected nomad life, into a supernatural account which was quite incompatible with it.

100 Since the command regarding the census was given a month after the erection of the tabernacle (Num. i.1) while the half-shekel redemption money was used in its construction (Ex. xxx.11f., xxxviii.25), it is natural to infer that both levy and census were made as of a fixed date, probably that of the erection of the tabernacle, which was set for the first day of the first month. All the males who had, or would have at that time, reached the age of twenty being subject to the tax and included in the census.

101 The attempt has been made to bring these census figures into accord with what many modern scholars consider the historically probable by asserting that they are due to a mistake: the word *eleph* which usually means "thousand" should have been understood in the sense of "family" or "tent." By this means Petrie reduced the total of 603,550 to "598 tents, 5,550 people" (*Internat. Stand. Bible Encyc.*, p. 912; cf. *Palestine & Israel*, pp. 42f.). It is a sufficient answer to this solution, that all the calculations are obviously based on the assumption that *eleph* means thousand. In the case of the half-shekel tax, it would mean reducing the 100 talents 1775 shekels to a paltry 2775 shekels, or increasing the per capita tax from a half-shekel to more than 100 times that amount.

102 The issue is put very clearly by C. J. Elliott, as follows: ". . . although it may be fairly alleged that the miraculous supplies of food and water were neither required nor bestowed to the extent which some have alleged, it must not be forgotten that the miraculous elements of the history are closely interwoven into its entire fabric; and hence, whilst it is open to unbelievers to deny the historical truth of the whole of the history, the impossibility of the sustenance of life, both in regard to the people and the cattle, without miraculous intervention, so far from furnishing any argument against the account which is given in the Book of Numbers, must rather be regarded as an indication of the historical truth of a narrative in which miraculous intervention is alleged both to have been required, and also to have been vouchsafed" (Ellicott's, *Bible Commentary*, Vol. I, p. 481).

103 *Introduction*, p. 184.

104 Cf. *American Journal of Semitic Languages and Literature* (1939), pp. 337-49. Irwin says of Deut. xxviii. 45-57: "There can be no doubt that, as Puukko concludes, this passage in Deuteronomy is a *vaticinium ex eventu;* it is no prophecy but an actual account of the invasion of Judah and the siege of Jerusalem. To our astonished eyes there appears here an eyewitness of those terrible days" (p. 347). Being convinced that this account must have been written "soon" after the event described, that it is written in the style of Deut., and that it is intended to be "a commentary on the epilogue of the code [chap. xxviii], Irwin finds in it "an objective criterion" for dating the code. It proves, according to Irwin, that the code in the epilogue of which this "eyewitness" account has been inserted must be pre-exilic, even if only by a very narrow margin. Thus, by critical interpretation and manipulation, Moses, who uttered the prediction centuries before, is metamorphosed into the "eyewitness" who beholds the fulfilment of his prophecy!

105 *Deuteronomy, the Framework of the Code* (1932), p. 204. Similarly, Menes says of Huldah's prophecy recorded in 2 Kgs. xxii.15-20: "That here, vss. 17, 19, 20, the Exile is predicted and that accordingly it [the passage] must be post-exilic will certainly be denied by no one" (*Die Vorexilischen Gesetze Israels* [1928], p. 75). In other words, a man would be a fool if he regarded Huldah's prediction as really a declaration regarding the *future*.

106 *Introduction*, p. 755.

107 P. 319, n. 21.

108 *Idem.*, p. 300.

109 *Idem.*, p. 307.

## NOTES TO APPENDICES (Pp. 289-304)

1 In the analysis given below subdivisions of verses are usually indicated simply by "*a*" and "*b*". For fuller details the reader is referred to the *Introduction* itself.

2 Cf. W. H. Green, "Primitive Chronology," in *Bibliotheca Sacra*, April, 1890; also B. B. Warfield, "On the Antiquity and Unity of the Human

Race," in *Princeton Theol. Review*, Jan., 1911 (reprinted in his *Studies in Theology*, pp. 235-258).

3 Yahuda (*Die Sprache des Pentateuchs*, pp. 251ff.) has proposed a quite different etymology (*mo-she*, "seed of the sea"). The different estimates of Yahuda's work expressed by Petrie (favorable, cf. *Palestine and Israel*, p. 62) and Albright (unfavorable, *Stone Age*, p. 181), are an illustration of the wide difference of opinion often to be found among archaeologists as regards not unimportant matters in the field of their researches.

4 Cf. R. D. Wilson, *Is the Higher Criticism Scholarly?*, pp. 18ff. This booklet of about fifty pages (published in 1922 by the Sunday School Times Co., Philadelphia) is now in its ninth edition. It sets forth in popular form some of the cogent reasons which led this great scholar to reject the conclusions of the higher critics. It may also serve to introduce the reader to Dr. Wilson's more elaborate works: *Studies in the Book of Daniel*, Series I. (1917), Series II. (published posthumously, 1938), *A Scientific Investigation of the Old Testament* (1926), and the numerous articles from his pen which appeared from time to time over a period of a quarter of a century (1903-1929) in *The Princeton Theological Review*.

5 A striking illustration of the uncertainty which may attach to the meaning of a proper name is the name Lazarus, given to the sick beggar in Lk. xv.19ff. Lazarus is usually explained as being the OT name Eleazar meaning "God (*El*) helps." But some scholars in interpreting the parable give it the meaning "Helpless" (taking the "l" as standing for "lo" [not]). Both meanings may be regarded as appropriate. Lazarus was a helpless beggar; but when he died he was carried to Abraham's bosom. If both of these meanings were attached to the name in NT times, it would be doubly appropriate here; and it is significant that the beggar is given a name, since names are exceptional in parables. It is also interesting to note that in the modern (Arabic) name of Bethany (*El-Aziriyeh*), which is apparently derived from Lazarus, the initial letter is taken in a still different sense, as the definite article (*el*) in Arabic.

# INDEX I

## Authors and Subjects

# INDEX II

## Texts

## THE AUTHOR

Oswald T. Allis is a Philadelphian; a graduate of the University of Pennsylvania (A.B.), Princeton Theological Seminary (B.D.), and University of Berlin (Ph.D.). In 1927 Hampden Sydney College conferred on him the honorary degree of Doctor of Divinity.

Dr. Allis taught in the Department of Semitic Philology at Princeton Theological Seminary, first as instructor and then as Assistant Professor from 1910 to 1929, during the last twelve years of which period he was Faculty Editor of *The Princeton Theological Review*. He was then for seven years Professor in the Old Testament Department of Westminster Theological Seminary. Since 1929 he has been an Associate Editor, now Editorial Correspondent, of *The Evangelical Quarterly* (Edinburgh).